ASSESSMENT FOR EQUITY
AND INCLUSION

ASSESSMENT FOR EQUITY AND INCLUSION:
EMBRACING ALL OUR CHILDREN

A. LIN GOODWIN

TRANSFORMING TEACHING
SERIES

ROUTLEDGE
NEW YORK   LONDON

Published in 1997 by
Routledge
29 West 35th Street
New York, NY 10001

Published in Great Britain by
Routledge
11 New Fetter Lane
London EC4P 4EE

For permission to use copyrighted material, grateful acknowledgement is made to the copyright holders on page 336, which are hereby made part of this copyright page.

Copyright © 1997 by Routledge

Printed in the United States of America on acid-free paper.

Library of Congress Cataloging-in-Publication Data

Assessment for equity and inclusion: embracing all our children / [edited by] A. Lin Goodwin.
     p. cm. — (Transforming teaching series)
    Includes bibliographical references and index.
    ISBN 0-415-91472-8 (hardbound: alk. paper) — ISBN 0-415-91473-6 (pbk.: alk. paper)
    1. Educational tests and measurements—United States.   2. Multicultural education—United States.   3. Educational equalization—United States.   4. Minorities—Education—United States.
I. Goodwin, A. Lin.   II. Series.
LB3051.A7667   1996
371.2'6—dc20   96-27641
                                               CIP

To my mother,
Lucy Marie Huang Armstrong,
who taught me about fairness,
justice, and love.

CONTENTS

ACKNOWLEDGMENTS

I would like to thank the many people who helped this book come to be. First, thank you, Jim Fraser and Celia Genishi, for pushing me to take this book on in the first place; without your encouragement, I might still be stuck at the "thinking about it" stage. I am also grateful to my friend Sabrina Hope King for her willingness to chip in when I needed help; help like yours is hard to find, especially over the summer. Nina Asher deserves a special acknowledgment for her expert handling of the many details that needed particular care while I was on the other side of the world. Many thanks too to Kristine Little Iglesias and Shabiya Wahabodeen who generously lent much-needed hands when I felt overwhelmed. Finally, to my co-authors and contributors, thank you for your hard work and good humor in the face of my constant nudging. We all made a great team.

SERIES EDITOR'S FOREWORD

James W. Fraser

In bringing the material together that is contained in *Assessment for Equity and Inclusion: Embracing All Our Children*, A. Lin Goodwin has produced a book of great value to teachers. Goodwin, and the extraordinary team of authors whom she has brought together, argue passionately for a means of assessment that will build an inclusive school and ultimately an inclusive society. The chapters here represent a powerful rejection of the most common use of the term assessment—the ranking and separating of students according to perceived academic ability based on test scores. At the same time, this volume provides committed teachers with much more than powerful arguments. These chapters explore the subtleties of alternative means of assessment and provide very specific examples of successful efforts, by teachers, to develop their own systems of assessment. Ultimately this volume points the way to the development of a new paradigm of education—a school where a rigorous definition of academic success is matched with a deep, and successful, commitment to the inclusion of all students in that success. The methods of assessment, as the whole curriculum and structure of the school, these chapters argue, must serve that end.

As the voices in this volume remind us so clearly, whether teachers like it or not, assessment is an ever-present reality in their lives. School districts and states require various forms of assessment. Teachers properly want to make their own evaluations of their own work and that of their students. At the same time, it has become virtually common knowledge among progressive educators that most of the forms of assessment available today do more to sort and label students—and usually to track them by race, class, and gender—than they do to help the teaching and learning process. As Goodwin notes, one response to this problem has been a rage for alternative assessments that is really one form of alternative assessment—student portfolios. While portfolios can be useful, they are far from the panacea that they are sometimes viewed as being. Teachers need a much richer mix of forms of assessment. And teachers equally need a clear and coherent way to deal with and critique the forms of assessment that are mandated for them. The essays in this volume provide teachers with a set of invaluable practical and theoretical tools for responding to this issue.

I am especially pleased that Goodwin's volume is launching Routledge's *Transforming Teaching* series. This series was born of a need voiced by many educators for materials that mixed a rich theoretical background with specific practical examples of classroom transforming activities. Goodwin and her colleagues have met that need. Teaching and teacher education programs are in an intellectual crisis today. In spite of a decade of ferment and "reform," quality books for teachers concerned with their own professional development and for students in teacher education programs are in short supply. With some few wonderful exceptions, teachers, and candidates for the profession, are offered how-to materials geared for an apprenticeship-style education that preserves the status quo while offering very little in the realm of intellectual excitement or critical reflection on the role of the school in larger social changes. At the same time, very important intellectual work has been done in education in the last decade, but very few links have been made between that work and the materials available for those who work in thousands of schools and hundreds of teacher education programs across the country.

While each volume will take a different approach and focus on a different topic, all of the volumes in the *Transforming Teaching* series will be united in seeking to provide materials that give teachers a theoretical base and specific, concrete examples in practice. The series is committed to speaking in the voices of teachers and to addressing the concerns of teachers in the service of a rich, equitable, and inclusive schooling for all students. Rigorous theory must always be informed by practice, and indeed it is in the dialogue of theory and practice that both are refined. We will doom ourselves to an anti-intellectual mediocrity if we fail to ask the most rigorous and critical theoretical questions about both current practices and the kind of schooling that is ultimately needed for the development of an inclusive, multicultural democracy. But we will not build that new society if teachers do not have the practical tools in hand to do their work. *Transforming Teaching* seeks to meet both needs. If groups of teachers find these volumes to have done so, and if groups of students experience schooling as a more successful experience because of these volumes, then the enterprise will have been a success.

INTRODUCTION

A. Lin Goodwin

This volume examines assessment and the concept of alternative assessment from historical, theoretical, practical, and critical points of view. The intent of the book is to shed light on assessment by presenting thoughtful discussions about the theories and definitions of this concept, to share best practice framed by the decisions teachers make and the thinking they engage in, to explore perennial curriculum dilemmas that naturally emerge from assessment, and to discuss some of the issues and barriers that impede progress. Each chapter reveals how assessment and inclusion are naturally connected, and that equity in schooling relies on appropriate assessment.

Calls for increased standardization in the form of a common curriculum supported by a national testing system are competing with equally strident calls for highly contextualized assessments employing multiple measures for professional attention. It is no wonder that assessment has become the topic of choice for national professional meetings, education journals, and in-service staff development across the country. Thus, this book capitalizes on the many heated debates about assessment currently occurring at both state and national levels by thoughtfully informing the discourse on this important issue.

CURRENT CONCEPTIONS OF INNOVATION

The education profession seems never to be lacking new ideas or innovative strategies. In the past decade alone, the field has enthusiastically embraced critical thinking, multiple intelligences, the Madeline Hunter method, learning styles, constructivist classrooms, whole language, cooperative learning, and a myriad of other pedagogical theories and techniques. Yet, despite the openness with which educators have generally approached educational innovations, the field is, paradoxically, consistently accused of stagnation and intransigence. Indeed, educators are often characterized as stuck in their ways and unwilling to change. The root of this apparent contradiction may lie in the absence of rigorous, intellectual critique around new education ideas, or in practitioners' lack of accessibility to intellectual critique.

Without thoughtful consideration, new ideas land in schools that are poorly prepared to receive them. Educators are placed in the unfortunate position of hasty implementation that simply results in failure, frustration, and inaccurate application. These ideas are either prematurely discarded because they appear to be unworkable, or are adopted carte blanche without attention to contextual appropriateness. Ultimately, schools either revert to the status quo or juggle numerous innovations that are, too often, thoughtlessly adopted.

ALTERNATIVE ASSESSMENT WITHIN THE CURRENT CONTEXT

The latest education mantra is alternative assessment. It has become the vanguard of the educational reform movement and is frequently described in the educational literature as the answer to lagging academic achievement among America's youth. No doubt there is much evidence to support the fact that assessment, defined primarily as standardized testing since the early 1900s, has had a number of deleterious effects on schools, on instruction, and particularly on children who are poor or who are members of dominated groups. Indeed, it has been well documented that standardized tests assess low-level, decontextualized facts; are often used as the sole measure of achievement and capability, despite the fact that they provide a fragmented picture of the learner; and frequently drive curriculum and instruction, particularly in poor and low-achieving districts, so that children who need the most enriched instruction are subjected to meaningless drill designed to improve their standardized test scores. Clearly, education needs an alternative to this restrictive method of evaluation, which characterizes 80 percent of all system-wide tests used by school districts nationwide. Yet what is being forwarded in the name of alternative assessment has received little professional scrutiny. The field's efforts to alter a long pattern of standardized testing appear anemic and ad hoc.

As a society, however, we are uniquely positioned to make fundamental changes in schooling in both positive and negative directions. On the one hand, we have the opportunity to loosen the tenacious hold standardized tests have had on the curriculum since the early part of the twentieth century; conceivably, we could change the way we value and measure educational outcomes by creating alternatives that are more responsive to local contexts and to the ways that learners learn. On the other hand, there is a push for a national curriculum supported by a national testing system. Embedded in this movement is the possibility that assessment become more standardized and uniform. No doubt, most states in the nation have demonstrated their belief in assessment innovations by mandating some form of alternative assessment. But a current study of what these new directives entail has revealed precious little information, since most states are still in the early stages of conceptualization, experimentation, and implementation. Thus, while it may appear on the surface that the country is moving rapidly in new directions, we are always in constant danger of sliding back to the status quo due to the syndrome that typically plagues educational reform—hasty adoption without critique, dialogue, planning, or evaluation.

Thus the authors in this volume open up the discussion on assessment in general and alternative assessment in particular by initiating a frank, intellectual, and substantive discussion of this important concept. They help to expand the notion of "alternatives" by presenting multiple possibilities and descriptions of innovative practice. However, this is not a recipe book for alternative assessment; rather, it is a thoughtful analysis of this concept from theoretical as well as practical viewpoints.

The book is divided into four components. The first lays the groundwork by examining the legacy of assessment in this country, describing the politics of testing and assessment, and conceptually framing alternatives to assessment. In chapter 1, George Madaus, Stacey Raczek, and Marguerite Clark provide a historical context for assessment in this country and link what we have done in the name of assessment to the things we are trying and planning to do. Celia Genishi deconstructs the concept of assessment from modern and postmodern viewpoints and clarifies, in chapter 2, the meaning of alternative assessment. In chapter 3, Linda Darling-Hammond and Beverly Falk look at assessment from a policy perspective. What movements, endeavors, reforms are underway in the name of alternative assessment, and what are the political ramifications of change and innovation?

The second section focuses on best practice as described by practitioners. These discussions are undergirded by the questions that practitioners need to consider and the ways in which instruction will naturally change when alternative assessment practices are brought to bear. Steve Ellwood describes his successful attempt to "de-track" a ninth-grade algebra class so that all the students, regardless of baseline ability, could participate in algebra, which is one of the gatekeepers for college entry. Yvonne Smith and A. Lin Goodwin collaborate on the story of a masterful early childhood teacher at Central Park East I in New York City. Smith works with children who represent a range of diversities—ethnicity and race, language, socioeconomic status, religions—all of whom find success in her classroom. Mathematics is usually perceived of as a highly defined and objective discipline, one that lends itself to standardized testing. In her chapter, Paula Hajar dispels this myth by exploring the role of assessment in mathematics as a way of opening up the discipline to all students. In their chapter, Julie Savitch and Leslie Serling tell what happens when two teachers—one who teaches gifted students, the other who teaches nongifted children—combined their classrooms and "de-tracked" a gifted cohort of students to the benefit of *all* the children. Margaret Borrego Brainard presents the authentic and "alternative" practices that special educators have long employed. Her chapter bridges "regular" and "special" education to reveal the wealth of knowledge special educators can share about alternative assessment.

The third section of the book presents broader curricular dilemmas—how does the concept of alternative assessment interact with some of the perennial curriculum conflicts that have plagued the field, concerns such as the equity, excellence, and standards dilemmas, or what knowledge is of most worth? In chapter 9, Sabrina King argues that good teaching in urban areas must be context specific and that good urban education is qualitatively different from good education generally defined. She suggests, therefore, that the assessment of teachers who plan to work in urban settings needs to be as specific and deliberate. Nancy Dubetz, Martha Erickson, and Steve Turley are three teacher educators who engage in a dialogue that raises and explores assessment dilemmas in relation to the preparation of teachers. In terms of alternative assessment and inclusion, they ask, "Is the academy practicing what it is preaching?" A. Lin Goodwin and Maritza Macdonald discuss the conditions necessary for authentic assessment and practice to occur. Their chapter describes the kinds of teacher behaviors and thinking that can support the success of culturally and linguistically diverse students. Finally, Asa Hilliard discusses the intersection of culture, language, and assessment and how this has affected the ways in which African-American children are perceived of as learners.

The book ends with a presentation of issues or barriers that need to be dealt with if we are to realize the aim of alternative assessment practices and meaningful evaluation. Beatrice Fennimore looks at the relationship between child centeredness, advocacy, and assessment in order to help educators understand how assessment can be an advocacy strategy. In chapter 14, Ana María Villegas discusses the impact of diversity on the development of Praxis III, the latest version of teacher assessments designed to qualitatively measure teaching ability and competence. In her chapter, Valerie Ooka Pang analyzes her own practice as a teacher educator committed to equity. She posits that teacher educators can use dialogue as a way of assessing teachers' dispositions toward diversity and critical issues surrounding race, gender, and class. Jennifer Robinson talks about parents in relation to new ideas of assessment. Her chapter explores parents' fears and discusses ways in which parents can be included in the discussion on assessment. Vito Perrone closes the book by asking, "Can we measure learning that means something?" In chapter 17, Perrone raises teacher, school, and pedagogical issues in order to articulate a larger, more complete conception of learning.

Dual themes that frame the entire volume are diversity and equity. As stated earlier, assessment practices have been used to sort and categorize students in an effort to render instructing them simpler. This has resulted in inequitable tracking whereby children of color are more likely to be placed in lower or nonacademic tracks and are more likely to receive a watered-down, skills-based curriculum. Invariably, standardized assessment practices have placed poor children and children of color in a cycle of failure and frustration. The authors in this volume present ways to interrupt this cycle by presenting assessment as an avenue whereby children who typically measure up poorly can be included rather than excluded. Assessment ought to be a tool for child-centered instruction so that the needs of each child can be defined and addressed. Assessment should be used to build communities of learners rather than to separate children into isolated groups. Thus the title of the volume, which depicts how assessment, equity, and inclusion are inextricably entwined.

Chapter One

THE HISTORICAL AND POLICY FOUNDATIONS OF THE ASSESSMENT MOVEMENT

George F. Madaus, Anastasia E. Raczek,

and Marguerite M. Clarke

Since the 1920s, multiple-choice, standardized, commercial tests have been widely used to measure the achievement of American students. Over the decades, despite vigorous criticism from some quarters, these tests have been widely regarded as administratively convenient, inexpensive tools that could help solve an array of educational problems (National Commission on Testing and Public Policy 1990). In the late 1980s, however, a powerful movement called authentic assessment emerged (e.g., Mitchell 1992; Newmann, Secada, and Wehlage 1995; Wiggins 1989), seriously challenging the supremacy of the institution of standardized multiple-choice testing.

This chapter explores the history of the evolution of measuring a person's academic attainment, from performance testing to oral and written examinations to multiple-choice testing, and, with current reform efforts, full circle back to performance appraisal.[1] Our analysis is primarily limited to the context of tests, examinations, or assessments—whatever the noun—used in the policy arena. Other chapters in this volume will consider the use of such tests in the classroom. Thus, while we would generally agree with the use of performance-based assessment by teachers for decision making within the context of their classrooms for either formative or summative purposes, we shall not explore this dimension of the assessment movement except to note that the in-service and preservice infrastructure necessary to train teachers to develop and use such assessments currently is problematic.

We begin with a short recent history of the reasons for the increasing use of standardized multiple-choice tests in education, beginning in the late 1950s. We then look at the etymology of several of the key words used in the current debate—standards, assessments, examinations, and tests. Next, we posit testing as a technology, then describe the concept of a test and the various modes that can be used to test an individual. We then proceed to a historical description of the various modes of testing student attainment used over the centuries and why they receded from use or were discarded in favor of other modes. Finally, we offer a tentative prediction on the fate of the assessment movement in the policy arena.

A caveat is in order. Until the end of the nineteenth century, tests were what we now call "achievement tests." They concentrated on attainment within a syllabus, curriculum, or craft. This tradition of measuring achievement/attainment is the sole focus of this chapter, although the advent of the psychological testing movement in the latter part of the nineteenth century altered testing—including achievement testing—profoundly. The changes in achievement testing arising from the mental testing movement are beyond the scope of this chapter. Suffice it to say that early proponents of mental testing claimed, and it was widely believed, that testing could do more than assess what people learned; it could now measure their underlying—some said innate—mental ability or intelligence. This belief has, from the beginning of this century to today, influenced how some people envision student achievement/attainment and the school's role in fostering it. The controversy engendered by Herrnstein and Murray's 1994 book *The Bell Curve* is a case in point.

RECENT HISTORY

Beginning in the late 1950s, four social forces combined to create a bull market for standardized testing (Haney, Madaus, and Lyons 1993). First was recurring public dissatisfaction with the quality of education and several concomitant waves of educational reform. Witness the Sputnik brouhaha of the 1950s, continuing with the basic skills movement of the 1970s, the release of the National Commission on Excellence in Education's *A Nation at Risk* in the 1980s, and, finally, the *Goals 2000: Educate America Act* in this decade. In each of these reform waves, testing was seen as an important policy tool. Second was an array of federal and state legislation promoting or explicitly mandating standardized testing programs, beginning with the National Defense Education Act of 1958. Third was a broad shift in attention, signaled by the famous Coleman report (Coleman et al. 1966), from evaluating the inputs or resources devoted to education to measuring the outputs or results operationalized by student test performance on available multiple-choice tests. Finally, increased bureaucratization of society in general, and of schooling in particular (Wise 1979), made the technology of multiple-choice, standardized, commercial tests an attractive tool. Tests provided a means for categorizing people, educational institutions, and problems according to abstract, impersonal, and generalizable rules and helped to expedite formal and impersonal administrative procedures. These four factors were intimately related one to the other; for example, public dissatisfaction with the quality of education produced legislation that in turn contributed to increased bureaucratization (for details see Haney, Madaus, and Lyons 1993).

While space does not permit a development of how these four social forces impacted on the testing industry, impact they did. Haney, Madaus, and Lyons (1993) estimated that, by the end of the 1980s, between three and nine standardized tests were administered annually to each of the nation's 44 million students. They also calculated that the nation invested between $311 million and $22.7 billion annually in state and local testing programs.[2] To put these amounts in perspective, total national expenditure on elementary and secondary education in 1987–88 was about $169.7 billion (U.S. Department of Education 1991a); Haney and associates' testing cost estimates range from 0.18 percent to 13 percent of that figure.

An indirect indicator, developed by Haney (1986), documents the increased attention over the decades to testing's importance in the educational realm (Haney, Madaus, and Lyons 1993). To show growth in the volume of testing over time, he charted the number of citations under the rubric "testing" (as indicated by the number of column inches) from 1930 through 1985 in the *Education Index*. For comparative purposes, and because he argued curriculum issues should

FIGURE 1.1: Education Index Listings Under Testing and Curriculum
Source: Haney, Madaus, and Lyons 1993; Madaus and Raczek 1995; Education Index, 1932–1994

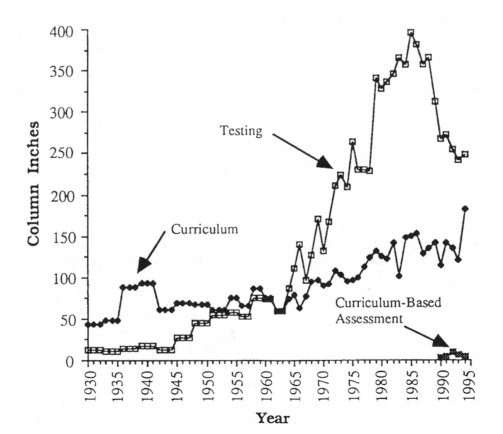

be a central focus of schooling, the number of citations under "curriculum" were also charted.[3] The Haney data shown in Figure 1.1 are updated through 1994.

Figure 1.1 shows that the average annual number of column inches devoted to citations concerning curriculum has increased only modestly over the last 62 years—from 50 to 100 inches per year in the 1930s and 1940s to 100 to 150 in recent years. In contrast, column inches devoted to tests and scales have increased greatly, from only 10 to 30 in the 1930s and 1940s to well over 300 in the 1980s. The past few years have seen a decline in the number of citations regarding testing; however, the new rubric "performance-based assessment" was added to the *Education Index* in 1992 to reflect prevailing testing terminology, and those citations are not included in our update. We do include data for "curriculum-based assessment," another category that was implemented in 1990. While these indices are admittedly crude, the data certainly highlight the prominence of testing in the education literature, particularly since the mid-1960s.

As noted above, the authentic (alternative) assessment movement emerged in the late 1980s. The seeds of this movement were sown in 1983, when Americans heard Orwellian news from the National Commission on Excellence in Education that the country was "a nation at risk" (the title of their explosive report). Since then, the public schools have been routinely portrayed as self-serving, mediocre, failing, inferior to those of competitor countries, injurious to students, and endangering our economic competitiveness and future as a world power. *A Nation at Risk* (1983) introduced the idea of testing as a major policy tool to combat these ills. Subsequently, there were several proposals for and, in one case, legislation authorizing a national testing scheme of one sort or another (e.g., Boyer 1983; Educate America 1991; Public Law 100-297; U.S. Department of Education 1984; U.S. Department of Education 1991a). By the end of the 1980s, some reports (e.g., Commission on the Skills of the American Workforce 1990; National Center on Education and the Economy 1989; Secretary's Commission on Achieving Necessary Skills 1992) recommended that new national performance standards, measured by performance-based examinations (performance assessments, portfolios, and projects), be developed.

Assessment has been contrasted with "more artificial testing approaches" that "do not measure the ability to think deeply, to create, or to perform in any field" (Darling-Hammond, Ancess, and Falk 1995: 3, 6). Proponents argue that alternative forms of assessment must replace or, at the very least, complement the multiple-choice mode if teachers are to help students develop the conceptual and analytical skills needed to solve everyday problems and to prepare them for future vocational success. (Interestingly, it is the multiple-choice item that is most widely employed in the external testing programs of Japan, our economic arch-rival, to whom we are often compared unfavorably by some advocates of authentic assessment.) Advocates offer a litany of benefits associated with such assessments (albeit without much in the way of supporting evidence): they can drive the reform movement built around world-class standards; they are worth teaching to; they give teachers clear models of acceptable outcomes; they defeat negative test-preparation effects associated with multiple-choice tests; they have a positive influence on instruction and learning; they measure higher order skills; they motivate unmotivated students; and, finally, they are more equitable for assessing the progress of students who differ in race, culture, native language, or gender.[4]

Thus, alternative assessment has been promoted for two very distinct functions: as a high-stakes policy tool to drive educational reform, and as a tool for improving classroom instruction. Underpinning the alternative assessment movement is the belief that student learning and progress are best assessed by tasks that require active engagement—such as producing extended responses or some other tangible product that can be evaluated on its merits, investigating complex problems, generating material for portfolios, performing exhibitions, or carrying out experiments—rather than by having students select an answer from several alternatives. In part, this approach to appraising student attainment reflects a shift from a transmissionist view of learning to a constructivist one (Garcia and Pearson 1994).

Our premise, however, is that while assessment can assist in reform efforts, the nation cannot assess, test, nor examine its way out of its educational problems. Claims that authentic assessment is a "technological breakthrough" in solving such problems need to be treated with a healthy skepticism.[5] While performance-based, high-stakes assessments may well be preferable to multiple-choice tests in terms of forcing teachers and students to pay attention to certain neglected aspects of the curriculum and learning, we nonetheless need to be clear that as a policy lever such assessments are a variation on the old theme of measurement-driven instruction (MDI) (Popham 1983); the principal difference is the form of the measures. And, it should be noted, in the context of MDI, performance-based measures are as corruptible as any multiple-choice measure (see Madaus and Greaney 1985). Finally, as we develop below, "authentic assessments" are not new, novel, nor innovative. They predate multiple-choice testing by centuries as standard forms of examining and assessing attainment or skills and historically have had problems associated with their use.

ETYMOLOGY OF KEY TERMS

Presently, advocates of educational reform prefer the term "assessment" to that of the traditional word "test" when talking about the process of determining student achievement. "Standards," often modified by "world-class," is also a cardinal term in the reformers' vocabulary (see Ravitch 1995). The Oxford English Dictionary (OED) (Oxford English Dictionary 1993) reveals interesting etymologies for these terms.

First, in the OED the word *standard* has four general meanings pertinent to reform dialogue. In its oldest meaning (circa 1154), a standard may be a figure or object used as an emblem or symbol of a person or a group of people. Standard may also mean a model or example commonly accepted or adhered to; that is, a criterion set for usage or practice. These two meanings are implied in talks about, and efforts to develop, "world-class standards"—in particular, in academic disciplines. For example, the National Council of Teachers of Mathematics (NCTM) standards have been widely accepted and held as an exemplar for other academic disciplines to follow in developing a framework for teaching and learning (in fact, one variant of the latter meaning for standard refers to the "books or documents accepted by a church as the authoritative statement of its creed" [OED 1993]. The NCTM standards are analogus to this latter meaning). The NCTM standards are also important in a symbolic sense; they are emblematic of how serious most math educators are about educational reform. However, the demise of the standards developed by the National Center for History in the Schools (1994), also known as the national history standards, vividly illustrates the thorny problem of who gets to decide what will comprise the standards—the accepted emblematic canon for a discipline.

Two more contemporary OED meanings for the word standard seem to fit recent uses of the word. Standard can mean a level of excellence or attainment regarded as a measure of adequacy. It can also refer to something established as a rule or basis of comparison in measuring quality or value. Both of these latter meanings are implied, it seems, when reformers and policy makers use the normative term "world-class standards" and operationalize them through tests, assessments, or examinations.

Similarly, the OED also offers the following British meaning (circa 1870s): "Each of the recognized degrees of proficiency, *as tested by examination,* according to which school children may be classified" (italics added). As this meaning makes clear, when curriculum standards (or frameworks) are operationalized through assessments, tests, or examinations, such performance—often with a pass/fail cut score—becomes the *de facto* standard.

Currently, the term "assessment," modified by the adjectives "new" or "authentic," is for many an approbation, while the term "standardized, norm-referenced, multiple-choice test" is greeted with intolerance and disdain. Assessment has captured the linguistic high ground much like minimum-competency testing did in the last decade. Nevertheless, the positive images assessment conveys mask the many functions it may be asked to perform and the attendant side effects. In the OED, the word "assessment," meaning estimation or evaluation, dates back to 1626. However, its first link to education in the OED didn't occur until 1956, when it was used in England in contradistinction to the more traditional term "examination." The first American usage linked to education in the OED is a 1985 citation to a *Washington Post* article that opines that "test scores and core curriculum are not the answers. . . . That is why individual assessments are necessary."[6] (Of course, the term "assessment" has been used widely in the U.S. since 1968 when it described the first federally funded test of a national sample of students—the National Assessment of Educational Progress.) In the OED, the term "test" is considered an Americanism. The first OED reference is a 1910 one to Binet-Simon and implies a "simpler, less formal procedure than an examination."

Examination is the oldest of the three terms and the preferred one in Europe (it was however, used in the nineteenth century in America, e.g., by Horace Mann). The first OED reference to an academic examination is this interesting one from 1612: "Which worke of continiall examination, is a notable quickner and nourisher of all good learning." Variations on this aphorism about the close connection that has always existed between teaching, examinations, and learning have appeared regularly down the centuries right through the measurement-driven instruction era of the 1970s and '80s.

There are subtle but interesting differences between OED definitions of the verbs examine, test, and assess. *Examine* implies an attempt to investigate, inquire, and probe, to understand and learn about what the student has attained. To *test* implies putting the students through an ordeal designed to reveal their attainment. To *assess* implies determining or fixing an amount, evaluating and judging student attainment. However, the way these three terms are actually used in the reform movement differs somewhat from the OED definitions. Current usage of the word "assessment" in the reform movement certainly encompasses evaluating or judging student attainment. But on closer reading, it seems many advocates of assessment are actually asking that we *examine* students for attainment. Further, whether advocates agree or not, most current proposals for assessment involve determining or fixing the amount of learning in order to make high-stakes accountability decisions.

WHAT IS AN ASSESSMENT/TEST/EXAMINATION?

Strip away the linguistic veneer; whatever noun you choose—assessment, examination, just plain test—they all encompass the same basic technology. This section describes that technology.

We begin answering the question, "What is an assessment/test/examination?" by asserting that whatever one calls it, the process is a technology and needs to be understood and evaluated as such. (For simplicity we shall use the term test in what follows.) Testing, embedded in our system of education, fits various definitions of technology (Madaus 1994, 1995a). Most simply, testing (like any technology) is something put together for a purpose, to satisfy a pressing and immediate need, or to solve a problem. But testing, like most modern technologies, also involves specialized arcane knowledge, hidden algorithms, and technical art, and like many current technologies is a complex of standardized means for attaining a predetermined end in social, economic, administrative, and educational institutions (Ellul 1990; Lowrance 1986; see also Basalla 1988; Boorstin 1978; Marx 1988; Staudenmaier 1985, 1989; Winner 1977, 1986 for further definitions of technology).

There are a number of reasons why it is important to think about testing as a technology, not the least of which is that it opens up new ways of evaluating testing based on an extensive literature from the fields of history and philosophy of technology. While exploring these rich connections is beyond the scope of this chapter, we will mention one important one (see Madaus 1993 for a more detailed evaluation of testing from the perspective of technology). The literature on technology reveals that all technology, including testing, is inextricably embedded in a moral context. Special technologies, such as the steam engine, the assembly line, electric power, the media (Lowrance 1986; Winner 1977, 1986), and testing (Foucault 1977; Winner 1977), have conferred power on those who control them. Moral and ethical issues associated with the use of this power inevitably arise. Kula (1986) has documented that historical attempts to make weights and measures equitable have failed without accompanying reforms in such things as feudal rights, provincial particularism, and equity before the law. Testing systems designed to make high-stakes decisions about individuals will produce unjust measures if we do not put into place corresponding reforms in social and educational delivery systems.

Available evidence clearly shows that many large, sophisticated technological systems are in fact highly compatible with centralized, hierarchical, managerial control (Winner 1986). And, as we saw above in our discussion of the growth of the testing industry, testing is no exception to this rule. Both standardized testing and authentic assessments used as instruments of public policy confer, on those who control them, real power over the actions of teachers, students, and administrators; real power over the curriculum; real power over what is taught and learned, and how material is taught and learned (Madaus 1985a, 1988, 1990; Madaus and Kellaghan 1992; Madaus and McDonagh 1979). Ellul argued that "technique comes with its own effects quite apart from how it is used" (1990: 35). Therefore, the nature of the effects and their consequences for schools, teachers, and pupils—particularly for those poorly served by the present system—need to be analyzed and evaluated carefully. Further, the seats of power associated with policy uses of testing need to be illuminated by historical and contemporary analysis in any attempt to craft an ethical and just system of test— or assessment-driven educational accountability.

Our values and social relations determine not only how tests are used but also the nature of the tests themselves. The entire test-development process—the domain we decide to measure, the cultural background and specialized training of test developers, the material chosen for inclusion, the design of the individual items, the language and idioms used, the directions given, the validation process, and so on—stacks the testing "deck" in favor of certain values and groups in our society and unintentionally assures that other values and groups are dealt a weaker hand.

The question remains, "What is a test?" Despite their extensive experience with tests—and precisely because they are so familiar and ubiquitous—many Americans, including many who regularly give and use tests in education, business, and the government, would be hard put to answer the question accurately. The technology of testing rests on three fundamental ideas: (1) test focuses on a particular domain of interest; (2) test is a sample of behavior, products, answers, or performance from the larger field of interest; and, (3) test permits the user to make inferences about the larger domain of interest and then, based on the inference, to describe or make decisions about the test taker and, after aggregation, about groups of test takers or institutions. Let us consider briefly each of these ideas.

A Test Focuses on a Particular Domain of Interest

A test is designed to measure or assess a particular body of knowledge, skills, abilities, or performances that are of interest to the test developer and eventual user. This area of interest is technically called the test domain or universe (we shall use the term "test domain" in what follows). A test domain should be defined so that a person can readily decide whether a particular aspect of knowledge, or a particular skill, task, ability, or performance, clearly falls within the domain. For example, a rather straightforward test domain might consist of fourth-grade arithmetic problems, which in turn might be divided into subdomains or facets, representing the basic operations of addition, subtraction, multiplication, and division. We might further specify any of the four facets. For example, we might limit the addition facet to problems involving three or fewer digits with no carrying. The four major subdomains could also be divided into numerical computational problems and word problems. Once we are satisfied with the domain specification, a test can be constructed to assess either the entire domain of fourth-grade arithmetic or some facet of it.[7]

The statement that a test is designed to measure or assess a domain of interest seems so obvious that one might ask, "Why bother even to mention it?" There are three reasons. First, the concept of a test domain is central to an understanding of the two remaining concepts embodied in a test as discussed below. Second, too often people fail to question whether the domain is the correct one, given the uses to which the test will be put. And third, there is an enduring, serious problem associated with the names given to some domains. Let us examine briefly these last two reasons.

At first blush, it seems a truism that people should question whether a given domain, and hence the test that represents it, is the correct one for their intended purposes. Nonetheless, too often an inappropriate domain is used. For example, consider the important domain of reading literacy needed for job performance. Reading is regarded as a basic job skill, and some employers use a standard, school-related, or academic basic-skills reading test to screen job applicants. However, there is research that shows that the pertinent domain for reading on the job may be different from the domain of reading necessary in schools, and that the ability of school-based reading tests to predict job performance varies enormously from job to job (Datta 1982; Stedman and Kaestle 1987). Thus, it is always important to question critically the appropriateness of a particular domain for a particular use.

The name given to a test domain is also critical, since the connotative power of the domain's name, and hence the test's name, can carry powerful cultural meanings that may mean quite different things to different people. The worrisome, intractable problem associated with a domain's name is that many people take the name literally. As a result, subsequent test performance takes on the entire generalized semantic, affective, evocative, connotative, emotional, rhetorical, and metaphorical baggage associated in people's minds with the name. Plus, naming a domain also affects attitudes about test use, sometimes at a profound level. For example, people generally resist the use of an "intelligence test" to retain children in kindergarten. However, when the same sort of test is called a "readiness" test, the practice becomes defensible and ultimately acceptable.

A Test Is a Sample of Performance from the Domain of Interest.

A test samples behavior, products, answers, or performance from the larger domain of interest. If one considers the domain of fourth-grade arithmetic, it becomes apparent that so many different problems or questions could be posed that students could never be asked to solve them all. Thus, a sample of problems is selected, representing the important parts of the domain, to constitute a test of the domain.

The items sampled from the domain are the basic building blocks of a test. Basically, there are two supra types of test items—selection and supply. Selection items require a person to choose an answer from a range of alternatives (e.g., the multiple-choice or true/false question) and involve recognition on the part of the examinee. Most standardized commercially available tests use selection questions, because they generally permit a larger sample of domain behavior than do supply questions, thus increasing the reliability of the test, and because they can be efficiently and cheaply scored by machine, thus facilitating the testing of large numbers of students.

Advocates of authentic assessment clearly eschew the selection modality in favor of supply-type tasks. Supply items involve production and can be presented in written or oral form. They require an examinee to: furnish an answer (e.g., the essay or short-answer question); produce a tangible product that can then be evaluated according to some preset criteria (e.g., the production of a piece of writing or a painting); generate material for portfolios; or perform certain physical acts like speaking, fixing a carburetor, conducting a chemistry experiment, singing, dancing, diving, and such, which are evaluated according to predefined criteria.

Both the supply and selection modalities of testing require agreement on what is to be valued in a student's response (Myford and Mislevy 1994). In the selection mode however, these judgments of what response is to be valued are built into the test *before* the student ever sees the test. "The objectivity of 'objective tests' refers simply to the virtually uncontested agreement among observers as to whether, under pre-specified testing conditions, a student marks predetermined correct options (: 1)."

In the supply mode, on the other hand, a student's response generally is not simply and unambiguously classified as right or wrong (although this does happen in the case of fill-in-the-blank or computational items). Instead, judgments are made about the quality and appropriateness of the performance *after* the fact. In authentic assessment used in summative decisions, therefore, it is "essential to establish a common framework of meaning among judges—shared standards for recognizing what is important in performance and mapping it into a summarizing structure" (Myford and Mislevy 1994: 1). Finally, it is essential that teachers, who often also act as the judges of the targeted performance, know and understand the framework of meaning—that is, the criteria used to evaluate the performance. Students should also understand the criteria used.

A Test Is Used to Make Inferences About the Larger Domain of Interest

Implicit in what has gone before is the concept that it is the domain, not the test, that should be of interest in any testing situation. An examinee's performance on the particular small sample of items drawn from the domain—the test—is of interest only insofar as it permits the user to make a more general inference about an examinee's performance relative to the entire domain.[8] And, based on the inference, the test user describes and/or makes a decision about a test taker or group of test takers. The appropriateness or correctness of an inference about a person's performance relative to a domain made on the basis of test performance is called *test validity* and is the central, and most important, concept in testing.[9]

FASHIONS IN TESTING: FROM SUPPLY TO SELECTION, BACK TO SUPPLY

Ecclesiastes' moral, "What has been is what will be, and what has been done is what will be done; and there is nothing new under the sun" certainly subsumes the technology of testing.[10] Every modern technology has ancestors, and the ancestry of testing is one of the oldest. In this section, we shall consider this ancestry in China, then in Western Europe, and finally in the United States.

The establishment in 210 BC of the Chinese system of civil-service examinations is the first example of testing employed as a national administrative technique.[11] The Han dynasty, faced with the need to consolidate government, lessen patronage, and select men of merit for government office at all levels, designed a series of extremely competitive tests along with standardized procedures for administering and scoring (Loewe 1986). While the predominate mode of testing was through a series of written essay questions and the production of poetry (Chaffee 1985), Cheng claims that "the true-false, the ingenuity test, the picture-completion test, the verbal question test, all have fore-runners" in the Chinese system (quoted in Thorndike and Lohman 1990: 1).

Two experiences from China—more than 900 years apart—with external examination systems are worth recounting. First, Fan Zhong Yan in 1043 pointed to the negative effects of the civil-service examinations on imagination and on the pursuit of studies of practical utility because these characteristics were not assessed by the examinations (Little 1993). While the civil-service exam system lasted until the beginning of this century, it failed in the end because the civil servants were unable to deal with practical issues of Western technology and modernization (Kracke 1963; Nivison 1963). The second experience, in 1977, relates to the then newly introduced tertiary entrance-examination system whose disadvantages quickly became apparent. The examination was found to dominate teaching and learning activities in Chinese secondary schools at the expense of things not examined (Meng 1993). Both stories illustrate the enduring historical fact, noted above, that teachers and students attend to those topics most likely to appear in important examinations.

In Europe, the medieval guilds examined apprentices by having them supply a relevant product as final proof of competence. The Waterford apprentice bowl is a contemporary example of this process: in this piece, apprentice glass cutters produce each cut in the Waterford crystal repertoire. In medieval universities, the *viva voce*, or oral disputation, was the testing design of choice. The apprentice scholar demonstrated his mastery of a traditional form of rhetoric by responding to a set of previously known questions. The student's "ability to remember . . . knowledge [and] present it in eloquent form, and a tacit conformity to orthodoxy, educational and social" were qualitatively evaluated by the masters (Hoskins 1968: 68). There was face-to-face interaction between judge and judged. Passing the exam meant that the judge approved of the performance, and the examinee was included within the community that the judge had been authorized to represent (Staudenmaier 1989).

In 1444, students in Treviso, Italy, were primarily the children of merchants, who wanted to ensure that their children could carry on the family business. The town fathers, therefore, fixed the schoolmaster's salary according to the primary students' level of attainment in a *viva voce* examination on the grammar curriculum of that day (Aries 1962). This use of oral supply-type testing is the first Western example of holding teachers accountable by student test scores. This practice came to be called *payment by results* (PBR). PBR, based on the interesting belief that all students can learn if properly taught (Madaus and Kellaghan 1992), emerged again in the eighteenth century in Ireland (Burton 1979); in the nineteenth century in Australia (Hearn 1872), England (Bowler 1983; Montgomery 1967; Sutherland 1973), Ireland (Madaus 1979; Rapple 1992), and Jamaica (Gordon 1968); and in the twentieth century in the United States: with performance contracting in the 1960s (Levine 1971), attempts to link merit pay to student test performance in the '80s (Lerner 1981; Shanker 1986), and privatization schemes in the '90s (e.g., Educational Commission of the States and National Education Goals Panel [ECS/NEGP] 1995a, 1995c, 1995d).

From the sixteenth century well into the twentieth century, the most widely used form of oral examination in Europe by far was the catechism. Luther, and subsequently Canisius and Bellarmine, examined children with oral questions—known in advance—to ensure the transmission of religious orthodoxy; answers were evaluated as factually right or wrong. The Protestant Reformation, and the subsequent Counter Reformation, perhaps mark the beginning of a general interest in schooling for young children, and the catechism may be the first *widespread* use of a formal technique to evaluate a child's attainment of a fixed body of knowledge (Tynan 1985).

The next important development in European testing was the emergence of the written exam.[12] Written exams were found in the fourteenth century, and in Jesuit schools in the sixteenth century (Farrell 1938; Perreiah 1984), but it wasn't until the latter part of the eighteenth century, when paper was more readily available, that they were systematically introduced in European schools. Foucault argues that the introduction of the written examination marks "the beginning of a pedagogy that functions as a science," since the exam defines what is expected and forces students to reveal periodically how their learning is progressing (Foucault 1977: 187). An impetus for the switch from the oral to the more readily *standardized* and more *efficient* written mode of testing was the need at Cambridge and Oxford to examine attainment in mathematics (Hoskins 1968; Montgomery 1967; Wiseman 1961).

The late eighteenth century saw another important technical development in testing that marked the first step in the development of the field of psychometrics as we know it today: William Farish's innovation of assigning *quantitative marks* i.e., a number) to performance across the oral disputation and written portions of the university examination. The shift to a quantitative mark for "correct" answers that were aggregated to arrive at an individual's overall score permitted the seemingly more "objective" ranking of examinees. It also allowed for such scores to be averaged and aggregated across individuals (Hoskins 1968; Madaus and Kellaghan 1992).

The written examination was not unknown in the United States. In 1845, Horace Mann supplanted the oral exam in the Boston public schools by the written essay exam. Mann recognized that a written examination allowed examiners to pose an identical set of questions simultaneously, under similar conditions, in much less time, to a rapidly expanding student body, thereby producing comparable scores (Madaus 1990).

Like many policy-makers down the decades, Mann also had a political motive in introducing the written exam. In his attempt to abolish corporal punishment, Mann and his confidant Samuel Gridely Howe recognized that school-by-school test results gave them political leverage over recalcitrant headmasters. In a letter, Mann told Howe that:

> Some pieces should be immediately written for the papers, containing so much of an analysis of the answers, as will show that the pupils answered common and [memory] questions far better than they did questions involving a principle; and it should be set forth most pointedly, that in the former case, the merit belongs to the scholars, in the latter the demerit belongs to the master. All those abominable blunders . . . [in] orthography, punctuation, capitalizing and grammar are the direct result of imperfect teaching. Children will not learn such things by instinct. They will not fail to learn them, under proper instruction. . . . One very important and pervading fact in proof of this view of the case, is the great

difference existing between schools, on the same subject, showing that children could learn, if teachers had taught. (Massachusetts Historical Society Documents 1845)

The political and policy ideas in this letter are distinctly contemporary: publishing school-by-school results in the newspaper; holding teachers and administrators accountable for poor results; and distinguishing between lower- and higher-order thinking skills in the curriculum and examinations.

Mann's use of testing as a political and administrative technique needs to be viewed in conjunction with a larger social movement of that time: industrial capitalism's developing commitment to standardization, uniformity, precision, clarity, quantification, and rational tactics (Staudenmaier 1985, 1988, 1989; see also Madaus 1993 for a discussion of this development in technology). The overt link between commerce and education, however, has much older roots. It may be traced to the sixteenth century, when the foundation of the factory model of schooling was laid by Peter Ramus (1515–1572) and his followers. He introduced an approach to education that had as its controlling concept a method described as a kind of intellectual commercialism—knowledge was pursued as a commodity rather than as a path to wisdom (Ong 1971). The Ramist curriculum was built around the knowledge and skills congenial to the artists' and burghers' commercial merchandising views (Ong 1971). It was, after all, the commercial class who hired schoolmasters to educate their children (Aries 1962). The Ramists' "method" regarded knowledge in terms of "intake" and "output" and "consumption"—"terms which were not familiar to the commercial world in Ramus' day. . . . but which [did] refer to realities present within that world" (Ong 1971: 173–74).

The link between commerce and education grew stronger in the nineteenth century. For example, consider Karl Marx's criticism of Dr. Kay's pamphlet *Recent Measures for the Promotion of Education in England.* Kay's thesis—one reminiscent of present educational arguments—was that all social ills are attributable to neglected education and that schools should serve as propagators of business culture. Here is Marx's description of the Kay argument:

> From lack of education the worker fails to comprehend the "*natural laws of commerce,*" laws which *necessarily* lead him to pauperism. Hence he resists. This can only "*disturb* the *prosperity* of English manufacturers and English commerce, shake the mutual confidence of businessmen, *diminish* the *stability* of political and social institutions." (Marx 1967: 343; emphasis in original)

In nineteenth-century America, the expansion of public education was related in part to industry's need for literate workers and the desire to teach punctuality, regular attendance, and other useful job-related attitudes (Parenti 1978), and the factory metaphor for schools was greatly admired. Tyack describes its use: "Like the manager of a cotton mill, the superintendent of schools could supervise employees, keep the enterprise technically up to date, and monitor the uniformity and quality of the product" (Tyack 1974: 41). The factory model, with its techniques of conformity and dressage "by location, confinement, surveillance, the perpetual supervision of behavior and tasks" (Kritzman 1990: 107), came to be held in high esteem by educators well into the twentieth century; indeed, versions of it are still used (e.g., Doyle 1991). And the written test became an important technique for superintendents to monitor output and hold students and educators accountable.

The short-answer and the multiple-choice modes[13] gained prominence early in this century: partly in response to their administrative convenience; partly in response to classic studies showing that the marks assigned to essay questions were highly subjective and hence unreliable (Starch and Elliot 1912, 1913); and partly in response to the growth of the scientific management movement's application to education, which required that growing numbers of children be tested to measure a district's efficiency (Callaghan 1962).

In 1917 Otis developed a group-administered IQ test, the Army Alpha. His innovation was spurred by the fact that the sheer number of examinees that needed to be tested—almost 2 million recruits—demanded a more efficient, manageable, easily scored, and easily recorded technology than that offered by the Binet, which had to be individually administered, scored, and interpreted by a trained psychologist (Sokal 1987). This supply technology was quickly adapted to achievement tests immediately after the war and helped give commercial testing a foothold in the publishing industry.

In 1926 the College Entrance Examination Board adopted the multiple-choice format, and in 1937 it dropped the writing component of the SAT partly because of the *cost* of scoring (Angoff and Dyer 1971). In 1955, Lindquist's invention of the high-speed optical scanner, coupled with the multiple-choice item format, made it economically feasible to mount the large-scale district and state multiple-choice testing programs of the '60s, '70s, and '80s (Baker 1971).

More recently, in 1992 the Graduate Record Examination Board announced that they would offer a new computerized Graduate Record Examination (GRE), overcoming the problem of being able to offer only a limited number of fixed-date, large-scale administrations. The chairman of the GRE Board, Gene Woodruff, opined that this new computer-adaptive testing is more efficient, allowing better measurement in less time (Woodruff 1992).[14]

These changes in assessment technology over the last two centuries were all geared in one way or another to increasing efficiency, and, as the numbers of examinees increased, making the assessment system more manageable, standardized, easily administered, objective, reliable, comparable, and inexpensive. In the United States such changes led to the streamlined, machine-scorable, standardized multiple-choice test as the technology of choice for policy makers. (And computer-adaptive testing holds the promise of eventually making that technology even more efficient.)

As noted above, the multiple-choice format is now viewed by many reformers as impeding the reform process.[15] The advent of the authentic assessment movement brings us full circle in the evolution of the testing mode used to implement public policy. We also noted above the putative claims made about the benefits associated with the adoption of authentic assessment. However, such claims are circular: they presume what is to be proven. The historical perspective on modes of testing and why changes came about is a cautionary tale. It should make educators and policy makers "think more deeply, more completely and on the basis of an enormously enlarged experience about what it may be possible or desirable to do now . . . [and it] should arm [people] against surrendering to the panaceas peddled by too many myth makers" (Elton 1991: 72–73). Let us examine more closely the implications of this latest development in the technology the nation chooses to use to test, assess, or examine student attainment.

WHITHER ASSESSMENT AS A TOOL IN EDUCATIONAL POLICY?

Advocates of reestablishing the older supply-type assessment modes as a policy tool have ignored a number of features of this technology that historically were viewed as seriously problematic. Likewise, they have ignored contrary contemporary evidence from Great Britain's implementing its national curriculum and associated high-stakes assessments (see Madaus and Kellaghan 1993; Nuttall 1992; Nuttall and Stobart 1994). Five issues emerge from a historical and contemporary review. First, the performance/supply mode is more inefficient, difficult to administer, time consuming, and disruptive to school organization and routine (Madaus and Kellaghan, 1993). Second, it is not as easily standardized in terms of support for a school's teachers who are administering assessments and the actual administration itself, leading to a lack of comparability of results (Madaus and Kellaghan 1993). Third, it samples a considerably smaller portion of pupil performance, thus raising questions about the generalizability of results to the larger domain of interest (see Dunbar, Koretz, and Hoover 1991; Gao, Shavelson, and Baxter 1994; Koretz, Linn, Dunbar, and Shepard 1991; Koretz, Stecher, Klein, and McCaffrey 1994; Nuttall 1992; Shavelson, Baxter, and Gao 1993; Shavelson, Baxter, and Pine 1992). Fourth, it is by its very nature considerably more costly (for contemporary cost figures see Koretz, Madaus, Haertel, and Beaton 1992; Madaus and Kellaghan 1991a, 1991b, 1993). Finally, some critics point out that the lack of norms for performance assessment tasks is a serious drawback. For example, *The Daily Report Card*, published by the Educational Commission of the States and the National Education Goals Panel, reported in March 1995 that Georgia state legislators are moving closer to removing the current curriculum-based state assessment and replacing it with a norm-referenced test. The decision marks a departure from the national trend to improve schools by measuring student achievement against objective standards rather than general norms (ECS/NEGP 1995b). These historical, practical, technical, and cost issues cast a wintery prognosis over the feasibility—however desirable—of deploying a predominantly performance assessment-oriented national or statewide testing system to make high-stakes decisions about large numbers of individual students (e.g., all fourth graders).

There are other potential pitfalls overlooked by those proposing a national testing system. There is the complex issue of what gets measured. While there is a consensus in some curriculum areas about what students should know or be able to do in a broad sense (e.g., the NCTM standards), there is, nonetheless, great disagreement in many other areas of the curriculum (such as history, social studies, arts, literature, and aspects of science) about what is important, what is permitted, what is taboo—in short, disagreement about what should comprise the canon in a given discipline and who gets to decide (Madaus 1995b). How do we reach an accord in these value-laden curricular areas—and should we? These are nontrivial questions facing the assessment movement, since the issue of what is included in the canon can become victim to the current cultural civil war between what Connolly (1993) describes as the forces of pluralism and fundamentalism.

According to Connolly, pluralism may be broadly defined as a way of looking at the world so as to embrace divergent viewpoints and sectors in society. Pluralists are sometimes labeled liberals or multiculturalists. Pluralists are dissatisfied with "the dominance of the white Anglo-Saxon perspective in the academy" (Piore 1995: 44). An example of a pluralist position can be seen in the 1991 report of the Social Studies Syllabus Review Committee in New York State in which the authors argued that "the main objective of public education should be the protection, strengthening, celebration and perpetuation of ethnic origins and identities"; that "previous ideals of assimilation" should be put aside; and that the curriculum should highlight instead "the racial and ethnic pluralism of the nation" (Piore 1995: 47).

We use the term "fundamentalism" in Connolly's sense, which is broader than the more popular conception of religious fundamentalism. Fundamentalists hold a worldview more exclusive in terms of what they include in their version of a healthy society; fundamentalists are boundary setters. "Conservative" is a label often used to categorize people in this camp, who may be further divided into "moral" and/or "fiscal" conservatives (Edsall 1995). As opponents of cultural pluralism, many fundamentalists feel that the role of the curriculum is to maintain national unity: "the single (and Eurocentric) interpretation of history creates the nation" (Piore 1995: 47). The fundamentalist response to the 1991 Social Studies Syllabus Review Committee report, foreshadowing attacks on the U.S. history standards, was that "the report 'reverses the historic *theory* of America' not the historic facts"; (47–48; emphasis added). And one fundamentalist critic asserted that a "viable nation has to have a common culture to survive in peace" (47). Mutual understanding is unlikely or nearly impossible between the forces of pure pluralism and pure fundamentalism. Conflict is inevitable and it threatens the movement toward national content standards and authentic assessment geared to these standards.

The debate over the history standards is a classic example of the cultural divide between the forces of pluralism and fundamentalism. Initially, establishing content standards seemed relatively straightforward. Experts in the various disciplines would develop national standards for what students should know and be able to do at key points in their schooling. Problems soon arose, however, in value-laden curricular areas such as history and English. Controversy raged over what and whose knowledge was of most worth and should be included in the curriculum. It was this ideological, rather than technical or educational, battle that was at the center of the history standards debacle (Pyne 1995).

In late October 1994, the UCLA National Center for History in the Schools released voluntary standards for the study of American and world history for elementary, middle-, and high-school students. A wave of negative reaction followed, spearheaded by Lynne Cheney, who focused on what she perceived as the excessive inclusiveness and anti-Western bias in both the U.S. and world history standards. She argued that this bias supposedly created an untrue, but politically correct, version of history (Cheney 1994). Cheney's negative review received exceptionally wide exposure because, when chairwoman of the National Endowment for the Humanities (NEH), she lobbied for history standards, funded the project, and selected its leaders.

Cheney's attacks were answered by a number of apologists, whose views were summed up by Nash, the primary defender of the beleaguered standards. Some pointed out that the project's "inclusiveness" was a positive factor with a good balance between women, minorities, and white males (see Henderson 1994). Others argued that the standards did not make judgments but posed a limitless number of provocative themes (Gugliotta 1994). Still others claimed that the standards did not fail—as critics charged—to include the great people, events, and accomplishments that have traditionally been a central part of U.S. history in the schools (Nash and Crabtree 1994). The negative arguments, however, won the day when, on January 20, 1995, the Senate voted 99 to 1 to reject the history standards.

Toward the end of February 1995, a counterinitiative to the UCLA history standards emerged. The conservative Family Research Council (FRC) released its own vision of what American children should know about U.S. history—a vision that appealed ideologically to conservative groups and individuals like Cheney. Also around this time, more articles analyzing the motives of the antistandards camp began to appear (e.g. Rich 1995; Wiener 1995a). It was argued that Cheney and the congressional conservatives, who denounced the history standards and the NEH, were actually guilty of trying to dictate to teachers "a patriotically correct version of our nation's past" (Wiener 1995b). Defenders pointed out that, on the one hand, Cheney and the standards' critics argued against government involvement in the standards while, on the other, they wanted to dictate what kind of history is considered patriotic enough to be taught in schools. As late as July 1995, however, a different charge—this time of antiscience and antitechnology—was leveled against the history standards (Park 1995). The neglect of science in the standards (except in a section that lists professions from which women have been systematically excluded) is, according to Park, a reflection of what he perceives as the postmodern, antiscience stance of the authors of the standards' documents.

The ideological battle over who and what should be included in the history standards had repercussions in other subject areas (Diegmueller 1995). In December 1994, the U.S. Department of Education dropped its plans to fund a new English/language-arts project—another area of potential ideological controversy. Prior to this, the department had refused to continue funding the initial English/language-arts project, claiming the draft standards were vague and dwelt too much on opportunity-to-learn standards.

Another contemporary example of the tension between pluralism and fundamentalism in deciding what gets measured comes from Albert Shanker (1993). He points out that the ultraright has already successfully blocked or altered some outcome-based education (OBE) legislation because of concerns about the proposed outcomes. (Outcome-based education programs are those whose educational success is determined by looking at student performance on indicators of various kinds, e.g., achievement, truancy, dropout rates.) Outcome- or performance-based education is currently under attack in Pennsylvania, Kentucky, Virginia, Alabama, and California by parents concerned that the movement incorporates values antithetical to their beliefs (Asimov 1994d). Such sentiments are exemplified by the words of the leader of one Texas-based parents organization; "I don't know if you can link [OBE] with communism, but there is a thread there" (ECS/NEGP 1995e).

Another potential pitfall, even if there is agreement on the content to be measured, is that specific assessments designed to measure content are not immune from the tension between pluralism and fundamentalism. Consider the power of Christian conservatives, who lobbied successfully to change the tenth-grade California Learning Assessment System (CLAS) English test by having a question removed that concerned the Alice Walker story *Roselily*, which conservative Christian critics saw as antireligious. Also stricken from the test were instructions asking students to express their feelings about stories they read on the test. A representative of the Traditional Values Coalition (TVC) successfully argued that it was not the role of the school to test children on their feelings (Asimov 1994a). The other side of the pluralistic/fundamentalist conflict is illustrated by the reaction to the TVC of twenty-five teachers, members of the English/Language Arts CLAS development team who, in a letter to the editor of the *San Francisco Chronicle*, opined that the expunged works "epitomize the high quality literature we hope to bring to our assessment of California's diverse students" (Letters to the Editor 1994: A22). The TVC and CLAS development team views are diametrically opposed to one another.

But it was not just the Christian right that was offended. Another Walker story, *Am I Blue*, was rejected from CLAS on the grounds that it was "anti-meat-eating" and also because tenth graders should not be asked to comment on the fact that animals have to be killed to put meat on the table (Asimov 1994b; Editorial 1994). Still another essay by Annie Dillard, *An American Childhood*, about a snowball fight, described as a "charming and delightful reminiscence," was purged from the eighth-grade test as too violent for children to contemplate (Asimov 1994c; Editorial 1994). Once we get beyond the National Council of Teachers of Mathematics Standards, we can expect controversy over the content of questions or exercises used to assess attainment relative to whatever standards emerge.

A third potential pitfall revolves around whether the testing industry will be able to service the needs of those wishing to construct a state/national high-stakes exam system within reasonable cost frameworks. The industry is relatively inexperienced with performance, portfolio, and product assessments (the 3Ps), and, even more importantly, is used to making its profit from the sale of answer sheets and scoring services—a "Give 'em the razor, sell 'em the blades" business approach (Lyman 1989). Further, it is not clear whether testing companies now have the size and capabilities to develop, score, and report on a national testing program that involves census testing (that is, testing all students at a given level) using the performance and product modes and at various grades. This would be a massive undertaking, one that dwarfs the United Kingdom's effort to assess the national curriculum using "authentic/new" assessments.

A fourth problem area relates to how we provide an infrastructure for teacher preparation around alternative assessments if they are to be used in high-stakes situations. (Needless to say, such an infrastructure is even more crucial if we hope to reap the benefits ascribed to using alternative forms of assessment by teachers for decision making within the context of their classrooms.) Teachers are key to the successful implementation of any testing system. A 1993 poll for the Ford Foundation revealed that teachers are well aware of the proposals for federal or state outcome-based accountability systems. The poll showed that most teachers (more than 70 percent of those polled) believed the new approach will make their school more accountable for the outcomes of their teaching. A large majority, however, also believed that the new reforms will "end up by rewarding school districts which figure out how to get their students to test well, but not necessarily to learn more" (Harris and Wagner 1993: 27). Most of the teachers were skeptical about the standards and assessment agenda helping either the educational process, themselves, or their students.

These survey data reveal the need for substantial in-service training for teachers. However, in-service training around assessment issues currently leaves a lot to be desired in most districts. We need to consider a series of questions including: How can we equip current teachers with the skills they will need to deal with a high-stakes "authentic" assessment system and the instructional issues surrounding it? Who will do the in-service training? What will the content of such courses include? When will it be done? and who will pay for it? How will we handle inservice in large, medium, small, urban, rural, rich, and poor districts? The problems are equally daunting at the preservice level. How do we integrate the assessments, as well as the content and behaviors measured by them, into teacher-preparation institutions so that the next generation of teachers will be comfortable with assessment demands? Are current testing/measurement/assessment textbooks appropriate for such training? How can current education and arts faculty be trained to incorporate the issue of standards and assessments into preservice curricula?

On the positive side, changes in testing's technology should point us in a different, more fruitful direction. That is, these practical limitations and potential pitfalls should make us rethink how we conceive of and design a politically unavoidable, absolutely necessary, state/national educational accountability policy. We need to consider how matrix-sampling techniques, and other survey and reporting technologies developed by the National Assessment of Educational Progress, might allow us to use the 3Ps efficiently. This approach to accountability could supply policy makers with rich information about school and district performance without the downsides associated with census testing.

If the use of census testing is unavoidable, then we should look more closely at how such exams are handled in European countries, where there is considerable variation in policies. In Europe, examinations set by the government or some sanctioned external examination body generally are given at ages 16+ and 18+ for certification and admission decisions; external exams are not given in the primary grades as has been proposed in this country.[16] European countries offer exams across a wider range of subject offerings—thirty or more—than do U.S. reform proposals. European countries predominantly use the essay mode with some multiple-choice exams, not the "new" assessments proposed in this country. In Europe, social, family, health, and educational delivery systems make for a much more level playing field than is the case in this country (Madaus and Kellaghan 1991a, 1991b). Recently, the American Federation of Teachers (AFT) called for a common national curriculum and a national examination for all high-school students, arguing that American students do less well than those in Europe because they lack clear goals (West 1995). The AFT claims that national academic guidelines and tests in France, Germany, and Scotland motivate students to work hard and meet high standards. Proposals like this may indeed have merit, but they must be carefully evaluated in terms of European cultural and contextual issues, which are quite different from those here. They also need to be carefully scrutinized in terms of benefits ascribed to the programs, such as their motivational power (see Kellaghan, Madaus, and Raczek 1995 for a discussion of motivational issues in testing).

CONCLUSION

As we argued above, testing, assessment, or whatever noun you use to describe measuring student attainment, is a technology. Like other successful and almost indispensably useful technologies, testing is accepted and taken for granted as one solution to perceived educational problems. Nonetheless, perhaps the "central problem of technology—is how to come to terms with solutions" (Boorstin

1978: 39). While the application of the assessment technology can solve problems, it also creates them. One scholar of technology puts it this way: "Americans [need to realize] that not only their remarkable achievements but many of their deep and persistent problems arise, in the name of order, system, and control, from the mechanization and systematization of life and from the sacrifice of the organic and spontaneous" (Hughes 1989: 4). And Daniel Boorstin (1961) counsels us to be "suspicious of all mass medicines for national malaise. . . . The bigger the committee, the more 'representative' its membership, the more collaborative its work, the less the chance that it will do more than ease or disguise our symptoms" (iv).

The idea that any testing technique—be it a new test design or a national test or system—can reform our schools and restore our nation's competitiveness is the height of technological arrogance and conceals many of the negative possibilities of such a move under the guise of a seemingly neat technological fix. Thus, it is important that we submit generalized negative claims about public schools and accompanying proposals to reform them—such as alternative assessments—to a relentless, thorough examination. We need to treat critics' fixed beliefs and unexamined ideological response to reform as hypotheses to be tested. Until then, our schools will continue to be the object of facile cures and fiddling reformism.

NOTES

The authors gratefully acknowledge support for this work from the Ford Foundation (Grant 910-1205-2).

1. Material for this chapter was drawn, in part, from previous works by one of the authors. See Madaus 1993; Madaus and Tan 1993; Haney, Madaus, and Lyons 1993.
2. There is obviously a huge range in these low and high estimates. The primary reason for the difference is because the costs of student and teacher time devoted to test preparation are included in the high estimate. See Haney, Madaus, and Lyons 1993 for more information.
3. Figure 1.1 was constructed by measuring the number of column inches devoted to lines concerning testing and curriculum in every volume of the *Index* from 1932 through 1994. Over these volumes there were some changes in the index rubrics concerning testing and curriculum. See Madaus and Raczek 1995, and Haney, Madaus, and Lyons 1993 for details.
4. For claims about the value of authentic assessment, see, for example: Boykoff-Baron 1990; Commission on the Skills of the American Workforce, Educational Leadership 1992; FairTest 1992; Garcia and Pearson 1994; Grace and Shores 1992; Guay 1991; Herman, Aschbacher, and Winters 1992; LeMahieu 1992 (personal communication, December 23, 1992); Mitchell 1992; National Council on Education Standards and Testing 1992; Newmann 1991; Popham 1993;

Resnick 1991; Wiggins 1989, 1990, 1993; Wolf 1992. For an analysis of the claims about the motivation and equity see Kellaghan, Madaus, and Raczek (1995); and Madaus, Raczeck, and Thomas 1996.

5. We agree with John Kenneth Galbraith's argument that we make a serious error "in undue generalizations as to the quality of American education" (Galbraith 1992: 181). We do have some very real and serious educational problems. But those problems are, by and large, *particular*, not *general*, circumscribed, and specific to certain groups of students—the poor, inner-city children, cultural and linguistic minorities, immigrants, and, in many cases, the non-college-bound.

6. In the OED, under the rubric *assessment board, centre* is an interesting 1948 reference to the book *Assessment of Men*, an interesting, unfortunately long out-of-print book that described the training and selection of candidates during World War II for the Office of Strategic Services (OSS), the predecessor to the CIA. The assessment situations used to select spies to be dropped behind enemy lines are fascinating. The training and selection described in the book were earlier depicted in the 1946 semidocumentary movie *13 Rue Madeleine*, starring James Cagney.

7. Test domains, of course, are not limited to academic achievement or curricular areas. A test domain might focus on such things as job-related skills for a particular occupation, or on one of a wide range of more abstract traits such as "intelligence," "motivation," "honesty," teacher "competence," "functional literacy," musical "aptitude," mathematics "problem solving ability," reading "comprehension ability," visual "memory," "self-esteem," "psychopathic deviation," and spatial "ability." Many tests used in education, psychology, medicine, business, government, and the military purport to measure these and a multitude of other abstract domains technically called constructs.

8. Sometimes, inferences may also be made about a domain other than the one covered by test items. For example, the SAT—composed of items designed to tap verbal and mathematics skills—is often used to predict (make inferences about) future college performance.

9. Volumes have been written about test validity and test validation. Basically, test validity refers to the degree to which a particular inference, and any resultant description or decision about an individual, group, or institution, made on the basis of test performance, is appropriate or meaningful. According to the 1985 Standards for Educational and Psychological Testing developed by the American Educational Research Association, the American Psychological Association, and the National Council on Measurement in Education, "Validity is the most important consideration in test evaluation. The concept refers to the appropriateness, meaningfulness, and usefulness of the specific inferences made from test scores."

10. This quote from Ecclesiastes was used by Henry Petroski (1990) in describing the development of the technology of the pencil. Petroski observed that while every technology has unique aspects in its development, there is nonetheless a sameness in how they all evolve, and this sameness is captured in verse nine of Ecclesiastes.

11. Jesuits brought the idea of the Chinese technique back to France, influencing the development of the French civil-service exam system on which our own was modeled (Webber 1989).

12. China, where paper was invented, had written exams from the beginning of its civil-service testing.

13. Samelson (1987) names Frederick Kelley the inventor of the multiple-choice item in 1914. However, Thorndike and Lohman (1990) credit the Chinese with the development and use of the selection/multiple-choice item type.

14. This latest move to efficiency via new technology is not without its problems. For example, we need more information on the differential validity of computer-administered exams; it is not a simple transformation from one mode to another (see Madaus 1985b for a discussion of issues involved with the use of computers in testing). Computer administration also requires a change in traditional test-taking strategy—no longer can an examinee go back and change an answer, or skip an item considered difficult and return to it later. Also, employees of Stanley Kaplan—the largest test preparation company in the U.S.—who took the computerized adaptive version of the GRE have charged that they were able to memorize most of the items (Schrof and Pollack 1995), which certainly facilitates the job of test preparation companies.

15. The evidence supports this view; there is little doubt that the high-stakes multiple-choice testing programs of the 1970s and 1980s have had an overall deleterious effect on teaching and learning (Darling-Hammond 1991; Jaeger 1991; Lomax, West, Harmon, Viator, and Madaus 1992; McLauglin 1991; Shepard 1991; Stake 1991).

16. England and Wales are the sole exceptions to this general rule. See Nuttall 1992; Nuttall and Stobart 1994; and Madaus and Kellaghan 1993 for a discussion of the British Standard Assessment Tasks given at age seven.

REFERENCES

American Educational Research Association, American Psychological Association, and National Council on Measurement and Education (1985). *Standards for educational and psychological testing.* Washington, DC: American Psychological Association.

Angoff, W. H., and H. S. Dyer (1971). The admissions testing program. In W. H. Angoff (ed.), *The College Board Admissions Testing Program: A technical report on research and development activities relating to the Scholastic Aptitude and Achievement Tests,* (1–14). Princeton, NJ: Educational Testing Service.

Aries, P. (1962). *Centuries of childhood: A social history of family life.* New York: Vintage.

Asimov, N. (1994a). Alice Walker story pulled from state test. *San Francisco Chronicle,* February 19, pp. A1, A13.

———— (1994b). State rejects another story by Alice Walker. *San Francisco Chronicle,*

February 19, pp. A1, A13.

———— (1994c). Wilson endorses removal of Walker, Dillard stories. *San Francisco Chronicle*, March 3, pp. A1, A15.

———— (1994d). Parents fear new exams part of attack on values. *San Francisco Chronicle*, March 7, pp. A1 and A13.

Baker, F. (1971). Automation of test scoring, reporting and analysis. In R. Thorndike (ed.), *Educational measurement*, 202–234. 2d ed. Washington, DC: American Council on Education.

Basalla, G. (1988). *The evolution of technology*. New York: Cambridge University Press.

Boorstin, D. J. (1961). *The image: Pseudo-events in America*. New York: Vintage.

———— (1978). *The republic of technology*. New York: Harper & Row.

Bowler, R. (1983). Payment by results: A study in achievement and accountability. Ph.D. dissertation, Boston College, 1983. Ann Arbor, MI: University Microfilms International No. 8314852.

Boyer, E. (1983). *High school: A report on secondary education in America*. New York: Harper & Row.

Boykoff-Baron, B. J. (1990). *Performance assessment: Blurring the edges among assessment, curriculum, and instruction*. Washington, DC: American Association for the Advancement of Science Forum for School Science.

Burton, E. (1979). Richard Lowell Edgeworth's education bill of 1799: A missing chapter in the history of Irish education. *Irish Journal of Education 13*(1), 24–33.

Callaghan, R. E. (1962). *Education and the cult of efficiency*. Chicago: Chicago University Press.

Chaffee, J. W. (1985). *The thorny gates of learning in Sung China*. Cambridge: Cambridge University Press.

Cheney, L. V. (1994). The end of history. *Wall Street Journal*, October 20, p. 22.

Coleman, J. S., E. Q. Campbell, C. J. Hobson, J. McPartland, A. M. Mood, F. D. Weinfeld, et al. (1966). *Equality of educational opportunity*. Washington, DC: Office of Education, U.S. Department of Health, Education and Welfare.

Commission on the Skills of the American Workforce (1990). *America's choice: High skills or low wages!* (0-9627063-0-2). Rochester, NY: National Center on Education and the Economy.

Connolly, W. E. (1993). *Fundamentalism in America*. Paper presented at the meeting of the Sapporo Seminar in American Studies, July 1992 (revised 1993), Sapporo, Japan.

Darling-Hammond, L. (1991). The implications of testing policy for educational quality and equality. *Phi Delta Kappan 73*(3), 220–225.

Darling-Hammond, L., J. Ancess, and B. Falk (1995). *Authentic assessment in action: Studies of schools and students at work*. New York: Teachers College Press.

Datta, L. (1982). Employment-related basic skills. In H. F. Silberman (ed.), *Education and work*, 140–168. Chicago: University of Chicago Press.

Diegmueller, K. (1995). Running out of steam. *Education Week*, April 12, pp. 4–8.

Doyle, D. P. (1991). Empowering teachers. *Atlantic Monthly*, September, p. 15.

Dunbar, S., D. Koretz, and H. D. Hoover (1991). Quality control in the development and use of performance assessment. *Applied Measurement in Education* 4(4), 289–303.

Editorial (1994). State board failed to pass a simple test. *San Francisco Chronicle*, March 3, p. A16.

Edsall, T. B. (1995). He's not running for preacher. *Washington Post National Weekly Edition*, July 3–9, p.12.

Educate America, Inc. (1991). *An idea whose time has come; A national achievement test for high school seniors!* Morristown, NJ: Author.

Educational Commission of the States and National Education Goals Panel (1995a). The firm: Private management and public education: Hartford. *Daily Report Card News Service* 3(282) (January 4).

———— (1995b). Georgia: Moving towards norm-referenced tests. *Daily Report Card News Service* 3(309) (March 13).

———— (1995c). Sherman (Texas) school district: Beginning to see the light. *Daily Report Card News Service* 3(314) (March 24).

———— (1995d). Wilkinsburg, PA: On the map with charter run by firm. *Daily Report Card News Service* 3(314) (March 24).

———— (1995e). Teaching techniques: Storm thunders in Fort Worth. *Daily Report Card News Service* 5(5) (June 19).

Ellul, J. (1990). *The technological bluff.* Grand Rapids, MI: Williams B. Eerdmans.

Elton, R. G. (1991). *Return to essentials: Some reflections on the present state of historical study.* Cambridge: Cambridge University Press.

FairTest. (1992). Primary language record. *FairTest Examiner* 6(3), 9–11.

Farrell, A. P. (1938). *The Jesuit code of liberal education: Development and scope of the Ratio Studiorum.* Milwaukee, WI: Bruce Publishing Company.

Foucault, M. (1977). *Discipline and punish: The birth of the prison.* New York: Viking.

Galbraith, J. K. (1992). *The culture of contentment.* Boston: Houghton Mifflin Company.

Gao, X., R. J. Shavelson, and G. P. Baxter (1994). Generalizability of large-scale performance assessments in science: Promises and problems. *Applied Measurement in Education* 7(4), 323–42.

Garcia, G. E., and P. D. Pearson (1994). Assessment and diversity. In L. Darling-Hammond (ed.), *Review of Research in Education 20*, 337–91.

Gordon, S. C. (1968). *Reports and repercussions in West Indian education 1835–1933.* London: Ginn and Company.

Grace, C., and E. F. Shores (1992). *The portfolio and its use: Developmentally appropriate assessment of young children.* Little Rock, AR: Southern Association on Children Under Six.

Guay, D. A. (1991). Tracking student progress. *Thrust for Educational Leadership* 21(2), 45–48.

Gugliotta, G. (1994). Curriculum guidelines play down traditional heroes and focus on negatives, critics say. *Washington Post,* October 28, p. 6.

Haney, W. (1986). College admissions testing and high school curriculum: Uncertain connections and future directions. In *Measures in the College Admissions Process: A College Board Colloquium.* New York: College Entrance Examination Board, pp. 32–52.

Haney, W., G. F. Madaus, and R. Lyons (1993). *The fractured market place for standardized testing.* Boston: Kluwer.

Harris, L., and R. F. Wagner (1993). *Testing assumptions: A survey of teachers' attitudes toward the nation's school reform agenda.* Report prepared for the Ford Foundation. New York: LH Research.

Hearn, W. E. (1872). *Payment by results in primary education.* Melbourne: Stellwell and Knight.

Henderson, K. (1994). The making of the history standards. *Christian Science Monitor,* November 18, p.15.

Herman, J. L., P. R. Aschbacher, and L. Winters (1992). *A practical guide to alternative assessment.* Alexandria, VA: Association for Supervision and Curriculum Development.

Herrnstein, R. J., and C. Murray (1994). *The bell curve: Intelligence and class structure in American life.* New York: Free Press.

Hoskins, K. (1968). The examination, disciplinary power and rational schooling. *History of Education 8,* 135–146.

Hughes, T. P. (1989). *American genesis: A century of invention and technological enthusiasm.* New York: Penguin.

Jaeger, R. M. (1991). Legislative perspectives on statewide testing: Goals, hopes, and desires. *Phi Delta Kappan 73*(3), 239–242.

Kellaghan, T., G. F. Madaus, and A. E. Raczek (1995). *The use of external examinations to improve student motivation.* Report prepared for the Ford Foundation.

Koretz, D. M., R. L. Linn, S. B. Dunbar, and L. A. Shepard (1991). The effects of high-stakes testing on achievement: Preliminary findings about generalization across tests. In R. L. Linn (Chair), *Symposium on the effects of high-stakes testing on instruction and achievement,* American Educational Research Association and National Council on Measurement in Education, Chicago.

Koretz, D. M., G. F. Madaus, E. Haertel, and A. Beaton (1992). *Statement before the Subcommittee on Elementary, Secondary, and Vocational Education Committee on Education and Labor, U.S. House of Representatives,* February 19,1992.

Koretz, D. M., B. Stecher, S. Klein, and D. McCaffrey (1994). The Vermont portfolio assessment program: Findings and implications. *Educational Measurement: Issues and Practice 13*(3), 5–16.

Kracke, E. A. (1963). Sponsorship and the selection of talent. In J. M. Menzel (ed.), *The Chinese civil service: Career open to talent,* 84–91. Boston: D. C. Heath.

Kritzman, L. D. (ed.) (1990). *Michel Foucault: Politics, philosophy, culture: Interviews and other writings 1977–1984.* New York: Routledge.

Kula, W. (1986). *Measures and men* (R. Szreter, trans.). Princeton, NJ: Princeton University Press.

Lerner, B. (1981). The minimum competency testing movement: Social, scientific, and legal implications. *American Psychologist 36*(10), 1057–66.

Letters to the editor (1994). The CLAS test process. *San Francisco Chronicle*, March 4, p. A22.

Levine, D. M. (ed.) (1971). *Performance contracting in education. An appraisal: Toward a balanced perspective.* Englewood Cliffs, NJ: Educational Technology Publications.

Little, A. (1993). *Towards an international framework for understanding assessment.* Paper presented at the Conference on Learning, Selection and Monitoring: Resolving the Roles of Assessment, sponsored by the International Centre for Research on Assessment, Institute of Education, University of London, July.

Loewe, M. (1986). The former Han dynasty. In D. Twitchett and M. Loewe (eds.), *The Cambridge history of China*, 103–198. Cambridge: Cambridge University Press.

Lomax, R. G., M. M. West, M. C. Harmon, K. A. Viator, and G. F. Madaus (1992). *The impact of mandated standardized testing on minority students.* Boston: Center for the Study of Testing, Evaluation, and Educational Policy, Boston College.

Lowrance, W. W. (1986). *Modern science and human values.* New York: Oxford University Press.

Lyman, R. (1989). Give 'em the razor, sell 'em the blades. *Graphic Arts Monthly,* (January), 74–76.

Madaus, G. F. (1979). Testing and funding: Measurement and policy issues. *New Directions for Testing and Measurement 1*, 53–62.

———— (1985a). Public policy and the testing profession—You've never had it so good? *Educational Measurement: Issues and Practices 4*(4), 5–11.

———— (1985b). *The perils and promises of new tests and new technologies: Dick and Jane and the great analytical engine.* Paper presented at the October 1985 ETS Invitational Conference on the Redesign of Testing for the Twenty-first Century, New York.

———— (1988). The influence of testing on the curriculum. In L. Tanner (ed.), *Critical Issues in Curriculum*, 8–121. Chicago: University of Chicago Press.

———— (1990). *Testing as a social technology: The inaugural Boisi lecture in education and public policy.* Chestnut Hill, MA: Center for the Study of Testing, Evaluation and Public Policy, Boston College.

———— (1993). A national testing system: Manna from above? A historical/technological perspective. *Educational Assessment 1*(1), 9–26.

———— (1994). A technological and historical consideration of equity issues associated with proposals to change the nation's testing policy. *Harvard Educational Review 64*(1), 76–95.

———— (1995a). A technological and historical consideration of equity issues associated with proposals to change the nation's testing policy. In M. T. Nettles and A. L. Nettles (eds.), *Equity and excellence in educational testing and assessment.* Boston: Kluwer.

———— (1995b). *Do we have a crisis in education? The fashioning and amending of public knowledge and discourse about public schools.* Division D Vice Presidential

Address, presented at the Annual Meeting of the American Educational Research Association, New Orleans, April.

Madaus, G. F., and V. Greaney (1985). The Irish experience in competency testing: Implications for American education. *American Journal of Education 93*(2), 268–94.

Madaus, G. F., and T. Kellaghan (1991a). *Student examination systems in the European Community: Lessons for the United States.* Contractor report submitted to the Office of Technology Assessment, United States Congress.

———— (1991b). National testing: Lessons for America from Europe. *Educational Leadership 49*(3), 87–93.

———— (1992). Curriculum evaluation and assessment. In P. W. Jackson (ed.), *Handbook of research on curriculum,* 119–54. New York: Macmillan.

———— (1993). The British experience with "authentic" testing. *Phi Delta Kappan,* (February), 458–59, 462–63, 466–69.

———— (1994). National curricula in European countries. In E. Eisner (ed.), *The hidden consequences of a national curriculum.* Washington, DC: American Educational Research Association.

Madaus, G. F., and J. T. McDonagh (1979). Minimum competency testing: Unexamined assumptions and unexplored negative outcomes. *New Directions for Testing and Measurement 3,* 1–15.

Madaus, G. F., and A. E. Raczek (1995). The extent and growth of educational testing in the United States: 1956–1994. In H. Goldstein and T. Lewis (eds.), *Assessment: Problems, developments and statistical issues.* London: Wiley.

Madaus, G. F., A. Raczek, and S. Thomas (1996). *Performance assessment and issues of differential impact: The British experience—Lessons for America.* Paper presented at the second conference on Equality and Educational Assessment sponsored by the Ford Foundation, Washington, DC, May 12–14.

Madaus, G. F., and A. G. Tan (1993). The growth of assessment. In G. Cawelti (ed.), *Challenges and achievements of American education,* 53–79. Alexandria, VA: Association for Supervision and Curriculum Development.

Marx, K. (1967). Critical notes on the "King of Prussia and social reform." In L. D. Easton and K. H. Guddat (eds.), *Writing of the young Marx on philosophy and society,* 338–60. Garden City, NY: Doubleday.

Marx, L. (1988). *The pilot and the passenger: Essays on literature, technology, and culture in the United States.* New York: Oxford University Press.

Massachusetts Historical Society Documents (1845–1846). Horace Mann Papers #8. Reel 8 (August 29, 1845).

McLauglin, M. W. (1991). Test-based accountability as a reform strategy. *Phi Delta Kappan 73*(3), 248–51.

Meng, H. W. (1993). *The role of assessment in China: A shift in direction from selection to monitoring.* Paper presented at the Conference on Learning, Selection and Monitoring: Resolving the Roles of Assessment. Sponsored by the International Centre for Research on Assessment, Institute of Education, University of London, July.

Mitchell, R. (1992). *Testing for learning: How new approaches to evaluation can improve American schools.* New York: Free Press.

Montgomery, R. J. (1967). *Examinations: An account of their evolution as administrative devices in England.* Pittsburgh: University of Pittsburgh Press.

Myford, C. M., and R. J. Mislevy (1994). *Monitoring and improving a portfolio assessment system.* Princeton, NJ: Educational Testing Service.

Nash, G., and C. Crabtree (1994). A history of all the people isn't PC. [Letter to the editor.] *Wall Street Journal,* November 21, p. 25.

National Center on Education and the Economy (1989). *To secure our future: The federal role in education.* Rochester, NY: Author.

National Center for History in the Schools (1994). *National standards for United States history: Exploring the American experience.* Los Angeles: Author.

National Commission on Excellence in Education (1983). *A nation at risk.* Washington, DC: U.S. Government Printing Office.

National Commission on Testing and Public Policy (1990). *From gatekeeper to gateway: Transforming testing in America.* Chestnut Hill, MA: National Commission on Testing and Public Policy, Boston College.

National Council on Education Standards and Testing (1992). *Raising standards for American education.* Washington, DC: U.S. Government Printing Office.

Newmann, F. M. (1991). Linking restructuring to authentic student achievement. *Phi Delta Kappan 72*(6), 458–63.

Newmann, F. M., W. G Secada, and G. G. Wehlage (1995). *A guide to authentic instruction and assessment: Vision, standards and scoring.* Madison, WI: Wisconsin Center for Education Research.

Nivison, D. S. (1963). The criteria of excellence. In J. M. Menzel (ed.), *The Chinese civil service: Career open to talent,* 92–106. Boston: D. C. Heath.

Nuttall, D. L. (1992). Performance assessment: The message from England. *Educational Leadership 49*(8), 54–57.

Nuttall, D. L., and G. Stobart (1994). National curriculum assessment in the U.K. *Educational Measurement: Issues and Practice 13*(2), 24–27, 39.

Ong, W. J. (1971). *Rhetoric, romance and technology.* Ithaca, NY: Cornell University Press.

Oxford English Dictionary (Version 1.0b) [CD-ROM] (1993). Oxford: Oxford University Press.

Parenti, M. (1978). *Power and the powerless.* New York: St. Martin's Press.

Park, R. L. (1995). The danger of voodoo science. *New York Times,* July 9, p. E15.

Perreiah, A. R. (1984). Logic examinations in Padua circa 1400. *History of Education 13*(2), 85–103.

Petroski, H. (1990). *The pencil: A history of design and circumstance.* New York: Knopf.

Piore, M. J. (1995). *Beyond individualism.* Cambridge, MA: Harvard University Press.

Popham, W. J. (1983). Measurements as an instructional catalyst. *New Directions for Testing and Measurement 17,* 19–30.

——— (1993). Circumventing the high costs of authentic assessment. *Phi Delta*

Kappan 74(6), 470–73.

Public Law 100-297 (1988). *Augustus F. Hawkins-Robert T. Stafford elementary and secondary school improvement amendments of 1988.* 102d Congress.

Pyne, J. (1995). When history meets politics. [Letter to the editor.] *Record,* April 5, p. C06.

Rapple, B. A. (1992). Payment by results (1862–1897): Ensuring a good return on government expenditure. *Journal of Educational Thought 25*(1), 183–201.

Ravitch, D. (1995). *National standards in American education: A citizen's guide.* Washington, DC: The Brookings Institution.

Resnick, L. B. (1991). *Memo to Governor Roy Romer.* Interim report of resource group on student achievement and citizenship, Pennsylvania. February 1.

Rich, F. (1995). Cheney dumbs down. *New York Times,* February 26, p. 15.

Samelson, F. (1987). Was early mental testing: (a) Racist inspired, (b) Objective science, (c) A technology for democracy, (d) The origin of multiple-choice exams, (e) None of the above? (Mark the RIGHT Answer). In M. M. Sokal (ed.), *Psychological testing and American society, 1890–1930,* 113–27. New Brunswick, NJ: Rutgers University Press.

Schrof, J. M., and K. Pollack (1995). Click goes the mouse: Despite a shaky start, computerized tests appear to be the wave of the future. *U.S. News and World Reports America's Best Graduate Schools,* pp.17–18.

Secretary's Commission on Achieving Necessary Skills (1992). *Learning a living: A blueprint for high performance.* Washington, DC: U.S. Department of Labor.

Shanker, A. (1986). Power vs. knowledge in St. Louis: Professional under fire. *New York Times,* October 26.

———— (1993). Outrageous outcomes. *New York Times,* September 12, pp. E7.

Shavelson, R. J., G. P. Baxter, and X. Gao (1993). Sampling variability of performance assessments. *Journal of Educational Measurement 30*(3), 215–32.

Shavelson, R. J., G. P. Baxter, and J. Pine (1992). Performance assessments: Political rhetoric and measurement reality. *Educational Researcher 21*(4), 22–27.

Shepard, L. A. (1991). Will national tests improve student learning? *Phi Delta Kappan 73*(3), 232–38.

Sokal, M. M. (ed.) (1987). *Psychological testing and American society: 1890–1930.* New Brunswick, NJ: Rutgers University Press.

Stake, R. E. (1991). The teacher, standardized testing, and prospects of revolution. *Phi Delta Kappan 73*(3), 243–47.

Starch, D., and E. C. Elliot (1912). Reliability of grading high school work in English. *School Review 21,* 442–57.

———— (1913). Reliability of grading work in mathematics. *School Review 21* 254–59.

Staudenmaier, J. M. (1985). *Technology's storytellers: Reweaving the human fabric.* Cambridge, MA: MIT Press.

———— (1988). *Technology and faith* [audiocassette recording]. Kansas City: Credence Cassettes.

———— (1989). U.S. technological style and the atrophe of civic commitment. In D.

L. Gilpi (ed.), *Beyond individualism toward a retrieval of moral discourse in America*, 120–52. South Bend, IN: Notre Dame Press.

Stedman, L. C., and C. F. Kaestle (1987). Literacy and reading performance in the United States, from 1880 to present. *Reading Research Quarterly 22*(1), 8–43.

Sutherland, G. (1973). *Elementary education in the nineteenth century*. London: London Historical Association.

Thorndike, R. M., and D. F. Lohman (1990). *A century of ability testing*. Chicago: Riverside.

Tyack, D. B. (1974). *The one best system: A history of American urban education*. Cambridge, MA: Harvard University Press.

Tynan, M. (1985). *Catholic Instruction in Ireland 1720–1950*. Dublin: Four Courts Press.

U.S. Department of Education (1984). *The nation responds: Recent efforts to improve education*. Washington, DC: U.S. Government Printing Office.

——— (1991a). *Digest of education statistics 1990*. Washington, DC: U.S. Department of Education, Office of Educational Research and Improvement.

——— (1991b). *America 2000: An education strategy: Sourcebook (ED/OS91-13)*. Washington, DC: Author.

Webber, C. (1989). The mandarin mentality: Civil service and university admissions testing in Europe and Asia. In B. R. Gifford (ed.), *Testing policy and the politics of opportunity allocation: The workplace and the law*, 33–60. Boston: Kluwer.

West, P. (1995). A.F.T. decries lack of standards, "gateway" exam. *Education Week*, July 12, p. 7.

Wiener, J. (1995a). The critics who didn't actually read the National Standards for History. *San Francisco Examiner*, January 18, p. A15.

——— (1995b). "Patriotically correct" history isn't honest. *Los Angeles Times*, March 12, p. A7.

Wiggins, G. (1989). A true test: Toward more authentic and equitable assessment. *Phi Delta Kappan 70*(9), 703–713.

——— (1990). The case for authentic assessment. *ERIC Clearinghouse on Tests, Measurement, and Evaluation* (December) (ERIC Document Reproduction Service # ED 328 611)

——— (1993). Assessment: Authenticity, context, and validity. *Phi Delta Kappan 75*(2), 200–214.

Wilson, H. W. (1932–1944). *Education Index*. New York: Author.

Winner, L. (1977). *Autonomous technology: Technic-out-of-control as a theme in political thought*. Cambridge, MA: MIT Press.

——— (1986). *The whale and the reactor: A search for limits in an age of high technology*. Chicago: University of Chicago Press.

Wise, A. E. (1979). *Legislated learning: The bureaucratization of the American classroom*. Berkeley, CA: University of California Press.

Wiseman, S. (1961). *Examinations and English education*. Manchester: Manchester University Press.

Wolf, D. P. (1992). *Assessment as an episode of learning.* Paper presented at the conference Diversifying Student Assessment: From Vision to Practice. Sponsored by the Newton Public Schools and the Center for the Study of Testing, Evaluation, and Educational Policy, Boston College, November.

Woodruff, G. L. (1992). Computers to improve testing for colleges. [Letter to the editor.] *New York Times*, April 24, p. A34.

Chapter Two

ASSESSING AGAINST THE GRAIN: A Conceptual Framework for Alternative Assessments

Celia Genishi

The purpose of this chapter is to provide a conceptual framework for understanding current movements in assessing student learning.[1] I focus on contrasts between objective (traditional) assessment and its alternatives, placing both approaches within a postmodern context. Postmodernism is invoked in order to highlight the multiplicity of perspectives that current forms of assessment must accommodate and the shift in power relationships that equitable assessment implies.

Equitable assessment also implies a different view of the human being from that associated with traditional approaches. This contrasting view (called *intersubjective*) presents the test taker as an active thinker, capable of "reading" people and situations, including tests. Teachers too are active thinkers who can play a major role in the process of reforming assessment. This role is highlighted through the inclusion of the voices of two teachers, who discuss the special challenges presented by students whose first language is not English. Teachers like these go "against the grain" as they assert their power and authority as primary assessors of learning.

The chapter is organized as follows: the contrast between traditional assessment and its alternatives; an objective versus intersubjective perspective on assessment; the challenge of equitable assessment of "different" children, especially those who are linguistically different; teachers' descriptions of their individual-focused assessments; and a summary of the current state of assessment and teacher/assessors—teachers who assess.

ASSESSING LEARNING IN THIS POSTMODERN TIME

From an academic point of view, the societal context in which we live is postmodern, that is, eclectic, without fixed standards, and full of shifting, multiple perspectives. It is also postmodern in a philosophical and political sense: in the arts, education, and the social sciences, for example, there is a generally skeptical attitude toward standards or toward canons that have been viewed historically as standards. In the "modern" era, there were "grand narratives of legitimation" (Lyotard 1984) or broadly accepted explanatory theories of human development, literature, science, and so on. There was a belief that human beings were progressing toward some undefined better state, following known and accepted standards.

In the postmodern era, these standards are still known but no longer accepted without question. Along with standards, relationships of power have become fluid, and those who had the power to assert standards and theories underlying them now face multiple challenges. Thus a theory of human development that is based on research only on males or on children in the Western hemisphere is questioned. And a literary canon consisting primarily of writers of European ancestry is no longer the only legitimate body of work to be studied. Writers of diverse (non-Western) backgrounds are increasingly recognized as credible.

The postmodern is not only reactive or critical of existing theories and power relationships; it is also potentially an active force. In the arts, the postmodernist "searches for new presentations, not in order to enjoy them but in order to impart a stronger sense of the unpresentable" (Lyotard 1984: 81). Lyotard's vantage point is aesthetic and philosophical, but his definition of the postmodern calls to mind one of the great challenges of assessment, how to present the unpresentable, or how to present what sometimes seems unpresentable: *what a human being knows and how s/he is doing as a learner.* What is known and how one is doing both imply some processes that are hidden from view (within one's head/mind) and that are inherently unstable since one's knowledge and learning are constantly changing.

In education, the grand narrative of objective assessment or measurement presents learning as a sequential process that is assessed by discrete, statistical methods. Part of that narrative is a set of textbook definitions (often elaborated upon and debated by researchers) for the basic terms related to what a person knows or has achieved as a learner. These definitions are clearly asserted, as in the following examples (Keeves 1994):

- *assessment*—a term reserved for determinations about people, usually individuals (sometimes small groups)
- *evaluation*—"operations associated with nonperson entities, such as curricula, programs, interventions, methods of teaching, and organizational factors" (363)
- *measurement*—assessing or evaluating by assignment of a numerical quantity.

Thorndike and Hagen (1977: 9) state that measurement in any field involves three general steps:

1. identifying and defining the quality or attribute that is to be measured
2. determining a set of operations by which the attribute may be made manifest and perceivable
3. establishing a set of procedures or definitions for translating observations into quantitative statements of degree or amount.

The traditional way to measure the identified quality or attribute in school settings is to create a *test*, or the set of operations that make the quality or attribute perceivable. What makes a test a "measure" is the translation of a learner's performance (e.g., quality of spelling, quality of work on a social studies assignment) into a number or quantitative statement.

The legitimacy of these definitions and the theories and practices they imply has been challenged for decades (e.g., Baratz and Baratz 1971; Dobzhansky 1973; Gould 1981), but it is within the last ten years that traditional ways of assessing students have changed in notable numbers of schools in the United States. Thus the grand narrative of objective assessment or measurement now competes with narratives/ theories in tune with contemporary school-reform efforts.

THE RELATIONSHIP OF THE ASSESSOR TO THE ASSESSED

An Objective Perspective

Traditional measurement, including standardized testing, has been a persistent feature of the school experience in the United States largely because it is seen as objective. The assumption is that students taking a standardized test take it under virtually the same conditions and that their responses will be scored in identical ways. Thus the score for any individual taking the test is objective. When the test is psychometrically sound, it is also reliable (accurate and consistent) and valid (measuring what it claims to measure). It allows for comparison of an individual with a group norm and for comparison of groups with each other. (For purposes of this chapter, I use *objective* in an inclusive sense, incorporating the definitions of reliable and valid into that word.) From this perspective, there is no relationship between the assessor and the assessed. It should not matter who administers the test, nor does it matter who is taking the test. Objectivity is inherent in the test or instrument.

This traditional view of assessment also implies a particular definition of intelligence, a unitary one, by which the score or battery of scores on an objective measure captures the test taker's level of general intelligence. We might say this view is clearly out-of-date and has been replaced by much richer theories of intelligence, for example, Gardner's theory of multiple intelligences (Gardner 1983, 1993). However, the recent work of Herrnstein and Murray (1994) suggests that old views manage to survive, since the authors proclaim not only a traditional unitary definition but also a racist account of the genetic origins of intelligence.[2]

Figure 2.1a presents a schematic representation of the traditional process of assessment: the assessor (whether a teacher, researcher, or stranger administering

Figure 2.1: Contrasting Views of Assessment

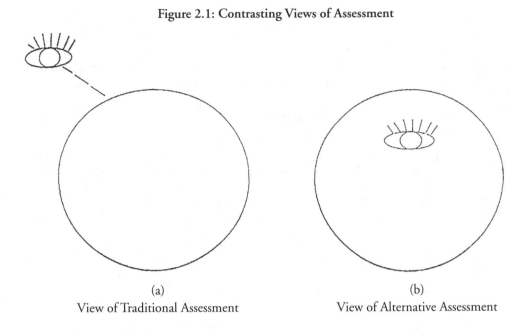

| (a) | (b) |
| View of Traditional Assessment | View of Alternative Assessment |

an individual or group test) is a detached "eye" and views the testing event from an objective distance, outside the universe of the person assessed. That distance assures the objectivity of the score. In theory, then, all scores on standardized tests are "relationship free." Yet in practice, each of us can probably provide an example of how objectivity in testing can be violated because of characteristics of the test, the person assessed, or the testing situation.

An Intersubjective Perspective

For a number of years, the objective perspective with respect to testing and learning in general has been under scrutiny. An alternative perspective is not "anti-objective" or purely subjective, but it is a contrasting conception of the person or learner and thus the relationship between the assessor and assessed. In the United States many trace the contrast to developmentalists Piaget (Piaget and Inhelder 1969) and Bruner (Bruner, Olver, and Greenfield 1966; Bruner 1996). Both theorists posit learners not as empty vessels or *tabula rasa* to be filled with knowledge, but as thinkers and constructors of their own understandings of the reality around them.

Bruner has termed a cornerstone of this conception to be "intersubjectivity," or

> the human ability to understand the minds of others, whether through language, gesture, or other means. It is not just words that make this possible, but our capacity to grasp the role of the settings in which words, acts, and gestures occur. We are the intersubjective species par excellence.

It is this that permits us to "negotiate" meanings when words go astray. (Bruner 1996: 20)

The search for intersubjectivity and negotiation of meaning takes place between parent and child and teacher and learner in what Bruner calls "a subcommunity of interaction" (Bruner 1996: 20).

Earlier theorists in psychology and sociology have made similar points (Kelly 1955; Mead 1934/1962). Kelly (1955), for example, posited a personal construct theory as the foundation for his work as a clinical psychologist. Some basic assumptions of the theory are that:

1. human existence is defined by action and change over time
2. no one can experience a reality that is free of interpretation or "construing" (either a single event in one's life or the kind of assessment that one uses/develops in the classroom)
3. to be an interpreter of experience one needs to have an active mind; every person cannot help but construe patterns in the continuum of life and actively construct a theory about it.

Kelly's theory placed as much emphasis on the person's capacity for imaginative interpretation as on intellectual theory making. For this reason, his theory seems appropriate as an adjunct to other less interpretive perspectives on intersubjectivity. The student or teacher who interprets a test as an opportunity to demonstrate competence, for example, is construing that event very differently from the one who sees it as an event full of anxiety, offering the potential for failure. According to Kelly, every participant would construe that event in a unique way. Like all interactions, then, assessment events involve a search for intersubjectivity and a negotiation of shared meaning.

In the classroom, intersubjectivity is relevant not only to testing situations but also to learning in general. Teachers continually try to grasp what is or is not in the mind of the learner. In fact, many might call this the fundamental task of teachers' assessments: reading the learner's mind or determining "where the learner is." Students, too, continually engage in the process of figuring out "what the teacher wants," especially when being assessed.

When teachers view the task of assessment as their own, they often rely on observation of various kinds to make a determination. Classroom observation (by means of note taking, anecdotal records, electronic equipment, checklists, and so on) contrasts with the objective observations of researchers. The teacher plays multiple roles with respect to learners whose lives are entwined with the teacher's. S/he is not an objective or passive observer but instead an active participant. Unlike the objective assessor, the teacher/assessor lives in the same universe—the same educational space—as the person observed and assessed (see Figure 2.1b). Teachers are necessarily the "eye" within the circle of the classroom; they seldom have the luxury of stepping outside the shared space and observing from a distance.

Indeed, since the 1970s, educators and researchers (Almy and Genishi 1979; Bissex and Bullock 1987; Bussis, Chittenden, and Amarel 1976; Bussis, Chittenden, Amarel, and Klausner 1985; Carini 1975; Glesne and Peshkin 1992; Guba and Lincoln 1989; Perrone 1975) have written about the impossibility of separating the observer, often the teacher, from what s/he observes, often students and their behavior. Carini (1975) illustrates a method of observation and record keeping called *documentation* that depends on the observer's dwelling in a particular setting over time.

This method is grounded in what Bruner calls an intersubjective view of the person; each person is capable of experiencing and interpreting situations for her or himself. Because of its emphasis on setting, the method is similar to that of participant observation, used often by anthropologists and ethnographers as they study a culture or settings within a culture (Erickson 1986). Participant observers, like classroom participants, cannot stand apart from the phenomena around them; instead they try to see patterns in what occurs. Eventually, they interpret what they see, and their interpretations are drawn from immersion or participation in the setting.

Intersubjectivity and Objective Assessment

Contemporary classrooms provide examples of how both teachers and children interpret testing situations. Consider McCarrier's report of some kindergartners' responses to practice items on a standardized achievement test, administered to see if the school can qualify for special government funding:

> One item requires children to choose the picture of something that starts with the same sound as doll. There is a picture of a dog, and a few children say, "woof, woof," or "arf, arf," apparently thinking that this is the sound a dog makes. Nothing in the children's manner suggests that they are making a good joke. Another example: when the children are to choose groups of letters that look just like the group of letters in the test question, some children ignore the order in which the letters appear. They might match BOT with TOB or OTB. The children's responses are reasonable from the child's perspective but of course are not correct from the testmaker's. (Genishi 1992: 6)

Thus the objectivity of this reading test is threatened by children whose capacity for intersubjectivity "reads" the purpose of the items—the mind behind the test—in unexpected ways.

This capacity to understand others' thoughts and grasp the role of settings is also corroborated by unlikely observers. For example, a century ago Alfred Binet, whose name is synonymous with measures of intelligence, worried over how human beings' suggestibility could affect the objectivity of measurement (Gould 1981). As he measured the circumference of skulls to see if skull size was correlated with intelligence (craniometry), he discovered that his measurements were consistently higher than those of one of his students'. This discrepancy led him to measure the same skulls a second time, after which he found that his measurements had all decreased in size. He concluded that "self-suggestion" was at work; our ability to interpret situations for ourselves and be influenced by our interpretations can make suspect seemingly straightforward measures. In fact, Binet's self-revelation soon led him to abandon this approach to intelligence testing.

Another pioneer in measuring intelligence, H. H. Goddard (renowned primarily for his study of the Kallikak family), used the intelligence tests that Binet developed to test immigrants to New York City in the early 1900s (Gould 1981: 165–66). His procedure was to have two women identify "the feebleminded by sight" and then test the identified group with the Binet scale. According to Goddard, in 1913 between 79 percent and 87 percent of the adults tested were determined to be "feebleminded," or functioning below the level of a twelve-year-old. Gould's comments on this procedure:

> consider a group of frightened men and women who speak no English and who have just endured an oceanic voyage in steerage. Most are poor and have never gone to school; many have never held a pencil or pen in their hand. They march off the boat; one of Goddard's intuitive women takes them aside shortly thereafter, sits them down, hands them a pencil, and asks them to reproduce on paper a figure shown to them a moment ago, but now withdrawn from their sight. Could their failure be a result of testing conditions, or weakness, fear, or confusion, rather than of innate stupidity? (Gould 1981: 166)

Goddard did not consider the role that the setting might play in the testing process, nor did he take into account his own suggestibility—based on his belief that human beings could be easily sorted into groups of superior or inferior intelligence. Yet he was confident of the validity of his scores and took credit for the deportation of numerous immigrants in 1913 and 1914.

Although testing is no longer done at entry points for immigrants, Gould's comment is striking in light of current dilemmas regarding the testing of populations who clearly differ from a mainstream "norm." These examples from history show how an objective test may be interpreted or "grasped" in a multitude of ways, because each test maker and test taker may view both the testing situation and test items quite differently from others.

THE SEARCH FOR INTERSUBJECTIVITY WITH "DIFFERENT" LEARNERS

The current assessment scene is a postmodern one, full of multiplicity. It portrays some educators struggling to allow for the variation in test takers' prior experience with and interpretation of tests. The scene also includes different ways of assessing, necessitated by new theoretical understandings about the nature of intelligence and how it might be assessed, as well as by the diversity of learners.

The Challenges of Testing Language

"Diversity" incorporates individuals' different approaches to learning (motoric, verbal, visual, etc.), variations in the ease with which they learn, and the range of their social, ethnic, linguistic, and economic backgrounds. Currently, about 30 percent of all public school students are children of color (Banks 1991), and they constitute more than 70 percent of total school enrollments in twenty of the country's largest school districts (Center for Education Statistics 1987). According to the 1980 U.S. Bureau of Census:

> The language minority population . . . in the United States was about 30 million (projected to reach 40 million by the year 2000) with a school-age population of 3.5 million children. The population of limited English proficient (LEP) students, which was 2.4 million in 1980, is conservatively projected to reach about 3.5 million by the year 2000. (cited in Trueba 1989: 3)

In states like California, by the year 2030, 50 percent of students will not be English speakers on their first day of school (Garcia and McLaughlin 1995).

Thus one of the greatest challenges of assessment is that of addressing the needs of non-English speakers or, as some refer to them, English-language learners (ELLs) (LaCelle-Peterson and Rivera 1994). In terms of intersubjectivity, many teachers in the United States are initially unable to draw on their own verbal or linguistic knowledge to infer what is in or on the minds of ELLs. Teachers may see a poignant reflection of the immigrants Goddard tested (Gould 1981) in their immigrant students, who may indeed have neither held a pen in their hand nor seen a standardized test "bubble sheet" before.

Methods for assessing/categorizing ELL students grow out of a tradition of test development that roughly coincides with researchers' understanding of children's language acquisition (Rivera and Simich 1981). For example, objective language tests based on behaviorist theory measure "discrete-point" elements such as pronunciation, vocabulary, and grammar (Henning 1987). These tests often require students to identify objects, repeat sentences, or respond to specific oral directions, and have been criticized over the years since language skills are rarely acquired or used in isolation. Moreover, ELLs are often required to take tests in English just as they are beginning to learn the language so that their failure is nearly assured. And although much energy has been put into the development of language proficiency measures, "comprehensive, flexible assessments don't currently exist" for ELLs (LaCelle-Peterson and Rivera 1994: 66; see also Duran 1993).

Teachers' Searches for Intersubjectivity: Learning from Student Performance

Comprehensiveness and flexibility with respect to language assessment are elusive in the context of objective tests. The current focus on developing alternative performance-based assessments (Darling-Hammond 1994; Wiggins 1993) for all aspects of the curriculum has led to more comprehensive, equitable, and flexible teacher-created alternatives, or ways of tapping student performance—*what learners can actually do in classrooms in the course of the day*. Some schools and school districts provide guidelines for the collection of samples of varied performances. The samples are based primarily on teachers' observations and on products from students (Copeland 1994). For example, required samples of art, math, or oral language may be collected three times during the year (fall, winter, and spring). Or there may be teacher-selected and/or student-selected pieces that demonstrate ability or skill not included in the required samples or that reflect a unique aspect of development. In classrooms with ELLs, teachers' focus could initially be on the processes of becoming familiar with the classroom and second language, rather than on discrete samples or forms of language.

Marla Powell's Prekindergarten

Marla Powell's prekindergarten classroom is a setting in which the teacher has developed her own guidelines for performance-based assessment and so watches learning processes as closely as products. In this bilingual situation, many of the children come from Spanish-speaking families. Here, teacher-created assessments are enriched by the teacher's knowledge of the children's language *and* culture. Marla Powell relates a story of assessment that is culturally aware and strives to detect what ELLs are learning:

> A learning environment which involves a language other than English may also involve a cultural perspective that is outside of the mainstream. Thus the teacher in a bilingual classroom will need to be "fluent" in two cultures, as well as in two languages. This fluency, or cultural literacy, is a prerequisite for quality teaching, which includes quality assessment.
>
> Before a teacher can begin to assess and evaluate young students, she must be able to understand and interpret the children's expressions. This understanding is limited if she considers only the grammar of the language and is not familiar with the children's culture. One example might be the use of the term *maestra*, literally "teacher." In many Dominican families, this term is seen as one of respect and honor. To many teachers raised in the U.S., *maestra* might be interpreted as a generic and not very respectful term, leading them to say, "My name is Ms. So-and-so." If a child continued to use *maestra*, how might she or he be viewed by a teacher out-of-touch with the students' background?

I've also learned about the importance of being aware of current trends within the children's lives. Examples range from Barney to the Power Rangers, popular action figures. While screening a child last week (a school district requirement), I noticed that although he couldn't name the colors, he could say "Jason" and point to the red crayon and "Tommy" and point to the green crayon (Jason is the red Power Ranger, Tommy, the green one). If I did not know anything about the Power Rangers, I would have dismissed these comments as meaningless. . . .

One of the most important endeavors of the early childhood teacher who wants to improve her assessment skills is to get organized at or before the beginning of the school year. I have learned that this is imperative to conducting fair and timely assessments. I make a schedule which lists, month-by-month, the types of assessment I will conduct. (Genishi and Borrego Brainard 1995: 57)

Most of Ms. Powell's assessments are done on an ongoing basis. She focuses on every aspect of the curriculum, from early literacy experiences to free play to spoken language in an informal interview with each child, and embeds her interpretations of children's progress in her knowledge of their culture. In her own words:

One very critical aspect of assessment in a bilingual classroom is that it *must* be ongoing. Children may make a gradual move toward greater usage of a second language or may make a more rapid change. Some children may continue to choose their dominant language in a large group setting, while using their second language in less formal, and possibly less pressured, settings. In order to assess a child's current level, a teacher must be continually observing and recording a child's linguistic attempts, in varied settings. (Genishi and Borrego Brainard 1995: 58)

Ms. Powell defines her role in the classroom broadly. She sets up an environment that offers a range of activities to children with whom she fortunately shares two languages. Each child, though, is a person whom she must come to know, with whom she continually negotiates shared meanings.

Cira Focarino's First Grade

Cira Focarino is a first-grade teacher in a "regular" classroom in which almost all the children are Chinese. Unlike Ms. Powell, she does not share the children's first language and thus relies on nonverbal as well as verbal means of establishing intersubjectivity. She is an acute listener as well as one who maintains an ongoing written dialogue with her children as they keep journals throughout the year. Journal keeping is the core of her language arts curriculum, because it enables children to use a variety of abilities—speaking, drawing, writing, socializing for pleasure, asking for or giving help—as they become writers and readers in a "sub-community in interaction." The process of joining the larger English-speaking and writing community is gradual and is a real challenge for the six children in her class who are ELLs, or ESLs as they are called in Ms. Focarino's school. In her words, ESL learners rely on nonverbal abilities:

> In the beginning of the year, the journal may be a picture which is more developed than the "story." I'll use their story picture to aid in completing the word story. But the picture is a valuable story as is, until they [the children] are willing or able to tell about the picture in words. (Genishi, Dubetz, and Focarino 1995: 130)

Like Ms. Powell, Ms. Focarino watches for nonverbal cues from the children as she makes assessment decisions about when ESL learners are ready to accept correction of errors (editing) in their journals:

> To differentiate between the students who are just coping and those who are ready to tackle the editing . . . it is mostly a nonverbal thing that I get from the kids, like it's their body tensing if I have their journal right there and they're sitting in the chair, how comfortable they are. Also . . . if they're writing the same sentences over and over again, and don't change their subjects and don't change the length of their journals, that shows me that they're not confident to go further. . . . If I see growth, then I know they're ready for like just a tiny bit of editing. . . . I just get that whole sense of who can take not a piece of criticism, but a correction. . . . Some kids will only write correctly spelled words. . . . Some of the kids are just not ready. . . . It's just on a one-to-one. Everybody's different. (Genishi, Dubetz, and Focarino 1995: 130)

Making progress in literacy learning involves risk, since children share their successes and errors with the rest of the class during "journal share." Like other teachers whose assessments are integral to their curricula, Ms. Focarino watches for the times when learners are ready to take risks, to share publicly what's in their minds.

RESPONSIVENESS, TENSION, AND PRESSURE: SUMMARIZING THE CURRENT ASSESSMENT SCENE

The conceptual framework presented in this chapter was built upon the contrast between a "modern" view of assessment and a "postmodern" one. The modern view of objective assessment depicts the frequent use of standardized tests, administered at different grade levels to show what learners know and/or have learned. Scores on these tests stand for what is in the minds of students, and the "typical" student is assumed to be an English speaker. S/he is of average intelligence and learns to read and do math. Taking an objective test does not present problems for this mythical student.

A postmodern view of assessment portrays educators who question whether this mythical student ever existed. They see not the "typical" student but individual students with widely varying backgrounds and needs. Their variability presents such a challenge to traditional views of assessment that educators now consider whether to discard the frame surrounding those views. A new frame must take on a different shape and size to fit the diversity of learners in United States schools.

A postmodern frame must accommodate the fundamental shift in ways of looking at the person—both the person who is the assessor and who is the assessed. Both are capable of actively constructing their own theories of the world and their unique interpretations of situations. Classrooms are places where teachers and learners ideally work to interpret situations in similar ways; they work toward intersubjectivity and shared meanings. This work is especially challenging when learners do not yet share the language of teachers.

Thus this view of persons in classrooms implies a scene full of complications. Assessment is no longer synonymous with testing, and the "eye" of Figure 2.1 is not safely external to the teacher-learner relationship but a part of it. Objectivity in the usual sense cannot be assumed because the teacher/assessor is embedded in the interactions that are the bases for assessment. Instead a search for intersubjectivity becomes central as teachers' roles expand to include that of primary "human instrument" for ongoing assessment, for trying to present what learners know or are learning (Lyotard's "unpresentable").

The Tension of Responding to the Individual and the Group

Teachers who take on the challenge of responding to individuals with all their variability soon sense a tension between the pull of individuals and that of the group, the class as a whole. They realize that the task of teaching is multifocal, focusing simultaneously on the individual and the group. Cira Focarino, the first-grade teacher, illustrated this tension as she kept in mind individual difficulties and successes at the same time she knew that her curriculum required learners to engage in whole-class, public displays of their work. Marla Powell, the prekindergarten teacher, placed individual performances within a larger cultural frame— that of children's popular culture and their social and linguistic backgrounds.

We sense that for many teachers, regardless of the age of the student, the individual's needs come consistently to the foreground. Thus for them objective tests that compare individuals to an abstract group norm have little relevance. The group that matters most to them is the one made up of the individuals they attempt to assess daily. From the point of view of traditional assessment, teacher/assessors are most comfortable challenging the assumptions of objective tests; that is, they go against the grain. They resist the idea that the "eye" inside the classroom is less accurate than the one outside.

Pressures to Be Postmodern

The conception of the person as an active thinker and interpreter strikes many as sensible, not postmodern. Yet the conception of the teacher as thinker-interpreter-assessor is one that challenges traditional ("modern") assumptions. The teachers who take on the challenge—who go against the grain—not only add to their workload; they also take on authority and power that have not traditionally been theirs. Thus they invite additional pressure into their professional lives.

Alternatives to traditional assessment have been part of the educational scene for enough time that there are now significant signs of backlash. For example, the media reflect desire for old-fashioned accountability and for clear teaching methods and standards (Klein 1996), rather than general guidelines that encourage teachers to make their own curricular choices. Thus the teacher/assessor who proclaims that her/his ways of assessing learners are as valid as standardized measures is under pressure to "prove" this point.

Teachers on their own cannot respond to this pressure. Administrators and policymakers have critical roles to play in this regard (see Darling-Hammond and Falk, this volume). It is clear from teachers' and researchers' writing about assessment (e.g., Genishi 1992) that teacher/assessors are hardworking. They are working against the grain in multiple ways: creating their own curricula instead of relying on publishers, assessing individual children with such time-consuming means as careful observation and portfolios, and staying after school every day to keep up with parental concerns, paperwork, and so on.

Teachers do this because they reject the traditional view of teacher-as-complier and follower-of-other-people's-rules. They are part of a postmodern activist movement in which they are changing the culture of teaching (Hargreaves 1994). Still, if we take seriously our own capacities for intersubjectivity and shared meaning, we would have to conclude that in teachers' minds there must be many questions about feasibility and endurance. Teacher/assessors must be asking the question, "For how long will I have the energy to do it all?" Our communal task for the future must be to figure out ways to share the teachers' load—to support teacher/assessors as we join them in going against the grain to create more equitable assessment for all learners.

NOTES

1. Because alternatives to traditional assessment in the United States counter almost a century of reliance on standardized tests, I echo and acknowledge Marilyn Cochran-Smith's title, "Learning to Teach Against the Grain." Hers is an article that casts the role of teachers as both educators and agents for change, participants in the political activity of teaching.
2. There have been many criticisms of this book, including a recent collection edited by Kincheloe, Steinberg, and Gresson (1996).

REFERENCES

Almy, M., and C. Genishi (1979). *Ways of studying children.* New York: Teachers College Press.

Banks, J. A. (1991). Teaching multicultural literacy to teachers. *Teaching Education 4*, 135–44.

Baratz, S. S., and J. C. Baratz (1971). Early childhood intervention: The social science base for institutional racism. In R. H. Anderson and H. G. Shane (eds.), *As the twig is bent: Readings in early childhood education*, (43–52). New York: Houghton Mifflin.

Bissex, G. L., and R. H. Bullock (1987). *Seeing for ourselves: Case-study research by teachers of writing.* Portsmouth, NH: Heinemann.

Bruner, J. (1996). *The culture of education.* Cambridge, MA: Harvard University Press.

Bruner, J. S., R. Olver, and P. M. Greenfield (1966). *Studies of cognitive growth.* New York: Wiley.

Bussis, A. M., E. A. Chittenden, and M. Amarel (1976). *Beyond surface curriculum: An interview study of teachers' understandings.* Boulder, CO: Westview.

Bussis, A. M., E. A. Chittenden, M. Amarel, and E. Klausner (1985). *Inquiry into meaning: An investigation of learning to read.* Hillsdale, NJ: Lawrence Erlbaum.

Carini, P. F. (1975). *Observation and description: An alternative methodology for the investigation of human phenomena.* Grand Forks, ND: University of North Dakota.

Center for Educational Statistics (1987). *The condition of education.* Washington, DC: U.S. Government Printing Office.

Cochran-Smith, M. (1991). Learning to teach against the grain. *Harvard Educational Review 61*, 279–310.

Copeland, S. (1994). *The use of early childhood developmental portfolios for kindergarten screening and changing teaching practice.* Unpublished dissertation proposal, New York, Teachers College, Columbia University.

Darling-Hammond, L. (1994). Performance-based assessment and educational equity. *Harvard Educational Review 64*, 5–30.

Dobzhansky, T. (1973). *Genetic diversity and human equality: The facts and fallacies in the explosive genetics and education controversy.* New York: Basic Books.

Duran, R. (1993). Testing of linguistic minorities. In R. L. Linn (ed.), *Educational measurement*, 573–87. 3d ed. Phoenix, AZ: Oryx.

Erickson, F. (1986). Qualitative methods in research on teaching. In M. Wittrock (ed.), *Handbook of research on teaching*, 119–61. 3d ed. New York: Macmillan.

Garcia, E., and B. McLaughlin (eds.) (1995). *Meeting the challenge of linguistic and cultural diversity in early childhood education:* Yearbook in early childhood education (vol. 6). New York: Teachers College Press.

Gardner, H. (1983). *Frames of mind: The theory of multiple intelligences.* New York: Basic Books.

Gardner, H. (1993). *Multiple intelligences: The theory in practice.* New York: Basic Books.

Genishi, C. (ed.) (1992). *Ways of assessing children and curriculum: Stories of early childhood practice.* New York: Teachers College Press.

Genishi, C., and M. Borrego Brainard (1995). Assessment of bilingual children: A dilemma seeking solutions. In E. Garcia, and B. McLaughlin (eds.), Meeting the challenge of linguistic and cultural diversity in early childhood education: *Yearbook in early childhood education*, vol. 6, 49–63. New York: Teachers College Press.

Genishi, C., N. Dubetz, and C. Focarino (1995). Reconceptualizing theory through practice: Insights from a first-grade teacher and second-language theorists. In S. Reifel (ed.), *Advances in early education and day care*, vol. 7, 123–52. Greenwich, CT: JAI Press.

Glesne, C., and A. Peshkin (1992). *Becoming qualitative researchers: An introduction.* White Plains, NY: Longman.

Gould, S. J. (1981). *The mismeasure of man.* New York: Norton.

Guba, E. G., and Y. S. Lincoln (1989). *Fourth generation evaluation.* Newbury Park, CA: Sage.

Hargreaves, A. (1994). *Changing teachers, changing times.* New York: Teachers College Press.

Henning, G. (1987). *A guide to language testing: Development, evaluation, research.* Cambridge, MA: Newbury House.

Herrnstein, R. J., and C. Murray (1994). *The bell curve: Intelligence and class structure in American life.* New York: Free Press.

Keeves, J. P. (1994). Methods of assessment in schools. In T. Husen and T. N. Postlethwaite (eds.), *The International Encyclopedia of Education*, 362–70. 2d ed. New York: Elsevier Science.

Kelly, G. A. (1955). *The psychology of personal constructs*, vol. 1. New York: Norton.

Kincheloe, J. L., S. R. Steinberg, and A. D. Gresson, III (eds.) (1996). *Measured lies: The Bell Curve examined.* New York: St. Martin's.

Klein, R. (1996). Text and subtext. *New York Times*, March 18, p. A15.

LaCelle-Peterson, M.W., and C. Rivera (1994). Is it real for all kids? A framework for equitable assessment policies for English Language Learners. *Harvard Educational Review 64*, 55–75.

Lyotard, J. F. (1984). *The postmodern condition: A report on knowledge.* Minneapolis: University of Minnesota Press.

Mead, G. H. (1934, rpr. in 1962). *Mind, self, and society: From the standpoint of a social behaviorist.* Chicago: University of Chicago Press.

Perrone, V. (ed.) (1975). *Testing and evaluation: New views.* Washington, DC: Association for Childhood Education International.

Piaget, J., and B. Inhelder (1969). *The psychology of the child.* New York: Basic Books.

Rivera, C., and C. Simich (1981). Issues in the assessment of language proficiency of language minority students. *NABE Journal 6* (1), 19–39.

Thorndike, R. L., and E. P. Hagen (1977). *Measurement and evaluation in psychology and education.* 4th ed. New York: Macmillan.

Trueba, H. T. (1989). *Raising silent voices: Educating linguistic minorities for the 21st century.* New York: Newbury House.

Wiggins, G. P. (1993). *Assessing student performance: Exploring the purpose and limits of testing.* San Francisco: Jossey-Bass.

Chapter Three

SUPPORTING TEACHING AND LEARNING FOR ALL STUDENTS: Policies for Authentic Assessment Systems

Linda Darling-Hammond

and Beverly Falk

Over the last decade, educators, policymakers, and the public have begun to forge a consensus that the schools in our nation must better prepare students for the demands of the twenty-first century. A major goal is to support schooling that will encourage *all* students to construct, integrate, and apply their knowledge; to think critically and invent solutions to problems; and to respond creatively to unforeseeable issues that will confront them in the complex world of tomorrow.

In pursuit of higher levels of learning for a greater range of students, local, state, and national efforts have focused on articulating rigorous standards of student achievement as a basis for new curriculum and assessments. The best of these, like the standards of the National Council of Teachers of Mathematics (NCTM), articulate core ideas and critical skills in the discipline in a way that is sufficiently pointed to be meaningful for guiding practice without being overly prescriptive. The worst repeat the mistakes of the competency-based education movements of the 1970s by specifying hundreds of discrete objectives that reduce subject matter to tiny subskills and factoids—too reductionistic to be useful for thoughtful teaching (Darling-Hammond 1994a).

Along with the challenges of developing educationally useful standards, there are many dilemmas that confront policymakers and educators as assessment strategies are redesigned. These include developing challenging curricula based on these common standards that are responsive to the differing perspectives of diverse populations; building the capacities of teachers to use a range of strategies that will help students to achieve the standards; designing new forms of assessment that better support and reflect what is being taught; and creating systems for curriculum, assessment, and schooling that support student learning rather than merely pointing out deficiencies with new measures (Darling-Hammond 1994b; Mitchell 1992; Rothman 1995).

Changes in curriculum and assessment practices have been successfully undertaken in many classrooms. Many teachers have developed assessments that ask students to solve problems and express ideas in deeper and fuller ways than traditional approaches have allowed. They involve students in empirical inquiry and library research projects, compiling portfolios of writing and mathematics work, producing video and oral-tape recordings, and conducting experiments (Darling-Hammond, et al. 1993; Darling-Hammond, Ancess, and Falk 1995).

This kind of teaching and assessment has remained limited in its development, however, because its approach is generally not compatible with the approach to teaching needed to prepare students for the high-stakes tests used by most districts and states (Darling-Hammond and Wise 1985; Falk and Larson 1995; Moss 1994; Wiggins 1993). These large-scale testing systems, used to decide if students should graduate, be held back, or be placed in special programs or tracks, have strongly influenced classroom practice (Allington and McGill-Franzen 1992; Darling-Hammond 1991, 1992; Koretz 1988; Shepard and Smith 1988; Smith et al. 1986). Because the tests rely heavily on multiple-choice questions that ask students to recall facts from large bodies of knowledge, they have focused instruction on superficial content coverage rather than on in-depth study. Instruction has begun to mimic not only the content but also the limited formats and low cognitive demands of tests: the passive recognition of answers from those arrayed in a list, rather than the production of ideas or performances (Glaser and Silver 1994; Wiggins 1989, 1993). In addition, pressure to teach to standardized tests has made it difficult to effectively teach diverse groupings of students who bring different starting points, understandings, and styles of learning to the learning enterprise (Darling-Hammond 1989, 1991, 1994b; Falk, MacMurdy, and Darling-Hammond 1995; Garcia and Pearson 1994).

Many states now recognize that in order to alleviate the tension between testing and good teaching, large-scale assessment systems must change to better reflect more authentic performances. This is, however, more easily said than done. This chapter focuses on the host of issues, problems, and challenges that must be addressed if large-scale assessment systems are to support and encourage powerful teaching that responds to new standards for student learning as well as to the diversity of ways in which students learn. Based on the experiences of a number of states that have already begun this work, we outline nine principles to guide the construction of large-scale assessment systems. We then describe how the New York State assessment system is seeking to bring these principles to life. And we conclude with a discussion of the conditions and supports needed for schools and districts to effectively and equitably educate all students.

PRINCIPLE 1: BASE ASSESSMENTS ON STANDARDS FOR LEARNING

High-quality content and performance standards that outline what students should come to know and be able to do over the course of their education should guide the development of new assessment systems. Basing assessment on standards should promote greater clarity about the kinds of content and performance that are valued and assessed, thus promoting equity by giving teachers and students the opportunity to work toward meeting the standards. States like Kentucky, Maryland, and Vermont that have developed standards-based assessments are beginning to see substantial improvements in the quality of student work in areas like writing and mathematics the longer the assessments are in use.

Assessments designed to measure student achievement of standards are very different from the norm-referenced tests still used in most testing programs. Norm-referenced tests are designed to compare students to one another rather than to evaluate their performance in relation to specific standards. Items on norm-referenced tests are designed to ensure that student scores will fall out along a bell curve; thus, those items on which too many or the wrong subset of students do well are excluded from the test, regardless of their relation to curriculum or goals for learning. Devices such as time limits and distractor questions (deliberately placed to distract students from the right answer) are used to sort out the "best" performers. This approach to test construction is not compatible with the standards-based reforms that seek to clarify what students should know and be able to do, and then give them opportunities and information for developing their performance (Darling-Hammond 1994b).

Items or tasks on standards-based assessments are developed to provide indicators of student attainment of valued learning goals. While student performance may vary greatly, the tasks are designed not to preclude some students from achieving mastery but to provide information about how much they have thus far learned. In addition to providing more information about actual student learning, one of the advantages of standards-based assessments is that they contribute to clarity of purpose and rigor in developing a curriculum (Darling-Hammond 1994b; Resnick 1989). They ask all of those involved in educating students to be clear and purposeful about articulating their goals. They push all those involved in curriculum decisions to ask and answer the fundamental question: "What will students really know and actually be able to do as a consequence of engaging in particular learning activities and demonstrating what they know in particular ways?"

Standards-based assessments offer all students the opportunity to demonstrate how they have mastered valued goals for learning. Because they start with learning goals and end with performance standards, providing descriptions of varying levels of achievement, they allow students to demonstrate a range of abilities, from beginning competencies to distinguished performance.

PRINCIPLE 2: REPRESENT PERFORMANCES OF UNDERSTANDING IN AUTHENTIC WAYS

Anyone familiar with schools in districts that emphasize high-stakes testing knows the powerful hold that tests have on curriculum, instruction, and learning. What is tested is what is valued. Unfortunately, the converse is not always true. When California's new curriculum framework in mathematics was being piloted some years ago, a set of case studies found that its implementation in the classroom was undermined both by teachers' lack of knowledge about how to teach for understanding, rather than for rote recall, and by the state's continuation of traditional standardized testing. As one teacher explained: "Teaching for understanding is what we are supposed to be doing. . . . It's difficult to test, folks. That is the bottom line. They want me to teach in a way that they can't test. Except that I'm held accountable to the test. It's a catch-22" (Wilson 1990: 318).

If schools are to have incentives to support powerful learning, assessments must be good representations of the kinds of learning desired. Multiple-choice proxies for performance will never support instruction that builds students' capacities to think well, write clearly, express themselves persuasively, find resources, solve problems, and design new products and ideas.

Earlier approaches to curriculum informed by behaviorist learning theory have shaped most current standardized tests, which test lower-level cognitive skills on the belief that, once mastered, these might add up to thinking skills (Resnick 1987). We now know that learners accrue basic facts and skills in more powerful ways while they build conceptual understanding and skilled performances, which help them create mental maps of how the world works. Higher-order thinking is the foundation that makes factual and other kinds of learning possible, rather than the reverse. Thus teachers must focus on more holistic performances and ideas as a basis for content learning, and they must understand a great deal about students' thinking in order to do so (Piaget and Inhelder 1970; Resnick 1987; Sternberg 1985).

Thus, support for meaningful learning requires the development of "authentic" assessments (Shepard 1995; Wolf 1989) that examine "performances of understanding" (Gardner 1991). Such assessments should, to the greatest extent possible, look directly at student work; measure applications of knowledge and skills in real-world contexts; and require higher-level thinking and complex problem solving.

Authentic assessments vary in different contexts. In early grades, they may focus more on the process of learning, relying heavily on observation and documentation of learners' growth over time in natural contexts. These kinds of assessments, like the Primary Language Record (Barrs et al. 1988) in use in Britain, California, and New York, yield information about how each student is progressing in relation to developmental criteria along an articulated continuum for a discipline or age group (NAEYC 1988).

In upper grades, assessments may continue to include observations of student growth while they focus increasingly on the products of student learning, using a range of projects, performances, and exhibitions to evaluate student achievement according to articulated criteria that are important for actual performance in that field (Wiggins 1989). While considerations of cost and comparability pose some constraints on assessments that are used for reporting purposes—for example, that tasks use common prompts that can be scored in comparable ways—they can still demand performances much like those students would undertake in real-life contexts.

PRINCIPLE 3: EMBED ASSESSMENT IN CURRICULUM AND INSTRUCTION

Testing students once a year does not ensure learning nor does it necessarily support responsive teaching. Teachers must understand the kinds of work required by new assessments—and they must deeply understand their students' paths to learning—if they are to build curriculum and teaching that help develop students' capacities to succeed. This process is encouraged if assessments are embedded in the processes of teaching and curriculum development, rather than added on as an unrelated appendage at the end of the year.

The importance of ongoing assessment to the process of effective teaching has been made more clear by recent advances in cognitive research. This research reveals that, far from being *tabula rasa* who can be easily imprinted with information and ideas, learners actively construct knowledge throughout all of their life experiences. In addition, individual students learn in different ways, at different rates, and from the vantage point of their different experiences (Garcia and Pearson 1994; Gardner 1983; Kornhaber and Gardner 1993). Because of this, no highly specific, predetermined curriculum can ever be equally effective for all students. To be successful at helping all students achieve, teachers must meet students where they are and create a bridge between their individual talents, interests, and experiences, and common, challenging learning goals. This means that teachers must have the knowledge, skills, resources, and flexibility to figure out what students know and how they think and then to use a variety of pathways to respond to what they find out.

In many countries, and in some reform-minded states and restructuring schools in the United States, assessments are tightly interwoven with teaching. Curriculum-embedded assessments may include portfolio collections of student work in various subject areas, developed and revised over time. They may also include extended tasks and projects that call on students to analyze, investigate, experiment, cooperate, and present their findings in written, oral, or graphic ways. The information they provide about students' strengths and approaches to learning helps teachers shape and adapt instruction to the needs of individual students (Darling-Hammond, Ancess, and Falk 1995; Einbender and Wood 1995).

Assessment systems like those in Vermont and Kentucky have successfully used portfolios to guide, inform, and support instruction while also providing evaluations of student learning and progress. Systems in parts of Canada, Australia, Great Britain, and Europe include student work samples developed throughout the year as part of the assessment systems for graduation. These systems do much more than deliver tests and report scores. They also:

- inform the ongoing life of classrooms, requiring teachers to assume new roles in instruction as well as assessment
- provide information that is useful for instruction and that encourages reflective practice
- examine the process as well as the products of learning so that teachers can assess students in a cumulative, longitudinal fashion
- communicate expectations and support student motivation and self-assessment as well as teacher assessment of student growth
- identify students' strengths, abilities, and progress as they are unfolding, opening up possibilities for further growth rather than precluding access to future advanced instruction.

PRINCIPLE 4: PROVIDE MULTIPLE FORMS OF EVIDENCE ABOUT STUDENT LEARNING

A system of assessments should provide opportunities for students to demonstrate what they know and are able to do in a variety of ways. It should assure that multiple forms of evidence about student progress and achievement are available, and that they are used in concert to make judgments about students (Price, Schwabacher, and Chittenden 1993). All of these forms of evidence should be consistent with teaching that fosters meaningful learning. Test preparation, in other words, should always mirror and support good instruction (National Forum on Assessment 1995).

No test is ever a perfect measure of the domain or skills it hopes to tap. Thus, individual assessments should always be treated as partial and fallible. Assessments in the system should complement each other so as to serve multiple purposes. First among these is providing evidence about what students know and can do, the strategies they use, and their strengths and needs. This knowledge can help teachers diagnose student needs and adapt their teaching strategies to be responsive to individual differences.

A second purpose is to provide teachers, students, families, and school systems with information about how students have progressed over time, what standards for learning they have mastered, and what further challenges they need to take on to progress through the continuum of achievement.

A third purpose is to provide information about the progress of groups of students across schools, districts, or states. This information keeps track of how students are doing across different locales and different populations. Such information can help educational agencies evaluate their own success in educating all students equitably.

As it is now, in order to fulfill these different purposes for assessment, teachers often have to subject students to overtesting, intensive test preparation, and conflicting messages about the kind of learning that is valued. In many situations, teachers collect rich information that can be used for instruction but that cannot be used to demonstrate achievement for other purposes beyond the classroom. Even though the accumulated data of observational records, collections of student work, and curriculum-based projects offer a fuller and richer picture of progress than any one test can provide, for accountability purposes most districts and states require students to take standardized tests. The "catch-22" is that preparation for these tests often precludes students from having the time to engage in the projects and other extended activities that offer opportunities for in-depth learning and demonstrations of student understanding.

In designing systems of assessment, classroom work that is useful for teaching should be able to be sampled for other purposes as well. And assessments used for comparable reporting should be compatible with high-quality classroom teaching rather than a deflection from what many teachers call "real" teaching and learning (Darling-Hammond and Wise 1985). In addition, the assessment system should use multiple forms of evidence to make important decisions about a student's future. Decisions about program placements, promotion, and other matters should always take into account several kinds of information about performance, rather than being based on any single test or piece of work.

PRINCIPLE 5: EVALUATE STANDARDS WITHOUT UNNECESSARY STANDARDIZATION

One of the major challenges in developing large-scale assessment systems is to support learning and respond fairly to the differences that exist across groups while at the same time providing comparable and reliable evidence for public accountability purposes (Darling-Hammond, Ancess, and Falk 1995; Falk and Larson 1995; Moss 1994; Wiggins 1993). Serving these dual purposes creates a tension. Part of the tension has to do with the fact that in order to use assessments to compare student achievement across large groups, a certain amount of standardization of the assessment must take place. This standardization is necessary to ensure that the student work being compared is measuring the same standards of learning and represents the same quality of achievement across sites (an issue that is not problematic when using standardized tests in multiple-choice formats where achievement is easily measurable because there is only one possible right answer).

However, efforts to make authentic assessments more standardized to answer reliability and comparability concerns generally affect both their validity for drawing inferences about individual students and their usefulness for teaching. Standardization, by necessity, makes assessments become less accessible to some students and moreso to others, as students are differentially familiar with the contexts selected for displaying knowledge (Darling-Hammond 1994a; Moss 1994;

Wiggins 1993).

When differences in living and learning experiences are ignored or wished away, they can become sources of hidden bias in testing. One psychometrician testifying about cultural bias in testing gave as an example a set of reading questions from a test, developed in Minnesota but used in California, that happened to use sledding as a referent. Almost no children in southern California could answer the questions correctly, as they had never seen or heard of a sled.[1] The example seems obvious, but the problem is nearly unavoidable. All problems, items, and prompts have referents with which children from different communities will be differentially familiar. Research illustrates that when test references differentially tap students' life experiences—whether these deal with regattas or piñatas—students' differential performances will be conditioned not by their underlying competence but by their contextual knowledge (Garcia and Pearson 1994).

New systems must find ways to design assessments that are responsive to variations in students' different learning contexts, while also eliciting the same kinds and levels of achievement. Tasks that use different performance modes and that involve students in choosing ways to demonstrate their competence become important for this goal (Kornhaber and Gardner 1993; Gordon n.d.). Substantial teacher and student involvement in and control over assessment strategies and uses are critical if assessment is to support the most challenging education possible for every student, taking full account of his or her talents and ways of knowing. As Gordon puts it:

> The task is to find assessment probes which measure the same criterion from contexts and perspectives which reflect the life space and values of the learner. . . . Thus options and choices become a critical feature in any assessment system created to be responsive to equity, just as processual description and diagnosis become central purposes. (n.d.: 8–9)

This can be done by designing assessments based on uniform standards and scoring them using standardized processes. Uniform standards and rubrics create a validity path from standards to tasks to student scores. Then, elements of content, context, procedures, or format might vary according to the precise learning situation. Students' mastery of valued skills can often be assessed allowing choices of content: pieces of literature to be analyzed; types of models to be developed; topics for research projects or experiments to be conducted. This has long been the case in tests like those used for Advanced Placement in some subjects and in some Regents tests in New York State. It is also the case with work samples collected in assessment systems like Vermont's and Kentucky's portfolio systems and those in several countries worldwide.

The objective of maintaining high standards with less standardization will demand teachers who are able to evaluate and eliminate sources of unfair bias in their development and scoring of instructionally embedded assessments; and who can balance subjectivity and objectivity, using their knowledge of students in selecting tasks and assessment options while adhering to common, collective standards of evaluation. These same abilities will be crucial for other assessment developers. In many respects, even greater sensitivity to the sources of bias that can pervade assessment will be needed, with forms that frequently eliminate the anonymity of test takers, drawing more heavily on interpersonal interaction in tasks, and on observations on the part of teachers.

PRINCIPLE 6: INVOLVE LOCAL EDUCATORS IN DESIGNING AND SCORING ASSESSMENTS

Efforts to ensure that *all* students learn in meaningful ways that result in high levels of performance require that teachers know as much about students and their learning as they do about subject matter. However, teachers' understandings of students' strengths, needs, and approaches to learning are not well supported by external testing programs that send secret, secured tests into the school and whisk them out again for machine scoring that produces numerical quotients many months later.

Teachers learn about the deeper structures of curriculum, the nature and nuances of student thinking, and the connections between teaching and learning from firsthand encounters with assessment design and the evaluation of student work. Involving teachers in this work is powerful professional development: it helps them learn to teach more effectively, while also ensuring that their knowledge of students and curriculum is incorporated in assessments.

In other countries, teachers have always been involved in developing and scoring assessments, some for widespread common use and others for classroom use. Teachers evaluate the work of their own and each others' students. This kind of involvement in assessment creates the possibility that teachers will not only develop a curriculum aimed at challenging performance skills but that they will also be able to use the resulting rich information about student learning and performance to shape their teaching in ways that can prove more effective for individual students (Darling-Hammond 1994a).

In addition, evidence from restructuring efforts indicates that when schools wrestle with setting standards and evaluation, the collective struggle to define directions, to evaluate progress, and to "map backward" into new curriculum and teaching possibilities creates an engine for change that is absent when assessment is entirely externalized. If authentic forms of student assessment are shaped and implemented by members of the whole school community, they can enable the kinds of teacher, parent, and student learning that are needed to support the classroom and schoolwide changes required for student success (Darling-Hammond, Ancess, and Falk 1995).

It is for this reason that the locus of assessment development and implementation is as important as the nature of the assessment tools and strategies. Assessments that are externally developed and scored cannot transform the knowledge and understandings of teachers—and of school organizations, even if they are more performance based than are current tests. Assessment reforms can increase student success by increasing organizational learning if they change not only the kinds of tasks students are asked to engage in but also the kinds of inquiries schools and teachers are called upon to undertake as they bring assessment into the heart of the teaching and learning process. At the core of an assessment system, then, is the principle that assessment should inform and support teachers' efforts to understand student learning and schools' efforts to improve the educational opportunities they provide.

Local involvement in assessment should also involve students, their families, and community members in two-way communications that provide information about student progress and school performance. Assessment systems should develop mechanisms for regular dialogue and exchange of ideas among all concerned with the educational enterprise. Methods for communicating to parents and the public could include exhibitions of students' work, such as displays and demonstrations of what they have learned and accomplished. As in the town meetings and recitations conducted at schools in the early days of this country, people should be able to see what schools are doing and what their students can do as a result. These processes of communication should provide opportunities for community members to participate in discussing and evaluating what schools are doing.

PRINCIPLE 7: LET THE INNOVATORS OF THE SYSTEM LEAD

Local innovations generally precede large-scale change, and they produce a great deal of learning about possibilities and pitfalls that should inform system-wide initiatives. Those responsible for system policies should consciously seek to learn from local innovations, and should develop ways for schools to share knowledge about successful practices.

Governments often fail to learn from or support promising local work because the "assumption of hierarchical intelligence" (Darling-Hammond 1994a) implicitly demeans such work, presuming that decisions made by higher levels of government are always superior to those made by localities. This presumption has created much of the regulatory gridlock schools now experience. It is an assumption that has been increasingly brought into question by the lessons of restructuring businesses that have learned the importance of encouraging frontline inventiveness.

Designers of new assessment systems should seek out and build upon promising local assessment practices as well as document local successes so that school people and members of the public can learn more about how to support student learning. To promote innovation, states and/or districts should also sponsor research and information about new forms of teaching, curriculum, and assessment so that widespread access to these resources is available.

Because teachers and schools, just like students, are at different stages of development and implementation of new teaching and assessment practices, states and districts should actively support existing innovative work. Freedom from policies that constrain promising experimentation should be granted to those individuals, schools, or districts that have made progress in developing high-quality assessment systems and mechanisms for accountability. In this way, reform efforts can be complemented rather than overridden by new policies and processes.

PRINCIPLE 8: PROVIDE PROFESSIONAL DEVELOPMENT THAT BUILDS THE CAPACITY OF TEACHERS AND SCHOOLS TO ENACT NEW TEACHING AND ASSESSMENT PRACTICES

If new standards and assessments are to promote higher levels of achievement rather than merely documenting high levels of failure, teaching must become much more effective and powerful. Consequently, professional learning must be an ongoing part of the process of developing and evaluating curriculum and assessments. Teachers need information, expertise, and time to work together on the development and implementation of new curriculum and pedagogy. As teachers consult with one another in collectively developing, analyzing, and evaluating student work, they learn about student learning and gain insights and understandings about their own teaching and learning processes as well. Systems like Vermont's that have organized occasions for teachers to work together on developing and scoring tasks and evaluating student work have found that the nature and quality of instruction are improving (Murnane and Levy 1996). In places where professional development has been an afterthought, however, assessments have provoked anxiety and high rates of failure rather than greater empowerment and more successful schooling.

PRINCIPLE 9: JUDGE SCHOOL PERFORMANCE BASED ON PRACTICES AS WELL AS LONGITUDINAL PERFORMANCE DATA FOR INDIVIDUAL STUDENTS

While assessment systems, old and new, purport to address issues of accountability, this purpose cannot be fulfilled only by looking at student test data. As Oakes argues, information about resources and school practices is essential "if [policymakers] want monitoring and accountability systems to mirror the condition of education accurately or to be useful for making improvements" (1989: 182). Those who would attempt to use standards in the quest for accountability and improvement can themselves be held accountable for making sound decisions only if they address questions of *why* outcomes appear as they do and make necessary changes in the conditions that influence learning.

Assessment of student outcomes must be accompanied by other evaluations of school inputs and practices likely to produce the valued outcomes. These include information about (1) how well school personnel are using professional knowledge and practices to meet the needs of their students; (2) the extent to which students have equitable access to appropriate resources and materials that support their learning; and (3) whether schools have structures and vehicles in place to address collectively the problems and issues that arise in the course of teaching. Because all of these aspects of schooling critically affect how students are achieving, they must continually receive attention, along with the assessment of student achievement (Darling-Hammond 1992). School review processes, much like the Inspection system developed in England, provide this kind of information about the quality of teaching and the opportunities for learning that are made available in a school. School- and district-reporting systems must also include this information.

In addition, to be helpful for drawing inferences about school quality, statistics about student learning gains should be based on longitudinal assessments of the performance of the same group of students over time, rather than on school average test scores. Because these average scores are sensitive to the population of students taking the test, such a measure creates incentives for schools to keep out students whom they fear may lower their scores—children who are handicapped, with limited English-speaking skills, or from educationally disadvantaged environments. These outcomes have already been reported from high-stakes uses of school test scores for making decisions about school rewards and sanctions. They include labeling large numbers of low-scoring students for special education placements so that their scores won't "count" in school reports, retaining students in grade so that their relative standing will look better on "grade-equivalent" scores, excluding low-scoring students from admission to "open enrollment" schools, and encouraging such students to leave schools or drop out (Allington and McGill-Franzen 1992; Darling-Hammond 1991, 1992; Koretz 1988; Smith et al. 1986; Shepard and Smith 1988).

Needless to say, this kind of policy creates a distorted view of accountability, one in which beating the numbers by playing shell games with student placements overwhelms efforts to serve students' educational needs well. Equally important, these policies further exacerbate existing incentives for talented staff to opt for school placements where students are easy to teach and school stability is high. Capable staff are less likely to risk losing rewards or incurring sanctions by volunteering to teach where many students have special needs and performance standards are more difficult to attain. This compromises even further the educational chances of disadvantaged students, who are already served by a disproportionate share of inexperienced and underqualified teachers.

THE NEW YORK STATE ASSESSMENT SYSTEM: A FRAMEWORK TO SUPPORT MEANINGFUL LEARNING

Over the last several years, New York State has been developing a comprehensive system of learning goals and standards, curriculum frameworks, new assessments, and support strategies that embody many of the principles we have described. The school-reform initiatives launched by Commissioner Thomas Sobol and the Regents in the early 1990s, and more recently enacted in policy by Commis-

sioner Richard Mills, explicitly aimed to loosen input regulations while supporting the attainment of more challenging learning goals for all students through a
process of "top-down support for bottom-up reform," a phrase that became one
of the mottos of the reform process. New York's *New Compact for Learning* began
with the precept that "all students can learn" and promised to "focus on results,"
"provide the means," and "provide authority with accountability." Like initiatives
in a number of other states, the goal is to encourage schools to focus on improving outcomes rather than on implementing procedures—on doing the right
things, rather than on doing things right. In an extraordinarily highly regulated
environment, this strategy poses many challenges as well as possibilities.

In order to fully understand the assessment system's redesign, a sense of history and context is helpful. New York State has a long tradition of administering
an extensive array of examinations to students. In the elementary grades, these
have been used for program assessment as well as for identifying individual students in need of special supports and services. Local districts have also frequently
used scores to make decisions about grade promotion. Average scores at the
school level have been used to identify schools in need of intervention.

In the high schools, state examinations linked to specific courses and syllabi
have traditionally focused on extensive content coverage, strongly influencing the
nature of instruction in the disciplines. High-school graduation in New York
State relies on two types of exams and diplomas. Students receiving a local
diploma must pass six Regents Competency Tests; those seeking a Regents
diploma must pass at least eleven examinations. The two types of exams, originally created to address differences in student abilities, have created a two-tiered
structure and tracking system that determines access to curriculum in New York
high schools. While the Regents track includes more difficult content, both examination systems provide few opportunities for students to demonstrate higher-
order thinking skills and application of knowledge in a range of different ways.

The exams represent primarily the recall and recognition of factual information on multiple-choice tests, which students widely claim they forget within
weeks. The few writing tasks are short essays on tightly bounded topics. Students
complete the Regents curriculum without ever writing a paper of more than a
few paragraphs, reading a primary source in history, doing a research project, or
designing a science experiment. Teachers argue that there is little time for these
"frills" in the press to cover all of the facts that might be tested at the end of the
term.

Many of the exams are also antiquated in their conceptions of subject matter
and counterproductive to the acquisition of higher-order thinking and performance skills. Mathematics experts claim that it is impossible to teach to the
NCTM standards in the current Regents curriculum. Alan Schoenfeld's (1988)
study of mathematics Regents courses found that the more successfully teachers
taught for the test, the more they were forced to teach "bad mathematics." The
same is true of most of the current science Regents courses. None of the currently
proposed national science standards can be achieved in the existing Regents

courses, where students memorize science facts rather than applying scientific methods to original problems or conducting independently designed research.

The redesign for the New York State system supports a more robust view of learning. It is intended to promote and reflect learning experiences that call on students to synthesize and apply knowledge and skills to analyze, critique, question, and invent. The assessments in the system are designed to model and mirror good instruction, providing a framework that encourages and reflects meaningful learning (New York State Curriculum and Assessment Council 1994). All of the examinations will be performance oriented and will include a curriculum-embedded component to allow more in-depth work on more extended tasks. Some Regents assessments will allow students to demonstrate attainment of state standards through experiments, designs, and problem solutions in which students perform, explain, and show the products of their work.

The system's redesign also hopes to remedy the discrepancies in opportunities to learn that are prevalent among students with differing backgrounds in New York State, while providing a means for all students to demonstrate learning in broader ways than traditional measures have allowed. Under the system's redesign, all students will take examinations designed to measure attainment of the state's standards in core areas defined by new curriculum frameworks. At the high-school level, all students will take a set of four or five common Regents examinations. After fulfilling these requirements, students will have choices to pursue more advanced-level courses and exams and to branch out into other areas of study. The natural range of student abilities and performance will be addressed by allowing students to sit for the required examinations at different points in their school careers—some students can move rapidly through the core curriculum to take on more demanding and challenging work, while others can proceed at a slower pace. But all students will have access to the same core curriculum entitlement.

The redesign of the assessment system is intended to move the state from a testing program that focuses on summative evaluation using primarily multiple-choice forms of testing to a system of performance assessments used in the service of ongoing teaching and learning. The new system emphasizes the integration of assessment with curriculum and instruction, featuring a blend of state and local work and on-demand and curriculum-embedded assessments. This integration is intended to encourage the use of teaching and assessment strategies that help teachers, parents, and students gain a rich understanding of what students know and can do, as well as how they think and learn. The system will use a variety of assessment strategies to enable students to capitalize on their strengths while also challenging them to perform and communicate in different ways. It should allow educators to evaluate the success of programs while providing data that indicate attainments across the state and within districts.

State and local assessments are intended to work together to serve a number of different purposes: providing information to students, teachers, and parents about individual students' progress in ways that help inform teaching and learning; providing information to the state and local school boards about the outcomes of programs and the performances of groups of students in ways that can inform the further development of state and local policies and identify schools in particular need of improvement; and communicating expectations and standards about valued knowledge, skills, and abilities that can support program development. The system is designed to address these purposes through a smaller number of higher-quality state-administered assessments that stimulate, complement, and build on local work supportive of student-centered learning. This is a key point: the system aims to incorporate instructionally useful, curriculum-embedded work while meeting the technical requirements generally applied to large-scale testing systems.

Components of the Assessment System

Under the redesign of the system, each examination includes both an on-demand test and common curriculum-embedded tasks.

The *on-demand* components are performance-oriented standardized examinations administered at a given point in time. These assessments are time-bound, not timed, but can vary in duration, lasting anywhere from several hours to several days. The test component calls on students to demonstrate what they know and can do by answering questions in writing or orally, conducting experiments or other short-term investigations, or producing products ranging from essays to graphs, charts, and computer simulations.

Curriculum-embedded tasks include classroom projects that are part of the ongoing teaching/learning process: collections of written products, extended investigations or experiments, and research projects. These kinds of assessments can be conducted at various points in the year as teachers deem appropriate, taking anywhere from several days to weeks to complete. In addition to their use for state assessment purposes, the projects in the extended-task component of the state assessments can become part of a local K–12 collection of student work, used by local districts to assess individual student progress and to inform the teaching process.

In addition to these state examinations, local districts are to develop their own sets of complementary assessments to document students' continuous progress and to inform teaching and support learning. Districts and schools that have made progress in developing and using performance-oriented assessments can fold the curriculum-embedded component of state assessments into their existing local systems. In districts and schools where performance-oriented assessments have not yet been developed, local assessments can be built on the models provided by the state examinations.

To assist schools and districts in developing such assessments, the state is compiling an Assessment Collection that includes prototypes of promising practices developed in the field. Technical assistance and professional development will be needed to assist districts in developing performance-based assessment systems for local accountability and curriculum reform and to assist districts in aligning these local assessment procedures to the state standards.

Establishing Reliability and Validity

Both the on-demand and curriculum-embedded components of the proposed state assessments are evaluated by a scoring process drawn directly from the standards outlined in each curriculum framework. The scores students receive on each component are to be combined to determine each student's score on the examination as a whole. Scores will be differentiated into multiple levels of performance (for example, beginning, proficient, accomplished, and distinguished). A proficiency standard would illustrate the minimum score that a student must achieve to be considered competent enough to pass; an accomplished standard could be set to identify performances that represent a strong command of the subject and skills being evaluated; and a distinguished standard could acknowledge exceptional performance.

In New York, as in many European countries, all teachers whose students are tested are involved in scoring the assessments. This has the value of providing ongoing engagement in assessment that supports teachers' understanding of the standards and examinations. It also creates issues of reliability in scoring that need to be addressed. All teachers who score performance tasks will participate in scoring protocols and moderation exercises so that common understandings can be developed about what constitutes achievement of the standards. Moderation and auditing procedures will support the reliability of teacher ratings of student performance. Common rubrics and moderated scoring will also promote shared understanding about assessment and performance, contributing to the profession's knowledge base.

The validity of the state examinations is established by evaluating whether they are good measures of the knowledge and skills embodied in the content and performance standards of the curriculum frameworks. Validity also rests on the premise that standards are understood by teachers and inform the curriculum (that is, provide the necessary opportunities to learn) to meet the state standards. Demonstration of consequential validity will ultimately require showing that the use of the assessments encourages the kinds of learning that the frameworks intend. Validity data are obtained through disciplinary expert reviews of the standards and assessments as well as through questionnaires to teachers and students that elicit their views of assessments and their impact on student learning and on teaching.

Raising Standards and Providing Flexibility

Including performance elements in the assessments will raise expectations by requiring that students take on more challenging work than they do in the current system. Standards will also be raised at the high-school level by eliminating the dual examination system and replacing it with a unitary set of exams for all students. Merging the two systems will ensure that all students undertake more intellectually rigorous tasks and will not track some students out of challenging courses solely because of the structure of the testing system. The expectations of the new Regents examinations—for students to demonstrate not only attainment of knowledge but its application as well—will apply to all students. However, performance levels on these more challenging tasks will vary and will allow a much higher ceiling, thus enabling more advanced students to demonstrate very high levels of attainment, while all are challenged to undertake more authentic and challenging performances.

Flexibility in the programs will be achieved through expanding the format of the Regents examinations to incorporate extended tasks as a key component and by tying examinations to standards for learning rather than to specific course configurations. Thus, local schools or districts may choose to use a variety of course configurations that prepare students to succeed on the assessments.

The extended-task component will allow students to work on in-depth curricular tasks that are designed to elicit critical thinking and to demonstrate a student's command of major concepts in a particular field of study and in a variety of ways. Extended tasks for each discipline will have a common format, common guidelines, common criteria, and uniform scoring rubrics. Depending on the discipline, they may include a collection of written work or a research paper. Similarly, a project that integrates math, science, and technology might be submitted for Regents credit to supplement on-demand examinations in mathematics and science, and might include an experiment or exhibition across several disciplines or interdisciplinary courses in the three areas.

Local Portfolios

In addition to the Regents examinations, New York's Council on Curriculum and Assessment has urged that students assemble a graduation portfolio that reflects their performance over the course of school. The state university system's Task Force on College Entry-Level Knowledge and Skills also recommended that students assemble a portfolio of performance-based assessments as data for college admissions and placements (SUNY 1992). Included in the portfolio could be a compilation of tasks from Regents examinations as well as other work samples that might include:

- evidence of learning in fields like the arts and technical fields not included in the state testing system
- more extensive work in areas of specialization
- evidence of learning through an internship or other work-related learning experience
- an independent research project
- an oral presentation and defense of one or more major products.

Building choices into the overall assessment system while streamlining the core graduation requisites in this way should allow students of diverse talents and abilities to develop and demonstrate what they know and are able to do well, while ensuring that a standard of achievement for all has been achieved in essential areas of knowledge. This strategy might also allow the award of a Regents diploma with a recognition of distinguished performance in a particular field (math, science, art, foreign language) or with an overall distinction, reflecting outstanding achievement.

Developing and Piloting the Revised Assessment System

Moving the assessment system from the idea stage into operational form requires consideration of many factors. How do you "unfreeze" an existing system to enable change and create capacity for new practices? How do you inform the public about changes that are taking place? How do you build the capacity of state and local agencies to understand and use a new assessment system? How do you create new infrastructures and provide the resources and supports that are needed to ensure that the change initiative takes root and stays alive in the face of budgetary constraints and political pressures?

Strategies for Unfreezing the System

In order to create an atmosphere that invites change, a variety of strategies were initiated to "unfreeze" the old system. One strategy was to permit leading-edge schools and districts to experiment with new forms of assessment through waivers from existing tests and approval of options. These included a Regents Option project that invited and helped schools develop curriculum-embedded assessments that could be credited to up to 35 percent of the existing Regents examination score; state and local participation in the New Standards pilot examinations; and the establishment of New York State "partnership schools" that received comprehensive waivers to create fully developed assessment systems. As a result of these "invitations to invention" offered by the state, a climate and culture of systematic experimentation has developed. Many schools throughout the state eagerly volunteered to create new curriculum and assessment possibilities. Through involvement in these initiatives, both individual teachers and schools have increased their capacities to teach and assess in new ways.

Alternative Equivalent Measures

To encourage continual innovation, renewal, and growth, the new assessment system will continue to accept some alternative measures of student learning. This will encourage schools or districts that are developing new strategies for teaching and assessing to pursue work that might be promising models for others to use. Thus there is a means within the new system—as there was in the old—for some assessments or assessment systems to be approved as options if the alternatives are shown to be of at least equivalent rigor to the existing state examinations and meet the state standards in the curriculum framework. In addition to locally developed options, external tests like the College Board's Pacesetter or Advanced Placement examinations, or the International Baccalaureate exams might be used as substitutes for state-developed examinations. Decisions about the appropriateness of alternative examinations would be made by a state-established committee of recognized curriculum and assessment experts.

Constructing Prototype Exams

New York State has a tradition of teacher involvement in assessment development and use. The new system of performance-based assessments is building on this tradition by involving teachers (who represent different geographic locations and the population diversity in the state) in creating new assessments. Teachers with expertise in developing and using performance assessments form the core of assessment development teams. In addition, promising work that is already being carried out in other state and national projects inform the assessment development process. A precondition to using any of these assessments, however, is that they be aligned with the standards outlined in the state curriculum frameworks.

The first phase of this process has been to construct prototype examinations for piloting. The rationale for developing full-blown prototypes is to allow the State Education Department to signal the field about the nature of the new examinations—their philosophical underpinnings as well as their form and content. Pilots examine the content validity of tasks, the reliability of scoring methods and rubrics, the length and difficulty of the exams, and their impact on students, teachers, and schools.

Capacity Building to Prepare for New Assessments

Teacher involvement in exam development and scoring is a key aspect of capacity building. The state provides training for teachers to learn how to score the new assessments, a process that allows teachers to look carefully at student work and gain information about students and their learning, which can help shape their teaching. Assessing student work against the new standards also helps teachers to consider how important dimensions of the disciplines can be assessed and the criteria that signal excellent and competent performance. The conversations about student work build shared understanding and a common language as well as inter-rater reliability.

Another capacity-building step is the circulation of prototype pilot assessments to all districts, along with scoring rubrics and student-work samples that represent different levels of achievement of the standards. Study and discussion of the new assessment prototypes provide teachers, administrators, parents, and the public with the opportunity to learn about the new assessments and their implications for teaching and learning.

An infrastructure will also need to be created to establish a statewide core group of lead teachers working across the different regions of the state. Ideally, these teachers will be among those first involved in constructing assessments, creating criteria and rubrics, scoring them, and teaching others to do the same. They

15. The students in the 5th grade at the Elm Street School wanted to find out how many students in each grade attended summer camp. They took a survey and tallied the results shown in the table below.

Grade	Attended Camp
1	‖‖ ‖
2	‖‖ ‖‖‖
3	‖‖ ‖‖ ‖‖
4	‖‖ ‖‖ ‖‖ ‖‖‖
5	‖‖ ‖‖ ‖‖ ‖‖ ‖

Use their data to construct a graph on the grid provided.

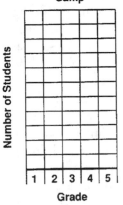

Students Attending Camp

Number of Students

Grade

Write one or two sentences that tell what you learned from the graph.

_____

_____

_____

_____

_____

_____

Excerpt from New York State Elementary Mathematics Pilot Assessment 1996

could then return to regional centers to lead other teachers in scoring local student work. These centers could become the locus of these and other professional development activities for the assessment system of the state.

Initial Findings

The first state assessments to be developed in pilot form were in mathematics and English language arts, plus a set of extended tasks in mathematics, science, and technology (MST). In 1995 and 1996, nine pilots were launched in the elementary through high school grades involving 12,000 students in more than 400 schools. These will be further refined in the coming years. Preliminary findings from the first two pilot years indicate that the exams offered reliable and valid ways for students to demonstrate their achievement while also providing information that is useful for teachers to use in instruction. With a combination of short answer and extended response tasks, inter-rater reliabilities of .83 to .96 were obtained on the on-demand tests, and reliabilities of .65 to .75 were obtained on the MST projects. This demonstrates that the work can be scored with a high degree of agreement. More important, an overwhelming majority of the teachers who administered the pilots felt that the examinations were accurate, fair, and useful measures of the standards in their disciplines. Because the tasks asked students to show their work (see example), many teachers reported that they learned much about their students:

> Students were able to show me what they know instead of bubbling in an answer that they guessed.

> The really important part of the test was that the kids showed the work. It made me see how they were thinking.

Many teachers also reported that the exams supported needed changes in their teaching:

> The exam serves as a guideline for teachers.

> The assessment requires teachers to teach differently.

> The exam gave me a look at my students but also at myself as a teacher. I thought I was teaching math before but this test made me realize that I need to make things more real and practical. It gave me a chance to see what I need to do in my teaching.

> The test really modeled good practice!

A majority of teachers also reported that their students enjoyed taking the exams.

> Most of my students enjoyed the assessment because they believed that this was a better instrument to measure what they know.

The students really enjoyed this. I think they liked being able to have as much time as they needed. Most importantly, I think they enjoyed it because they could really relate to the questions.

My students were eager to do the assessment and enjoyed the challenge.

This was an engaging activity. It was an authentic task that got the students involved.

The test allowed the struggling kids to do *something* while the "most intelligent" child in the class also found it challenging because in order to do well he had to think. It provided an opportunity for all students to show us their best work.

The kids had a great time. They learned a great deal. They changed over the days that they did the project. It was a wonderful experience!

Students responded positively to the new content and format of the tests. They reported that they liked the new exams because the exams assessed their skills and abilities better, allowed them to express their ideas more fully, were challenging and engaging, related to their lives, gave them enough time to show what they could do, and provided them with a learning experience:

I like this test, and I think it's better because it shows more what you are.

You can explain what you think instead of what *they* think.

I get to actually write and spell instead of filling in those blanks. Filling in the blanks is not helping you to read and write.

I liked all parts of the test because they were all interesting.

It was hard and fun and it gave me a sense of accomplishment.

This was a good challenge to your ability!

It is interesting to learn while you are doing a test.

As educators understand more about how to help a greater range of students achieve at higher levels of performance, we are challenged also to expand our definition of what constitutes sound assessment. We need to develop assessments that do not constrict teaching and learning and that support what we know is needed for learning: opportunities to use and apply knowledge, to inquire, to analyze, to critically evaluate, and to pose and solve problems. We need to make these assessments an integral part of the learning experience, allowing students to demonstrate in a variety of ways what they really know and can do. Only when meaningful student work is made a part of the assessment process can there be valid and equitable evaluation of the skills and abilities of all students.

The redesign of the New York State assessment system offers one model of how to enact these principles. The beginnings of the system that are described here promise to provide opportunities for students to demonstrate what they know and can do in both standardized and nonstandardized settings. The new assessment system responds to the need to provide information about student learning that is valid and useful for teaching and learning as well as for reporting measures of learning to the public for accountability purposes. In addition, it is motivating and enjoyable to both teachers and students, a compelling reason to continue this kind of development. Hopefully, future assessment development work in New York and elsewhere in the country will heed the unsolicited advice of one of the students who participated in taking the pilot examination:

> This test is better than other tests. You should make more tests in the future just like it.

NOTE

1. Personal communication with Stephen Klein.

REFERENCES

Allington, R. L., and A. McGill-Franzen (1992). Unintended effects of educational reform in New York. *Educational Policy* 6(4): 397–414.

Barrs, M., S. Ellis, H. Hester, and A. Thomas (1988). *Primary Language Record.* London: Inner London Education Authority/Centre for Language in Primary Education.

Darling-Hammond, L. (1989). Curiouser and curiouser: Alice in testingland. *Rethinking Schools* 3(2): 1, 17.

———— (1991). The implications of testing policy for educational quality and equality. *Phi Delta Kappan* 73(3): 220–25.

———— (1992). *Standards of practice for learner-centered schools.* New York: National Center for Restructuring Education, Schools, and Teaching (NCREST).

———— (1994a). National standards and assessments: Will they improve education? *American Journal of Education* 102(4): 478–510.

———— (1994b). Performance-based assessment and educational equity. *Harvard Educational Review* 54(1): 5–30.

Darling-Hammond, L., J. Ancess, and B. Falk (1995). *Authentic assessment in action: Studies of schools and students at work.* New York: Teachers College Press.

Darling-Hammond, L., L. Einbender, F. Frelow, and J. Ley-King (1993). *Authentic assessment in practice: A collection of portfolios, performance tasks, exhibitions, and documentation.* New York: National Center for Restructuring Education, Schools, and Teaching.

Darling-Hammond, L., and A. Wise (1985). Beyond standardization: State standards & school improvement. *Elementary School Journal* 85(3): 315–36.

Einbender, L., and D. Wood (1995). *An authentic journey: Teachers' emergent understanding about authentic assessment and practice.* New York: National Center for Restructuring Education, Schools, and Teaching.

Falk, B. (ed.) (1994). *The Educational Forum 59*(1). Issue on Authentic Assessment.

Falk, B., and J. Larson (1995). *An invitation to invention: Top-down support for bottom-up reform of assessment in New York State.* Paper presented at the Annual Meeting of the American Educational Research Association, San Francisco.

Falk, B., S. MacMurdy, and L. Darling-Hammond (1995). *Taking a different look: How the Primary Language Record supports teaching for diverse learners.* New York: National Center for Restructuring Education, Schools, and Teaching.

Garcia, G. E., and P. D. Pearson (1994). Assessment and diversity. In L. Darling-Hammond (ed.), *Review of Research in Education 20*: 337–91. Washington, DC: American Educational Research Association.

Gardner, H. (1983). *Frames of mind: The theory of multiple intelligences.* New York: Basic Books.

——— (1991). *The unschooled mind.* New York: Basic Books.

Glaser, R., and E. Silver (1994). Assessment, testing and instruction: Retrospect and prospect. In L. Darling-Hammond (ed.), *Review of Research in Education 20*: 393–419. Washington, DC: American Education Research Association.

Gordon, E. (n.d). Implications of diversity in human characteristics for authentic assessment. Mimeograph.

Koretz, D. (1988). Arriving in Lake Wobegon: Are standardized tests exaggerating achievement and distorting instruction? *American Educator 12*(2): 8–15, 46–52.

Kornhaber, M., and H. Gardner (1993). *Varieties of excellence: Identifying and assessing children's talents.* New York: NCREST.

Mitchell, R. (1992). *Testing for learning: How new approaches to evaluation can improve American schools.* New York: Free Press.

Moss, P. A. (1994). Can there be validity without reliability? *Educational Researcher 23*(2): 5–12.

Murnane, R., and F. Levy (1996). *Teaching the new basic skills.* New York: Free Press.

National Association for the Education of Young Children (1988). NAEYC position statement on developmentally appropriate practice in the primary grades, serving 5 through 9 year olds. *Young Children* (January): 64–84.

National Forum on Assessment (1995). *Principles and indicators for student assessment systems.* Cambridge, MA: FairTest.

New York State Curriculum and Assessment Council (1994). *Learning-centered curriculum and assessment for New York State.* Albany, NY: New York State Education Department.

Oakes, J. (1989). What educational indicators? The case for assessing the school context. *Educational Evaluation and Policy Analysis 11*(2): 181–99.

Piaget, J., and B. Inhelder (1970). *The science of education and the psychology of the child.* New York: Penguin.

Price, J., S. Schwabacher, and E. Chittenden (1993). *The multiple forms of evidence study.* New York: NCREST.

Resnick, L. B. (1987). *Education and learning to think.* Washington, DC: National Academy Press.

———— (1989). *Tests as standards of achievement in schools.* Paper presented at the Educational Testing Service Conference, The Uses of Standardized Tests in American Education, New York.

Rothman, R. (1995). *Measuring up: Standards, assessment, and school reform.* San Francisco, CA: Jossey-Bass.

Schoenfeld, A. (1988). When good teaching leads to bad results: The disasters of "well taught" mathematics courses. In T. L. Carpenter and P. L. Peterson (eds.), *Learning mathematics from instruction: Educational Psychologist, Special Issue* 23(2): 145–66.

Shepard, L. (1995). Using assessment to improve learning. *Educational Leadership* (February): 38–43.

Shepard, L. A., and M. L. Smith (1988). Escalating academic demand in kindergarten: Counterproductive policies. *Elementary School Journal 89*: 135–45.

Sizer, T. R., J. P. McDonald, and B. Rogers (1992–1993). Standards and school reform: Asking the basic questions. *Stanford Law and Policy Review 4*(Winter): 27–35.

Smith, F., and colleagues (1986). *High school admission and the improvement of schooling.* New York: New York City Board of Education.

State University of New York (1992). *SUNY 2000: College expectations—Report of the Task Force in College Entry-level Knowledge and Skills.* Albany, NY: Author.

Sternberg, R. J. (1985). *Beyond IQ.* New York: Cambridge University Press.

Valencia, S., E. Hiebert, and P. Afflerbach (1994). *Authentic reading assessment: Practices and possibilities.* Newark, DE: International Reading Association.

Wiggins, G. (1989). A true test: Toward more authentic and equitable assessment. *Phi Delta Kappan 70*(9): 703–13.

———— (1993). *Expanding student performance: Exploring the purpose and limits of testing.* San Francisco: Jossey-Bass.

Wilson, S. (1990). A conflict of interests: The case of Mark Black. *Education Evaluation and Policy Analysis 12*(3): 309–26.

Wolf, D. P. (1989). Portfolio assessment: Sampling student work. *Educational Leadership* (April): 35–39.

Chapter Four

The POWER of POSSIBILITIES

Stephen C. Ellwood, IV

INTRODUCTION

I remember the moment as if it were yesterday. I placed the last piece of adhesive tape on a small orange oak-tag rectangle centered on my desktop. I then stepped back to view it. One word was printed on the oak tag surface: "INVICTUS." It was the last word I wanted to leave in my classroom of five years. I grabbed my briefcase and slowly walked to the classroom door. The July heat, even in New England, had made the classroom feel like an oven. As I glanced up at the door, I noticed one last thing to take home with me—a green oak tag poster hanging over the entrance to the classroom. The words on the poster captured the meaning of much of the events of my classroom: "Through This Door Walk The *Best Students* In The World! (Don't Forget It.)" I slipped the poster under my arm, picked up my briefcase, and stood in the doorway looking at the empty classroom. The quiet was almost intolerable. My classroom was rarely quiet, rather it was usually filled with student voices as they actively pursued learning with meaning. I had fully expected to retire from teaching in this small K–8 elementary school, yet here I was silently saying good-bye to the room where I too pursued learning with meaning. In a month, my wife, six-year-old son, and I would be loading a U-Haul in preparation for our move to Harvard University where I, at age 39, would pursue a master's degree of education. How had life changed so fast? What were the events and the meaning of those events leading up to this moment? Specifically, how had equity and inclusion redefined my meaning of teaching and assessment? This paper is the reflective pursuit of the answers to these questions.

I will employ an operational definition of reflection to examine the "meaning making" that occurred in my classroom. Throughout my teacher education, early years of teaching, and finally my five-year tenure at Riverdale,[1] my pedagogy and assessment strategies had changed, with inclusion and equity serving as benchmarks for that change. I will examine this change through the lens of reflection.

Schon's "reflection-in-action" (1983: 62) describes my thinking as I examined my pedagogy and assessment practices during my eight years of teaching. Schon made it clear that reflection-in-action occurs during "the zone of time in which action can still make a difference to the situation" (62). Clearly, I am presently beyond this temporal frame, yet this paper will document, in retrospect, my reflection-in-action as a professional educator.

Schon's "reflecting *on* action" (1983: 278) provides an operationalized definition of reflection—a lens from which to construct meaning of the past. Reflecting on action, according to Schon, is looking back on an event after the event is completed. I will now reflect back on the meaning of my life in the classroom, focusing on teaching mathematics at the junior-high level.

BEGINNINGS

My university teacher-training program culminated in the student-teaching experience. I was quite nervous about student teaching and its sink or swim connotations. During the semester prior to student teaching, I took two reading-methods courses from a superb education professor. She was very reform minded and wanted each of her students to question the status quo in schools. Dr. Rose Smith also had little tolerance for learning that departed from a sound cognitive rationale.

Dr. Smith was nudging me to reflect beyond the "how" of teaching and forcing me to ask "why" more often. Prior to Dr. Smith's courses, I saw teaching as a responsible career enabling me to help young people to learn, but there were other motivators as well: As an outdoor-recreation guide, I would have plenty of time in the summer to guide people on canoe trips. Teaching would not be easy, but I presumed that it would not consume me like my first career choice of medicine surely would have. Without codifying van Manen's three "levels of reflectivity" (1977: 226), I now realize what journey Dr. Smith was leading me on. Initially, van Manen noted that "the practical is concerned mainly with means rather than ends" (226). At the next tier, van Manen stated: "It is assumed that every educational choice is based on a value commitment to some interpretive framework by those involved in the curriculum process" (226). Van Manen described his ultimate tier as that in which "the practical addresses itself, reflectively, to the question of the worth of knowledge and to the nature of the social conditions necessary for raising the question of worthwhileness in the first place" (227). LaBoskey defined van Manen's tiers of reflectivity as "practical-technical, social-political, and moral-ethical" (LaBoskey 1994: 12). Despite Dr. Smith's passionate pleas for reform that included my responsibility for being a change agent, the realities of student teaching overshadowed van Manen's notion of critical reflection. I maintained van Manen's "means rather than ends" focus and concentrated on how to plan, teach, and maintain discipline in the classroom.

The "practical-technical" focus came to the forefront throughout student teaching and during my first few years of teaching. Dr. Smith's message, however, remained alive yet dormant in my subconscious and would later replace the "practical-technical" mentality. Equity and inclusion are not practical issues.

They cut right to the moral fiber of classroom life.

Student teaching, however, was a practical matter. The nuts and bolts of teaching—memorizing the daily schedule, learning names, and negotiating entry into the school occupied a lot of time. I spent the first half of student teaching—(about) seven weeks—at the fourth-grade level (Riverdale Elementary School) and then moved on to a large K–8 school to a seventh-grade science placement (Centerville Elementary School). The students at this school were ability grouped into five tracks: Advanced, Standard 1, Standard 2, Standard 3, and Basic.

My first reaction to tracking was quite positive; it seemed to make sense. The students were sorted into tracks that, at least on the surface, eliminated the need to plan for varying abilities in the same classroom. I learned to alter my pedagogy for each different track—slowing things down considerably for the Basic group.

Implicitly, I accepted the belief that ability was inherent and stable within individual students. I also accepted that this ability could be reliably assessed. At this point in my evolution as an educator, I viewed assessment through van Manen's lowest tier—a pragmatic lens. Quickly accepting that ability could be assessed for sorting purposes, I focused on questions such as: How many grades do I need in the rank book each quarter to combine for an average? Do I weight test grades over homework and classwork grades?

Gardner (1983) discussed this stable view of intelligence when he introduced his multiple intelligences theory. Citing Berlin, borrowed the term "'hedgehogs'" from the poet Archilochus:

> The hedgehogs not only believe in a singular, inviolable capacity which is the special property of human beings: often, as a corollary, they impose the conditions that each individual is born with a certain amount of intelligence, and that we individuals can in fact be rank-ordered in terms of our God-given intellect or I.Q. So entrenched is this way of thinking—and talking—that most of us lapse readily into rankings of individuals as more or less "smart," "bright," "clever," or "intelligent." (Gardner 1983:7)

The macroscopic consequences of rank-ordering students, operationalized as tracking in schools, was the least of my concerns. My job was to get an "A" in student teaching. The reality was clearly written—without an "A," I could forget about getting a teaching job. Getting the "A" entailed many things, but first and foremost, I had to demonstrate that I could control the class.

Britzman explained the control issue in teaching:

> Both teachers and students implicitly understand two rules governing the hidden tensions of classroom life: unless the teacher establishes control there will be no learning, and, if the teacher does not control the students, the students will control the teacher. This power struggle, predicated upon the institutional expectation that teachers individually control their classes, equates learning with control. . . . Teachers tend to

judge themselves, and others tend to judge them, on the basis of their success with this individual struggle. (1986: 449)

My solution to the "struggle" was to be firm. I knew from my student experience that certain teachers required students to behave. And so I decided, early on, to be a firm disciplinarian. Prior to graduation, an experienced teacher offered me some advice regarding survival: "Handle your classroom discipline problems yourself; don't involve the office, for this is seen as a sign that you are struggling to maintain control."

With that in mind, I began my first year of teaching at a rural junior/senior-high school. My responsibilities included seventh- and eighth-grade math and science. Again, the students were neatly tracked, this time into A, B, and C classes. Again, I saw this as normative and sensible—students' innate ability could be assessed allowing for subsequent sorting. My role in assessment was grounded in the practical need to assign a grade for each student in math and science. If asked to discuss assessment at this point in my teaching career, I would have taken out my rank book and pointed to the homework, quiz, and test scores. My charge was to teach math and science and assess the students' learning via selected graded homework, quizzes, and tests. I prioritized, however, being firm and maintaining control.

As I reflect back, I see that my initial teaching style was a mirror image of the schema of teaching that I had developed during my own K–12 education. Upon reflection, I realize that Lortie's claim that "there are ways in which being a student is like serving an apprenticeship in teaching" (1975: 61) was actualized in my rookie year. Britzman also acknowledges this connection, which, she argues, leads to control-oriented, self-reliant teachers. She sees teacher education as a cog in this dysfunctional cycle that results in "technicians" (Giroux cited in Britzman 1986: 455) rather than the teacher becoming a "transformative intellectual" (Aronowitz and Giroux, cited in Britzman 1986: 454).

"Technician" is an accurate descriptor of my first year of teaching. Often, I followed the design embedded in my psyche from first grade onward: check and troubleshoot the homework, present new material, assign the next homework, and monitor students as they begin the assignment. This pedagogical stance was couched in a strict atmosphere that demanded student compliance.

Ironically, my teaching style was not normative among my colleagues in the junior-high wing of this small junior/senior-high school. The rest of the junior-high staff were warm and quite tolerant of students' behavior that I saw as "testing" or "pushing back the limits." As I look back, I realize that this cohort of junior-high teachers was tolerant of my strict disciplinarian ethos. I noticed that one teacher in particular was very student centered. Before and after school, students "hung out" in Ray Thomas's classroom not only for academic concerns but for familial and social needs as well.

Ray did me a great favor during the second half of my first year of teaching. One day while eating lunch with the junior-high teachers, I chose to complain about a particular student's attitudes and actions. Ray looked at me and said firmly, "If you had to grow up in his world you couldn't have done any better!" He picked up his tray and left the cafeteria. I was surprised but not offended; I just sat reflecting on the meaning of Ray's words. Intuitively, I knew he was right.

As my first year of teaching was coming to a close, I found myself watching Ray's interactions with students as often as possible. His frequent smile, inviting demeanor, and caring affect were ever present. I was enjoying teaching but Ray was basking in it. Furthermore, I wanted what he had—a great rapport with his students and a meaningful role in their lives within and beyond the classroom. As the year ended, I found myself smiling more and relaxing my tight grip on classroom control. Teaching and learning became the foreground issues and discipline became more of a background concern. As the classroom atmosphere became more relaxed, teaching became more enjoyable and, I would also argue, so did learning.

During the subsequent summer, I was offered a math position at Centerville Elementary School. Given that this would cut my commute in half, I seized the opportunity. My initial reaction to the relocation was to again become discipline focused. It was as if the stress associated with the change had brought to the surface the discipline-focused teacher-in-control paradigm lodged in my subconscious biography (Britzman 1986).

Centerville was familiar given that I had completed the second half of my student teaching there. A teachable moment occurred on day one. This time, unlike with Ray, the teacher was a student. I was responsible for teaching math to the seventh-grade Advanced, Standard 2, and Basic classes, as well as the eighth-grade Standard 3 and Standard 1 classes. The Basic class members took their seats. As I began my introduction, a student introduced his class: "We're the Basic class, we're the dummies." In knee-jerk fashion, I responded, "No, no, you're not dumb; don't say that about yourselves." The students stared at me as if to say, "Why don't you prove that to us?" As the class left the room, those words "We're the dummies" echoed repeatedly in my mind. Later, the eighth-grade Standard 3 class filed into the room. I read each student's name to begin placing faces with names. I came to Alec Strasburg, called his name, and stopped in disbelief. Trying to hide my disbelief, yet needing to know, I asked, "Are you John Strasburg's son?" He nodded in the affirmative. I stared at him—this time I'm afraid my surprise may have shown. How could a prominent citizen's son be in Standard 3? The children of professionals always were in the Advanced or Standard 1 tracks. The voice within said "don't look surprised" and I moved on to the next student.

By the end of my first day at Centerville Elementary School, I had for the first time consciously experienced two realities of which I had previously been unaware. First, the students internalize the meanings of the track names and hierarchy, and second, the tracks reveal a ranking of socioeconomic status—not just academic achievement. Alec Strasburg presented me with a negative case—a seemingly out-of-order example which allowed me to see the "regular" orderly correlation of student track placement with socioeconomic status. Two students had brought to the fore the unpleasant realities of tracking.

As a result of my continued reflection on these two experiences, I would never again blindly accept this system of assessing and sorting students. Dewey defined reflection: "*Active, persistent, and careful consideration of any belief or supposed form of knowledge in the light of the grounds that support it and the further conclusions to which it tends constitutes reflective thought*" (1933: 9). The students' internalization of track labels such as "dummies" as well as the socioeconomic status ranking made evident by Alec Strasburg's seemingly out-of-order placement were not "*grounds that support it*"—"*it*" being the assessment and sorting of students via tracking.

Although my first day at Centerville revealed more than one teachable moment for me, these moments were not idiosyncratic; rather, they were common tracking exemplars. Oakes's research is seminal to the tracking debate, and it grounded my experience with Alec Strasburg: "Poor and minority kids end up more often in the bottom groups; middle- and upper-class whites more often are at the top" (Oakes 1985: 13). Centerville was a 99.9 percent white rural community with a small population. Alec's lower-track placement made explicit the relationship of tracking to socioeconomic status. The realities (I would argue brutalities) of tracking are clearly summarized by Oakes:

> First, students are identified in a rather public way as to their intellectual capabilities and accomplishments and separated into a hierarchical system of groups for instruction. Second, these groups are labeled quite openly and characterized in the minds of teachers and others as being of a certain type—high ability, low achieving, slow, average, and so on. Clearly these groups are not equally valued in the school; occasional defensive responses and appearances of special privilege—i.e., small classes, programmed learning, and the like for slower students—rarely mask the essential fact that they are less preferred. Third, individual students in these groups come to be defined by others—both adults and their peers—in terms of these group types. . . . Fourth, on the basis of these sorting decisions, the groupings of students that result, and the way educators see the students in these groups, teenagers are treated by and experience schools very differently. (3)

During my two-year tenure at Centerville Elementary School, Oakes's descriptors slowly became apparant in the way an out-of-focus projection of a slide on a screen slowly comes into focus.

Track placement at Centerville was not totally inflexible. Limited mobility was achieved through the junior-high wing meetings, during which teachers could advocate for students' track changes. Unfortunately, changing to "lower" tracks predominated faculty requests. Parental requests were inverse; they wanted their children in "higher" tracks. I often agreed with the parents. If there was any chance that a student could achieve in a higher track, the chance needed to be afforded. Furthermore, I rarely supported the suggestion that a student move "down" a track. My conscience kept reminding me that we had to find a way to facilitate each student's success rather than condemning them to a "lower" tier.

My resistance to "downward" track mobility was the beginning of my divergence with the teaching status quo based on my moral belief that school must be the place where opportunity unfolds for young people. Dr. Smith's call for reform, heard but not initially heeded, was coming to life within me as my definition of teaching was evolving to van Manen's third level: "The question of the worth of knowledge and to the nature of the social condition for raising the question of worthwhileness in the first place" (1977: 227). Rather than envisioning assessment as a labeling and sorting tool or as the grading of homework, quizzes, and tests, my idea of assessment as a tool for student empowerment was coming more and more into focus. Assessment was beginning to be defined by me as a starting point in working with students.

In an effort to assist my students in mathematics, I began a morning tutoring program. Often, the students arrived at school and played on the playground for thirty minutes or longer before the morning bell signaled the start of the academic school day. This was the perfect time to give students the extra help they needed. Large numbers of students were often found working in my classroom before school, and I quickly found that I couldn't work with each student who needed help. Consequently, I began matching students with peer tutors, who received extra credit for their tutoring. Inter as well as intratrack pairings evolved. For the first time (beyond the Winter Carnival) I saw a heterogeneous group of students in one classroom. During my second (and last) year at Centerville Elementary School, the room swelled with students each morning.

At a staff meeting, concerns surfaced regarding the amount of student traffic in the hall in the morning. The concern was that students were abusing their use of the building—an interesting concern given the natural match between school buildings and children! I realized that I was going to have to be careful about giving each student a small yellow piece of paper known as a "pass." Since students with a pass were allowed into the building, I chose to comply and write the passes. The pass concept concerned me regarding the not-so-hidden message to students from the faculty: "We don't trust you." This assessment of students as deviant unless watched closely was the antithesis of my emerging view of assessment as student empowerment. The resulting message became clear: changes made within my classroom could have institutional effects beyond the boundaries of my classroom. I would have to negotiate these effects with the adults in schools if I was going to help my students succeed. My image of the school, like my image of teaching and assessment, was coming into focus; the school as a political arena was becoming more apparent each day.

In the spring of my second year at Centerville, the opportunity surfaced to transfer to Riverdale Elementary School, a small K–8 elementary school where I had begun my student teaching. The school, with fewer than 150 students in a town of less than 1,000 residents, offered me the chance to teach students grouped heterogeneously. Each grade constituted a class with class size averaging between twelve and twenty students. Also, I'd be teaching math and science; the disciplinary diversity was appealing. All was not euphoric, however, as the question from a Centerville colleague revealed: "Riverdale Elementary School is the cesspool of the district. Why would anyone in their right mind want to teach there? The Riverdale students have a terrible attitude." Another significant learning: tracking is not just a student phenomenon!

RIVERDALE

Riverdale Elementary School presented me with a self-perceived valuable opportunity. Here was the chance to teach multiple subjects to a small group of students. The average class size is about 14, and this small K–8 school features one class per grade.

Also, this was the town where I had resided for seven years with my wife, and now my one-year-old son was going to grow up here. Although we were not from Riverdale, we had chosen Riverdale to be our home town. My commuting distance would be drastically shortened, but beyond that, this was the chance to contribute to my community.

In many ways Riverdale Elementary represents an era gone by. The teaching and support staff are all, with rare exception, native to the community. The students and staff develop meaningful relationships based on nine years of interaction in a close environment that facilitates prolonged and regular contact. The school serves as the town meeting hall and location of all indoor recreation.

If there was one theme that all the Riverdale students and teachers would probably have agreed on, it was their sense that the resources in this school district were inequitably distributed. Centerville is literally the educational center of the geographic area. A small university campus is located near the center of the town. Centerville High School, a large comprehensive high school, collects students from three elementary schools: the large Centerville Elementary School, which I was transferring out of, and two small "outlying schools," of which Riverdale is one." The Riverdale students comprise but a small percentage of their freshmen class; the overwhelming majority come from Centerville Elementary. Centerville Elementary School is a large and relatively new building that has a modern industrial-arts room, a large library, and a large home-economics room. An additional building to house these features, on a smaller scale, was being built at Riverdale, but this did not ease the general disdain of the Riverdale residents for the perceived privileged educational opportunities of the residents of Centerville.

The inequity was not just perceived. Centerville fielded two teams in every sport, while Riverdale fielded one. Centerville drew on a much larger student body and therefore a much larger talent base. Riverdale students often left the playing field with their hearts in their hands, althouth there were notable exceptions to this pattern in the sport of basketball. Years of inequity, however, leave slow-to-heal scars; many of the residents of Riverdale were reflexive in their contempt for the Centerville schools.

The inequity stretched beyond athletics and facilities and reached into my classroom, particularly in the domain of mathematics. After the school board approved my transfer to Riverdale, the superintendent suggested that I spend a day there to familiarize myself with the routines and receive some guidance from the teacher I was later to replace. During the afternoon, the eighth-grade students filtered into the room for their math instruction. My antennae were on "alert" as I prepared to glean ideas from the observation. The students took out their books, that identified them as members of one of two within-class ability groups. Within-class ability groups result when a teacher reorganizes a class of students with heterogeneous math abilities into smaller groups—each smaller group consists of students of apparent homogeneous ability. Those students with red books, the overwhelming majority, were working on the Centerville analog known as standard math. Four or five students, seated in a group, took out their Algebra I books. I recognized this book immediately, as I was using it at Centerville Elementary to teach algebra to the eighth-grade Standard 1 class, who were learning algebra at a slow pace this year and would most likely take Algebra I in the ninth grade at Centerville High School. In short, it appeared that no student in the room had the book to prepare for entry into Algebra II as a high-school freshman.

The teacher who was orienting me to her class is a professional educator for whom I have great respect. She explained that she worked with some of the algebra students before school to give them more opportunity to work with the subject. Also, upon reflection, I realized that the preponderance of non-algebra based math was not unique to Riverdale; three of the five tracks at Centerville Elementary School were also non-algebra based.

As students entered the ninth grade at Centerville High School, the math curriculum offered many potential courses. As we know, the power track includes two options: Algebra I, or for those who already have a solid algebra background, Algebra II. The high-achieving math students from Centerville dominated the Algebra II census; this was partly a statistical reality based on the overwhelming size of Centerville Elementary School compared to Riverdale Elementary. Taking Algebra II at the ninth-grade level allows for the completion of a calculus-focused course at the twelfth-grade level and a head start on college math. Early in my tenure at Riverdale, I asked my former cooperating teacher, who was still teaching at the school, to name some of the students from Riverdale who had gone onto the "primo" Algebra II course as high-school freshmen. He could name only one student! It appeared that the road to high-school calculus was rarely traveled by Riverdale students.

Algebra-based math provides the language of power and possibility for the future. I committed myself to giving this language to my Riverdale students—now! I defined assessment as a beginning point, a sketch of students' present domain-specific skills, and from this beginning I also defined assessment as empowerment: sketches of progress to build upon. These became more focused foundations of my emerging definition of assessment.

The issue of curricular opportunities for students has attracted the attention of numerous scholars. Linn and Songer have argued that math and science are under-represented in course selection:

> In spite of the societal norms and anomalies that discourage women in mathematics and science, by far the most serious issue with regard to the social context of learning in America today is that far too few students altogether are being attracted to mathematics, science, and technology. Advanced courses in these domains are optional, and a small number of students are choosing them. (1991: 409)

I would add to Linn and Songer's observation: Students must be given the "power of possibilities." If students are not given the powerful language of algebra in junior-high school, they will then have difficulty gaining access to the upper-level math courses in high school.

Lee, Bryk, and Smith's review of the secondary school literature is also revealing regarding this issue of possibilities:

> A clear and strong finding emerges from the recent spate of analysis using HS&B [High School and Beyond] data: Student course taking and tracking are the most powerful predictors of academic achievement, far stronger than the effects of either personal background or a wide range of student attitudes and behaviors. . . . These research results have clear implications for policy: Efforts to improve academic achievement in secondary schools must center on the policies and practices through which students are exposed to subject matter. (1993: 217–18)

Lee, Bryk, and Smith make it clear that the power of possibilities is enormous. If students are shunted away from rigor early in their academic career, the "power of possibilities" will drastically diminish, leaving only a handful of survivors in high-school advanced-math courses.

A poster on the door to my classroom at Riverdale indicated that my students and I were going to confront these age-old practices that limited the power of possibilities. The poster, in the eloquent words of Robert Frost, noted the challenge about to begin:

> Two roads diverged in a wood, and I—
> I took the one less traveled by,
> And that has made all the difference. (1946: 223)

My initial teaching assignment at Riverdale included seventh-grade social studies, math, science, and art as well as eighth-grade math and science. In my second year at Riverdale, seventh-grade social studies was deleted from my teaching responsibilities, art was moved to the eighth-grade level, and sixth-grade science was added to my course load. Also, current events, study skills, and health were staggered into my teaching schedule at various times over my five-year tenure at Riverdale Elementary. I enjoyed the diversity of subjects, but I also realized early on that math was going to be where I not only "talked the talk" but "walked the walk" regarding my distaste for tracking and my intuitive sense that math could successfully be taught to heterogeneously grouped students. The key question was: How do I go about teaching junior-high math in such an environment while preparing as many students as possible for algebra-based high-school math?

Although this appears to be a question embedded in van Manen's initial tier of reflectivity—described by LaBoskey as "practical-technical" (LaBoskey 1994: 12)—the question actually originates from van Manen's uppermost tier of reflectivity, described by LaBoskey as "moral-ethical" (12). If algebra and the subsequent algebra-based high-school math courses leading to calculus had powerful connotations regarding high-school track placement and college entry and course selection, how could I give my students this math language of power? Assessment was becoming a "moral" issue for me. How could I assess students' math abilities while keeping the doors to algebra open to everyone? My "ethical" stance was rooted in my belief that the power of possibilities was the inherent right of every child.

"Walking the Walk"

As the seventh-grade students filed into class, I took a deep breath and prepared to introduce myself. This was the beginning of my true teaching career in Riverdale. I introduced myself and discussed my policies regarding homework, grading, discipline, and so on. Despite my evolution as a more humanistic teacher, I retrenched into a firm mode as I began at Riverdale. Upon reflection, I infer that the stress of making a career move again surfaced the teaching schema learned while making my way through school as a student (Britzman 1986). This was short-lived, as the humanistic style returned and was ultimately deepened.

I ended my introduction on a high note. I talked about my decision to teach at Riverdale Elementary School. I declared that I saw this as a special school with special students. This was my community and I wanted to put my effort into helping my community. It all sounded so good I could hardly make myself stop! Fate intervened, I didn't really have to try to stop; a student from the back of the room ended the sermon abruptly. She stated with anger: "This is a terrible school. The Centerville School has all the nice stuff! Its not fair at all." Another student sat back in her chair and resolutely asked: "What are you doing here?" As I probed for meaning, she made it clear that she could not understand why anyone would want to work in this school. I countered with talk about the small class sizes and the lack of a long bus ride to get to school. These were tangible advantages to going to school in Riverdale. But their minds were made up: Centerville was privileged. They believed that the school district was not equitable in dealing with Riverdale, and my pep talk was not going to change their minds.

Later, I responded in more detail to the negativism. What came out of my mouth was to become my motto for the next five years: "We must focus on ourselves. As long as we focus on Centerville, we're going nowhere. Together we will work hard and learn a lot. My goal is to get you folks into the upper-level math and science courses in high school. My goal is to prepare you so well for high school that you will walk proudly into Centerville High School knowing that they should be grateful that you're there. You're the best!" The room fell silent. I realized in an instant, as did they, that I was asking them to join me in changing a social order that had helped them define themselves as second rate. They felt excluded not included, less than not equal. I told them that hope resided with us. The silence in the room convinced me that they were willing to follow me down the tough trail of self-definition in the face of inequity. Our work in math became the pulse of our development.

My goals for the math program were twofold: (1) meet the students' math needs in a heterogeneous environment, and (2) move as many students as possible from arithmetic to algebra. This would enable them to pursue the power tracks in high school in preparation for college. The teaching of math and the related assessment of student learning became the operationalization of the power of possibilities. Assessment would involve assaying the students' present math skills in a fluid context; I would have an initial "snapshot" of their math skills, but this would not define and limit their math curriculum. Assessment was to become a starting point, never an end.

My first attempt at teaching heterogeneous math was centered on the formation of within-class ability groups. I explained to the seventh-grade students that the first few weeks of the school year would involve a series of tests that would enable me to assess their math skills. Each math class began with a brief review of a concept, e.g., adding fractions with unlike denominators; the students were then asked to complete a series of problems based on this concept. The students added, subtracted, multiplied, and divided whole numbers, fractions, mixed numbers, and decimals and finished up the testing regime with a group of word problems. The scores for all of the tests were averaged for each student, and if that average fell at least near 70 percent, I placed them in pre-algebra. They anxiously awaited the distribution of textbooks signaling the distribution of students into within-class ability groups. My first class of about twelve seventh-graders resulted in three students in standard math (arithmetic) and the rest in pre-algebra.

I explained to the students that these groups were not fixed. Mobility between groups was expected. The standard math students asked if they could make it into pre-algebra. I told them that they would move into pre-algebra the minute they mastered the needed arithmetic skills. I encouraged them to work hard toward that goal. I asked the sixth-grade teacher to give me some advice on placement, since she had taught these students math last year; I also learned what material she had covered. I examined the students' previous achievement-test scores, although these scores carried the least weight in the decision.

As for the eighth-graders, the departing teacher whom I replaced was able to advise me regarding which students were ready for algebra. Based on my snapshot assessment of the students' skills (with open-ended possibilities for the future) as well as my above-stated goals, the overwhelming majority of the class were given the opportunity to study algebra. Again, I wanted to include the maximum number of students in an algebra-based curriculum. Based on my belief in inclusion, I refused to send any students to the "resource room" for math during the regular math class; two mainstreamed students who had previously received their math instruction in the resource room comprised the standard math group, the majority of the class were in an Algebra I group, and four students constituted the advanced algebra group. I envisioned the two standard math students remaining mainstreamed as ninth graders in high school, the Algebra I students slowly working their way through the fundamental concepts in algebra and succeeding in high school Algebra I, and the four advanced students succeeding in high school Algebra II. These were lofty goals for my math curriculum as well as for the students' first year of high-school math, but they also bore the teeth marks of inclusion.

The students, particularly the seventh-graders, initially struggled with the math class routine. They needed to learn how to learn without a teacher constantly standing over them telling them what to do. Unfortunately, this is a skill often delayed until the college years. I explained to the students that they were experiencing a new way of teaching and learning, one that sometimes required them to work ahead in math without my immediate presence. If their assignment was finished, they were to move on to the next section of their book, using the other students in their group as resources. With practice, the students learned to push ahead in their studies, rather than doodling or catching up on gossip while I was working with another group. Kids are amazing when they get the chance! We had a goal to stretch ourselves and we never lost sight of that goal.

Based on my belief that individuals must have goals to aim for, individual goal writing was incorporated into our class routine. This also helped to keep the focus on our self-empowerment rather than being focused on Centerville. As a member of the district alcohol and drug education team, I had learned about the "whole-person model" from the Division of Alcohol and Drug Education Services of the State Department of Education. The whole-person model is based on the sum of the social, emotional, mental, and physical components of one's life. The functional underpinning of the model is the thesis that health is achieved by balancing the four components.

Early in the school year I distributed an index card to each student to record goals. I presented the whole-person model and explained the four components. Myself included, we then wrote two goals for each component of the whole-person model and put the index card in our desk. Each morning, while I completed my homeroom duties such as taking attendance, the students read their goals silently to themselves. At the end of each nine-week ranking period, those students who wanted to talk about their goals were welcome to do so. We updated our goals for each ranking period (see Ellwood, cited in Woolfolk 1993, 1995). Ultimately, this brought assessment to its most fundamental location: each student's consciousness. Assessment is most powerful when it becomes internally driven. Its power then becomes a personal power rather than one handed out or taken away by someone other than oneself.

During my tenure at Riverdale, I worked to foster a sense of us being in this together in other areas as well. I opted to go out with the students at lunch recess and play touch football or soccer or basketball. I began opening up the gym in the evenings once or twice a week for the students to have basketball games, in which I participated along with a student teacher or parent volunteer. As time passed and "we" became a comfortable pronoun for students and teacher, the roar of snowmobile engines could be heard on Sunday afternoons as a handful of students stopped in at my house to warm up, visit, and watch NBA basketball. Yes, I had followed Ray Thomas's lead and understood clearly that teaching was not so much about getting control but about giving it to students. To have control of one's life, a person first needed to have the power of possibilities.

As the first year in Riverdale wound down, I mistakenly believed that I had designed a solidly successful pedagogical stance for teaching math to heterogeneously grouped students. But shortly after the following school year began, I received a phone call from the mother of my highest achieving algebra student. After listening to his mom, I paid a visit to Darin. Darin was in the most advanced freshman math track—Algebra II. The transition to the large Centerville High School had sent a shock wave through him. He said very little, yet I likened his experience to my first year in college—panic! Darin now was competing with homogeneously tracked students in many of his classes. The familiarity of the last nine years was being shattered by the strangeness of the first two weeks of life in a comprehensive high school. I explained to Darin that he had nothing to prove to anyone, especially me.

Shortly thereafter, Darin changed from Algebra II to Algebra I. The other three students attempted to hang on and remain in the fast lane. I assisted two of the students with their homework over the phone, while the third student regularly stopped by my classroom after school for extra help. Unfortunately, all three girls changed courses to the slower paced Algebra I before the year ended. To add insult to injury, the high school math teachers required the girls to complete the Algebra I assignments not completed while they were in Algebra II.

My response to the above was to intensify the individualized approach. I created multiple within-class ability groups (as many as seven per class of about fifteen students), with students receiving complete individualization when needed. Despite the relatively small class sizes, staying in tune with each student's progress and staying planned was an enormous task. Was the emphasis on the individual too narrow as a pedagogical focus? Initially, I would have argued that it wasn't, but change was becoming a constant in my development as a teacher.

During the latter half of this year, the math department scheduled a regular departmental meeting to be attended by all of the math teachers in the district encompassing grades seven through twelve. These meetings were generally a source of contention for me, as the high-school teachers complained about the poor skills possessed by the students we were sending them. This meeting was not about contention; it was about conflict. The high-school math teachers expressed their disdain for my students' placements at what they considered to be inappropriately high tracks for most. The guidance counselor showed me the dismal results of my attempt to give my first Riverdale eighth-grade graduates the power of possibilities. Almost all of the students had left their original placement for a less challenging math course. Most distressing and potentially most damaging was the fate of the two students whom I had mainstreamed from the resource room the year before. They had fallen from the mainstream at Centerville and were now back in the resource room.

One high school teacher bellowed in anger: "Do you expect me to change my curriculum? I'm given a curriculum to work with and I can't just change it to work with your students!" I asked why not? He continued as if he hadn't heard me. His next comment was beyond belief. He complained that inappropriately mainstreaming students caused him to remain at school beyond the time he normally left the building. Sending the students back to the resource room required him to attend a Pupil Evaluation Team Meeting once for each student at the end of the school day. My inappropriate placements were extending his work day! The nightmare continued as an algebra teacher complained of the lack of books and seating room in the classes to handle the volume of students I was sending them. I countered, "Why don't you just add another section?" The math department chair made it clear that the schedule wasn't that flexible. I asked, "What kind of extra help did you offer the students?" Proudly, the response came back, "We don't provide extra help if the student doesn't come to us first." I argued that the teachers must make the first move, especially for my students who were already intimidated by being at this large school. They did not agree. In support, my principal exclaimed, "I don't like what I'm hearing here. There is nothing wrong with asking a student to come in for extra help." By now it was obvious that neither side was going to give in. The meeting ended, so I thought, in a stalemate.

The following day I received a phone call from the math department chair to discuss the meeting; the high-school principal, on another phone, was a part of the conversation. Starting with a restatement of each side's concerns, the discussion changed when they made it clear that they were concerned about this issue becoming a community issue. At that point I began smiling because I knew I had gained some leverage. They did not want the Riverdale community to get up in arms and cry "foul." They agreed to try to work with me to improve the situation, although they weren't talking about overhauling their tightly tracked curriculum. The fact that they had called to try to work out the problem was a moral victory for our side. Ultimately, they placed the Riverdale students with a math teacher for their daily high-school study hall to facilitate extra tutoring.

The truism that education is political was becoming more and more explicit. A change in math curriculum, pedagogy, and assessment in one classroom in a small town was creating political concerns. If assessment is operationalized as personal empowerment with a goal of equity and inclusion, then change will occur in the form of more students pursuing academic rigor, forcing those in power to attempt to reestablish equilibrium. The political ethos of education is particularly discouraging, because it is not rooted in equity and inclusion and is set off-balance when equity and inclusion become explicit goals.

Within my specific context I realized, for the first time how foreign and abrasive an environment Centerville High School must have been for my students. Furthermore, I realized that I was going to have to change my frame of reference from the confines of my classroom to the expanded boundaries of the entire district. Equity and the resulting inclusion of my students in challenging high-school math courses was going to require a comprehensive effort. Power moves slowly to wanting hands, but it does eventually move if one keeps trying. The macro focus of interconnected social changes was not a new idea spurned by the math-department meeting; I had realized early on at Riverdale that I was involved in more than changing the math curriculum. The math-department meeting, as uncomfortable as it was, inspired me to a heightened conviction to continue to work for inclusion and equity.

My involvement in the district-wide alcohol and drug education team provided an opportunity to showcase my students as well as to facilitate awareness activities within the school. Three of my students attended a summer teen-leadership camp and, with my facilitation, became the "Support Team." Together, we planned awareness activities for the school that included activities to promote a positive school climate. Hat day, secret pals week, and a winter carnival ensued with a sense of enthusiasm and excitement worn expressively on the students' faces. The climate was changing as students began to take risks and venture into uncharted water. No event was perfect, yet with each endeavor "we"—my students and I—grew stronger in our sense of commitment and community.

The district-wide alcohol and drug education team began a series of community and school awareness presentations, often held at local schools. As one of the regular planners and presenters, I seized the opportunity to include my students and I called them the "Riverdale Players." They performed role plays and cofacilitated breakout groups. Other schools began to get involved, but key was the foundation laid by the Riverdale Elementary School. We had carved out a special place within the district that others could now emulate.

Also related to my involvement in the awareness team was the founding of the first student-support group in the district and possibly in the county. The three student peer leaders cofacilitated the group, which included about twelve total members from the sixth, seventh, and eighth-grades. The group met weekly during a study-hall time period. The group had a generic focus and included discussions of self-esteem building, maintaining healthy relationships, handling stress, and the like. There were multiple pathways to getting into the group, including staff, parent, and student referral. At the beginning of each year, I circulated parent permission slips to the parents of each sixth, seventh, and eighth-grader. The overwhelming majority of parents granted permission for their sons or daughters to participate in the student support group. Students and parents often called me directly requesting membership.

The group was very important to its members, who complained with vigor if a meeting had to be canceled due to an assembly or other event. Here students worked on learning about building their self-esteem and how to engage in healthy interpersonal relationships. The spin-off to the school was obvious; the message to the surrounding community was also clear: "Riverdale Elementary School is interested in the total well-being of your child." If the history of Riverdale had been marred by exclusion and self-doubt, the tide was turning toward the positive rewards of self-determinism. "We" were redefining "we." Positive momentum was replacing negative inertia; we were not finished but we were making progress.

From the beginning of my tenure at Riverdale, I attempted to maintain constant communication with parents. I explained to parents the importance of mathematics proficiency regarding the college preparatory curriculum at the high school. I made it clear to parents that we needed to focus on the long haul and prepare for high school now—when their child was beginning the seventh-grade. I also was explicit in describing where the power lay. After our first discussion, they knew that high-school course placement was up to them and their daughter(s) or son(s)—no one else. I reminded the parents of this often since the Riverdale parents often felt marginalized with respect to Centerville and, in general, parents need to be partners in education not adjuncts who only receive weekly cafeteria menus.

Every spring, the guidance counselor from the high school came to Riverdale to meet with each eighth-grader and plan their freshman-year classes. At that time I gave him a list of my recommendations for each student's high-school math and science placements. Throughout the year, this counselor also made weekly trips to the school to work with students, cofacilitate our support group, and provide career awareness. I took every opportunity to let him know how well the math program at Riverdale was going and how well the students were progressing. He was a reasonable man, but he was based at the high school where the math teachers also had his ear. I used my "airtime" to continue to sell my heartfelt belief that upward mobility in math at Riverdale needed to be continued at the high school. He expressed some doubts about my approach to the math curriculum but he also remained open to my beliefs; I continued to espouse them.

When my students met with the counselor during the spring of their eighth-grade year, they were well prepared. We had already looked at their options, reviewed the high-school tracks and textbooks, and often made a preliminary decision regarding high-school math. They knew that they had, along with their parents, the power to make the choice and that no one else could decide for them. At the spring parents' conferences, I had the same conversation with the parents. We reviewed the different textbooks and discussed the various track characteristics. I gave them my recommendation for their son or daughter and helped them see the components of the decision as well as its future connotations. Always, I leaned toward recommending the most challenging option, noting that preparation for college required rigor.

During the spring of my second year at Riverdale, I took a proactive stance regarding the students bound for Algebra II. I gave them each a copy of the textbook used at the high school and we started working our way through some of the material in the morning, about twice weekly before school. It was my understanding that the Algebra II teacher relied heavily on the textbook. If they could become familiar with the book, then this was one less shock to endure in September.

My second graduating cohort fared better than the first. There was still some course changing, but we increased our holding power somewhat. The memory that stands out was the Algebra II hurdle. Two students went on to Algebra II from Riverdale and completed the year! The barrier had been broken, and I could now declare to other students that it had been done.

As my second year in Riverdale was winding down, I noticed Dr. Rose Smith coming down the hall. She was not a common sight at Riverdale, so I asked her if she would stop in my room—I needed some advice. I explained my approach to individualizing the math program and I also explained that keeping up with each student's progress was becoming more and more difficult as I increased the level of individualization. She suggested that I look at the horizontal linkages between within-class ability groups and students and provide more common instruction. Following the whole-group instruction, I could then vary the assignment that I gave each student or group. She felt that this would facilitate simplicity while still meeting the needs of individual students.

At about the same time, a student approached me after class and illustrated the validity of Dr. Smith's comments. He was working in the back of the room on a series of division of decimal problems while I was providing instruction at the board to a group of students learning to add integers with mixed signs. As the class ended, Fred stepped forward to inform me that he had been listening and he too could add positive and negative numbers. He then picked up a piece of chalk and demonstrated his accurate conclusion. I looked over his work sheet on decimal division. It became clear to me that dividing decimals required many more steps than adding integers of unlike signs, including moving decimal points, estimating, multiplying, subtracting, followed by multiple replication of the above steps. Yet, adding integers was generally a pre-algebra and algebra task. I began to realize that the within-class ability groups and individualized instruction had allowed me to provide more upward mobility for students toward algebra, yet I had not broken free of the false belief that students need to master the basic arithmetic skills before going on to algebra. Fred had shown me otherwise. Accepting Fred's demonstration and reflecting on Dr. Smith's advice resulted in a further curricular change.

I continued to diagnostically test the incoming seventh-graders regarding their basic arithmetic skills. But instead of immediately breaking them into groups, I distributed a standard math and a pre-algebra book to each student. In reality, the books are quite similar. Pre-algebra texts review the basic math skills and introduce the solving of equations and various other algebra skills. I provided whole-class instruction and then differentiated the assignment. Every student was exposed to algebra-based concepts such as solving equations. Different exercises and problems were assigned to different students or groups of students based on my perception of the level of difficulty each student or group could handle. The pre-algebra textbook was the text most frequently used. I then worked with groups of students or individuals based on their particular assignment. Before and after school I provided individualized instruction to those students who needed more one-on-one help than I could give during the math class. This included those students who were ready for more challenging material. I also employed regular problem-solving sessions during class, using heterogeneous cooperative learning groups. These groups solved word problems and worked on hands-on problems. At least once or twice a week, the students were working in cooperative learning groups, stretching their inquiry skills.

My eighth-grade curriculum also changed from a heavy reliance on within-class ability grouping and individualization. Both concepts remained but the overall curricular constellation changed. At the beginning of the year, each student received a standard math book, a pre-algebra book, and an Algebra I book. The message was clear: "We're all going to work on our basic math skills and we're all going to explore algebra." Both vertical and horizontal organizations of the curriculum were required to achieve these goals. The students worked in their within-class ability groups, solved word problems or hands-on problems in heterogeneous cooperative learning groups, and received whole-class instruction; time was alloted somewhat equally between all three instruction modes. The vertical within-class ability groups allowed students to focus their efforts on mastery of concepts enabling them to pursue a challenging high-school math track, e.g., Algebra II. The two horizontal components focused on streams of math concepts needed by all students. The cooperative learning groups solved varieties of word problems and competed to build structures using manipulatives. Whole-class instruction centered on the basics of integers, solving equations, geometry, percents, and so on. Before each math period, I walked to the students' lockers and informed them of the books they needed that day. My fifth and final graduating cohort from Riverdale was living proof of the power of possibilities. In a class of about sixteen students, two went on to high-school Algebra II, a small number of students did not pursue algebra as freshman, and the rest went on to Algebra I. I have only followed one of these students—Sam—since leaving Riverdale, and in a recent phone conversation, he informed me that he and the other Algebra II student had successfully completed freshman Algebra II, sophomore Advanced Geometry, and were now juniors in Pre-Calculus.

As often as possible, I attempted to empower students through assessment.

The first time a topic was assigned for homework, the grade was considered "optional." Students looked at the grade and decided whether or not to include it in their average. I believe that homework, a follow-up of work begun in school, should allow students the freedom to struggle with the material without having to pay with their average; after the material was fully fleshed out and practiced, I may have then required a later grade to stand. The students knew that extra-credit work was another avenue to boosting their average. Students who struggled on a test were often given a follow-up test—a second chance to demonstrate their mastery of the material. The resulting grade was the average of the two tests. If each member of a group being tested had a low grade on the test, I often discarded the test grades, retaught the material, and retested the students. I did not envision assessment as a sorting device; rather, I saw assessment as ongoing feedback to both students and myself.

From the beginning of my tenure in Riverdale until my last day in the classroom, I felt that I needed more time to teach math each day. My solution was to take advantage of before- and after-school slices of time. I used these times to work with individuals and within-class ability groups, and to begin working through the Algebra II text for those students choosing that high-school course. Parents were very supportive of my use of this extra time, as were the students. We were motivated, together, to achieve.

Since entering the teaching profession, I had redesigned my image of the "teacher." I was no longer a dispenser of information to lifeless automatons presorted into tracks. I saw myself as someone attempting to liberate children from inequity. Though some teachers complained that "The students belong outside!" their "traffic" in the hall was the sound of a small revolution of young people willing to study math when they could have been playing on the playground. They believed there was a higher ground for themselves. Together, we were actualizing Jesse Jackson's axiom: "You must have dreams bigger than your circumstances."

CONCLUSION

During my fourth year at Riverdale, I was named the State Teacher of the Year. The following year, I received one of the National Educator Awards sponsored by the State Department of Education and the Milken Family Foundation. These awards validated the work I was doing even while they heightened the tensions I was experiencing with some of my colleagues because I had "broken ranks" with the normative practices at the school and in the profession. To make matters worse, the principal who had supported my work and had often empowered me to new educational visions announced that he was leaving Riverdale. Later that year, I was accepted at Harvard Graduate School of Education; I too planned to partake of the power of possibilities.

During the twilight of my tenure at Riverdale, I made copies of William

Henley's (cited in Cook 1958) poem "Invictus," which was distributed to each of my students:

> Out of the night that covers me,
> Black as the Pit from pole to pole,
> I thank whatever gods may be
> For my unconquerable soul.
>
> In the fell clutch of circumstance
> I have not winced nor cried aloud.
> Under the bludgeonings of chance
> My head is bloody, but unbowed.
>
> Beyond this place of wrath and tears
> Looms the horror of the shade,
> And yet the menace of the years
> Finds, and shall find me, unafraid.
>
> It matters not how strait the gate,
> How charged with punishments the scroll.
> I am the master of my fate;
> I am the captain of my soul.
>   (95)

The last stanza encapsulated the meaning of our struggle. The human spirit cannot be denied.

I began this discussion with an examination of the meaning of reflection. Of reflection, Maxine Greene wrote:

> I am proposing, of course, that self-reflectiveness be encouraged, that teacher educators and their students be stimulated to think about their own thinking and to reflect upon their own reflecting. This seems to be inherently liberating and likely to invigorate their teaching and their advocacy. Also, it may well help in delineating possibilities never seen before—in the processes of futuring and choosing in which individuals must engage in order to create themselves. (LaBoskey 1994, x)

In eight years I had redefined my meaning of teacher. Three influential people—a reflective teacher educator, a mentor, and an inspiring leader—provided constant grist for my reflection mill. And long before I chose to be a teacher, I knew that Martin Luther King, Jr. was speaking to me. I was of a different race, yet the adversity of my youth left "overcoming" my only option. He was also speaking to my future students, who struggled for equity and inclusion in a bureaucratic system that sorted students and their futures with frightful ease.

In my journey from student teacher to Teacher of the Year, I had learned that assessment is so much more than organizing grades in a rank book and collapsing them into a quarter average. Assessment started as an initial snapshot of each student's math proficiency, but it also became more than that. Embedded in assessment was the question of how each student could become a speaker of the language of algebra, not who would have this privilege. Assessment became a tool for promoting equity and facilitating inclusion. Finally, assessment became the operationalization of the power of possibilities.

Last year, after a long night at the library here at Teachers College, Columbia University, where I'm studying for my doctorate, I returned home to a letter from Sam, a former Riverdale student. He discussed his athletic and academic accomplishments noting: "When you left you said I could do whatever I wanted and so far I am. . . . I'll make a deal with you, you keep on doing well in school and everything else you do and I'll do the same!" The "we" never ends—and neither does the "power of possibilities."

NOTE

1. Pseudonyms appear in place of proper names of people and places.

REFERENCES

Aronowitz, S., and H. A. Giroux (1985). *Education under siege: The conservative, liberal and radical debate over schooling.* South Hadley, MA: Bergin and Garvey.

Britzman, D. P. (1986). Cultural myths in the making of a teacher: Biography and social structure in teacher education. *Harvard Educational Review 56*, 442–456.

Dewey, J. (1933). *How we think: A restatement of the relation of reflective thinking to the educative process.* Rev. ed. Lexington, MA: D.C. Heath.

Frost, R. (1946). The road not taken. In L. Untermeyer, *New enlarged pocket anthology of Robert Frost's Poems*, 223. New York: Pocket Books.

Gardner, H. (1983). *Frames of mind: The theory of multiple intelligences.* New York: Basic Books.

Giroux, H. A. (1985). Critical pedagogy and the resisting intellectual, Part 2. *Phenomenology and Pedagogy, 3*(2); 84–97.

Henley, W. E. (1958). Invictus. In R. J. Cook (ed.), *One hundred and one famous poems: With a prose supplement.* (Rev. ed.) Chicago: Reilly and Lee.

LaBoskey, V. K. (1994). *Development of reflective practice: A study of preservice teachers.* New York: Teachers College Press.

Lee, V. E., A. S. Bryk, and J. B. Smith (1993). The organization of effective secondary schools. In L. Darling-Hammond (ed.), *Review of Research in Education,* vol. 19; 171–267. Washington, DC: American Educational Research Association.

Linn, M. C., and N. B. Songer (1991). Cognitive and conceptual change in adolescence. *American Journal of Education 99*; 379–417.

Lortie, D. C. (1975). *Schoolteacher: A sociological study.* (Paperback edition, 1977.) Chicago: University of Chicago Press.

Oakes, J. (1985). *Keeping track: How schools structure inequality.* New Haven: Yale University Press.

Schon, D. A. (1983). *The reflective practitioner: How professionals think in action.* New York: Basic Books.

van Manen, M. (1977). Linking ways of knowing with ways of being practical. *Curriculum Inquiry 6*; 205–28.

Woolfolk, A. E. (1993). *Educational psychology.* 5th ed. Needham Heights, MA: Allyn and Bacon.

———— (1995). *Educational psychology.* 6th ed. Needham Heights, MA: Allyn and Bacon.

Chapter Five

THE DEMOCRATIC, CHILD-CENTERED CLASSROOM: Provisioning for a Vision

Yvonne Smith and A. Lin Goodwin

Y*vonne Smith is a teacher of three-, four-, and five-year-olds at Central Park East Elementary School (CPE 1) in East Harlem, New York City. The public alternative school has a national reputation as a progressive, child-centered environment where children typically underserved by schools—children of color and poor children— thrive and succeed socially and academically (Bensman 1994).*

Yvonne has been an early-childhood educator in New York City for twenty-one years and has devoted eleven of those years to the children at CPE 1. As an African-American woman, mother, and teacher, her conceptualizations of teaching and learning and her visions for the children with whom she works are closely linked to her autobiography. Her roots are in the south—Virginia and North Carolina—where most of her family still lives, although she herself was born and reared in Manhattan on the lower East Side. As a child during the 1950s and then as an adolescent during the 1960s, she grew up surrounded by, and later participated in, many conversations that took place in her family—both immediate and extended—about education, civil rights, and democratic societies. She was educated in racially and culturally diverse public schools at the K–12 level as well as in college, and was a student at New York's City College during the 1969 student strikes for civil rights and open admission. Her two experiences with private schools, first as a student teacher at Riverside Church Nursery and then as the parent of a daughter who attended City and Country School were, she believes, pivotal in expanding her notions of what was possible in education. Her ideas were further shaped by experiences gained at the Workshop Center for Open Education at City College. Her thinking about teaching young children and about the profession as a whole continue to evolve as a result of her work at CPE 1, at the Prospect Center with Pat Carini, at the Center for Collaborative Education; and through her involvement with the Elementary Teachers Network at Lehman College, with the National Board for Professional Teaching Standards, and with student teachers.

Yvonne's cultural, political, and intellectual life experiences support and drive her practice as a progressive, child-centered, democratic educator. This is her story about how she uses assessment as a way to look carefully at kids in order to come to know them, their needs, and their dreams. Observing and assessing children closely gives Yvonne the precious clues and cues she needs to create a learning environment that invites all children in and allows them to build their senses of themselves as powerful, capable, and cared-for human beings. The story is written, for the most part, in her own words, and is derived from an extensive interview I conducted with her. As the behind-the-scenes narrator, I have organized and structured this piece and placed it within a conceptual framework. However, while we consider this piece to be a collaborative endeavor, it is Yvonne's voice you hear.

ASSESSMENT IS LEARNING ABOUT CHILDREN

Before I begin to think about assessment, I have to think about the setting and the situation that the kids are entering, because there should be a place in my classroom for just about any four- or five-year-old child. They each should be able to—I want them all to be able to—find a place to be in the classroom and ask who they are. So the setting needs to be able to reflect who four- and five-year-olds are and needs to consider the physical, cognitive, emotional, and social dimensions of their development. The cliché is that young children learn by doing; I know very young children learn by interacting with their environment in their environment. They also learn by interacting with other people, the other children in the classroom as well as the adults who are in the classroom. So the setting that I create for them has to reflect all these understandings. It has to be a place that allows for working with natural materials like sand and water, as well as materials made of natural things; so there are wood blocks in the environment, there is clay in the environment, there are lots of manipulatives in the environment. The environment also provides children with multiple means for creative expression. So there is paint available, there are all sorts of art materials, there is an area for trying on roles and pretending through imaginative play. There is a large library of children's literature, stories that are going to support and extend the work children will do in each and every one of those areas and activities. We do a great deal of cooking because it is a very important and concrete way of recreating home for children. I want them to see their world represented in the classroom. Thus, the classroom is set up in such a way as to allow children to do many things independently, and to do things with the support of each other and with the support of the adults. They are encouraged to experiment and create on their own; it is not an environment where they can't touch, they can't do. It is a place that is appropriate to their range of interests and their range of abilities, starting from where they are and what they bring with them. My aim is to build an environment that is infused with possibilities so that the possibilities inherent in children can emerge.

Assessment that is responsive to the being who is coming into the classroom, the individual that each being represents, can't be a narrow, paper-and-pencil, limited way of looking at children. Watching is *the* important part for me in terms of assessment—I have to watch, I have to look carefully, I have to look constantly, I have to listen, and I have to always be making immediate decisions about what to do or not to do next. When do I need to ask a question? When do I need to make a comment? When do I need to suggest a person, a thing, a book that a child might go to? Sometimes watching tells me I just need to say, "So-and-so is doing such-and-such," or "Did you see such-and-such over there?" I watch so I know where to nudge and where to push, where to suggest and where to guide. I have this expression that people tease me about. I always talk about thickening the stew and stirring the stew. Assessment enables me to know when and how to stir the stew, to keep the ingredients mixed, to keep the flavors moving and coming out more fully. To me, assessment is constant and ongoing because my decisions aren't based on what is generally appropriate for the child. There is no "the child." There are these particular children, that particular child in my classroom, who, from the first day he or she walks in I begin to develop a sense of—and that takes lots and lots and lots of time. Assessment means coming to know children well and, based on that understanding, inviting them in.

This is not something that I can do alone. I'm fortunate in that I always work with another adult in the room as part of the classroom staff, and I have student teachers. But I also rely on the wider school community and, most important, each child's family. I am only one person and I see from my particular perspective, my particular point of view, and even though my understandings are always changing, they are still only my understandings. The other people in the classroom also have their perspectives, their points of view, their understanding, and it is that communal understanding that helps me to act. Assessment and figuring out what comes next, figuring out the meaning that children are making in their interactions, are not things that I could ever either want or hope to do by myself. In terms of making sense, having those other people to talk to is crucial for me. Finally, I am in constant conversation with the children about the sense they are making of their work, what it is they are learning and doing. They provide windows into their own learning and questions. All these perspectives and players are, in a sense, the ingredients in the stew.

So assessment for me comes back to observing children from where they are, day one when they come in, and continuing to observe them over time, because a child may come in one way one day, and I can never say I know all that that child is. The next day or later on in the same day, I'll see a different facet of that child. Children cannot be pinned down and defined. Each is an ever-evolving jigsaw puzzle, as it were, and the picture becomes clearer and clearer, but ultimately it will never be finished. All I can hope to do is to look, describe, and put in more pieces. Then, based on my knowledge and understanding of children in general and "the child," I begin to make sense of what *a* particular child is doing, a particular group of children is creating, and the meaning they are making in their interactions.

The thinking behind the organizational structure of Yvonne's classroom is in keeping with the philosophical tenets of progressive education and child-centered schools that permeate CPE 1 and the many other alternative schools that belong to the Coalition of Essential Schools (for a case study of CPE 1, see Snyder et al. 1992). The child-centered classroom is

> designed for self-teaching and discovery learning. The teacher structures the environment by setting up learning centers that stimulate the child's interest and arouse the child's curiosity and desire to learn. Each child is seen as an active experimenter who explores his or her environment and selects from it the materials and topics that stimulate his or her interest. (King, Cruz-Janzen, and Chipman 1994: 71)

However, philosophy and organizational structuring aside, the child-centered classroom comes alive, is enacted, so to speak, only when the needs of the children and the curriculum are continuously aligned and realigned. Assessment that is developmental looks "for instances that reveal the child's way of thinking and feeling as well as his or her behavior" (Almy and Genishi 1979: 185). Continuous assessment through observation is characteristic of authentic observation (Einbender and Wood 1995) and informs Yvonne's curriculum, her choices about materials and activities, her pedagogy, and her visions for and of children. It also enables children to tell Yvonne who they are so that she, in turn, can create comfortable places where they can fit in.

WHAT DO THREE-, FOUR-, AND FIVE-YEAR-OLDS CARE ABOUT?

During Open House night when families are invited into the classroom, they often ask me, "Well, what do the kids talk about? What do they do in here?" I often tell them, they're just like you, they talk about sex, religion, and politics. Of course this shocks parents and some parents go "AAAARRGGHHHH!" But then I describe what that means for three-, four-, and five-year-olds. The religion part of it is, what do you believe? What do you believe about what's going to make buildings stand up? What do you believe about how people are supposed to treat each other? What do you believe about how we three-, four-, and five-year-olds learn? What do you believe about who people are and how you treat them? And the political part of it is, I'm bigger than you and I'm going to take this block, this truck, this whatever, and how do you deal with the power issues? And we talk about that. They may be three, four, and five years old, but they live in the real world. They see that the people who hold the power are adults and—before the adults in terms of who they look up to—the teenagers. They observe adults and they watch television; they see and hear what's going on in the real world. They see the contradictions in what they are asked to do (not fight) and what exists in the world. They think, "I am supposed to use my words and not fight, but these adults out here are having a war." And they're trying to make sense of all of that. So, when the Rodney King verdict came in years ago and there were riots in Los

Angeles, the very next day we sat and talked about it, about why people were so angry, about why people would burn down their own community, why black people were angry with and fighting white people. Everybody knew something about it, had an opinion, and had very strong feelings about it. And we talk about all of that. We talked about the Million Man March in October 1995 because it lives in our community. I was able to say, "Amanda did not come in today because her father participated in the march and she stayed home in support of him and the other marchers." Some children had heard people and other kids talk about it. Some kids didn't know anything about it and were going to go home and ask about it. I had four-year-olds saying, "I'm going to listen to the news tonight on TV to find out about it," because they're in that world stew too. We can't pretend that life doesn't affect them and that they're not putting those pieces together also. And finally, the sex part is how they feel about themselves, who they like and who they don't like, how they relate to each other, and how they, as individuals and as a group, learn to work and live together.

My classroom is, I hope, a place for people and ideas, where thinking is taken very, very seriously, and talking with each other, all of us talking with each other about what it is we're thinking and feeling is very, very important. People will come in and say, "Yvonne, your children don't fight," and I always say, "Knock wood!" but I try to create an environment where that doesn't need to happen and where the discussion of the children's real issues doesn't need to go underground. Every year in the first couple of weeks of school, there comes a time when it's important to tell people what the one rule in the classroom is, and that rule is you can't hurt anybody's body or anybody's feelings. That covers just about anything. However, you can't have two coins in one pocket without there being some noise, and that noise, that conflict, is a part of life. So just as I work to create a room that is going to accept whoever walks in the front door, that is open to that diversity, I have to ensure that it also accepts conflict because that's a part of life. There has to be a process for dealing with it. So we do a lot of talking about what's happening with us, not just what's happening in the block area or what's happening in wet sand, but what's happening between and among us. And the children learn that they can talk it out, that there's nothing that happens that they cannot talk about. This rule allows a safe space for that to happen, and my job is to hold that space open and safe for us to begin to have these kinds of conversations. In the beginning the conversations are very basic; "I wanted this and so-and-so had it and I took it from him." We talk about how wanting something is okay. But then we move to; "How did you feel when so-and-so took it from you?" "It made me angry." "Did you tell him that? You need to tell him that." So we set in place a process for kids to say how they're feeling, and we accept and acknowledge their feelings because we are all entitled to our feelings. We then need to look beyond that incident to what else is happening, and I find that children have an incredible sense of what is right and wrong, what's acceptable and not, and how we're going to live with each other. Usually, some time before the end of October, something physical happens and we have to hold a meeting. One of the children or I will say, "Do you like it when you're hit? How do you feel when someone hurts your feelings? What kinds of things hurt feelings?" And we'll talk about these important questions so that we come to understand that it's not just the grabbing and the hitting, but that words are also very powerful and they can be very hurtful. So, being called "stupid" is talked about, and having somebody say "I don't like you because you're black"—and it happens—is talked about, or "I don't like you because . . . or I'm not going to play with you because . . . " Talking about everything allows all the unspoken stuff to come up to the surface, which means the kids develop language for describing behaviors that are exclusionary and hurtful, and they begin to do it when they're three and four and five years old. By October, November, I begin hearing from parents: "My child came home and said that when I yelled at them, I hurt their feelings." And I have to laugh because I know where it's coming from. And so I describe what happens in the classroom so that they begin to understand where what they are hearing at home is coming from, just as I talk with them about stuff that I don't quite understand that may be coming from home so that we begin together to build a picture of the life of this child. But we have to talk about all of it, so we've had discussions about AIDS and children whose families are dealing with AIDS. You would be amazed what three-, four-, and five-year-olds have pieced together, where families are courageous enough to talk with children. But you would also be amazed by what children whose families work so hard at protecting them begin to piece together. They know they're not supposed to know, so they talk about things among themselves, and sometimes they will bring it to the classroom or I'll hear about it and open it up so that we can talk about it together.

Yvonne reminds us that children, even very young children, care about the same things that adults care about. They may not articulate these things in the same ways adults do, nor label them using the same words, but what is important to them is what is basic to human existence: being loved and cared for, figuring out what to value and believe in, finding a place in the world, learning to live with others. By listening and watching, Yvonne is able to pick up on and then build classroom talk around the questions that children are asking. She finds that children ask painful and powerful questions; they want to know about the real world because they are not immune to it, rather they are in the midst of it all. By empowering children to talk about the real-world events that they see and hear about, Yvonne engenders "a critical capacity within the classroom while promoting the integration of students, families, communities, and the world" (McCaleb 1994: 14).

Many scholars have written about the political nature of schooling and education (Freire 1971; Giroux 1983; hooks 1994; Nieto 1992). Schools have the capacity to oppress or to liberate. For many poor children and children of color, schools have arrested rather than transformed their intellects, development, and sense of wholeness. Schools and teachers often perpetrate "silencing" (Fine, cited in Kornhaber and Gardner 1993) by attempting "to ignore prominent aspects of nonschool life that children carry with them to class" (Kornhaber and Gardner 1993: 11). Transformative education or pedagogy, in contrast, is centered in "dialogue and problem posing" and children are offered opportunities for "analyzing and debating problems on a daily basis. The classroom [becomes] the microcosm where democracy is learned, practiced, and constantly reinvented" (McCaleb 1994: 13–14).

CHILDREN'S STORIES: WHAT HAPPENS WHEN CHILDREN ARE INVITED IN?

Helping Tom[1] Ask His Questions

From the day he walked into my classroom eight years ago, Tom was a builder. He would spend all day in the block area if I let him. My classroom was up on the third floor and right outside our window was the Amtrak train. When the train went by, Tom would go and get a milk crate and stand and watch it. What began to happen then in the block area was the re-creation of the scene outside the window—schools, tall apartment buildings, streets, people on those streets, elevated trains. Later came questions about, well, how did the train get up there, and, further downtown, how does the train go back underground? But what came first was the activity, the action, the actual putting together of blocks and trying to figure out how to re-create in the classroom what he was seeing outside. And I watched as the scientific part of building began to intrigue him. For him the central question was, "How do you make this work? How do you build this so that it will stand up in real life?" This meant making a lot of trips outside to allow him to observe and to help him figure out what his real questions were. I watched him re-create ramps, stairs, pulleys so that he could have elevators, all in the classroom. When Tom was in third grade, I kept hearing from his teacher about this kid in her classroom who was this incredible builder. I kept hearing about him and hearing about him, until finally she said "Tom." I said, "I know Tom, I can talk to you about Tom as a builder in pre–K." And so that was in third grade. For fourth grade he went to another teacher. Last year, in fifth grade, he worked again with his old third-grade teacher, and he's still building. He's building with Legos, and he's building to scale, and he's building all kinds of different things. I mean, you can see Tom in college in architecture. To me, that's a concrete example of a child who at four and five was asking himself real-life questions. People would walk into the classroom and say—they say it to me all the time and I still have a hard time dealing with it—your children are just playing. If I didn't have the eyes to look at that play and see not only the very real work that's involved in that play, but also the very real questions that are involved in it, I wouldn't be able to support it enough and then we would not be able to see in Tom the next Frank Lloyd Wright. I am convinced that for Tom, in some way, shape, or form, building is a real direction, a real passion in his life. It may not become his life's work, but somehow he'll always be doing it. For me, teachers must find the real questions that kids are asking, the real cognitive questions. We have to develop, we have to find the social setting that will allow a kid like Tom to develop his knowledge and understanding within a community so that he is not out on whatever track by himself. I want to build people and support kids who can work together and see themselves as part of a larger unit, so that their passion, their work is what makes the community rich and worth living in. From pre–kindergarten to now sixth grade, I have been able to follow this child and see the surprising turns that he has made, as well as see how something that started in my classroom just keeps going. Ultimately, we don't know where or how he's going to end up, but we have been able to identify some very strong threads in his life. So we have been able to support him and help him ask his questions about the things that he wants to know about and that he's able to talk about. Yes, we struggle with him over punctuation and grammar and pulling things together and finishing things. But there is this very strong learner here, a kid who sees himself as a person with ideas and with ways and means of following those things through and sees the adults that are in the school as resources and supports for him—not as the enemy to subvert, but as people who are going to help him find his questions and develop them.

Carmen[2] Is More Than Her Language Problem

On the first day of school, when the whole class was sitting in a circle and I asked the children to begin to think about and make choices about where they were going to work, Carmen's response came in her own language, and I couldn't understand a thing she said. She was a child who did not speak English and didn't speak any language. She had her own vernacular. In any other setting, she would have been placed in a special education class. When she answered where she wanted to work, I looked at her family and I saw their looks of panic and of just absolute total fear. Carmen spoke nonsensical words, sounds, phrases—not even phrases, just syllables. So, I brought her up to the chart and I pointed to what the choices were, and she pointed to one and I said, "Do you want to work in play-dough?" and she was able to repeat play-dough and go and work there.

After a while, she began to incorporate some recognizable words into her language; for example she would say, "Bllllllll play-dough," so I would know that Carmen wanted to work in play-dough. Slowly, more and more language from the classroom just came in. I believe that in a classroom that didn't allow children to sit and talk with each other about their work, about their lives, and wasn't set up to encourage that talk, to demand that of children, her language would not have grown as quickly and as richly as it did. In our classroom, she was just another child. It's not that we all sat down and said, "We have to teach her this, we have to teach her that, we have to teach her everything." People don't do that with babies, they talk with babies and they encourage babies to talk to them, and they accept the language that babies offer and they don't correct it. And that's what we in the classroom, the adults and the children, did with Carmen. She was as patient and understanding of us as we were of her. She was well aware that she didn't talk like we talked. But I think she also knew that that was okay, that our belief was that she had the capacity to do it, and in fact she did. At the end of her first year, she could hold a conversation with you. At the end of her second year,

Carmen spoke English, and her language didn't make her stand out. She needed and continues to need support in speech and language, but she spoke English.

We did try to get Carmen the speech and language help that she needed by going to the division of special education. The meeting was not held until the end of her first year, because it took that long to get all of the paperwork done. So, at the end of May, we went to the Committee on Special Education in her home district, the Bronx (pre-kindergarten referrals are handled in the child's home district). Carmen was not at the meeting and so the committee could only rely on what had been written about Carmen; they did not know her. I remember it was a Thursday, and the committee recommended that, based on what they had read, Carmen needed to be removed from my classroom by the following Monday. She would be placed in a self-contained special education classroom in Queens with a limited number of students, eight children with three adults. She would remain in this classroom from the end of May until the end of June, and then in September she would be transferred to another school. I remember two people from the special school were there, the classroom teacher and one of the administrators. There was also a parent who served as an advocate for families. I had accompanied Carmen's grandmother to this meeting and we didn't know the family advocate, we were just meeting the people from the school, and we had just met the person from the committee. I was blown away by the realization that they were going to make all of these decisions for a child they had never seen, that they were simply basing their decision on paperwork. Thank goodness the family has to accept and agree to any recommendations before anything can happen. They can always say no. We talked with the people from the special school and asked what the classroom would be like, who the other children in the classroom were, what her day would be like, what activities were offered. At the same time, I described the setting she was in. In the end, what the other school people said was that they could not offer art, they could not offer music, they could not offer her a classroom of children whose language would serve as a model for her. Carmen would be in a classroom with children with similar language issues. So my question was, "Where in school is she going to hear what it is we want her to be able to do? And where are the activities and the experiences around which this language will develop?" In the end we came to an unspoken agreement of sorts, where they tacitly agreed with us by saying to Carmen's family that they could not offer her all the things she was already getting. Carmen stayed with me for another year. She began writing her name and reading words in the environment. In first grade, along with everyone else in first grade, she began reading. She came to visit, and showed me her books and read to me, and this was a kid who two years before wasn't talking English.

Without the observing and the interactions and the day-to-day support; the day-to-day assessment; the documentation of all we observed so we could sit and examine what was happening today, what had happened in the past, and think about what was next for her, who was next for her—I wouldn't have been able to support her growth in so many ways. I had been presented with this kid, and I had to begin to see who was there because Carmen is more than her language. She had this incredible sense of design and what couldn't she do with magic markers! We took many pictures of her work. Even though she couldn't talk to us in words, she talked to us in pattern blocks, and this carried over into the artwork that she did and the paintings that she did. She began by re-creating similar kinds of designs and then began drawing pictures and eventually began creating words to begin to describe her stories, to begin to describe the process of what her thinking was. So Carmen was more than just a child who had a so-called language problem. She was a thinker and a doer, and it was my responsibility to provide the setting that would allow all of Carmen to develop and support the work in language that she obviously needed.

> Learning happens best when a teacher is able to engage a student in important dialogue; when the teacher listens carefully, not only to the big messages, but to the vibrations of what that youngster is all about, and says to himself or herself, "This youngster is capable of great things." (Brown 1991: 207)

These two stories are very different but they both illustrate practice that embraces all children and begins where they are, utilizing all that they bring with them. By watching and listening, Yvonne was able to help Tom identify and pursue his own questions. These questions became a driving force in Tom's education—they enabled Tom to direct his own learning. But more than that, they served as intellectual anchors for Tom so that he was always connected and engaged, always thinking. Most important, his questions came to define him as a learner, as conceptually powerful, as motivated. As Yvonne helped him to be successful, he naturally saw himself as successful and others, in turn, saw him as successful and capable too.

Carmen brought very different challenges and needs. Her language problems would have surely resulted in special education placement had she not entered a rich, welcoming environment in which Yvonne's goal is to discover children's gifts. Thus, despite her difficulties, which were never minimized, Carmen came to be known also as someone with strengths, as someone complex and multidimensional. The classroom allowed Carmen to communicate in many "languages" and through many activities. She was able then to use these authentic and personally meaningful experiences—her own work—to gradually develop cognitive connections between her language and the language of the classroom. Rather than being evaluated as a child without language, she was seen as a child who had the capacity for language. Yvonne's task was to unlock that capacity.

There is a large body of research documenting the constraining effect low teacher expectations or misguided teacher assumptions can have on the performance of learners (Brophy and Good 1986; Irvine 1991; Dusek and Gail 1983), especially those considered "culturally deficient" (Carter and Goodwin 1994). African-American and Latino children like Tom and Carmen are often "compared to a White standard in order to demonstrate the various ways in which they are deprived or deviant" (Carter and Goodwin 1994: 298). Thus, they are defined by their deficits and often seen as incomplete (Delpit 1995). What is clear from these stories of two very different learners is that Yvonne expected each child to be successful and saw each one as a whole, complex person. She then set about creating a classroom culture and providing appropriate experiences that served as scaffolds for each child's learning and needs by respecting each one's questions, desires, and strengths. We see that "when students are treated as competent they are likely to demonstrate competence" (Ladson-Billings 1994: 123) and that real "learning engages the whole person and becomes a form of meaning making" (Einbender and Wood 1995: 15).

MULTIPLE ENTRY POINTS FOR DIVERSITY

Diversity is a given. As teachers, we must, as much as possible, try to be aware of how our classrooms and curricula situations are structured so that there are many different points of entry for different people, entry points that are acceptable to them. Classrooms must offer opportunities for equitable participation, they should model the ways in which we value one another. For example, around the issue of snack and how families contribute, there are some parents who can make financial contributions and they do. There are other parents or families who make contributions of things and time that are just as important, and we talk about these contributions within our group as holding equal value. Last year, I had a grandparent who always knew whenever there was a sale on for the things we needed in the classroom or used for cooking. We could always count on her to find us the best prices, and that was her way of making a contribution. Another parent's contribution has been a dynamite bottle-cap collection, with which this year's group of children has done incredible sorting. I can't honestly say that somebody's dollars are more valuable than all the different kinds of bottle caps that she brings, because in terms of use and learning, five dollars is here and gone, but every time she finds a different kind of bottle cap, something happens to the discussions that go on during math time; they become more complex and thoughtful. To me, the bottle caps initiate the most valued experience, yet they are not looked on as having value, particularly within our society.

Birthday parties become another forum for community participation, individual valuing, and personal contribution. For me, the focus of a birthday party is on the growth that a child has made and will continue to make, so our birthday parties are celebrations of that. Everybody gets a cake or cupcakes and something to drink, whether it comes in from home, or we bake it in school, or we run across the street because we realize it's a child's birthday and for whatever reason the family didn't tell us about it. So the trappings of each celebration look the same. A birthday is not about all the stuff that somebody can bring in. It's about who this kid was and now is, what she or he has learned to do and say. We talk about what this kid was doing at one, two, three, four, five, six, seven. Families come in and we talk about milestones and significant moments. You hear what somebody's first words were, when they stopped using diapers, when they stopped using the bottle, and we all sit and hear that from the child's family. That is what's of value: that child, in relation to his family, in our classroom circle, here. Every year, the family first talks about what a child has learned to do at home. Then, I can talk about how this child has been growing in school since he started school here. I'll say a little bit and the child will say a little bit about what she's done, and the family will share too, and the other children chime in as well. So, we trade memories and in doing so emphasize how valuable each one of us is, how we live our lives. For children whose families don't celebrate birthdays, we find ways of acknowledging them in other ways. We always have a very open conversation in class about when this person's birthday comes, we're not going to have a party, but we will acknowledge that they are a year older. We're not going to ignore them.

Celebrating how we live our lives naturally must include all the traditions and customs each group holds dear. One of the things that we had struggled with at CPE 1 was how do we celebrate and acknowledge what happens in December, those unspoken December holidays? How do we acknowledge whether you celebrate the Indian Festival of Lights or Kwanzaa or Hanukkah or Christmas or you don't celebrate any of those but you acknowledge the return of the sun to the sky and the celebration of our internal lights somehow? One of the things I came up with was the Festival of Lights. The letter that goes home asks for people to come, to bring food from their family, from their cultures, but more important to bring stories and talk about what does and does not happen in their homes at this time. So, for some families it is a happy time, some families have said it was a stressful time, other families have talked about how it was a sad time for them because they were very poor or something difficult happened. Good or sad, those are their memories, strong enough that they haven't been forgotten and they still evoke a lot of deep feeling. So it's not that we celebrate only the good and the joyous; we celebrate the whole of our lives, the good and the bad, and in sharing we communicate and connect with one another.

One example of the connections that result from the stories we share is the bacalao story. One year in November, because of Puerto Rican History Month, the class next door was cooking Puerto Rican food. They had rice and beans and then they started cooking bacalao. I wanted to try it too, so I got the recipe from another teacher. But before we started cooking dried salt fish, I showed the children the dried fish and asked if they knew what it was. They could see that it was a fish and where the bones had been, and the kids in our classroom who were Puerto Rican said it came from Puerto Rico. And then the Dominican children started saying, Oh yes, we have bacalao also. Then Taleah says, "Bacalao? In my family, this is called salt fish." So we talked about that. Now, I had an Italian child in the classroom, so I said to her, "Go home and ask your family about bacalao and see if Mommy or Daddy has anything to say about that." She came in the next day and said, "You know, my Daddy *did* know about bacalao and he talked about grandma." This went on during all of November and into the beginning of December as other children in the classroom and other countries were brought into the conversation. Even my experience helped to build connections. When I was learning how to cook it from one staff member, I began getting different advice from another staff member about how it's "supposed" to be cooked! Soon the two women were arguing with one another about the correct recipe. So, in our Festival of Lights celebration, I told this story about how something that came from one part of our community, in fact, existed someplace else and in other places in the community. From the back of the room came a voice saying, Bacalao? Bacalao? Who's talking about my bacalao? And the accent was Israeli. So in this celebration, we found out that in Israel, also, they eat dried salt fish.

People talked and talked about how they celebrated Christmas in the Caribbean. People talked about what it was like in the African-American South. One man from the North and Midwest talked about what happened in his region. Another told a wonderful story about being Jewish in predominantly Catholic Colombia. By sharing the stories, people who don't celebrate any of the holidays were also able to get into that holiday spirit and talk about what it looked like in their homes, talk about the good times, talk about the bad times. We sing every song we know that has light as a theme, and then some we like that don't. People bring the songs, they bring instruments, they bring whatever they want to contribute. Since there is no one way but infinite ways for people to enter into the activity, we are able as a community to acknowledge the differences, acknowledge the pain, acknowledge whatever is in people that they want to bring out and share with the rest of the community. We light candles all over the place—we haven't burned down the school yet—and people say that it's one of their favorite times to just be able to come, to be able to sing and tell stories. Absolutely wonderful. It was in the telling of one of those stories during this festival that one kid turned to his family because they ate bacalao, and said, Puerto Rican? Does this mean I'm Puerto Rican? And his mother said, "How could he have not known all this time that he was Puerto Rican?" So she looked at him, and she said, "Yeah." And he said, "YES!!" The stories that come out of this event are just so rich and poignant, we are constantly reminded that we can't take anything for granted. We have to continue to look at what we choose to acknowledge and then how we choose to acknowledge it. It is not a perfect world, it will never be a perfect world, but we are as inclusive as we can be and we try to be aware of it and change it when we're not. We need to be aware of and conscious of the choices that we make and what each choice means within the community. And there's no one way, there are no right and wrong answers to some of these difficult questions. It is just trying to find the best possible way to come together based on who the community is.

"[Community] lies in sharing the truth" (Tinder 1980: 31). Yvonne supports community in her classroom by creating spaces for the public sharing of private lives.

In this space, her students—with their families—"authenticate their own experiences" (Giroux 1983: 203).

In the current press for multicultural education and culturally responsive pedagogy, there is much emphasis on the more superficial aspects of diversity—holidays and contributions. This is juxtaposed against a conservative backlash that is decidedly less tolerant of diversity and is threatening to retard some of the progress made in civil rights after the 1960s. Affirmative action is under siege, scholarships earmarked for "minorities" are being scrutinized, and racially biased incidents are on the rise, particularly in schools and on college campuses (Campbell 1996; Feinberg 1996; Wilkerson 1992). Education is usually touted as the first line of defense against prejudice, discrimination, sexism, homophobia, and inequity. If we can educate our children to get along, we believe we can be a better society. Yet schools have also been shown to be instrumental in perpetuating educational inequities by failing to provide equal opportunities for children of color and poor children to learn, grow, and succeed (Fine 1991; Goodlad 1984; Kozol 1991; Oakes 1985). It takes powerful measures to counteract the negative social press facing children from marginalized groups.

The authentic integration of school and home cultures requires that teachers build pathways that allow students to navigate the cultural boundaries between two often very different social contexts. Through the use of personal narratives, Yvonne encourages children and their families to "gradually impart meaning to the events of [their] own lives" (Greene 1994: 14). Because personal storytelling "is a pervasive, orderly, and culturally organized feature of social life in every culture and . . . is a major . . . mechanism of socialization" (Miller and Mehler 1994: 40), every family and child Yvonne works with can contribute meaningfully to the life and history of the classroom. In addition, by supporting her students and their families to share stories of individual growth and accomplishment, Yvonne encourages children to develop a

> growing awareness of their own history as learners in the classroom. . . . [T]he children not only make autobiographical claims concerning the self as learner in the classroom, but [establish] an alliance with peers through matching claims to similar autobiographical experiences as learners. (Miller and Mehler 1994: 50–51)

Each child is empowered to define him or herself as an accomplished learner; everyone celebrates community growth.

THINKING ABOUT TEACHING AND ASSESSMENT

To teach you have to be reflective. Someone said to me when I had first begun teaching: What you teach is who you are; everything else they'll learn in books. I really heard that. I know when I go into my classroom, I have to bring all of me in and be aware of who I am, what my thinking is, what my feeling is about teaching and learning as a teacher and learning and teaching in terms of kids. Do I really believe that people have the capacity to learn? If I really do, if that is my religion piece, that piece I truly believe in, then I have to dismantle all of those excuses that I've laid out there for why people can't learn and reaffirm that my starting point is my belief in students' capacities. If students are at the center of my work, then I have to ask myself what my role needs to be in relation to the community, their community. This means I must be very open about engaging the community in what I'm trying to create in my classroom and my school. I can't say I don't have the time, I can't say I don't have the patience, I can't say I can't. If I believe this and I'm committed to doing this, I have to engage the wider community and show that even if I am not of the community that I'm working in, that I'm for the community I'm working in. Communities know, not only by your commitment—because good intentions alone are insufficient—but by what you do, whether what you're saying and offering is really what you say it is. The same thing is true of multiculturalism. If I believe in diversity and see it as a positive quality, I have to find ways of being in some way, shape, or form connected to the community that exists within the school as well as outside the school. While this does not mean that I am involved in everything, I must be connected to all the pieces and people that make up the community and remember that it is not just me and my classroom. I am part of the community and, just as I want my kids to be committed members of the community, I have to be committed to the community of people that I work with. This allows us to be a school, not simply a collection of classrooms. Though we may be very different in our individual classrooms, people—children, families, the community—can see the common threads, the values and beliefs that tie us together, just like the threads that wove through Tom's school life. These threads of commitment must be evident in all that we are as a school. They also give some meaning to our work and the knowledge and understanding that we are building.

When I think about the larger ideas or goals of assessment, I must ask, "Why do I assess? What am I trying to find out and why?" If my goal in teaching were solely to transmit academic information, I could test the group—yes, even at three, four, five years old—and then structure "lessons" that would accomplish this. The academic aspect of education is a part, an important part of what I do and why I assess. But it is only part of what I assess and teach.

Checklists, or standardized tests, or any of those kinds of instruments give you large collections of data. However, real assessment lies in making sense of the information that is accumulated. Now, I can make some kind of sense of a collection of notes, but when I sit and talk about what a kid is doing and what it means, and I can describe his work within a larger picture, a different kind of understanding gets built. Assessment means uncovering kids, making children more visible. It means helping them articulate their own desires and questions and then providing the supports that allow them to follow those questions.

If I were to evaluate Tom's work, for instance, and give it a number or give it a letter that would tell him whether it was or was not good enough, what are we supposed to do with this information? But if I can describe his work, just describe what is there, it means I can talk about the things that he does in this way, the things that he struggles with, the things that come easily for him. This kind of descriptive assessment gives us something meaningful to hold onto, something substantive to look at, to discuss as we think about next steps for the child. It encourages new questions: Now what? Where might we go with this? We can then involve the child and ask; How do you feel about this? Does this seem to express to you who you are? Of course, the "you" in this includes the child, her family, and the wider school community.

It is important for me to know the Toms and Carmens as individuals. It is in this way that I provide for their learning and growth. But it is equally important that they come to know themselves and each other since they exist as part of a group. School, education, this work that I do, is not only about them as individuals but about each of them/us as members who sit equally yet uniquely in the group.

That group is a small society where children begin to know themselves and each other as members of a community. Just as each child has interests and work, so does the group. Each has individual work based on interests, questions, and issues; together they share through the arts, which offer alternative means of expression and insight into who they are. Their social interactions are the politics of their lives as they learn to share space, materials, ideas, and each other. The process of inquiry provides the means for discussion and exploration with materials that enable them to seek meaning and understanding.

It is important that my work begin with individuals and that these individuals be visible. But it is equally important that each member contribute to the shaping of the group and, *most equally* important of all, it is the work of the group and the commitment to the group that I observe and document over time. It is that vision—of a participatory group—that I try to make provisions for and that I hope my teaching and asssessment support. It is a never-ending complicated process. Actually, it's never always easy and it's never always impossibly difficult; it's a mix. It is what makes the stew interesting, and it's never boring, never, never.

Gloria Ladson-Billings in her book The Dreamkeepers *(1994: 38–98) outlines the pedagogical practices, attitudes, goals, and beliefs that define culturally relevant teaching. Some of these practices and beliefs are particularly illustrative of Yvonne's pedagogy. Practitioners like Yvonne who use culturally relevant practices:*

- *see themselves as part of the community*
- *believe that all students can succeed*
- *help students make connections between their community, national, and global identities*
- *see teaching as "digging knowledge out" of students*
- *encourage a community of learners*
- *[expect students] to teach each other and take responsibility for each other*
- *[take] student diversity and individual differences into account.*

According to bell hooks, "making the classroom a democratic setting where everyone feels a responsibility to contribute is a central goal of transformative pedagogy" (1994: 39). When children and all the cultural knowledge that they bring with them are respected and valued, the classroom becomes a safe place that embraces rather than rejects the lives they lead in their own communities. It is in this kind of classroom community that "commonalities among worlds can override differences" (Phelan, Davidson, and Yu 1993: 60); community becomes "a contributor to the creation of self" (Genishi and Dyson 1994: 240). In such an environment, assessment is a means to find out what children know, can do, and care about; it is not used to categorize, label, or define them as incapable. Yvonne's reflection on her practice provides us with an image of the classroom as a democratic, culturally relevant, and caring community that extends beyond the walls of the school. As a witness to her practice, I know that children are loved, respected, and valued by her, by one another, and by the larger school community. I can also say that the culture of her classroom is deliberately designed to support the work and development of three-, four-, and five-year-olds and to further their inquiry through multiple modalities and via numerous intellectual pathways. It is a classroom where "young people may be helped to build bridges among themselves . . . [and] provoked to heal and transform" (Greene 1993: 194).

NOTES

1. Tom is a pseudonym selected by "Tom" himself.
2. Carmen is a pseudonym selected by Yvonne.

REFERENCES

Almy, M., and C. S. Genishi (1979). *Ways of studying young children.* New York: Teachers College Press.

Bensman, D. (1994). *Lives of the graduates of Central Park East Elementary School: Where have they gone? What did they really learn?* New York: National Center for Restructuring Education, Schools and Teaching.

Brophy, J., and T. L. Good (1986). Teacher behavior and student achievement. In M. C. Wittrock (ed.), *Handbook of research on teaching,* 3d ed., 328–75. New York: Macmillan.

Brown, R. G. (1991). *Schools of thought.* San Francisco: Jossey-Bass.

Campbell, D. E. (1996). *Choosing democracy.* Englewood Cliffs, NJ: Merrill/Prentice-Hall.

Carter, R. T., and A. L. Goodwin (1994). Racial identity and education. In L. Darling-Hammond (ed.), *Review of Research in Education,* vol. 20, 291–336. Washington, DC: American Educational Research Association.

Delpit, L. (1995). *Other people's children.* New York: New Press.

Dusek, J. B., and J. Gail (1983). The bases of teacher expectancies: A meta analysis. *Journal of Educational Psychology 75*: 327–46.

Einbender, L., and D. Wood (1995). *An authentic journey; teachers' emergent understanding about authentic assessment and practice.* New York: National Center for Restructuring Education, Schools and Teaching.

Feinberg, W. (1996). Affirmative action and beyond: A case for a backward-looking gender- and race-based policy. *Teachers College Record 97*(3): 362–99.

Fine, M. (1991). *Framing dropouts: Notes on the politics of an urban public school.* Albany: State University of New York Press.

Freire, P. (1971). *Pedagogy of the oppressed.* New York: Continuum.

Genishi, C. S., and A. H. Dyson (1994). Conclusion: Fulfilling the need for story. In A. H. Dyson and C. S. Genishi (eds.), *The need for story: cultural diversity in classroom and community*, 237–44. Urbana, IL: National Council of Teachers of English.

Giroux, H. (1983). *Theory and resistance in education: A pedagogy for the opposition.* Cambridge: Harvard University Press.

Goodlad, J. I. (1984). *A place called school.* New York: McGraw-Hill.

Greene, M. (1993). The passions of pluralism: Multiculturalism and the expanding community. In T. Perry and J. Fraser (eds.), *Freedom's plow*, 185–96. New York: Routledge.

———— (1994). Multiculturalism, community, and the arts. In A. H. Dyson and C. S. Genishi (eds.), *The need for story: Cultural diversity in classroom and community*, 11–27. Urbana, IL: National Council of Teachers of English.

hooks, b. (1994). *Teaching to trangress.* New York: Routledge.

Irvine, J. J. (1991). *Black students and school failure.* New York: Praeger.

King, E. W., M. Cruz-Janzen, and M. Chipman (1994). *Educating young children in a diverse society.* Boston, MA: Allyn and Bacon.

Kornhaber, M., and H. Gardner (1993). *Varieties of excellence: Identifying and assessing children's talents.* New York: National Center for Restructuring Education, Schools and Teaching.

Kozol, J. (1991). *Savage inequalities: Children in American schools.* New York: Crown.

Ladson-Billings, G. (1994). *The dreamkeepers.* San Francisco: Jossey-Bass.

McCaleb, S. P. (1994). *Building communities of learners.* New York: St. Martin's.

Miller, P. J., and R. A. Mehler (1994). The power of personal storytelling in families and kindergartens. In A. H. Dyson and C. S. Genishi (eds.), *The need for story: Cultural diversity in classroom and community*, 38–56. Urbana, IL: National Council of Teachers of English.

Nieto, S. (1992). *Affirming diversity.* New York: Longman.

Oakes, J. (1985). *Keeping track: How schools structure inequality.* New Haven: Yale University Press.

Phelan, P., A. L. Davidson, and H. C. Yu (1993). Students' multiple worlds: Navigating the borders of family, peer, and school cultures. In P. Phelan and A. L. Davidson (eds.), *Renegotiating cultural diversity in American schools*, 52–88. New York: Teachers College Press.

Snyder, J., A. Lieberman, M. Macdonald, and A. L. Goodwin (1992). *Makers of meaning in a learning-centered school: A case study of Central Park East 1 Elementary School.* New York: National Center for Restructuring Education, Schools and Teaching.

Tinder, G. (1980). *Community: Reflections on a tragic ideal.* Baton Rouge, LA: Louisiana State University Press.

Wilkerson, I. (1992). Two neighborhoods and a wall called race. *New York Times,* June 21, p. 1.

Chapter Six

AWAKENING TO THE MATHEMATICIAN WITHIN: One Teacher's Story

Paula Hajar

Like many people, I grew up with great misperceptions about what mathematics was about and what it meant to be good at math. Had I not become a teacher, I might have gone to my grave with no idea at all of its possibilities for enjoyment and pleasure. However, as a teacher-in-training in the early 1970s, I had the luck to have these math misperceptions corrected by what might be called "math re-education." Now I find teachers struggling to replace their own negative formative math experiences with something better for their students as they confront the new standards of the National Council of Teachers of Mathematics (1989, 1991), which demand that children know the "why" of math as much as they know the "how." Even before the standards were in place, however, I think many had felt the need to develop the kind of classroom practice that would excite their students' interest in math and interrupt the cycle of math underachievement that seems to have become a commonplace among Americans. (In the 1991–1992 International Assessment of Educational Progress, out of fourteen countries participating, thirteen-year-olds in the United States scored nearly at the bottom, surpassing only Jordan. [National Center for Education Statistics, 1992.])

I will begin by reviewing three common (and I think destructive) mythologies about math, and then describe the pedagogical training that began some twenty-five years ago that helped me and others like me make the personal transformations that seem to be on the agendas of many elementary-level math teachers today. In doing so, I hope to offer something to the conversation about how teaching to a more valid kind of math knowledge can suggest new ways to awaken *all* children to their mathematical powers and to give us new ways of assessing math understanding.

One myth I absorbed early in my schooling was that in math memory was key, and that to be good at math one had to have good recall of discrete mathematical facts and be able to choose the appropriate procedures to perform on the problems given. There was always the danger that memory would fail, of course, leaving one adrift and helpless in a sea of facts and formulas. (Occasionally, as an aid to memory, "tricks" were offered, but rather than being offered for their insights into "how math worked," they were usually presented simply as tricks, also vulnerable to the lapse of memory.)

Closely related to the myth about the importance of memory was the myth that math was primarily about discrete questions and correct answers (Romberg 1992). Unlike the way most other disciplines were taught in school, math was often atomized, both from topic to topic and within topic; witness the ubiquitous flash cards and the rather senseless memorization of multiplication tables. (Rarely, even within the study of arithmetic, were we invited to look at how a topic functioned as a whole. And rarely did we students have a sense of how tiny a sliver of the whole field of mathematics the topic we were studying was. Rarely were we given the opportunity to see it in its larger context.)

A third myth, related to the others, was that speed was intrinsic to math competence. To do well in math meant to find the right answers quickly. Those who were more thoughtful or required more time were penalized, and even math "discussions" were geared to privilege those who were quickest to find the right answer. (The absurdity of this becomes clear when the speed criterion is applied to any other subject: our admiration does not soar particularly when we refer to artists, writers, scientists—even block builders—as speedy, and slowness or deliberateness in any of those activities is not necessarily an indication of lack of competence, but often of thoughtfulness.)

Math, in fact, was unlike any other subject we studied. In English we wrote essays, for which we crafted several drafts; the focus was on creativity and thoughtfulness. In history we did research, weighed evidence and information; we often worked outside of class and in consultation with other students, experts, and reference materials. The focus was on creating a critical synthesis. Even in science, often thought of as a companion discipline to mathematics, we did experiments and wrote lab reports; even here, speed seemed of secondary importance, and thoughtfulness and synthetic thinking were valued. But in math we did pages and pages of similar exercises, with half the answers at the back of the book, and corrected the homework. Thinking in mathematics usually went unexamined unless the "answer" was "wrong." If it was "correct," "assessment" needed to go no further.

Given this configuration of math beliefs, the standardized math test was the perfect tool to use to assess math competence (although it could persuasively be argued that these math beliefs were themselves the product of the standardized testing phenomenon). At any rate, standardized testing has been the assessment mode of choice for decades (Haney, Madaus, and Lyons 1993; National Commission on Testing and Public Policy 1990), and test scores have bred an elitism that would be unconscionable in any other subject (and is unconscionable in this subject as well).

For the last half decade or so, critics have been insisting that standardized test questions favor the knowledge base of boys and students in the majority culture over that of girls and people of color (American Association of University Women 1992; Oakes 1988; Sadker, Sadker, and Long 1989). In fact, in 1992, girls' SAT scores in mathematics trailed boys' scores by 45 points (almost unchanged since 1966, when the gap was 47). The differences between the scores of white students and those of minority students were even greater: Mexican-American high-school seniors scored an average of 70 points lower than white seniors as a whole; for Puerto Rican high-school seniors, the gap was 77 points, and for blacks it was 91 points (College Entrance Examination Board 1992, cited in National Center for Educational Statistics 1993).

For decades, standardized test scores have determined high-school, college, and graduate-school acceptances, access to scholarships, and in many cases employment opportunities. Because of their lower standardized test scores, women and minorities are often discouraged from continuing math study; as a result they are markedly underrepresented in fields that require a mathematical background (Armstrong 1980; Rivera-Batiz 1992).

There are two issues here: how the biases contained in the standardized tests create inequities for women and minorities in higher education and employment opportunities; and what standardized tests do to teaching and learning itself and to all who have to study the test-driven math curriculum. With regard to the second issue, we know at least anecdotally that the number of Americans who enjoy math and feel they do it well is alarmingly small, and that the preponderance of these are not women and minorities.

On the face of it, I would not seem to have been a casualty of the decontextualized questions of the tests and the other testing constraints, such as limitations on time. In fact, by all appearances I was one of the "successes" of the narrow math culture of the standardized test, for I broke 700 on my math aptitudes. Yet the testing knife cut both ways: though I was clearly anything but math phobic, I never felt I had the right to call myself a math star, for in my high school that label was reserved for those who scored a perfect 800 on their SATs. For the most part, the only entree to actually "being good at math" (not to mention "feeling good" about math) was to score not high, but highest, on tests.

Eventually I grew to resent the narrow way in which math competence was defined. The culture surrounding math seemed to have as its sole purpose the sifting and sorting of math students into elites and the rest of us, which ultimately served to cut the number of math enthusiasts to a handful and to deprive the vast majority of math students of enjoyment and continued participation in math study. It was almost by definition an elitist—not a human—discipline. For example, unlike in English, which is a lifelong pursuit, it seemed that only those with the top math scores had the right, if not the requirement, to continue math in college. Thus, like many of my classmates, at the end of compulsory math (in those years the twelfth grade), I saw no reason and had no desire ever to study math again. I was not, like some, disempowered by mathematics, but I was afraid that my luck would run out, that I was approaching the point at which I would begin to lose the honor grades. At that time, in the Darwinian test-driven culture that enveloped the study of mathematics, the pleasure and meaning in math lay primarily in getting the high test scores, not in any exploration of the discipline for its own sake or for intrinsic pleasures, as is the case with history or English. Thus, when math ceased to be a requirement (even though my test scores weren't bad), I could see no reason to continue, and I stopped.

When I returned as a new teacher to the study of math I was both thrilled and angry—thrilled to discover its possibilities for creative thinking and thrilled that it gave me a window onto the way my mind worked, and angry that, had I not had this good fortune to revisit math for professional reasons, I would have missed the chance to experience math in a way that exercised rather than suppressed my imagination.

This is the main point: in the climate of standardized math assessment, everyone—both the high and the low scorers—loses. The very experience that testing generates—learning a curriculum designed for an "objective" one-right-answer test, and having one's competency assessed almost solely by that test— drains the experience of learning math and its inherent potential for creative thinking, and discourages even those with a natural facility for the subject from pursuing it beyond what is required.

From the time I entered the teaching profession in 1971, I worked only in schools (two in succession) for whom critical attention to math pedagogy was pursued by the majority of the faculty with no less than a religious fervor. The experience of learning to teach math in this atmosphere radically transformed my understanding of the subject. Math became for me associated more with visualized patterns (Steen 1988a, 1988b) than with right or wrong answers, more about art than about arithmetic. It also became the starting point for all my conversations about ways to teach, and about ways to subordinate teaching to learning.

Both schools I taught in were heavily influenced by Caleb Gattegno, originally from Alexandria, Egypt, but by the end of his life a true cosmopolitan, who traveled the world giving seminars on literacy, second-language learning, and mathematics education. Gattegno had worked both with Piaget and with the Belgian educator Georges Cuisenaire, whose colored wooden "Cuisenaire rods" have gained fame as a remarkable math manipulative. (The Cuisenaire rods are a centimeter thick and of ten graduated lengths, from one to ten centimeters, each length having a different color; see Figure 6.1.) Gattegno, in collaboration with Cuisenaire, had been responsible for developing the more sophisticated ways of using the rods to teach math concepts (Gattegno 1971: 2). Teachers who studied with Gattegno learned to construct concrete models of mathematical ideas; later they would encourage their students to play with and manipulate these models, build similar and related ones, and extrapolate from the understanding they got from them to situations that they could imagine. (Reflecting and imagining were core activities in this practice, emphases I will return to later.) The focus was not only on math as computation but also on math as art, as a way of thinking about

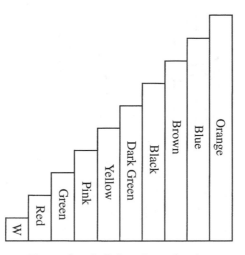

Figure 6.1: A Cuisenaire rod staircases.

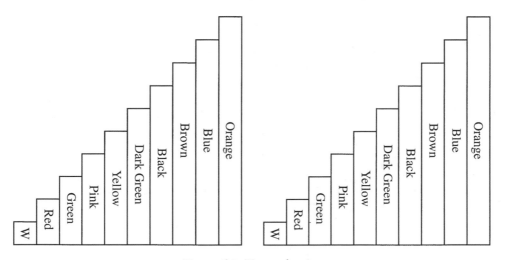

Figure 6.2: Two rod staircases.

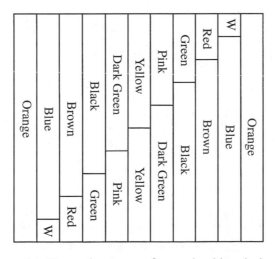

Figure 6.3: Two rod staircases, fit together like a lock and key.

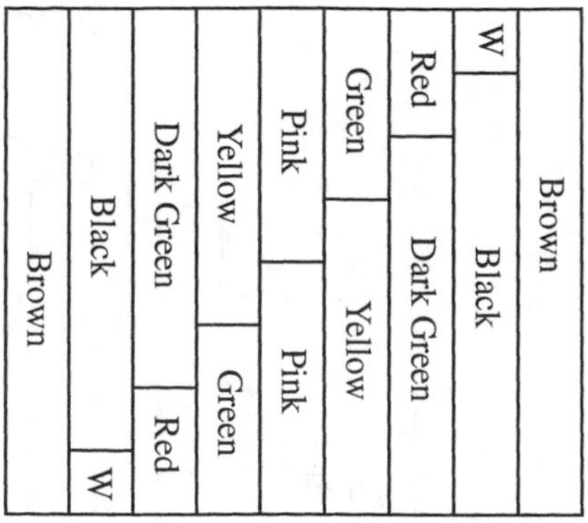

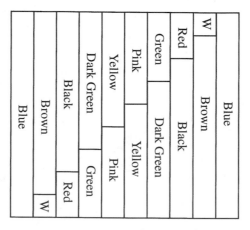

Figure 6.4: Complements of brown.

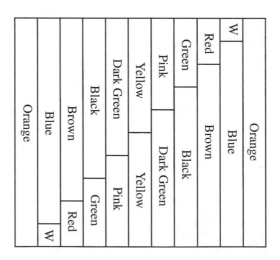

Figure 6.5: Complements of blue.

Figure 6.6: Examples of complements of 100: 55 + 45, using nine oranges (90) and another length equal to another orange (10).

situations, as a way of constructing and solving problems (Romberg 1992).

I remember quite clearly the exhilaration of the first full-blown math training workshop I ever attended. When I went to work as an assistant teacher in the first grade at a private elementary school in New York City, I was hired on the condition that I take a week-long math workshop at Gattegno's New York institute before school began in the fall. I remember thinking that this requirement was somewhat silly; after all, I had no trouble with mathematics, so why would my new school spend the money to get me in shape if I already was fit?

The first workshop afternoon was an epiphanal experience, for it allowed me to see for the first time that math was like a piece of art, or an artistic puzzle, with pieces that literally *did* fit together. At the direction of the workshop leader, as one of our first exercises we arranged the ten Cuisenaire rods into a staircase. Then we each made another staircase and rotated it so that it was upside down in relation to the first. Then we fit the second staircase to the first like a key into a lock. (See Figures 6.2 and 6.3.)

In this exercise I literally "saw" complementarity: that different pairs of rods are equivalent to a single length, that the pairs were reversible (that if a dark green and a pink were equivalent to orange, then a pink and a dark green were also); that as one rod of each pair got larger its mate got smaller; and finally that one could move the whole staircase over one position and create the complements of the next length. (See Figures 6.4 and 6.5 for a depiction of all the complements of the nine-centimeter blue rod and the eight-centimeter brown.) Through this exercise it was clear not only that math was visual, but also that a lot of math knowledge could be generated from a single observation or understanding.

For our study of the complements of one hundred, we each took ten of the orange ten-centimeter rods and made orange squares (these would be equivalent to one hundred white one-centimeter cubes). Then we covered them with random clusters of orange rods and one other rod. These would only partially cover the orange hundred square since they were equivalent to fewer than one hundred white cubic rods. (Examples: five oranges and a yellow, equivalent to fifty-five white cubes; or seven oranges and a red, equivalent to seventy-two white cubes.)

Each time we made a cluster we also imagined the complements of the cluster: how many oranges and what other rod would be needed to finish covering the orange square. (For example, five oranges and a yellow would need four oranges and a yellow for its complement in one hundred.)

Eventually we began writing down the number values of each original cluster and its complement. The pattern that emerged was something that in my twenty-three years of living and perhaps sixteen years of doing subtraction by the borrowing method, I had never noticed before: that complements of one hundred always add to ninety in the tens column and ten in the units column. The rods showed it visually: every pair of complements to one hundred had a total of nine orange rods, (which were equivalent to nine tens, or ninety), and two smaller-than-orange rods that were equivalent to another orange (or another ten). (See Figure 6.6.) It was easy to then see why forty-two would be paired with fifty-eight; thirty-seven with sixty-three, twenty-one with seventy-nine, and so on. Working at the blackboard, we extrapolated to other powers of ten (a thousand, a million, etc.) and discovered the pattern continued; that is, in every column but the units, the numbers added to nine; in the units column, the pairs added to ten. Thus to make a thousand, 345 was paired with 655; 231 was paired with 769, and so forth. (The reason was obvious: the numbers were adding to 900 plus 90 plus 10.) We realized with a slight shock that all we needed to know to be really good at this was the complements of nine and the complements of ten. We realized that we could find complements of a trillion with no more effort than finding complements of one hundred. It just took longer to say, and there were a few more words to know. (For a full discussion of complementarity and other aspects of the Gattegno approach to teaching mathematics, see Gattegno 1973, 1988.)

Complementarity was to become a cornerstone of the way I did subtraction and addition problems (and the way I taught them) because it gave the tools to transform all sorts of difficult problems into easy ones. In our study of subtraction that workshop week, it became clear that the number of equivalent subtraction problems—that is, pairs of numbers with the same difference—was infinite, and it became a game to transform the more difficult problems into easier ones. The problem 123 − 85, for example, could be transformed into 138 − 100, by adding fifteen (85's complement in a hundred) to both 85 and 123. The new problem yielded an equivalent difference, but the answer to 138 − 100 was much more obvious than the answer to the equivalent problem, 123 minus 85.

We used complementarity on addition as well, though differently; the challenge was still to transform hard problems, defined as those with lots of carrying, to the breezy ones that fairly sang out their answers. In the addition problem 74 + 89, for instance, one could shave 11 (89's complement in 100) from the 74 and give it to the 89; 89 would then become 100 and 74 would become 63. Since all that has happened is that 11 has been transferred between the two addends, the sum of the new problem, 100 + 63, is clearly equivalent to the original, and the answer is clearly 163.

Done this way, addition was no longer a matter of remembering hard sums that required carrying, in a system that was formulaic (and to many children—and adults—nonsensical) but of visualizing a kind of pouring process: one hand holds 89, the other, 74, and the second hand *pours* 11 into the first. One can *feel* that 89 has been increased to 100 and that 74 has shrunk to 63.

Another highlight of my math "transformation" was the discovery of the uses of doubling. Becoming adept at doubling faster than a calculator enabled us to generate a very healthy chunk of the multiplication tables. I "discovered" that the twos, fours, and eights tables were related by doubling—in fact, *were* doubles; and that the six table was the double of the threes. Multiplying by ten was just a matter of adding a zero; five was half of ten (taking half was called undoubling). Knowing how to double and undouble freed me (and my students) from ever having to "memorize tables" and it helped us generate all sorts of other multiplications. We learned not the "fives table" but how, in general, one multiplied by five (and by extension, 50 and 500, etc.); not the "eights table" but how, in general, one multiplied by eight. (And if one knew how to multiply by eight, was not the double of that, multiplying by 16, nearly as easy?)

The content and the way the curriculum was shaped exemplified the pedagogical principles we were learning. The focus on doubling was, among its other virtues, an example of the principle that topics would be easy—and more memorable—if taught so that they were interconnected in many ways, because then there would be many avenues from the known to the unknown. Another pedagogical principle of the approach was that anything we asked the children to spend time on—like the complements or doubling—should yield much in the way of mathematical returns, or power. I entered my classroom in the fall with the goal of designing lessons that would "get a lot from a little."

Promoting independence in the children was a third pedagogical principle, and we did it deliberately. We tried to teach in such a way that the children would develop criteria to decide, on their own, whether something was correct. Toward this end, one of the more powerful—and difficult—pieces of our teaching repertoire was the silent lesson. We tried to keep our verbal explanations to a minimum in order that the children might focus on making their own sense of the rod configurations we built or number patterns we wrote on the board. Silent lessons mobilized students' attention in a way the teacher's ordinary speaking often didn't. Silent lessons pushed students to figure out and articulate what was going on and what was predictable and "correct" about a situation. The silent lesson was for me the pedagogical ideal, and I idolized the teachers who could do it—even for ten minutes at a stretch. It was a tremendous challenge to all of us to try to overcome years of exposure to teaching as talking.

Another way we used silence in our teaching was to refrain from saying whether something was right or wrong. Stephen Smith, one of my colleagues at my second school (The Day School) remembers it as the most powerful part of his practice because it so strongly demonstrated respect for the children's intelligence. If we posed as the sole arbiters of correctness ("Right! Wrong!"), as had been typical of our own teachers, we would be robbing the students of their chance to exercise their own critical powers. Of course, many children would initially balk at this sort of teaching. They would scrutinize our poker faces, watching for clues of whether their answers were right or wrong; we had to work hard not to give anything away. When they did buy into what we were after, however, they developed pleasure in exercising their power more than their dependency, like six-year-old Michael in my first grade, who was known to cry, "No, no! Don't tell me! I can do this myself!"

Another highlight of my transformation and of my pedagogy was an emerging understanding of the role of students' mistakes. "Mistakes are the children's gift to you" was a strange and yet obvious truism that I heard perhaps at that first summer seminar, but certainly in my first few weeks as a teacher. "Study the mistakes: they tell you what you have to do next." We learned to milk the mistakes for their information. Mistakes told us what to stress, what structure to build in what way in order for a child to become more clear and aware of what was at hand. We teachers held math meetings on mistakes, but we also gave children opportunities to critique their own and each other's work for mistakes and to become articulate about why something was off. This is why we didn't say (or tried not to say) "Right!" or "Wrong!" but rather, "Does everyone agree with this? Does anyone not agree? Why?" and let the students articulate to each other their moves. We teachers made our own mistakes (occasionally planned, but often real) frequently enough that the students learned to critique what we did as well; we were so patently fallible in every aspect of our teaching that some children learned that they could only trust themselves, and this awareness sharpened their attention.

Another important step in my own trajectory of becoming-a-math-teacher was learning how to get children to use their imaginations in math lessons. No lesson was complete unless we asked students to imagine something that was an extension of a configuration they had constructed with the rods (but that they had not actually built). In this way we were helping them prepare for the abstract pencil-and-paper work they would do once the manipulatives were put away—they would be able to call up imagery to support their thinking.

A related pedagogical principle was to teach in such a way that the structure of the number system was revealed. Few lessons better employed both the focus on structure and the use of the imagination than the rod lesson about naming fractions. We would begin by having children measure one rod with another (for example, the seven-centimeter black rod and the white one-centimeter cube); from this we would give the language that, since seven whites were as long as black, one white was 1/7 of black. From there the children were on their own, and soon had many names for the white rod: it could be called 1/9 of blue, 1/10 of orange, 1/6 of dark green, 1/4 of pink, and so forth. (See Figure 6.7.) Giving

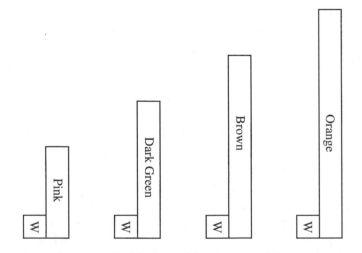

Figure 6.7: Rod images of fractions: ¼, ⅙, ⅛, and ⅒.

the white rod the value of one, and the other rods their value in relation to it, they could generate new fractional equivalences to one: 1/9 of 9, 1/10 of 10, 1/6 of 6, 1/4 of 4, and so on. Extending the pattern, children might put two oranges (equivalent to twenty of the whites) together, and generate another name for the white: 1/20 of 20. Building further, they could discover that it can also be called 1/25 of 25 and 1/100 of 100. If they listened they could use the melody of what they were saying to invent names for white they had not built but could be sure of, such as 1/237 of 237, 1/1000 of 1000, 1/9999 of 9999. Through this exercise they could learn the whole system of naming the fractions, and in learning the system would be liberated from having to experience every fraction personally; having built and touched a relative few and figured out the naming system, they could create an infinite number of fractional names for the number one—and later, any number.

What is being showcased here is the algebra of the situation, the fact that "one" can be expressed as—and is always equal to—1/x of x. This was the kind of awareness that allowed students to "get a lot from a little." With it they could see that they could generate their own knowledge, and that surprisingly little effort needed to be expended to generate, on their own, an infinite number of such equations. Particularly the youngest children, first graders, warmed to the challenge of creating fractional equivalences for a single number—expressions that they certainly would never have found in a workbook, where the curriculum dictated that they weren't even to *think* about numbers greater than 20 until they reached second grade. Six-year-olds were usually tickled with their creations, delighted that they could transform $1 + 1 = 2$ into $1/23 \times 23 + 1/89 \times 89 = 2/11 \times 11$.

Showcasing the number system was a particularly important part of the pedagogy. This was probably on my mind at the beginning of my third year as a teacher, when I began teaching a fourth/fifth-grade class at The Day School. For my first week there I decided that, rather than begin with a general review of material from past years, we would start with something that would revolve around an immediate experience. Thus I opened the first week of school with a curriculum unit on bases using the Cuisenaire rods. I decided to begin by working in base five, what I called the Yellow World, since the five-centimeter yellow rod was to be called "ten" (as opposed to our usual world in which the orange rod was called "ten"). I removed from classroom use all of the rods longer than yellow and told the children that in the game we would play, the only thing they needed to "remember" or accept for the sake of the game was that now the number after four was to be given the name "ten." (In this game we had "ten" fingers on each hand. Thus, in working with Cuisenaire rods, we would say that the yellow rod was worth "ten" whites.)

The first game was to build a staircase and count in the Yellow World. First we counted to ten (1, 2, 3, 4, 10) and then proceeded onward. What was the number we always gave the number right after ten? Eleven. After that? Twelve. Then thirteen, fourteen. The next length or step in the staircase consisted of two tens (two yellows). What was the name of two tens? Twenty. Two yellow "tens" and a white? Twenty-one. We continued with the staircase and the counting, on to forty, forty-one, forty-two, forty-three, forty-four, and then? What was the number after forty-four? We would now have another ten to add to the four tens we already had. That meant that we had "ten" tens. Ten tens are called one hundred.

Children generally enter into this game more easily than adults, who have much more invested in what they call "ten." But sometimes they would forget and use the words "five" or "six," and at those times we would furrow our brows and ask, "What does that mean? What language is that? Is that a word in our world?"

Other "explorations" consisted of counting by twos, and making predictions about which numbers would be even and which would be odd. We also generated complements of ten in the Yellow World (10 = 1 + 4, 10 = 2 + 3); and doubles (1 + 1 = 2, 2 + 2 = 4, 3 + 3 = 11, 4 + 4 = 13). Using what they knew of multiplication and fractions, children discovered other interesting facts of life in the Yellow World: for example, that if two threes equal eleven, then half of 11 is 3; and if two fours equal thirteen, then half of 13 is 4. Division, factors, prime numbers, fractional statements—all could be refigured in the new World—simply by starting from the single new "fact" of assigning the name "ten" to the number after four.

On subsequent days we worked in the Dark Green World (where the dark green rod, the rod one unit bigger than the yellow, was called ten), and later in the Pink World (where the rod one unit smaller than yellow was called ten). And so on, for the rest of that week.

Unlike traditional treatments of bases that focused on converting from one base to another (e.g., 6 in base ten equals 11 in base five), this one looked at operations and facts *within* the "world" of a single base. If we did cross boundaries (go from one world to another), it was to deepen our reflection on how the number system worked: what of the number system remained constant between one base and another and what changed and why. For example, we might ask what were the even numbers in the Yellow World and compare them to even numbers in other bases, and then examine the nature of even-ness. (Ten, for example, is an odd number in the Yellow World, as is one hundred.) Or we might notice that all the "tricks" we had learned about multiplying by nine in base ten (for example, that the digits of multiples of nine always summed to nine) could be applied to the fours table in the Yellow World and to the sixes table in the Black World.

Within a few days my new Day School colleagues had abandoned their beginning-of-the-year reviews and taken up the study of bases. As a culminating activity, my colleague Stephen Smith had his students write Travelers' Guides to the various worlds, to which they gave such titles as "How To Get Around in the Green World" and "Survival Tips for Life in the Brown World" and so forth.

Like the focus on structure, the emphasis on using imagination, and the curriculum-building dictum of "getting a lot from a little," the concept of equivalence bridged content and pedagogy. The curriculum was heavily laced with the concept, which we introduced to the youngest students as "another name for" (4 + 1 was "another name for" 5; 30 – 12 was "another name for" 18). Equivalence was everywhere in our teaching: trains of Cuisenaire rods were equivalent to other trains, fractions were equivalent to other fractions; the difference in one subtraction problem was equivalent to the difference in another. We continually wove the theme of equivalence into virtually all the topics we studied, so that the children would learn to see numbers and equations as members of a sometimes infinite series of equivalent expressions. One criterion in our assessment of students, in fact, was the facility with which they called into play these equivalences when faced with problems whose solutions were not apparent at first glance.

A fine example of this working was the case of a second-grade girl, Susan, who mistook the problem "What is 4/5 of 5?" for "What is 5/4 of 5?" The teacher, John Dexter, a former math staff developer and by then the headmaster of The Day School, was about to correct her and then decided not to, just to see what she would do. Within a few minutes he was supremely grateful that he had caught himself, for the solution she presented to him was a magnificent example of many of the goals we held for the children's math development; her solution was a series of equivalences that built a bridge from what she knew to the unknown.

In explaining her solution, Susan told John, "I didn't know what 5/4 of 5 is, but I did know that 4/4 of 5 is 5, because 4/4 is the same as one or a whole, and a whole of five is five. So that left me with 1/4 of 5. I don't know what 1/4 of five is, but do I know that 1/4 of 4 is one, so I added one to the 5 and then I had six. That left me with 1/4 of one, which I know is 1/4. So the answer is 6 1/4."

This explanation reveals two things: first, that Susan felt entitled to break the number into parts, that is, to rename it using equivalent expressions, (e.g., 5/4 became 4/4 plus 1/4); and second, that she had a facility with making those transformations. (In fact, this problem and its solution could lead to a whole set of problems of the type "8/7 × 9"; the solutions that could be solved by such transformations not only make sense but demonstrate in their shifting, adding, taking away, a problemsolving mentality—an "I-don't-know-this-but-I-do-know-that" kind of facileness.)

Such facility demonstrates what Kornhaber and Gardner describe as a "performance of understanding" (1993). It has to be cultivated continually, lest students get drawn in to the idea that math consists of algorithms and formulas. In my second year at The Day School (I was now teaching math in the middle school), I told a pre-algebra class of sixth graders to use their wits to figure out some algebraic equations with a single unknown. I gave out no rules; the students were simply to eyeball such equations as $3X + 15 = 63$ and ask themselves the question, "Given the fact that there is an equal sign here, what must be true of X?" Within a few days, working together, they'd generated more awarenesses about equations than they ever would have known if they had just "learned the rules."

Nowadays much is made of making math more "relevant" for children, and mathematics study is often tied to "real-life situations." I remember thinking occasionally in my days of teaching that I should spend more time on "story problems," and when I did, or when the children made up their own, I was always amazed that, considering how little time they actually spent on word problems, they were surprisingly adept at doing them; it was something, it seemed, they didn't need to practice. I surmise now that this was because story problems require a kind of translation—through visualization and talk—from a verbally described situation to numbers; and that the children working in our classes had been describing their mathematics, scrutinizing it, rearranging it by transformations, and, most importantly, visualizing it throughout their work with the Cuisenaire rods and other manipulatives. "Story problems" required nothing new (Romberg 1986).

Assessment came out of the activities, and our assessment was ongoing. If teaching was the process of learning what the students knew, assessment became a process of figuring out what to do next. The emphasis was on the students as individuals, their individual working and thinking styles, rather than on comparing students to a standard of achievement or to each other. Giving opportunities for feedback—either through talk or open-ended tasks—was as essential to assessment as it was to teaching. In fact, assessment was almost indistinguishable from practice; I may have given fewer than a dozen written "tests" in fourteen years of teaching. It was the building and conversation and creative writing that comprised the typical class that were our sources of feedback. At report-card time we sent home narratives describing how each child worked, what her style was, what strengths she relied on.

Observation was of course a key in assessment. Children built, they talked about what they built; we watched and listened. For example, we might ask the students to show with the rods various equivalences to 4/5. The teacher could simply look at what a child had built and know something of what he understood. If he was asked to speak about it (for example, "make some true statements about this pattern"), again, assessment was easy in that it revealed, in the language the student used, the level of understanding.

One of the more playful assessment modes—one that allowed students to explore and also relieved them of the fiction (and tension) that math by definition consisted of discrete questions and single right answers—was the restriction game. Among the variations were format restrictions, where the parameters referred to a class of problems. (Examples: Write as many subtraction problems as you can with the answer 121; using the fraction form, write as many equivalences for 1/2 of 16 as you can.) Another variation was to restrict the array of numbers and/or signs available. (Examples: Using the numerals 1, 2, and 3 and the operations + and ×, write as many equations as you can equivalent to 10.) Such restriction games were another way for children to explore the ways numbers function, and it allowed them to play and to experiment with patterns.

These restriction games were one form of the creative-writing exercises that we did in those days. In our classes, writing in math class did not mean, as it often does now, writing in journals about the experience of trying to understand a concept. Rather, at the end of a lesson, to assess what students understood of the material we had been working with, we often would ask them to make "inventions" (original equations) like the ones we had been working with. This was one way of assessing their ability to function with a topic, whether it was fractions as operators or equivalent subtractions. With creative writing we could find out what the students could do on their own with a point of the curriculum, and how they could integrate a new awareness with the old ones.

Because we taught to certain "milestones" such as complementarity, doubling, and transformations, as well as to certain key awarenesses—such as that specific operations were related (that addition was another way of expressing subtraction, and multiplication, division, factors, and multiplication of fractions were all different languages that described the same set of relationships)—part of our assessment activity was to monitor to what extent students used these awarenesses in solving problems. We did not teach algorithms, at least not in the early stages of inquiry, and avoided any "method" in which the sense was not apparent; we continually invited children to create their own ways of solving problems and then to share these ways with their classmates.

What we looked for, also, was evidence that the work that had been done in the concrete had found some place in their imaginations. Conversations that paralleled assessment activities encouraged children to imagine what they had built and then to describe what they saw in their imaginations. "Imagine you were to build that with rods." (Sometimes they did this with eyes closed.) "What would it look like? How many oranges would you use? If you made a red train just as long, how many reds would you need? How do you know?" Because they had already had the experience of building it actually, they had a real experience they could refer to. Seeing in the mind's eye, or reflecting, was valued more than remembering.

A current trend in thinking about math pedagogy is that real-life math is messy. Actually, it isn't math that is messy; it is real life that does not conform to rules and patterns. I think it is important to make this distinction: the situations in which we apply mathematical thinking are often very messy. Figuring out how to sort out information may feel confusing, as it feels whenever we try to make order out of chaos. (It is not so different, really, from organizing a history paper, or any other essay, including this one.) But the mathematics itself—the mathematical relationships—are not messy. What is true, though, is that there are many ways of describing those mathematical relationships, more than we are initially led to believe, and they are linked in ways we are often never taught.

One of the most important and interesting questions raised by the alternative assessment debate with regard to mathematics is, if one were to talk about true mathematical ability (and not simply adeptness at arithmetic and/or computation), what would it consist of? If we threw away the standardized tests, what would we look for to assess math competence and how would we look for it? I would offer that the following be part of the repertoire of mathematical functioning:

1. an awareness that numbers are systematic and have patterns, which makes extrapolation predictable and easier. For example, the ability to extrapolate that if 1/2 of 6 is 3 and 1/2 of 60 is 30, one can know, either by reevaluating the unit or by the sheer sense of the pattern, that 1/2 of 600 is 300, and that 1/2 of 6000 is 3000, and 1/2 of 60,000 is 30,000, etc.
2. an awareness of equivalence and a facility with using equivalence to solve problems; an example of this is when Susan noticed that 5/4 was equivalent to 4/4 plus 1/4; or when a "hard" problem like 302 − 289 is transformed to an equivalent but easier one, 313 − 300
3. an ability to visualize and imagine numbers and their relationships, which in this case means an ability to re-create in the mind's eye pictures of mathematical structures that students once built concretely, or are related to ones they once built
4. an awareness that it is possible to draw out information from mistakes.

What these assessment points have in common is that they are based on understandings of how math works (and that it *does* work) and on awarenesses of linkages between and among topics. These linkages are built, in the teaching and learning, through concrete experiences that bring the students' focus back, again and again, to the essence of the mathematics itself, its structure. The pleasure in the intrinsic "fit" of mathematics that this way of teaching generates sustains students' interest in mathematics in a way that high test scores about discrete math facts never can.

What is different about this way of teaching and assessing is that it looks quite closely at what children have already achieved and honors the various ways they naturally learn. It provides them with concrete experiences that not only are linked to conceptualizations of mathematical relationships but also furnish mental imagery for working with numbers on a more abstract level. It applies their experiences with the patterns of language to their work with learning the patterns of mathematics. In so doing it is a continuation of their natural ways of learning, which includes experimenting until they can make their own sense. With its emphasis on transformations, this way of thinking about math exercises the mind in ways that students can be conscious of and therefore talk about—beyond the test scores. In so doing, it honors the many ways that students think, and therefore invites students into the arena of experiencing themselves as mathematical.

To teach math this way, however, one does have to be "reborn" to the idea that math is the ultimate sense-making discipline, that in math, sense-making as a value supersedes speed or superficial formulaic efficiency, and that nothing is worth teaching or learning if it violates the learner's sense of truth. Thus understanding has to be born out of the learner's own experience.

One challenge of teaching (mathematics or anything) differently from the way one has learned it is to keep in mind that children bring none of the baggage that we who have a different math heritage bring to this different way of thinking about math. Never having invested any time in subtraction by borrowing, for example, they are much more open to using transformations to find differences. Never having been schooled in the speed culture of mathematics, they do not ask what is the worth of learning a way that might initially be slower but would make much more sense. They would not necessarily be comforted by the formulas that long ago became the crutches of their teachers' math repertoires. Transformations that they could see and that therefore made sense would be easier for them to adapt to and use than even for their teachers, since they wouldn't be burdened by any investments in the nonsensical old standbys.

What are some tools that assess math competence more accurately than the multiple-choice questions found on timed standardized tests? They include

1. *building*: exercises that give children the opportunities to build or demonstrate concretely (either with rods or other manipulatives) mathematical concepts
2. *imagining*: challenges to students to use their imaginations, and to extrapolate from the concrete to other imagined situations
3. *creative writing*: open-ended problems that allow children to generate knowledge, as well as to demonstrate their understanding of math as a system; and opportunities to create mathematical inventions (equations) that reflect the material they are working on
4. *sharing*: opportunities for children to talk about their mathematics and share their ways of doing it with others in the class.

ADVICE FOR TEACHERS AND TEACHER EDUCATORS

Clearly, whether one is a new or experienced teacher, revolutionizing one's own math teaching requires a tremendous personal effort and can only happen over an extended period of time. Workshops, in which groups of teachers meet together regularly over a period of perhaps at least a year to discuss their efforts in their classrooms and work on pedagogy are certainly better than solo efforts to revamp one's teaching and curriculum, and also better than one-shot exposures to new math pedagogy, such as summer math camps or weekend seminars (though these can be and usually are excellent starting points).

In any case, goals are as important as format here. In addition to rebuilding one's own mathematical understanding, including through the use of math manipulatives (the most common format of math workshops), such seminars could give participants opportunities to

1. study ways to create curriculum and curricular linkages that both make sense and save energy

2. study the pedagogical uses of mistakes and ways to let mistakes guide instruction

3. practice the pedagogy of silent lessons, in order to give more weight to creating awarenesses in children that do not rely on the teachers' verbal explanations, but rather encourage the children to generate their own language around math

4. learn techniques for observing and listening to children doing math, and develop a body of grounded knowledge about children's mathematical thinking to share in the seminar.

This chapter began with the theme of transformation: the transformation of my own perceptions about math and about what "doing math" was all about. The transformation happened almost by accident; after a lifetime of a "good education" I entered the teaching profession at the right place and met people who would transform my conception of mathematics and set me on the path to doing the same for children.

Today I meet adults about to enter teaching who actively want the same thing. They are well aware of their own hesitancies around mathematics and long for an experience that will make them feel comfortable enough with math at least not to set obstacles in the paths of their future students. What I and others like me know is that if they are going to immerse themselves in the business of teaching mathematics, then they are going to have to be ready to plan and assess mathematical activity not through the demands of a standardized test but by looking at what children actually do when they think about math and what they say about what they do. By honoring, in their teaching and their assessing, the multiplicity of ways that children talk and think and explain their math, teachers will be rehumanizing the discipline (Merseth 1993; Wheeler 1975), nurturing more speakers of the language of mathematics, and in that process, will be ensuring that a much greater proportion of their students will awake to their own mathematical creativity.

For too long, speed and memorization have held sway and served as the gatekeepers to higher mathematical pursuits. As Elliot Eisner says, "Assessment tasks should reflect the values of the intellectual community from which the tasks are derived" (1994: 204). Such values of the discipline of mathematics have been disfigured by the values of the standardized tests, and we need to restore them. Were reflectiveness to be honored, and that reflection to be about the patterns and liveliness of the structure of mathematics, rather than small answers to small questions, it is just possible that more of the disenfranchised (those who would rather reflect than speed, those who would rather understand than memorize) would count themselves in.

REFERENCES

American Association of University Women (1992). *How schools shortchange girls.* Washington, DC: Author

Armstrong, J. (1980). *Participation of women in mathematics: An overview.* Denver, CO: Education Commission of the States.

College Entrance Examination Board (1992). National report on college-bound seniors. In *National center for educational statistics digest of educational statistics 1993.* Washington, DC: U.S. Department of Education.

Eisner, E. (1994). *The educational imagination: On the design and evaluation of school programs.* New York: Macmillan.

Gattegno, C. (1971). *Now Johnny can do arithmetic.* New York: Educational Solutions.

——— (1973). *The common sense of teaching mathematics.* New York: Educational Solutions.

——— (1988). *The science of education. Part 2B: The awareness of mathematization.* New York: Educational Solutions.

Haney, W., G. F. Madaus, and R. Lyons (1993). *The fractured market place for standardized testing.* Boston: Kluwer.

Kornhaber, M., and H. Gardner (1993). *Varieties of excellence: Identifying and assessing children's talents.* New York: National Center for Restructuring Education, Schools and Teaching.

Merseth, K. (1993). How old is the shepherd? An essay about mathematics education. *Phi Delta Kappan 74*(7): 548–554.

National Center for Educational Statistics (1993). *International assessment of educational progress.* Washington, DC: U.S. Department of Education.

National Commission on Testing and Public Policy (1990). *From gatekeeper to gateway: Transforming testing in America.* Chestnut Hill, MA: Author

National Council of Teachers of Mathematics (1989). *Curriculum and evaluation standards for school mathematics.* Reston, VA: Author.

——— (1991). *Professional standards for teaching mathematics.* Reston, VA: Author.

Oakes, J. (1988). Tracking in mathematics and science education: A structural contribution to unequal schooling. In L. Weis (ed.), *Class, race and gender in American education,* 106–125. Albany: State University of New York Press.

Rivera-Batiz, F. (1992) Quantitative literacy and the likelihood of employment among young adults in the U.S. *Journal of Human Resources 27*(2): 481–91.

Romberg, T. A. (1986). Research on teaching and learning mathematics: Two disciplines of scientific inquiry. In M. C. Wittrock (ed.), *Handbook of Research on Teaching, Third Edition,* 850–73. New York: Macmillan.

——— (1992). Problematic features of the school mathematics curriculum. In P. Jackson (ed.), *Handbook of research on curriculum,* 749–88. New York: Macmillan.

Sadker, M., D. Sadker, and L. Long (1989). Gender and education equality. In J. Banks and C. H. M. Banks (eds.), *Multicultural education: Issues and perspectives,* 106–23. Newton, MA: Allyn and Bacon.

Steen, L. A. (1988a). Forces for change in the mathematics curriculum. *Wisconsin Teachers of Mathematics 34*(1): 3–7.

———— (1998b). The science of patterns. *Science 240*: 611–16.

Wheeler, D. (1975). Humanizing mathematical education. *Mathematics Teaching 71*(June); 4–9.

Chapter Seven

"I WOULDN'T KNOW I WAS SMART IF I DIDN'T COME TO THIS CLASS"

Julie Heiman Savitch and Leslie Anne Serling

Temper tantrums. Scissors flying. Toilets overflowing. One child trips and the other children ignore her cries, stepping over her to reach their destination. Parents scream at children other than their own. A typical day in Julie Savitch's first-grade classroom. Unusual behavior for Harbor Lane School.[1]

Harbor Lane School is a large public school located in the Chinatown of a large northeastern city. There are 1,200 children from prekindergarten through sixth grade. For each grade there are approximately six classes, one of which is a gifted class. Children assigned to gifted classes remain together from kindergarten through sixth grade, with few if any changes, although the teacher is usually different each year.

When the children are in prekindergarten (four years old), they become eligible to apply for the gifted program in this school. Through teacher recommendations and parents' initiative, children are sent to take an I.Q. test, which is followed by an interview. Since the test is in English, many of the students for whom English is a second language do not apply, due in large part to the language barrier. This confirms "the central role that language plays in assessment" (Sylvan 1994: 74). In addition, not all of the parents are aware of this program, and therefore many of the children who may be eligible are not tested. Consequently, though the school and the "nongifted" classes are 95 percent Chinese, the gifted classes are much more ethnically diverse and include children who are bused in from other neighborhoods.

Julie's first-grade gifted class in 1990–1991 had bad chemistry from the start. Neither the children nor the parents got along. After the kindergarten year, their teacher left the classroom to run a pull-out program. After their second-grade year, their teacher left the profession. The group's dynamics hindered their learning. Few strategies had worked within the classroom setting to alleviate the tension. No teacher was willing to take on the challenge they presented when they reached third grade.

The principal approached Julie with the suggestion that she teach this class again. Unwilling to perpetuate an unsuccessful situation, Julie declined but began talking to parents, teachers, and the students to generate alternatives for those children. The consensus was that the children should be split up. Julie and her colleague Leslie Serling, a third-grade teacher, had always worked well together on short-term projects; they also had very similar philosophies and personalities that complemented one another. They had been looking for an opportunity to collaborate on a more in-depth basis, and this third-grade class seemed to present them with such an opportunity. This chapter follows Julie and Leslie through the two-year collaborative journey they took toward untracking a gifted class.

A FRAMEWORK FOR CHANGE

Through hours of discussions and soul-searching, we created an unconventional plan that would benefit both the students and ourselves: we would divide the gifted class into two third-grade enrichment classes and collaborate to teach them both. Howard Gardner's theory of multiple intelligences offered a conceptual framework that guided us in this challenge (Gardner 1983). He writes that there are seven types of intelligence: interpersonal, intrapersonal, body-kinesthetic, spatial, musical, linguistic, and logical-mathematical. Gardner's expanded definition of giftedness supports our beliefs in a more inclusive classroom. Like Gardner, we believe that all children excel in one area or another and can therefore be teachers in their own right; we can all learn from each other. Rexford Brown, onetime director of communication for the Education Commission of the States, best summarizes our beliefs:

> Gardner's work has been important in attacking the monolithic notion of intelligence that has undergirded much of our thinking. We are beginning to see that education is not meant merely to sort out a few children and make them leaders, but to develop the latent talents of the entire population in diverse ways. (Cited in Winn 1990: 30)

This premise formed the basis of our curricular decisions, beginning with the way we rearranged the two class groups to the way we went on to structure our teaching around themes and learning centers.

In order to diversify the range of strengths in the two classes, we chose to complete the roster with children from the regular program, and change the configuration from one gifted class to two enriched classes. In our plan, we also took care to separate the volatile personalities, the shy and quiet children, the very needy children, and the outspoken voices. We attempted to create more balance in each setting.

The plan was presented to the other second-grade teachers, with a call for children whom they thought would be comfortable with children from the gifted program. We specifically asked for mature, independent, and motivated children who would help serve as positive role models. We wanted children for whom English was their second language, those who may have had trouble with the interview aspect of the original application process. We also wanted children who had strengths that were not scholastic or measurable by an I.Q. test.

However, since the second-grade teachers knew that the students they chose were going to be mixed with students from the gifted program, many of them chose children whom they deemed gifted in the traditional sense, the ones who were at the top of their classes academically. The majority picked children who did well on the standardized math and reading tests. Therefore, the two enrichment classes were more balanced than they had been previously but were not as heterogeneous as if we had chosen the children randomly. This reorganization resulted in one class with eleven children from the gifted class and sixteen from the mainstreamed population, and a second class with eleven from the gifted class and seventeen from the mainstream. Thus began our two-year commitment to untracking and team teaching for inclusion.

THE FIRST YEAR: 1992–1993

Since our decision to team came from our desire to work together and was not a mandate from the administration, we approached it with very positive attitudes. We knew we had similar teaching philosophies, which gave us a strong base from which to begin. Our first task was to discuss how our teaming would work. One of the essential features of an inclusive school is a cohesive sense of community that is accepting of differences and responsive to individual needs (Sapon-Shevin 1994/95). We began building our community of learning by first focusing on the relationship between the two of us before gradually extending the community culture we created to include all the children, first within each classroom and ultimately between the two classes.

Building Community Between Teachers

In anticipation of this challenging assignment, we came together over the summer to begin planning. We met with team teachers from other schools to see how they collaborated. We looked at our strengths and weaknesses to help us decide what shape our partnership would take. After numerous discussions, we decided to begin the transition slowly. Our teaming would consist of planning together, sharing our strengths, and encouraging one another to take risks. This summer meeting was the first of many future hours together; our partnership had begun.

Our discussions continued on a daily basis throughout the year. Since our principal supported staff collaboration, we were given five common preparation periods each week and adjoining classrooms. We were able to build a support system through our close proximity that took away the isolation that we have found to be so prevalent in our profession (Lieberman and Miller 1984). The easy access we had to one another and the daily time we had throughout the year were essential. We built our partnership through ongoing oral and written communication, team meetings, and dialogue journals. We spent our preparation periods as well as our lunches discussing curriculum, the children, and our own teaching. Though working together was extremely rewarding, it was not without occasional disagreements. Sharing the responsibility equally, compromising, and really hearing one another were lessons that we learned while working together, lessons that we knew our students would also need to learn.

Modeling Partnership and Collaboration for Students

In order to model collaboration for our students, we decided to make our partnership very visible. We consulted each other throughout each day on curriculum decisions, questions about the children, and suggestions for improving a lesson that one of us had finished but the other had not yet begun. We wrote parent letters together and shared materials, books, and ideas. The children witnessed our professional teamwork and friendship. They understood from our example that working together was a value that both of us held and acted upon. They in turn began to work together to solve math problems, on theme projects, and to edit each other's writing. They learned to talk to one another. The comfortable buzz of a productive learning environment permeated our classrooms. Collaboration was beginning to pervade the daily practice of our classrooms.

Dialogue Journals

We both kept dialogue journals, which helped us to expand our partnership in new directions. The pages of our journals enabled us to be more reflective on issues that could not be covered in a frenzied school day. In our journals, we folded the paper in half lengthwise. We wrote our reflections about journal articles, child observations, and teaching strategies on the left. Then we periodically switched journals and responded to one another's entries on the right. This allowed us to communicate on a deeper level. For example,

> JULIE: I taught these children in first grade, so I know the challenges that I will be faced with. I know the parents' and the children's personalities and how best to handle them. I feel confident that my previous experience will help us initially with this new arrangement. However, I am nervous about teaching third grade, since I have only taught first grade.
>
> LESLIE: I have taught third-grade for two years. I feel confident with my knowledge of the curriculum and the age group. I know that I will be able to contribute my experience to our team. I am relying on Julie to supply insights regarding the children and the parents.

We each responded in our dialogue journals to professional articles that were applicable to our situation, delving into topics such as untracking and gifted education. The articles often forced us to examine our own preconceptions and premises about gifted students. They led us to ask questions such as: What is the true difference between gifted children and average children? How can we label children at such a young age? Who is left out if selection is done so early? How can we change our assessment to be more inclusive? By reading critically and responding by free writing, our philosophies regarding inclusion and untracking became more focused. We began to widen our definition of giftedness even further, challenging each other to see the strengths in each and every child.

We also used our journals to write reflections about our experiences. A few times throughout the school year, we switched classes. In one instance in the beginning of the year, Julie expressed a reluctance to begin the literature discussions that Leslie was so proficient at facilitating. Leslie similarly expressed apprehension with cooperative learning, a strength that Julie had developed. We both felt that "our kids weren't ready." Was it that we were not ready?

We decided to switch classes, and try working with each other's students in the areas that we were comfortable. Julie did a cooperative learning lesson with Leslie's class, and Leslie had a literature discussion with Julie's class. Both lessons were extremely successful! We each wrote about the experience of teaching the other's students, including specific child observations and our ideas about class chemistry. We then traded journals and responded to those reflections. This method of debriefing was crucial to the experiment, because we were now beginning to see our students and ourselves through wider lenses. Our risk taking was supported by our dialogue journals, allowing us to broaden our teaching strategies. For each of us, the added insight of another teacher enabled us to see our students from a new perspective and thus assess our students in new ways.

Dialogue journals were so successful that we instituted them between our children and ourselves as a nonverbal form of communication. We introduced the journals by showing our students our own notebooks. The strength behind modeling was clear. They were all very excited to begin. We began by asking all of them the same question; What were their thoughts on cooperative learning? From that point on each journal took its own path. We collected and responded to half of the student journals once a week, giving our student teachers the opportunity to respond to the other half. Periodically we rotated the students whom we responded to, which allowed us to read all the journals over time. The journals allowed us to get to know the children and their opinions on a more personal and confidential level, which was crucial in our ability to assess them individually. Our insights deepened because of the one-to-one conversations we were having. These conversations could not have taken place otherwise with twenty-eight students in the class.

Building Community Within the Classroom

Our plan was to keep the two groups of children separate initially. It was important to develop a community within our own classrooms first, so the children would not be tempted to fall into old patterns with their former classmates. The sense of classroom community was created in a variety of ways, through the use of curriculum themes and by the physical layout of the classroom.

Theme-Based Learning

Teaching through themes involved taking a topic of interest and extending it throughout the different curriculum areas in order to tap into each of the seven intelligences.

The first theme in the fall of 1992 was Japan. We chose Japan because we wanted our Chinese students to learn about another Asian culture. The second theme the following year was water. Themes were a wonderful framework for inclusion and for fully exploring the different modalities of intellect outlined by Howard Gardner (1983). By redesigning our curriculum to be rich, complex, and concept based, we were able to frame learning tasks as complex problems, provide contexts that give meaning to facts, take informal knowledge seriously, allow for multiple answers, promote socially constructed knowledge, and require long-term projects (Oakes and Lipton 1992). Thematic study is much more accommodating of differences in students' prior knowledge and skills and allows all children to enter at their own level and extend their learning at their own pace. Since the children were coming in with a variety of academic as well as linguistic abilities, this was crucial.

Theme-based collaborative projects were also excellent ways to motivate students, gain their attention, and involve them in a variety of interactive activities. As a result, students worked together on projects that naturally promoted the use of both oral and written language to question, discuss, inform, negotiate, and communicate with others (Ernst and Richard 1994/95). Working with themes also allowed us to exercise our own creativity. We could brainstorm a plethora of ideas and choose those we wanted to implement in our own class using similar lessons but allowing for individuality.

Redefining our curriculum according to themes compelled us to redefine our assessment strategies in order to obtain an authentic picture of each child as well as of ourselves (Herman, Aschbacher, and Winters 1992). Alternate methods of assessment that we utilized included portfolio assessment, structured observations of students engaged in tasks, and videotaping. Videos in particular helped us to capture the change process and allowed us to revisit classroom discussions that we felt could be revealing. Often, they revealed unexpected results! For example, we each had our student teachers tape a discussion in our classrooms that began with the question, "What is cooperative learning?" By analyzing the tape together the next day, we shared helpful observations about each other's class. We noticed that in Julie's class, two or three children were clearly dominating the discussion. In Leslie's class, the discussion was more spread out and involved more children. We then collaborated on strategies to democratize Julie's discussions. The video camera provided a new way for us to look at our own teaching, as well as our students, together.

In keeping with Gardner's theories, the Japan unit included a wide variety of activities that allowed the children to discover and build upon their strengths. Most lessons were executed in cooperative learning groups, allowing for growth in the interpersonal realm. Throughout the unit, the children were required to write reflections about their learning process, including what they knew about Japan previously, what they wanted to learn, how they were going to attempt to learn it, and their thoughts and feelings about themselves as learners. This enabled the children to grow intrapersonally. The remaining five intelligences were explored through a variety of activity choices in both classrooms.

First, literature was woven throughout the three-month unit. Novels about Japan, such as *Meiko and the Fifth Treasure* and *Sadako and the Thousand Paper Cranes*, both by Eleanor Coerr, were shared in pairs and small groups. The students partnered to read, discuss, and pull vocabulary from the novels, thus creating meaning together and forming bonds of respect based on hard work and mutual interests. The children also worked in pairs to research topics of interest, including Japanese religions, toys and games, clothing, food, and architecture. They lent crucial support to one another during the investigative, writing, editing, and typing processes, as they created the written aspect of their projects. Finally, children were engaged in cowriting plays, constructing large-scale models, and cooking food. Through such activities, they employed mathematical thinking, examined spatial relationships, developed large and small muscle coordination, and gained important experience working in teams.

Physical Layout

The physical layout of the classroom was crucial to the promotion of collaboration. The desks were set up in clusters of five or six children. Each cluster had a Sharing Basket containing markers, pencils, erasers, scissors, and glue. These items were supplied by the children in the beginning of the year. The idea that there was no more "mine" and "yours," only "ours," was difficult for them to grasp at first. In time, the children became comfortable sharing, realizing that they had more materials when they combined them. This realization quickly spread to more intangible concepts, such as the sharing of ideas. We emphasized the importance of working together as a means of improvement. "Two heads are better than one" became our motto.

Within a few short months, our classroom community was firmly established. The children saw themselves as a cohesive unit, not as the "gifted" half and the "regular" half. The children recognized that every child in our class had strengths, and they worked hard to support each other in weak areas. Friendships began developing between the two groups of children, breaking down the cliques that had previously formed within the gifted class. Academically and socially, the children blended.

Building Community Between the Classes

Once the individual classroom communities were established, it was time to combine the two classes and expand our community. Learning centers, field trips, and our final project for the Japan unit, creating the Japan Museum, became the vehicles we used to foster this expanded community.

Learning Centers

During learning-centers time, we utilized the common areas outside our classrooms as well as both classrooms themselves. We combined our materials and shared space. In the alcove across from our rooms, we set up an architecture center with Julie's blocks from first grade. We shared the expense of a puppet theater for drama. Our art supplies doubled when we combined them in a single cupboard. By pooling our materials and books, we designed a science lab in a cleaned-out storage closet. Seeing our resources grow and building on ideas in our brainstorming sessions created real excitement for both of us.

We combined the two classes for learning-centers time, which happened twice a week for one hour each. During the first forty-five minutes, the children chose an area they wanted to explore. Each child had a learning-centers folder in which to keep track of the center he or she went to and when. We believe that while everyone is born with certain strengths and weaknesses in each of the cognitive areas, all children are capable of developing greater proficiency in all areas. Therefore, the students were responsible for trying *all* of the centers. Quite often, the students would hesitate to try a new center, only to make fascinating discoveries there. New interests were revealed and cultivated throughout this time as a result of the possibilities available to the children.

All the centers contained activities related to Japan. Since both classes were studying the same topic, the children had much in common on which to base inquiry and friendship. Students were also guided to work with new children regularly. We wanted to foster social growth by encouraging them to create new friendships. In addition, by grouping students with different strengths, children were exposed to new ideas and could learn from one another. Being able to be the teacher or expert in their area of strength fostered self-esteem in each child.

The last fifteen minutes of learning-centers time was devoted to reflection; children first wrote about what they had learned, and then shared their ideas, art projects, and creations aloud. Comments such as "I learned that the math center was more fun than I thought," or "I learned that Mon Fu is fun to play with!" and "I learned that Xiao Wen is really good at painting," were frequently heard. Working and playing together allowed the children to see that each person had strengths in different areas, and those differences were celebrated and valued. We wanted our students to gain respect for one another and to recognize that getting 100 percent on the math test was not the only thing valued in school; social skills, musical talent, and artistic ability were just as important. Learning centers offered a good vehicle for many personal discoveries.

The reflections that the children wrote were an important aspect of measuring growth. The learning-centers folders became a crucial assessment tool for both the students and ourselves, allowing us to see the children's range of interests and creativity, as well as their growth interpersonally and intrapersonally. By the end of the year, we had two classes full of children who knew how to self-evaluate and make decisions about their own learning based on their reflections. Self-assessment became habitual, and was woven throughout the curriculum.

Trips

The two classes were also combined for field trips. The trips enhanced our theme, while giving the students the opportunity to learn together outside the school environment. Upon returning, each child was responsible for writing a reflection about the trip, including what he/she learned, thought, and felt. Again, these pieces revealed important insights into the children's interests and thought processes. They also provided us with a number of authentic pieces of children's writing in order to see growth along stylistic, cognitive, and intrapersonal lines throughout the year.

Japan Museum

As their final project for the Japan unit, the children transformed both classrooms into a Japan Museum, with visual, dramatic, and written exhibits set up throughout the rooms. Exhibits included puppet shows, demonstrations, art projects, and creative writing. The administration, parents, and children from other classes were invited to attend the opening. The children were proud to be the experts as they answered questions and guided our visitors through the museum. The feedback was overwhelmingly positive. Every visitor was impressed with the learning that went on and with the creativity that emerged.

The Japan Museum also served as an authentic way in which to assess the children. We did not give them a test in order to see how much they had learned about Japan. We allowed the children to guide us through their learning process and demonstrate their learning in the modality that best suited them. Whether they expressed their learning through art, writing, or speech, their hard work and commitment to the unit was apparent to all of our museum visitors. Each child, whether initially from the gifted population or the regular population, became an expert about Japan. Assessing them in new, more meaningful ways allowed these children to grow, develop, and blossom in ways that united them.

As children collaborated through learning centers, trips, and preparing the Japan Museum, the two classes learned to work together and enhance their community. They looked forward to these opportunities to come together as a way to expand their social circle. The children began to see each other in new ways, focusing on one another's positive aspects. This was especially important for those children who had been in the previous self-contained gifted class. They were now able to work together in constructive ways, abolishing many of the negative interactions that had previously inhibited their learning.

Evaluation

In both classrooms, untracking had extremely positive effects on both the gifted and the nongifted children. Since children spent much of the day working collaboratively, each child had an opportunity to be the teacher in a strong area, and the student in an area in which he or she needed support. There was never an occasion in which the teachers were all of the gifted children and the learners were the "nongifted." There was *always* an even mix. This helped instill a positive self-image in all of the children.

Since the children mingled socially and academically from the start, it was difficult to tell which were from the initial gifted group and which were not. To test this theory, we asked all our five student teachers for their opinions. After being in our rooms for six weeks we asked them to identify the children they believed had been in the gifted class for the previous three years. All five student teachers had difficulty distinguishing the gifted children from the regular children; none of them had better than 60 percent accuracy.

Standardized test scores also reflected this mix. We found that the gifted children were spread throughout the range of scores in both classes. In Julie's class, the scores on the state exams for third grade were analyzed and found to be very revealing. On the Degrees of Reading Power (DRP) test given in May, four gifted and three mainstream children scored in the 97th percentile or above; one gifted and two mainstream children scored in the 49th percentile or below. The middle scores were mixed as well. In math there were similar results. On the California Achievement Test (CAT) taken in April, seventeen students scored in the 90th percentile or above, six who were gifted and eleven who were mainstream. Four scored below the 80th percentile, half of whom were gifted.

We did not use these standardized test scores to make decisions about the children, nor did we use them for the purpose of assigning labels. These scores do not reveal any signs of the children's growth, nor do they demonstrate giftedness. However, what intrigued us about these scores is what they say about the lack of equity in the methods of choosing children for a gifted program (Hilliard 1990). In the gifted program in our school, the teachers are uniformly innovative, reflective risk takers. They provide rich classroom environments from kindergarten through sixth grade, environments that may or may not be provided to the regular classes. The gifted classes are expected to take more trips, to have more projects, speakers, and performances. The children most needing the enrichment that gifted classes offer are often denied admission to the gifted kindergarten because they failed to make the necessary scores on standardized tests, failed the interview, or failed to even apply. We believe children should be given equal chances to be exposed to the highest and richest level of education throughout their schooling. As demonstrated by test scores and our daily observations, there were many children in our experimental classes who would not only fit into these gifted classes, but would thrive if given such opportunities. Both of us have always held high expectations for our students whether we worked with gifted, mainstream, or bilingual populations. We have found that our children rise to the occasion and enjoy the challenges we present. This was holding true once again this year.

The new chemistry that resulted from the two restructured classes created positive energy among the students. The change in students' behaviors was regularly noted by the other teachers (music, computers, library, gym) who worked with them. These teachers commented on how well the children were able to work together this year—a noticeable achievement compared to previous years. The students' social growth helped their academic performance and enabled them to change their reputation throughout the school. In the new setting, individuals stretched their minds and grew in ways that may not have been possible had the group remained static. The experiment was so successful that it was decided to keep the enrichment classes intact for the following year with two other fourth-grade teachers.

At the end of the year, we gave the students a survey to fill out about third grade. In response to "What was the most important thing you learned in third grade?" ten children answered math, and eleven children answered cooperative learning, stating, "How to be nice to other people," "How to divide the jobs so everyone is equal," and "How to share." When we asked, "Would you like to continue cooperative groups next year?" *every* child said "Yes" because "If you can't cooperate, you can't do special things," "Of course, I want to learn more better," "Two brains are better than one," "You can help each other," "I can work with my friends," "It's easier to work," "You get to meet other people," "You can share your feelings," and "Yes, because you get good ideas from other people." The students felt very positive about their ability to mesh as a classroom community. They had worked hard using cooperative learning strategies throughout our Japan unit to become a cohesive whole, and they were successful. We could see that there is, indeed, a strong relationship between inclusive classrooms and cooperative learning (Johnson, Johnson, Holubec, and Roy 1984; Sapon-Shevin 1990).

The benefits of splitting up the gifted class were apparent from the beginning of the year and multiplied as the year went on. At the end of the school year, we too reflected upon our students' growth since September and our satisfaction with the results of this experiment. We felt equally proud of our teaming efforts, having also explored new territory by working together so closely. We both felt that the teaming helped to take away much of the isolation that teachers face daily. It also gave us a forum for playing with ideas and encouraged us to take risks because we each felt supported by the other. Our work together laid the groundwork for a joint informal research project about untracking and its benefits. Daily conversations about student dilemmas, curriculum issues, and parent involvement created the parameters for continual staff development. Our commitment to collaboration and inclusion was solidified.

THE SECOND YEAR: 1993–1994

As stated earlier, traditionally at Harbor Lane School the gifted track stays together from kindergarten through sixth grade, with the 1992–1993 experiment breaking this norm for the first time. Since the upcoming gifted class was not experiencing serious disruptive problems like the class before them, we were not allowed to break them up and continue untracking in the same manner. There would be one third-grade class of gifted children. Julie had taught these children in first grade, so we decided that Leslie would take this class so students would be exposed to a different teaching style. Julie was assigned a heterogeneous mix of third graders. Now, we needed to discover a new road to untracking. With a successful year behind us, we were ready to embark on a different model of untracking for inclusion and to form new communities of learning for both our students and ourselves.

Our work the previous year had shown us the power connected to collaboration for both our students and for us. We wanted to continue to put our minds together and not be constrained by the labels "gifted" or "ESL" that were attached to the children in our roll books. It was important for us to uncover all of the talents our children had within them and to have them recognize the varied strengths in one another.

The Year Begins

Julie's new class was made up of twenty-five Chinese Americans and one Latino student. The majority of her students spoke Chinese at home. Three of the students were serviced by a daily, pull-out ESL (English as a Second Language) program. Leslie had twenty-two students; thirteen Chinese Americans and nine children from other ethnic backgrounds (Latino, African American, European American, and biracial).

These two neighboring third-grade classes were extremely different from one another and very different from last year's groups. Julie's class was not as verbal, since most of her students did not speak English at home. They were hesitant about sharing their thoughts and ideas. In addition, Julie had to simplify her language slightly to be understood. Yet, the students' social skills were well developed and, for most of them, collaboration came naturally. The opposite was true of Leslie's class. Strong personalities caused friction between classmates who had been together since kindergarten. Personality clashes were quite apparent now and contributed to a less-than-congenial community of learners. The children had already labeled one another as "the trouble maker," "the dummie," "the cry baby," etc. These labels stunted growth. The children obviously needed to learn to perceive one another differently. This class was very strong linguistically, however; most spoke English at home and were not shy about speaking their minds. This is not surprising, since precocious verbal ability is considered important for acceptance into our gifted program.

As we devised our plan for working together, we focused on the strengths of our individual groups. By exposing Leslie's students to children who were strong socially and Julie's students to children who were strong verbally, we could foster growth in both classrooms. All students would act as mentors. They would also learn patience and sensitivity. In addition, Julie's group would have the opportunity to learn in a more culturally mixed setting. With thoughtful grouping using cooperative strategies, we could maximize the possibilities for learning for this culturally and linguistically diverse group (Johnson and Johnson 1994; Duran 1994).

Teaming Strategies

We decided to continue with team planning for a thematic curriculum on water. However, we knew our populations had different needs, so our individual plans would necessarily have to reflect those needs. At the same time, the wide range of abilities between the two classes offered many opportunities for these children to collaborate and learn from one another.

We formulated a plan. Mornings would be spent with our own students in reading, math, and language arts. Our classes would be combined four afternoons a week, twice for learning centers and twice for enrichment activities centered on the study of water. In the learning centers, children could choose from a variety of activities. The enrichment activities, which were teacher guided and done as a whole class or in small groups, would serve as vehicles for science, social studies, hands-on math, art, and eventually writing. Since the two classes varied so widely in their levels of written language skill, we purposely held off teaming them for writing. We felt that stronger partnering skills were necessary for success. Thus we planned that all of the activities would be accomplished cooperatively; enrichment activities would bring half of each class together in order to create two groups with a heterogeneous makeup. This meant that the same enrichment activities could be done in both rooms with mixed groups. We were careful also to plan for multiple intelligences so there would be many options for learning. The variety of activities selected would allow children from both classes to rise as leaders. We believed that this approach would allow students to grow both academically and socially.

Cooperative Groups

At the start of the year, we carefully selected which students would work in which classroom for the enrichment sessions. This was accomplished by splitting up clashing personalities in Leslie's class and dividing up the ESL students from Julie's group. We strived to create a symbiotic chemistry to promote an optimal learning experience for all of the students. As the year progressed and the children grew in their ability to work cooperatively, we were able to move from prescribed groupings to simply describing the upcoming enrichment activity and asking children to choose which room they would rather work in. We found that we usually had about half of the students from each class volunteer to work next door—and not the same kids each time. The choices they made provided us with additional information regarding their growth.

Enriching Ourselves

Sharing students involved a lot of careful planning. Common preparation periods were once again a necessity. The enrichment sessions were carefully thought through and often debated. We kept in mind the range of abilities from both classes. We aimed to equitably create a setting that would provide a more even playing field on which *all* our students could develop. Much of our preparation time was spent organizing the activities, gathering materials, and deciding how the students would be grouped.

After each activity, it was important to debrief each other about what had worked and how we would modify instruction for the next time. Sometimes the activity went smoothly in one room but was more challenging to carry out next door. Leslie often questioned Julie about the intricacies of delivering clear directions for our science experiments. Through discussion, simple details (e.g., don't put out the materials until the activity has been explained) that made the difference between a fluid activity and one with rough edges surfaced. Teaching strategies multiplied as we gained insights from each other.

Debriefing time became invaluable for our growth individually and as a team. We exchanged observations about specific children, offering alternative perspectives that were always welcome. We came to understand that teachers "need one another as audiences and as 'friendly critics' for their ideas, insights, and implementations. They need serious and ongoing dialogue about the nature of learning and teaching" (Einbender and Wood 1995: 24). Together we experimented with different methods to further stretch children's learning and social development. We kept learning alongside our students. Our motto, "Two heads are better than one," was at work again.

The benefit of working next door to one another surfaced regularly as we touched base throughout each day. Often we joined forces for additional support while the enrichment sessions took place. If one of us reached a frustration level with our group, we sought out the other for a reassuring word. When amazing interactions were taking place, we were anxious to share them with our teammate. These moments could never be recaptured. In her journal, Julie wrote:

> The aloneness that I have experienced previously in the classroom is now gone. It feels good to have another teacher who knows my students well enough to discuss their learning process and to help me assess their needs. I used to have long conversations with myself about how to work with challenging children. Now I have Leslie.

Learning Flows

As the students engaged in cooperative learning, we assessed their needs by visiting with the groups, questioning them, and jotting down notes about students needing additional help. This allowed us to ascertain if certain concepts needed to be reviewed with the entire group, in which case we stopped and addressed everyone. We particularly wanted to make sure that the more verbal children did not take over. With coaching, Julie's students learned to be more assertive, to speak up if they wanted to contribute. The outspoken children came to realize that they could not always make the group decisions. We noted moments of shifting power when the voice of a shy child filtered through. The notion of compromise was slowly sinking in.

As we observed the mix of different learning styles, personalities, and skill levels, we reminded one another of how beneficial it is to teach in this cooperative, integrated way. During activities, ESL children modeled positive social interactions and working together successfully. When the groups shared their projects, the ESL students were provided with strong models of spoken English. Satisfaction with the group's efforts was evident by the pride in their faces as they spoke.

An even greater challenge was the assimilation of certain children into a congenial pair or group. We wanted the bossy children and the class clowns to realize on their own that they would not be popular choices in a group if they continued their behavior. Our goal was for these children to self-assess and to connect their behavior with the success of their groups, leading to a desire to change their actions. Toward the year's end, we were pleased with improvements in their social skills, which allowed them to be welcome group members. Their positive feelings about their participation and their pride in the group's accomplishments were reflected verbally and in their writing.

The students became accustomed to debriefing, discussing what worked well and how they could proceed differently next time. Their verbal accounts expressed an understanding of teamwork. As time passed, our students demonstrated more proficiency with the skills necessary for success with cooperative learning. At the conclusion of each project, we asked our students to reflect on what they had learned. This reflective writing was included in each child's portfolio and became an important part of our assessment process.

The students not only wrote about the results they had gathered but also their experiences of sharing the responsibility to carry out the experiment. A comment we read often was, "I learned that being a teacher is hard work!" There were many touching moments when our mature eight-year-olds encouraged their partners to join in and work with the group. We witnessed ultimate patience and creative thinking. Praise was offered for their gifts as teachers, and we came to appreciate our new role as facilitators.

Assessment Broadens

As our repertoire of teaching strategies expanded, our lens for assessment assumed a broader view as well. Cooperative learning naturally guided us to see and think about students' growth in different ways. We were no longer giving weekly tests or asking children to memorize facts. We were expecting them to do much more: learn collectively, take more responsibility for their learning, and demonstrate self-reflectiveness through the writing assignments that followed the activities. By removing the fear many kids have about taking tests, we opened up new avenues whereby they could demonstrate their knowledge in more creative ways. They knew we were not grading them on the number of correct answers or on perfect sentences. They knew also that best efforts and working well together were valued. Because we were concerned about social growth, leadership skills, and conceptual development, our conceptions of assessment stretched beyond the grade book. All of our students were being given an opportunity to rise. They also had the benefit of many eyes watching over them rather than two.

Testing Labels

In March, after having worked together for nearly seven months, we were curious to find out if our students knew that there was a designated "gifted" class and what the word "gifted" meant to them. Neither one of us ever used the term when referring to the children; we had no idea what their parents had told them. So we decided to ask them indirectly during a class discussion. Our experience the previous year told us that videotaping would provide added insights.

The opening question was, "What are some of the things we've done with Ms. Serling's/Ms. Savitch's class?" The students listed different enrichment projects, learning centers, and trips. Our next question was, "Do you see any differences between the two classes?" Their responses were extremely interesting! In Julie's class we got answers like, "We know the kids in here better." "Our room is bigger." Julie asked, "What about the children?" Responses: "Most of the children in Ms. Serling's class are white. They don't speak Chinese." "A lot of children in Ms. Serling's class take a bus because they live far away." "A lot of people in this class go to the after-school program. Not a lot from Ms. Serling's class—only Ronald." "We have more children than them." "Most of their hair is different colors." Then one boy shouted out, "Her class is a gifted class, ours is not." Julie asked, "What does that mean?" The child replied, "I don't know." Julie asked, "Raise your hand if you've heard her class is a gifted class." Five hands went up. "Does anyone know what that means?" Responses included: "Like if you're English, you get an English teacher." "I think her class are smarter." "They know times tables better." Julie asked, "What else does gifted mean?" Responses: "Is it if they don't do their homework they get sent to the principal's office?" "Every year they're in the same class." Apparently, though some children had heard of the word gifted, none actually knew why that word had been attached to a particular track of students.

In Leslie's class the responses were quite similar. Leslie: "We've done many projects with Ms. Savitch's class over the last seven months. Do you see any differences between the two classes?" Responses: "They have more children." "They have a different schedule." "I think we had some different spelling words." "They might organize things differently and have different things." "She has a different learning-centers chart." "Once she did the homework at a different time and is her class gifted?" Another student replied: "I don't think so, but I think she usually is. She usually teaches a gifted class." (This student is recalling her year in first grade with Julie as the teacher. She has labeled Julie as "gifted.") Leslie said: "Let's go back to Tanya's question." The student replied: "I think she is gifted . . . her class is gifted." "I think sometimes her class is gifted because they do just as hard work as we do and sometimes they do different work, but most of the time I think they're gifted because we do like the same things." "I think the class is not gifted because last year she [Julie] was in the gifted class and they moved her here so I thought she wouldn't be gifted any more." "I know her class is gifted." "In first grade her class is gifted. Don't all teachers stay like the same . . . like a gifted teacher always?"

Leslie inquired: "How many people think that Ms. Savitch's class is gifted?" All raised their hands! Leslie said: "Think about the children. How are they different?" Responses: "Almost everyone is Chinese." "The personalities." "Some of the children go to English as a Second Language." Leslie asked: "Why are we called the gifted class?" Responses: "Don't know." "This class is more challenging." "We were able to do harder stuff." "I think my mom decided I was gifted." Leslie asked: "Is there anything else different?" Answers: "They speak with an accent." "They speak Chinese to me. I don't know it." "They are a little shier."

In her journal, Leslie wrote:

> I am very surprised that my students didn't bring up their testing or have a different sense of their placement from things their parents may have told them. I was expecting my students to respond, "They're not as smart as us." or "They can't speak English very well." I was wrong and I am pleased!

In our debriefing session, we were both reassured that the "gifted" label was not prominent in the minds of our youngsters. We were happy that they had put the "gifted" label on Julie quicker than on themselves. After viewing the tape, we both agreed that this line of questioning was a fabulous way to get inside our kids' heads. Too often teachers hold on to perceptions that just aren't true. Their low expectations or inaccurate assumptions about children can lead to differential treatment of students, which can result in educational inequity and inappropriate instruction (Brophy and Good 1986; Irvine 1991).

Portfolio Assessment

When it came time to measure cumulatively students' progress for the report cards, student portfolios were our main tool for assessment along with our observations. We knew that all of our children entered the school year on different levels with a variety of gifts. The portfolio would document growth from September through June and included teacher-suggested, student-selected work (Valencia and Calfee 1991). Our students gained ownership of their portfolios early on. These portfolios comprised the children's work across the curriculum, with an emphasis on their reflective writing pieces. By looking at samples of their writing month after month, we could tangibly assess their growth in grammar, spelling, and sentence structure, along with their developing thought processes.

We wanted our students to become self-reflective learners. At the end of each marking period, we asked them to review their work to examine the growth they had made. Each wrote a reflection for the different curriculum areas, reviewing the strides they had made and how they wanted to improve in the upcoming months. These pieces went into their portfolios along with the reflections that they had been writing throughout the year; students became engaged in their own learning as they engaged in self-assessment (Kuhs 1994; Paulson, Paulson, and Meyer 1991).

Periodically, we had one-on-one conferences with each student about the portfolios. We began by asking them, "What does your portfolio say about you?" The responses included, "I am proud of my math, but I need to work on word problems," "I like chapter books now; I didn't in September," "I need to work on organizing my work," and "I am a good writer, but I need to work on editing." With practice, all of our students became quite comfortable with this self-assessment process. They were more accountable for their work, and we watched them take pride in their efforts as they became accustomed to "a portfolio culture in the classroom" (Asturias 1994: 699).

Parents in the Picture

Since our methods for evaluating the children had changed, we needed to change the way we conveyed this information to parents. Each parent-teacher conference was typically ten minutes long, taking place during one afternoon and one evening. Many of the children's parents did not speak English, therefore the conversations were translated. This significantly decreased the amount of time that anything of substance could be discussed. In addition, sharing the children's progress in the portfolios was difficult, since the parents could not read them. Frequently, the only question that the parents had was, "How is my child doing compared to the rest of the class?" Thus, it was time to develop an alternative.

"Portfolio Night" was born. Portfolio Night involved inviting six of the parents to come with their children for the sixty minutes that regular conferences would have taken. The children would be in charge. They would walk their parents through a shortened version of a typical day in our classroom, showing them the learning centers and much of the school work that never gets sent home. They would then show their parents their portfolios, discussing what they were proud of and what their goals were. Throughout this session, we would be walking around and touching base with each parent, answering their additional questions and discussing their child's progress. This alternative was explained in a letter home, giving the parents the option of coming to the standard conferences or Portfolio Night.

More than half of the parents chose to come to Portfolio Night, and it was extremely successful! We sent a questionnaire home with the parents to find out their reactions. The responses were uniformly positive, though some parents would have liked to have this option in addition to the standard conferences. All parents were able to see their children's commitment to education and pride in their work in a way that we would not have been able to express in a ten-minute conference. They appreciated the increased amount of time that they could spend learning about their children's progress. The parents who did not speak English had their children as their translators and therefore got a lot more out of the conference. The children were equally thrilled with the experience. As Tom said, "I got a chance to show [my parents] my portfolio and me and my mother were proud. . . . I got a chance to show my special work."

FINAL THOUGHTS

All of our children should be given the opportunity to produce special work. They should not be graded in the same exact way, because they all enter the school year with different skill levels and developmental stages. By opening up our curriculum thematically and holding high expectations for *all* of our students, learning was on fire. Everybody was invited into the learning process. Our curriculum and organizational changes benefited children on top, in the middle, and on the bottom of the achievement scale, because their positions continually fluctuated depending on the activity. It became clear to us that test scores do not represent giftedness and can potentially categorize children into bins that are not accurate and end up constraining rather than freeing educational and personal development.

By opening up our doors and our eyes, we unwrapped gifts that were hidden and screaming to emerge from their wrappings. We created a new definition of giftedness—one that includes everybody. How can we label children at such an early age when they haven't yet been given the chance to show us what they are capable of? By creating tracks, the children needing to be challenged the most are not being given that opportunity, when in actuality they are ready for the challenge. Are we as teachers ready to take this challenge on as we step away from our grade books and assess our students more holistically? As Howard Gardner states, "I believe as long as we have a narrow definition of intelligence—a very scholastic definition—most kids are going to think they're stupid, and they're going to miss the fact that they may have a lot of abilities that could be important vocationally and avocationally" (cited in Winn 1990: 30). We need to establish classrooms where all talents are nourished and children are supported so that they learn to trust in and nourish their own capabilities.

Reflecting on our own development, we both recognize the tremendous growth we have made over the past two years. By working as a team, we increased our teaching strategies and became more reflective learners. Our assessment procedures grew both vertically and horizontally. Lots of learning took place! Perhaps one of Julie's students said it best. In her dialogue journal she wrote, "I wouldn't know I was smart if I didn't come to this class."

NOTE

1. The name of the school has been changed.

References

Asturias, H. (1994). Using students' portfolios to assess mathematical understanding. *Mathematics Teacher 87*(9): 698–701.

Brophy, J., and T. L. Good (1986). Teacher behavior and student achievement. In M. C. Wittrock (ed.), *Handbook of research on teaching*, 328–75. 3d ed. New York: Macmillan.

Duran, R. P. (1994). Cooperative learning for language-minority students. In R. A. DeVillar, C. J. Faltis, and J. P. Cummins (eds.), *Cultural diversity in schools*, 145–60. Albany: State University of New York Press.

Einbender, L., and D. Wood (1995). *An authentic journey: Teachers' emergent understandings about authentic assessment and practice.* New York: National Center for Restructuring Education, Schools and Teaching.

Ernst, G., and K. Richard (1994/95). Reading and writing pathways to conversation in the ESL classroom. *Reading Teacher 16*(4): 320–26.

Gardner, H. (1983). *Frames of mind.* New York: Basic Books.

Herman, J. L., P. R. Aschbacher, and L. Winters (1992). *A practical guide to authentic assessment.* Alexandria, VA: Association for Supervision and Curriculum Development.

Hilliard, A. G., III (1990). Misunderstanding and testing intelligence. In J. I. Goodlad and P. Keating (eds.), *Access to knowledge*, 145–58. New York: College Board.

Irvine, J. J. (1991). *Black students and school failure.* New York: Praeger.

Johnson, D. W., and R. T. Johnson (1994). Cooperative learning in the culturally diverse classroom. In R. A. DeVillar, C. J. Faltis, and J. P. Cummins (eds.), *Cultural diversity in schools*, 57–74. Albany: State University of New York Press.

Johnson, D. W., R. T. Johnson, E. J. Holubec, and P. Roy (1984). *Circles of learning: Cooperation in the classroom.* Alexandria, VA: The Association for Supervision and Curriculum Development.

Kuhs, T. M. (1994). Portfolio assessment: Making it work for the first time. *Mathematics Teacher 87*(5): 332–35.

Lieberman, A., and L. Miller (1984). *Teachers, their world, and their work.* Alexandria, VA: Association for Supervision and Curriculum Development.

Oakes, J., and M. Lipton (1992). Detracking schools: Early lessons from the field. *Phi Delta Kappan 73*: 448–54.

Paulson, F. L., P. R. Paulson, and C. A. Meyer (1991). What makes a portfolio a portfolio? *Educational Leadership 48*(5): 60–63.

Sapon-Shevin, M. (1990). Student support through cooperative learning. In W. Stainback and S. Stainback (eds.), *Support networks for inclusive schooling: Interdependent integrated education*, 65–79. Baltimore: Paul H. Brookes.

——— (1994/95). Why gifted students belong in inclusive schools. *Educational Leadership 52*(4): 64–70.

Sylvan, C. E. (1994). Assessment in a multilingual school: The International high school. *Educational Forum 59*: 74–80.

Valencia, S. W., and R. Calfee (1991). The development and use of literacy portfolios for students, classes, and teachers. *Applied Measurement in Education* 4(4): 333–45.

Winn, M. (1990). New views of human intelligence. *New York Times Magazine,* April 29, 1990.

Chapter Eight

ASSESSMENT AS A WAY OF SEEING

Margaret Borrego Brainard

Many of those who currently advocate alternative assessment point out that the root of the word assessment is derived from a Latin verb *assidere*, which means "to sit beside" (Chittenden 1991; Herman, Ashbacher, and Winters 1992; Wolf, LeMahieu, and Eresh 1992). It is likely that their mentioning of this term is intended to point out that, in order to reveal what children really know, it is necessary to be close to them, perhaps even moving alongside them as they pursue the challenges of learning. As a special educator, I very much like the idea of being close enough to children in order to understand them, since many of the children I have taught over the years have not always been able to tell me what they know. Nevertheless, I prefer to extend my thinking beyond considering the adjacency of the teacher into an awareness of the perceptions s/he employs in assessment and evaluation, particularly that of seeing.

At the very simplest level, assessment is the ability to see children, to perceive what they can do in the hope of understanding how they learn. Observing children, formally or informally, provides teachers with a great deal of information about them, so much so that the necessity of collecting, recording, and organizing information eventually leads us to filter out extraneous details in the field of our vision in order to discern patterns in their behavior that help us plan our teaching. In looking for patterns, assessment changes from merely sitting beside children to sitting beside them with particular purposes in mind, or evaluation. When the purposes and expectations of evaluation come into play, teachers begin to regard their students through many different windows, from multiple perspectives, and through a variety of lenses. As evaluation grows in complexity, the view of children can seem relative, like figure/ground perceptions, where individuals are periodically regarded in the foreground mass of other students of the same age who represent standardized levels of competency. It is at this point that the real knowledge and understanding that children possess is, in my opinion, least visible.

Students are often referred to people like me for assessment and evaluation, especially when their parents and teachers are having a difficult time determining how they learn. The assumption is that, with our specialized knowledge, special educators are able to find out more about children than are their regular class-room teachers so as to help students overcome problems with learning. This is a fair assumption, since most of us have received special training in cognition and psychology, have gained a good deal of experience with working with unusual learners, and often have an opportunity to provide extra attention to children as individuals or in small group settings. Nevertheless, I've always been troubled by the notion that those of us who work in resource rooms or who travel from class-room to classroom to support students struggling with their work have such highly specialized skills that only we are capable of assessing and evaluating chil-dren's learning difficulties. The very term "referral" conjures up images of doctors and other specialists who examine, diagnose, and prescribe cures for a variety of ailments, using procedures that are reserved for a select group of professionals.

The exciting thing about much of the current interest in alternative assess-ment is that it helps to break down this medical model of education by providing teachers in a variety of settings with, among other things, knowledge about teach-ing and assessment practices that have been familiar to many special educators for a long time. The deliberate search for alternatives to traditional testing, influ-enced as it is by an increasing awareness of new theories of intelligence and learn-ing (Gardner 1983; Resnick and Klopfer 1989), implies a respect for individual differences that has always rested at the base of good practice among special edu-cators and, I believe, is shared by good teachers everywhere, regardless of their ar-eas of expertise. There is a great deal that these teachers have learned from their unusual students that can contribute to our understanding of how to alter assess-ment and evaluation practices in the future. After almost twenty years in regular and special classrooms, I have had the opportunity to collect some stories that might be useful to other educators as they contemplate creating new and altering old ways of seeing the children they teach.

When I first began teaching, I used to watch Jerry cut silhouettes out of con-struction paper. It was fascinating. He would hold a pair of small school scissors in the palm of his very large hand and, without even inserting his fingers in the handles, cut out delicate outlines of peoples' features freehand. His parents and other teachers never knew who the faces of the people were, whether they were real or imaginary, because Jerry rarely spoke directly to anyone. He would sit at his desk, slowly and deliberately cutting as he rocked back and forth reciting the daily weather report, without seeming to concentrate very hard on what he was doing, appearing to be oblivious to other activities in the classroom. He would deliver the morning's radio weather forecast almost verbatim with very little ex-pression in his voice except when he came upon a term he particularly liked, like "patchy clouds," which he would say with great volume, sometimes smiling as he turned his head and shrugged his shoulders.

Though I spent a lot of time observing Jerry, it took me a long time to see him. I was a novice teacher assisting in Special Class, a self-contained, experimen-tal program for children who were termed "educably mentally retarded." The classroom was laid out similarly to most open classrooms, filled with manipulative materials relating to many subject and skill areas, which were displayed on shelves lining the classroom walls.

Periodically, we would introduce new materials, and the children were free to select those that interested them. However, the teachers often chose particular materials for their students, since many of the children had motor difficulties and needed help with them or, like Jerry, were often content to do the same thing for hours on end and needed to be urged to explore new activities.

During the three years that I assisted with the class, two different teachers, Frances and Gloria, were the lead teachers in the program. They developed individualized curriculum and assessment procedures for Jerry and the other children in the class, some of whom had been diagnosed with cerebral palsy and Down's syndrome and others who, like Jerry, had shown extreme difficulties in learning for reasons that weren't necessarily all that clear to the teachers.

Frances and Gloria described Jerry to me as an "idiot savant." He was extremely bright in some ways, though his ability to learn school-related tasks was limited. It was as if he had some sort of selective mechanism in his brain that helped him acquire some kinds of knowledge and denied him access to other kinds of learning. Large and very tall for his age, Jerry moved very slowly, spoke rarely, and only began to respond verbally to direct questions toward the end of the time that I knew him.

Jerry resisted using the materials we presented to him, and would not interact with teachers long enough to allow us to use traditional assessment procedures to uncover what he did or did not know about the concepts underlying the activities we had designed. He preferred to work alone, cutting or doing paper-and-pencil tasks, though he was cooperative and willing to sit with the other children when encouraged to do so. In attempting to understand him, Frances and Gloria developed a system for recording everything he did. They would jot down notes on cards they carried in their pockets, or speak informally during recess or quiet moments in the classroom and then, daily, summarize all that he had done on a log that they kept at the teachers' desk. It was their hope that, gradually over time, they would begin to see patterns in how Jerry learned or at least determine if some activities appealed to him more than others so that they could plan appropriately for him.

It was in assisting with the collection of anecdotal information about Jerry that I first began to understand the value of documenting children's progress. I found that there was a great need to be organized about observations. It did no good just to sit and watch or even to sit and watch and record what I saw if I did not try to look for patterns.

One of the advantages of being in a self-contained special education class is that there is often time to develop systems for collecting observations. When attempting to determine how to teach particularly unusual learners, it has been important to just keep plodding along, gathering more and more records of what they do. It is often tempting to give up, to set aside recorded observations in a spare notebook or relegate them to a bottom drawer. Documentation has only really become useful when I have made use of what I've collected by thinking of my written observations as snapshots, images of children I have somehow captured on paper. Then, when I have systematically organized my records, much as I might organize pictures in a photo album into various categories, I have learned a great deal about my students. I have also found that, even when working in larger classrooms with many more children with far less time, there is real value in this sort of thinking. Just sorting brief anecdotal remarks and prioritizing them has helped me review what I've seen in a valuable way—even if the amount of time I've had to observe has been limited.

As we were collecting observations of Jerry, we tried to find activities that would interest him. Since he had shown such skill in memorizing the radio and television weather reports, the teachers would often give him work to do that involved memorization. He seemed to enjoy long repetitive drills, too, though we could rarely determine whether or not he was actually reasoning through the problems he did. One of his strengths was an ability to duplicate number patterns he had seen in print. He would read an example on a worksheet or in a math book and apply what he had read accurately to all of the practice problems on a page. His reading skills seemed to continue to improve, though he read by memorizing words on pages as if they were long lists rather than sentences. We could not be sure if he really understood what he was doing, since he would not answer our questions, though he could reproduce responses extremely well. If the teachers had chosen to do so, we probably could have given Jerry a series of worksheets or workbooks for his entire curriculum and it is likely that he could have completed each one accurately, provided he did not need to search for relationships between the skills he was practicing. We wanted him to begin to problem solve, though, and to manipulate materials that would help him discover relationships. Unfortunately, every time we would try to engage him in such tasks, he would politely ignore us and refuse to do that kind of work.

Our compromise was to allow him to work on drill sheets and his cutting, periodically inviting him to work with us and the other students as we explored new concepts. Meanwhile, Frances and Gloria noticed in reviewing their anecdotal records that Jerry did occasionally make comments during his weather reports that were related to what was actually happening around him. As a result, they decided to concentrate the daily log entries on verbatim records of these sometimes mumbled asides. Gradually, we noticed that he was repeating excerpts of the conversations that teachers had with other children as they introduced materials to them. When we focused on what he did when we were teaching near him, we began to notice that he was mimicking in very subtle ways the actions and words of the students who were near him. Encouraged, the teachers began to introduce materials to other students seated beside Jerry and gradually tried to pull him into their conversations. Though he would rarely respond to us directly, we found that eventually we were able to give him activities that called for real reasoning after we had introduced them to other children in his proximity. It was a kind of parallel teaching, but eventually it led us toward being able to help Jerry make all sorts of relationships, academic and social. He grew to be one of the strongest students in the class.

Gloria once told me, "You have to do whatever you can to figure out what the kids know—call it diagnosis or just keeping your eyes open—then teach to that. Then take a really hard look at what they've learned as a result of your teaching. If they haven't learned anything, start over, teach in a different way. If they've learned a little something, change your teaching in a way that will help them learn even more. The trick is to know lots of ways of teaching and lots of ways of looking."

The idea of combining the "teaching with the looking" is, in more formal terms, described as embedding assessment in curriculum and instruction. It is, in my opinion, what good teachers do, especially those who are faced with teaching a wide range of students well. They make use of "looking" at children to uncover indicators (Chittenden 1991) of what children know, and adapt their instruction accordingly. This approach is consistent with what Glaser calls "adaptive education" (Glaser and Silver 1994); though it seems to be fairly straightforward in theory, it can be tricky to put into practice.

It is tricky because we don't necessarily consciously separate out assessment from instruction when we use it to make adaptations, and everything tends to get jumbled together. It is all too easy to find at the end of a school term—or even a school year—that, while we have been adapting instruction according to our ongoing assessments of children all along, we have no clear record of how we've done it or just how the students have responded to what we've done. It is no wonder that, in those closing days before report time, we devise classroom tests that are often unsatisfying representations of what children know, because we haven't created systems for recording our assessments as we have taught. Part of the appeal of portfolios and other alternative assessments is that they can provide a tangible representation of such assessments, even though they do require space and special management. They are one way of storing the knowledge we have gained by adapting instruction in response to what we've seen our students do.

Perhaps it is because children with special needs, like very young children, can't always remember what they've learned at the end of a unit of study that special educators have tended to look for multiple ways to gather evidence of student learning over the years. It is as if we try to look at our students through many different windows, from a variety of angles, in varying degrees of light, in order to see them as they really are.

It can be especially hard to determine how children with severe learning needs approach new tasks. I have often wanted to reach inside the minds of such children. They are often unable to tell me anything about what I've taught them or why they don't understand what I have tried to explain to them. Sometimes, the only indications come from what they do or how they react to me. Relying on external behaviors in order to understand the internal processes of these children seems like a constant struggle at times, particularly when children grow weary of being watched or wish to engage only in the kinds of tasks they know they can complete well, as Jerry did. This calls for developing systems for assessing students that must be as accurate as possible. Anyone can come up with a way of registering whether or not children make mistakes, but it is finding ways to record how and why they make them that is difficult.

Airasian (1991) refers to the need to look through many windows in urging teachers to employ a full range of assessment practices, depending upon the choices one has made for one's students. Unavoidably, these choices are influenced by the personal definitions teachers may hold regarding what they believe their students need. Those personal definitions are greatly influenced by the values teachers have and by consideration of what I define as evaluation. Evaluation, while it may entail many of the same elements of assessment, is always conducted with a purpose or goal in mind. Whereas assessment is based upon seeing where the child is, evaluation is seeing where the child is in relation to where the teacher wants him/her to go, especially with reference to specific norms or standards in mind.

In evaluation, teachers collect data about a student's understanding, but they look at the data with reference to their own values or judgments. They regard the child through certain lenses, if you will, attempting to determine how close a child has come to attaining a particular goal or objective the teacher has set for him/her. Ideally, as Cryan (1986) notes,

> [evaluation] involves the acceptance of specific values combined with the use of varied observation instruments and measurement techniques to arrive at those value judgments. [It] is the teacher's comprehensive response to the uniqueness of each child. It is directly related to the objectives of instruction and provides not only information for reporting to parents and keeping student records but for the opportunity to improve curriculum. (345)

The value judgments that teachers form are linked closely to their understanding of what is good work for students to do (Gronlund and Linn 1990). This necessitates creating specific criteria upon which teachers can make these judgments.

In establishing criteria and/or standards toward which their students must strive, teachers must sometimes "see" very differently. In a way, it becomes necessary to envision the kind of learning they would like to see their students do. This is not always easy. It requires that teachers visualize good work and specify what they mean by good work. One way of doing this is through finding exemplars to work from, another practice often touted by advocates of alternative assessment, who describe "providing students with models of exemplary performance and encouraging them to . . . internalize high standards" through reflecting upon their work (Herman, Ashbacher, and Winter 1992: 16).

I have often thought that the mental picturing of good work, which I consider to be very similar to establishing standards, is easier when dealing with children who have extreme difficulty in learning than it is with other children. We want them to be able to behave in ways that are generally acceptable, to carry on conversations that are considered normal, to use a pencil, and so forth. As we consider children who have less difficulty learning, it is not quite as easy because it takes a lot of work to decide which standards to use, and determining whether or not students have reached those standards can often be a daunting task. Still, I think that the way special educators often think about standards setting can be particularly useful, since it involves a perspective that can be applied to many circumstances.

I worked for a time in a hospital that served children who had multiple handicaps. The children with whom I worked had severe language difficulties, termed at the time "childhood aphasia," and several of them also were coping with various neurological problems as well. They had numerous emotional problems that arose from their difficulties with communication, and the program was designed to offer them a steady, systematic procedure for learning to read and write based on repetition and drill. The idea was to incorporate the physical modality with language skills in the hope that, by involving their whole selves in the process of learning the vocabulary and sentence structure, they would be able to overcome some of their confusion in language processing and essentially learn language through making use of body memory.

According to the strict program we used, teachers would choose three words every couple of days, draw or reproduce pictures to go with the words, and introduce the vocabulary at the board, sitting with the children facing us in a semicircle. We would teach the children to form the words in cursive, using sweeping arm motions as we all phonetically sounded out each word. Every child would practice forming the letters of the words with the teacher's help as he or she said the word while the others looked on. We would continue through this type of word learning until eventually they were ready to learn sentences. As they began to learn sentences, we would repeat the procedure with whole sentences.

As any teacher could imagine, classroom management during this highly repetitive work called for a fair amount of energy and consistency. The children had to sit attentively while their peers practiced the words; take their turns; then return to their seats where they would continue to practice associating the words, sounds, and pictures in a variety of ways. Given that the children were also subject to seizures and emotional outbursts, keeping them on task was not always easy. It was necessary to set highly specific goals for the children in the social/emotional realm as well as in the cognitive areas.

According to the laws that had just been passed in the state where I was working at the time, it was necessary to write extremely specific behavioral objectives for each child. We were required to state behaviors and criteria for evaluating them in a highly specific manner and to maintain records with great care so that we could demonstrate exactly how close each child was to reaching goals we would set on a weekly and monthly basis. We had to break tasks down into small steps and determine the actual percentage of accuracy we hoped each child to obtain in reaching each objective. Thus, we would state such things as, "Adam will write the sentence 'The dog is near the house' with 80 percent accuracy by the end of the week" or "Adam will sit in his seat for approximately 60 percent of the time during follow-up activities."

Needless to say, such work was tedious and time consuming, but it did provide us with a highly systematic way of stating what we hoped to teach and of evaluating whether we had been able to teach it. Each week, as we would sit down to plan and list objectives, we would examine the evidence we had of the children having reached their percentages, readjust percentages that had expected too much or too little, and prioritize our objectives. Like many tasks, however, it became easier to do as time wore on. It was not a way of teaching that I would advocate, even though it did seem to be effective for the children in our program. Still, practicing those procedures influenced my thinking dramatically. When planning for students, I still say to myself, "What are my criteria . . . how will I know when my students reach the objectives?" I don't think I would really understand how important that clarity can be if it hadn't been for the time I spent having to be very certain of my criteria and standards.

Many teachers begin by envisioning the standards they wish their students to achieve and then systematically set objectives designed to assist their students in attaining them. The objectives should, in a way, act as the "mortar" that holds together the purposes teachers have with the outcomes of student learning (Engel 1981: 153). Evaluation in this sense is the act of determining whether the objectives have been met. In adaptive education, the teacher may change objectives when a student has not met them. The standards or broad goals of the curriculum must remain constant, however, and the revision of objectives should serve to find alternate routes to reaching high standards.

Sometimes, it is all too easy to get caught up in measuring objectives (Engel 1981) and to forget about the children. I think that is why we have grown to resist using behavioral objectives, especially those of us who have come to prefer a more constructivist approach (Brooks and Brooks 1993) toward teaching and learning. Still, my experience in working with severely emotionally disturbed children has led me to have a great deal of respect for the effective use of behavioral methods, particularly as they relate to assessing children who are trying to obtain specific social/emotional goals that are hard for them to reach. I have always felt that there are systematic ways of thinking associated with behaviorism that can be useful in any classroom. When I have worked as a consultant teacher in classrooms where teachers have needed to develop programs for students who have, for example, attention deficit disorder, or who behave inappropriately for one reason or another, the careful use of behavioral techniques has proved very useful. Many teachers use techniques rooted in behavioral psychology without really realizing it, like using the "time out" chair or awarding happy face stickers. Applied well and consistently, such practices can help to create a more positive atmosphere in the classroom, and they don't require feeding children M&Ms for good responses or meting out punishments. In fact, I regard behavior modification as one of many ways to integrate assessment with instruction.

I was part of a team of educators who worked closely with Michael and other students like him who seemed to have very little interest in communicating. Michael had suffered some severe traumas as a very young child and, though he was physically capable of speech and did echo what others said from time to time, he did not speak to other people or establish eye contact for more than a few seconds. While he was polite about moving to the classroom or the lunchroom when requested to do so, he would not engage in any sort of learning or even free play in the classroom. He tended to sit quietly, sometimes rocking back and forth, and do nothing. It was clear that he was aware of those around him; he simply didn't respond to them. He was, however, fascinated by the television, and he absolutely loved to dribble a basketball in the gym. Our goal for Michael was to assist him to interact directly in some meaningful way with another individual—child or teacher—and we used a behavioral practice called successive approximations to get him there.

A parent donated an empty television cabinet to our program. It was big enough for the children to sit inside of and use as a puppet theater from time to time. Michael loved it. He would sit and look into the empty cabinet for long periods of time, occasionally talking to it. When we noticed that Michael would watch children who were performing inside of the cabinet, we decided to see if there would be some way to get him to interact with one of the teachers if she sat inside of the cabinet and talked to him. We outlined a particularly methodical behavioral program for him based on rewarding him with time in the gym every time he would respond to someone who spoke to him from the cabinet. Slowly but surely, he began to establish eye contact, to respond physically, and finally to verbalize answers to simple questions that were directed to him from the TV cabinet. In time, we were able to use similar procedures to move Michael away from the TV cabinet into the classroom, to create situations where he would play parallel to other children and eventually interact with several others in the classroom.

Successive approximations require an extremely careful, deliberate approach. If a teacher chooses to employ them, she must be consistent, always carrying out the reward when the child responds, and that is not very convenient. It also requires good observation techniques and a very specific understanding of the objectives one is trying to reach. It is a little more palatable to employ these techniques with children who have severe learning needs, since much of the work with them is meant to prepare them to function in society, to exhibit basic prosocial behaviors. Nevertheless, there are times when they are appropriate for many other kinds of children who are struggling to control some behaviors that interfere with learning.

As teachers, we find it very difficult to take a more scientific and objective view of our students. The kind of evaluation that requires us to scrutinize our students from preestablished criteria, to see them as we might regard some organism in a laboratory experiment, is not appealing to most teachers. Though we often seem to feel obligated to approach evaluation as if we could rule out all kinds of subjectivities, the reality is that caring for our students often gets in our way. Consider the assignment of grades. Brookhart (1993) found that teachers often find it hard to separate grades from the social consequences they generate. Student self-esteem and effort are often factored in when teachers assign grades. For most of the teachers she surveyed, "a grade was a form of payment to the students. Students earned grades or points for the work they did. According to the teachers, grades functioned as the coin of the realm" (Brookhart 1991: 125). Grades were less often regarded as absolute indicators of academic achievement and more as a means of reward or punishment. Teachers, aware of the importance of motivating their students, were very conscious of the consequences of their grading.

Recently, there has been increasing interest in the "consequential validity" (Glaser 1990; Glaser and Silver 1994) of evaluations in order to address some of these issues. Ideally, consequential validity should look at "the extent to which an assessment tool and the ways in which it is used produce positive consequences both for the teaching and learning process and for students who may experience different educational opportunities as a result of test-based placements" (Darling-Hammond 1994: 11). This has been a concern for special educators for some time.

I don't believe that I am reaching into the realm of unreasonable generalizations when I say that most of the special educators I have known while teaching have felt that standardized tests are inadequate measures of many of their students' capabilities. Many regard them as necessary evils, however, since our funding is often dependent on using tests to "diagnose" children so that they can receive the services they deserve. Still, the teachers I have known—in both regular and special education—who have been most successful with children who seemed to learn differently from their peers have often chosen to develop a variety of authentic representations of their students' capabilities in addition to and in spite of the results they have obtained from normative testing. Even further, there is something we can all learn from those special education teachers who know the tests well, and who approach them selectively.

"I always have to tell myself to start with what I've got and, if all I've got on paper is standardized tests, then I start there," Jenny told me. We first met when she was teaching in a junior-high resource room in a middle-class suburb outside of a city in the Southwest. "You have to really think about beginnings, because there are so many ways to get sidetracked in this kind of work." Her work involved providing what was termed at the school "Reading/Language Enrichment" for students who came to her for forty-five minute periods when their classmates were attending English class. Most of the seventh, eighth, and ninth graders who worked with Jenny had been struggling with reading and writing throughout their school careers and demonstrated skills ranging from about a third/fourth-grade level up to fairly close to what the school expected for them at their own grade levels.

Petite and usually soft-spoken, Jenny was smaller than some of her students, though there was no doubt about her authority in the classroom. She used a lot of humor in her teaching and, like many special educators I have known, tended to find energy in being optimistic. Her focus on "beginnings" meant that she had to ask herself a lot of questions, and none of them had easy answers. Should she start by finding out her students' interests since, as early adolescents who had endured a lot of failure in school, they needed to find ways to persist in learning without becoming discouraged? Should she launch her students into a study of the content knowledge their peers were working on in the "regular" classes, carefully monitoring just how much they were able to understand, in order to prepare them for an eventual return to classes at their appropriate grade levels? Or should she start where her first inclination as a teacher was to begin, with determining just what her students knew about reading and writing and then building a suitable program for each student from there? Jenny's answer was to try to find a creative way to begin in all three areas at the same time, placing emphasis on different beginnings at different times, depending on the individual styles, time frames, and personalities of her students.

To gain a sense of her students' interests early in the school year, Jenny relied on a board game she had created that called for students to express their opinions about a variety of topics, everything from their favorite television shows to the sorts of places they liked to go to buy their clothes. She used the game mostly as an icebreaker to begin informal conversations among her students and to help them feel more comfortable in her classroom, though it did serve as a fairly useful interest inventory. She also read aloud from the texts that were being used in the other English classes and held discussions with her students immediately after her reading, which provided her with some insight into how much her students understood about the subject matter that their peers were studying in depth elsewhere.

The logical resources for her to use in planning for each student were the diagnostic reports that accompanied each child as a result of their referrals to special education; these included reading and analyzing standardized test results, among other things. One such report I remember clearly was for a student named Doug, who was a seventh-grade student new to that particular resource room. Together we read through the standard report format, which had been written by the school psychologist. It began as usual with a summary of his academic history based on interviews with his family and a review of his academic file. It then offered a brief description of which standardized instruments had been used to evaluate Doug, a report of his scores, and a general account of his behavior during one-on-one testing.

I knew Doug as a lanky seventh grader who loved motorcycles and seemed to know everything there was to know about them. The most notable element of Doug's approach toward his work was that he would give up easily. He rarely became upset; he simply tended to retreat from challenges, and it was not hard to pick up cues from him when he was about enter into one of those retreats. Jenny had developed various reading and writing activities for him based on a fairly substantial store of magazines about customizing and racing motorcycles in the hope that we could motivate him to persevere in acquiring new skills. He seemed to be working at about a fifth-grade level, according to our informal assessment of the work he had done in the resource room.

Doug had been administered a particular "battery" of standardized tests that we agreed were appropriate, given the kinds of difficulties he had shown in his reading and writing in class. We were familiar with the tests because, in our combined experience, we had each administered them enough times to be aware of the tasks involved in completing them. Students are asked to respond to a progression of items arranged from lower to higher levels of difficulty. The tester establishes a baseline capability of the student according to his/her ability to respond correctly to a certain number of predetermined concurrent items, usually five, and then proceeds to ask increasingly difficult questions, until the student responds incorrectly to another set of five or so questions, which are usually termed the student's "ceiling" level. After administering the tests, the tester determines the student's grade-level equivalency by comparing the number of errors the student has made between his/her base and ceiling levels to scores listed on a set of norming tables commensurate with the level at which he is expected to function, according to his chronological age and/or actual grade level.

The report described the results in terms of Doug's grade-level equivalency in such skills as word attack, comprehension, syntax, and vocabulary, among others. Doug's average grade-level equivalency was rated at a high third-grade to low fourth-grade level. We knew he could do better than that.

As we read the report, we talked about how we assumed Doug might have answered particular test items given what we knew about the reading he'd done in the resource room. As we continued to talk, we found ourselves discounting certain results and agreeing with others, wishing all along that one of us had been the one to administer the test, since we knew that it was likely that he would have responded differently if his tester had been someone with whom he felt comfortable. We knew how Doug's confidence tended to waver when he experienced failure and were certain that he had made errors that he wouldn't have made if he hadn't sensed the increasing difficulty of the questions. Another problem was that, because of the design of the evaluation instrument, Doug had been asked to demonstrate much of what he could do through providing responses to very few items in each skill or subskill area. He was the kind of student who needed a little "warm-up" time in his thinking. We knew the "real" Doug was not represented in his test results.

In the literature on alternative assessment, there are numerous references to the practical need to replace standardized tests with assessments that can be developed within schools (Wiggins 1993). Many see real value in the possibility of teachers and testers being one and the same, as Jenny and I did, when we wished we could have been the ones to see exactly what Doug did as he tried to answer some of the problems he confronted on the tests. Since she and I had administered many of the same assessment devices to other students in previous years, we were familiar with the thinking behind the subtests on which Doug had made his lowest scores. In the weeks that followed our reading of the report, we developed classroom activities designed to allow us to see firsthand just how Doug approached tasks that were, in our opinion, very similar to those that had given him most difficulty on the tests. In a sense, we reconstructed those subtests in our classroom practice over time. Had we been able to design the original tests based on what Doug would actually be doing in the classroom, we might have avoided repetition in diagnosing his needs and saved him anxiety during testing.

The program we eventually designed for Doug tried to answer all three of Jenny's questions about "beginnings." We selected some information from the test results, combined them with what we knew generally would be covered in the curriculum Doug's peers would be experiencing, drew on content and materials we could develop in the resource room based on Doug's interest in motorcycles, and developed a program we hoped would parallel that of the other seventh graders. It was not an ideal situation, but it came close to meeting his needs. Doug's attitude improved, as did his willingness to persevere, though he continued to work below grade level.

Since the time that I worked with Jenny, I have had many similar conversations with other special educators about the uses and interpretations of particular diagnostic tests such as the Woodcock-Johnson, the Brigance, Keymath, the ITPA (Salvia and Ysseldyke 1991), numerous subtests within I.Q. measurements, and others. Most times, these talks begin with general agreement that these instruments are useful because they are administered one-on-one and, recognizing that they are carefully normed, can provide some helpful information worth considering in the design of programs for children who struggle with many of the skills that other children often take for granted in classrooms. Still, as we enter into discussions of strategies for teaching that call for maintaining broader perspectives of individuals, many of the special education teachers I've known have tended to speak more selectively about the tests. It has been my experience that those who have administered the tests and used them to plan for children agree about which items are reliable predictors of students' performance and which items do not work at all.

There are often tasks on the tests that can provide very straightforward information about students' skills in such areas as auditory memory, like those requiring students to repeat a series of numbers in reverse order or reproduce complicated sentences aloud. More complicated items that require processing information in response to verbal prompts about visual stimuli are not always as easy to interpret, though. Teachers tend to see flaws in the design of these items, choosing to make use of those that they believe come closest to providing some means of recognizing patterns in students' responses and rejecting those that they have found to be unrelated to their own understanding of classroom work. Discussions in staff rooms and during planning periods often lead to evaluations of the merits of one type of item or another, comparisons of subtests across instruments, and the sharing of discoveries about how items meant to measure one skill are often useful indicators of a particular child's understanding of a completely different skill.

As professionals, we know that it is totally inappropriate to select items from a variety of different tests and create our own assessment instruments, since it would invalidate test results and delay student referrals. In our actual diagnosis of children's problems, however, I think that is what many of us do. We "cut and paste" test results in our minds, if not in actual practice. This is a very specialized way of seeing children, through the selective use of someone else's instrument.

Anyone who has worked with diagnostic standardized tests can tell that the test items have been carefully constructed by measurement experts who spend countless hours designing tests and administering them to many different populations. I know that such work takes a lot of energy, time, and knowledge. Still, when I try to imagine how to develop a truly useful instrument that is applicable to living, breathing children, I would like to invite some of these measurement experts to spend a few years working with the teachers of these children in their day-to-day practice. Wouldn't it be wonderful if, as Stiggins (1991) suggests, the test developers could work alongside the teachers to create test items that could be more closely associated with the actual work that goes on in classrooms and resource rooms?

I have great hope for assessment through professional collaboration. Sometimes, we learn most about students through crossing the boundaries of our expertise with other educators. Pat Carini (1979) has shown that the teaming of teachers to review students' learning is very effective, and I believe I have found some of my most satisfying successes as a teacher when I worked with other educators as a consultant teacher in assisting students with mild learning problems who were mainstreamed in regular classrooms.

I remember one particular staff meeting that I conducted to support a student, Jackson, when the history teacher told me, "This kid just doesn't get it. Even when you tell him that he doesn't get it, he doesn't get it. I mean, he's smart enough, you can tell that, but he just can't keep his mouth shut long enough to listen to what people are trying to say to him." "And his handwriting," the science teacher added, "I can barely grade his tests because his writing is so sloppy that you can't even tell what he knows and what he doesn't know."

The math teacher explained, "I've worked with him before and I know that, if he'll just calm down and think for a minute, he can get his work done. I know his mother understands that. She's helped him before. I don't understand why she's not helping him now."

Jackson's mother had stopped helping him do his work because he was a sophomore in high school and she had decided that he needed to learn how to do his work without her help or he'd never be able to make it to college. She had told me as much in an interview I had with her after I reviewed Jackson's file, which had indicated that he was probably a student who had an attention deficit disorder. Throughout his history in school it was clear that Jackson had struggled with his work, though he had developed fairly good organizational skills largely because his mother, a former teacher, had structured his life for him. He had never been particularly popular, largely because he tended to do and say things that seemed insensitive to his peers. No one could quite figure out what it was about him that seemed to make school so hard for him, but everyone tended to agree that Jackson just happened to be one of those people who was extremely hard to be around. He was really irritating, he talked too much, and it seemed as if he never finished anything unless someone pushed him to do it.

The staff meeting was usually the first step I took when students were referred to me so that I could determine what was and was not effective in the classroom for students. I also did diagnostic testing when appropriate, observed students, and interviewed them to determine how much they knew about their own learning. When I met with Jackson the first time, I presented an overview of attention deficit disorder and showed him how some of the patterns in his work indicated that he might very well have such a problem.

Jackson took it very well. He asked me a few questions for clarification and then said, "Okay. I get it. That sounds like what I've got. My parents say that if my grades are good at the end of the term, they'll give me back my car privileges. That's about six weeks. Can you fix it by then?"

While I found it understandable that Jackson approached his problem as he did, I was fairly amazed that his teachers tended to think similarly. Somehow they had the notion that, since he had been referred to me and I had come up with a tentative diagnosis, all we would need to do would be to prescribe medication or supply Jackson with a little extra tutoring. It took months for some of his teachers to understand that to "fix" anything at all, we would have to spend a lot of time trying to identify just what it was that Jackson needed and adapt his program accordingly.

We did just that. We had meeting after meeting where teachers would bring stories and samples of Jackson's work to our discussions, and we would try to recognize patterns and develop some idea of how to teach Jackson effectively. I provided some information to the teachers on attention deficit disorder and acted as a sort of liaison among them, Jackson's doctor who prescribed medication, and his family who were struggling in their own way to support Jackson as he slowly began to understand more about himself as a learner.

As a group, we found a number of solutions for Jackson. Eventually, most of his teachers allowed him to take monitored, untimed tests at a computer in my office. This seemed to help him tremendously. The history teacher allowed him to do some research based on collecting oral histories from people in his community. The math teacher worked steadily with Jackson, giving him additional tutoring time and helping him reflect on what he was doing in his learning log. The science teacher never really conceded to make any special accommodations for Jackson, although Jackson learned from her the necessity for being diplomatic in advocating for himself. In speaking with all of us, Jackson began to get the messages we all agreed to send him, and he gained a real understanding not only of what the obstacles seemed to be in getting through high school but also of the kind of learning that he could do best. He did make it to college and he understands that he is in charge of "fixing" himself now.

In the midst of working together to assist Jackson and other students like him, his teachers and I developed a variety of assessment practices and learned to see not only the students with greater clarity but also the power of our collaboration in adapting instruction. In addition, I like to think that the high-school teachers may have learned a little about learning difficulties from me. I'm certain that I learned a great deal from them about the differences in teaching and learning processes within each of the disciplines, or what Shulman (1987) has referred to as "pedagogical content knowledge."

We are all, in a sense, special educators if we respond to our particularly puzzling students by focusing upon their individual needs through developing systematic procedures for assessment and evaluation. Since the 1920s, teachers have been creating interesting ways to determine what their students know over and above what many of us regard as traditional forms of testing (Wolf, Bixby, Glenn, and Gardner 1994). There is no reason to believe we won't all continue to do so, especially now as we have begun to name these practices.

If, with the advent of current interest in assessment reform, we can find reasons to reach into our memories or examine our current practices to find new ways of seeing our students—especially the students who we have in the past regarded as unteachable—then we can all contribute to increasing the degree to which our schools can serve a wide range of different individuals, especially if we work together. I have already seen changes in that direction and I am certain I have much more to see.

REFERENCES

Airasian, P. W. (1991). Perspectives on measurement and instruction. *Educational Measurement: Issues and Practice 10*(1); 27–35.

Brookhart, S. M. (1993). Teachers' grading practices: Meaning and values. *Journal of Educational Measurement 30*; 123–42.

Brooks, J. G., and M. G. Brooks (1993). *In search of understanding: The case for constructivist classrooms.* Alexandria, VA: Association for Supervision and Curriculum Development (ASCD).

Carini, P. (1979). *The art of seeing and the visibility of the person.* University of North Dakota: North Dakota Study Group on Evaluation.

Chittenden, E. (1991). Authentic assessment, evaluation, and documentation of student performance. In V. Perrone (ed.), *Expanding student assessment*, 22–31. Alexandria, VA: (ASCD).

Cryan, J. R. (1986). Evaluation: Plague or promise? *Childhood Education 62*; 344–50.

Darling-Hammond, L. (1994). Performance-based assessment and educational equity. *Harvard Education Review 64*(1); 5–30.

Engel, B. (1981). Objecting to objectives. *Studies in Educational Evaluation 7*; 151–60.

Gardner, H. (1983). *Frames of mind: A theory of multiple intelligences.* New York: Basic Books.

Glaser, R. (1990). The re-emergence of learning theory within educational research. *American Psychologist 45*(1); 29–39.

Glaser, R., and E. Silver (1994). Assessment, testing and instruction: Retrospect and prospect. *Review of Research in Education 17*; 393–419.

Gronlund, N. E., and R. L. Linn (1990). *Measurement and evaluation in teaching.* New York: Macmillan.

Herman, J. L., P. R. Aschbacher, and L. Winters (1992). *A practical guide to alternative assessment.* Alexandria, VA: (ASCD).

Resnick, L. B., and L. E. Klopfer (1989). *Toward the thinking curriculum: Current cognitive research: 1989 Yearbook of the Association for Supervision and Curriculum Development.* Alexandria, VA: ASCD.

Salvia, J., and J. E. Ysseldyke (1991). *Assessment.* Boston: Houghton Mifflin.

Shulman, L. (1987). Knowledge and teaching: Foundations of the new reform. *Harvard Educational Review 57*; 1–22.

Stiggins, R. J. (1991). Assessment literacy. *Phi Delta Kappan 72*(7); 534–39.

Wiggins, G. P. (1993). *Expanding student assessment: Exploring the purpose and limits of testing.* San Francisco: Jossey-Bass.

Wolf, D. P., J. Bixby, J. Glenn, and H. Gardner (1994). To use their minds well: Investigating new forms of student assessment. *Review of Research in Education 17*; 420–84.

Wolf, D. P., P. G. LeMahieu, and J. Eresh (1992). Good measure: Assessment as a tool for educational reform. *Educational Leadership 49*; 8–13.

Chapter Nine

TOWARD THE DEVELOPMENT OF AN IMPROVED URBAN TEACHING AND EVALUATION PROCESS

Sabrina Hope King

As I sit down to write this chapter in my home, helicopters deployed by the New York City Police Department circle my block and apartment building. This continues for one hour and the noise at times escalates, causing me to stop my work and contemplate the reality of helicopters circling my residence. Such a scenario is similar to scenes I imagine in occupied territories or in war zones abroad.

INTRODUCTION

An ongoing debate exists as to whether teaching in urban[1] schools is qualitatively different from teaching in other school contexts (Weiner 1993; Haberman 1993). The evolving research base on the nature of urban school teaching as well as on urban life suggests that teaching in urban schools is absolutely worthy of discrete attention (Bey and King 1995). Calls for school reform emphasize the need to recognize the diversity among school contexts (Fullan and Hargreaves 1992) and to improve the preparation of teachers for urban school contexts (Austin and Abder 1995; Haberman 1991, 1993; Torres-Guzman and Goodwin 1995; Weiner 1993) as well as the development and evaluation of teaching (Darling-Hammond 1994; Darling-Hammond and Goodwin 1993; Lieberman 1995; Zumwalt 1986).

Given the realities of urban schools, it is not surprising that the majority of new teachers express an interest in teaching in suburban school contexts (Dilworth 1990). However, given that the numbers and needs of urban schools are increasing (King and Bey 1995; Noguera 1995), it is useful to consider the improvement of urban teaching practice simultaneously with the improvement of the urban teacher evaluation process. If the contextual factors of urban schools suggest a unique and "to-be-developed" urban teacher knowledge and practice base, urban teacher evaluation must be informed by and be a part of this reconceptualization process.

This chapter highlights some of the contextual factors of urban schools, provides examples from the research literature on successful teaching in urban schools, and offers recommendations on ways to develop a teaching and evaluation process based on the intersection of the two.

URBAN SCHOOL REALITIES

My experience as an educator in urban settings and a review of the literature on urban schools point to specific realities of urban environments and school contexts. It follows that educators in urban settings have to learn as much as they can about the perceptions and realities of the urban school experience in order to develop a useful framework from which to guide the development of a knowledge and practice base for successful urban school teaching.

While there are increasing efforts at restructuring urban schools into small schools (Fine 1994; Marquardt, Fountain, Gutknecht, and Stoddart 1994; Ayers, 1994; Meier 1995), traditionally, urban schools are large and anonymous and "filled with more cracks than safety nets" (Fine 1994: 2). Nationally, the largest urban school districts have the largest populations of students of color. In 1991, students of color made up 74.7 percent of the population of urban schools classified as Great City Schools, while teachers of color comprised 37.9 percent of full-time teachers in these schools (Council of Great City Schools 1993) and 24.9 percent of teachers in central city schools (NCES 1983).

Urban schools serve students from various socioeconomic backgrounds, including, but not limited to, students who are challenged by poverty. Urban school districts are often without resources considered to be basic by many suburban districts (Kozol 1991, 1995). In New York City, resources for schools were cut at the beginning of the 1995–1996 academic year even with all districts reporting student population increases (Steinberg 1995). While in many suburban Long Island, New York school districts students have access to individual calculators and computers in their classrooms (King 1995a), in one New York City school students report having to share single sheets of paper (King 1995b).

Urban schools often experience high student and teacher transition rates. In 1990–1991, while 15.8 percent of public schools nationally experienced difficulty in filling teacher vacancies with qualified teachers, the difficulty was greater for urban public schools, where almost one-fourth had teacher vacancies they could not fill (Council of Great City Schools 1993). Urban schools have less desirable teaching conditions (Natriello and Zumwalt 1993), and this affects the career plans of entering teachers (Dilworth 1990; Haberman 1993) as well as the teaching practices and career decisions of veteran teachers. In Milwaukee, Wisconsin, for example, 30 percent of beginning teachers quit by the end of their first teaching year (Haberman 1993). Urban schools typically offer the least attractive working conditions and experience the highest teacher turnover rates (Darling-Hammond 1990, 1995a). Teacher turnover of this magnitude plus inadequate school facilities leave urban students with the least opportunity to learn (Darling-Hammond 1995a).

Urban schools are full of students who have life experiences that are unfamiliar to many teachers and teacher educators (Kanpool and Yeo 1995). Student teachers often express disbelief at the life experiences of urban students (Stallings and Quinn 1991), which include making transitions from one country to another, from a rural to an urban setting, from one language to another, and from a home environment to a radically different school environment. Other experiences include living where violence, drugs, homelessness, hopelessness, racism, and lack of hope coexist with strong cultural institutions, including the family, which provide love, hope, and self-determination and which are rarely represented or even acknowledged in the culture of the school. Challenging experiences as well as the presence of viable communities are equally a part of the reality of the urban experience.

Urban schools are affected by additional challenges faced by urban communities such as poverty, crime, drugs, a high rate of teenage pregnancy, and disintegrating families (Gonzales and Picciano 1993). We know that incidences of societal ills including crime, drug addiction, welfare dependency (Wilson 1987), and HIV and AIDS (Kozol 1995) are increasing dramatically in urban areas.

These are the contextual realities of urban schools. The relationship of these realities to urban school practice (e.g., the causes, effects, and educational implications) is less definitive and needs to be articulated and addressed by all involved in urban school improvement. At the very least, it is reasonable to suggest that meaningful urban school practice requires a specialized urban teacher knowledge and practice base that is grounded in these realities.

What Is Good Urban Teaching Practice?

An evolving knowledge base on urban school teacher preparation and practice suggests that teachers in urban schools need to possess empowering teaching perspectives and strategies that are different from or more critical than those needed in other school contexts (Haberman 1988; Weiner 1993). Thus, while it may be tempting to characterize urban teacher practice simply as good teaching, urban teacher practice is distinguished not only by its urban reality framework, but also by individual teachers' belief systems regarding the realities and possibilities of the setting. When considering urban teacher practice, it becomes necessary to include approaches that enable teachers simultaneously to confront these beliefs and realities and to address the needs of the students by challenging any dichotomies or points of divergence that may exist among these variables. Much of the work on good urban teaching practice—indeed much of what we know about good teaching—rests upon teachers' convictions about the power of learning, the inherent capabilities of students, and possibility of personal transformation. The fact that many students who attend urban schools do not succeed in life, drop out of school, or fail to be engaged by the school experience makes it all the more critical to examine exactly what those teachers who are deemed successful in urban settings do.

Marquardt et al. (1994) suggest that the successful urban teacher must be proficient in the following:

1. creating and sustaining a learning environment for urban students that enables their success
2. experimenting to improve practice throughout their professional careers
3. utilizing problem solving, critical thinking, teamwork, and reflectivity
4. consistently and routinely adapting learning experiences to meet the unique needs of their students, paying particular attention to students' prior knowledge and learning styles
5. integrating multicultural education into those learning environments they create
6. acting as decision makers who make sound judgments, articulating the rationale for those judgments, and recognizing the value of modifying such decisions when presented with additional data.

Gonzales and Picciano (1993) urge urban teacher education students and teachers to contemplate the following questions as they prepare to become urban teachers:

1. How does a teacher engage students in subject matter content that the students may see as irrelevant to their lives?
2. How does the teacher communicate with and develop sensitivity toward students from very diverse social, ethnic, economic, and cultural backgrounds?
3. How does the teacher help close the gap for the students whose first language is other than English?
4. How knowledgeable must a teacher be about family dynamics that are often in sharp contrast to what are typically defined as traditional family values?
5. Can a good teacher really make a difference in a large urban school system?

Peterson, Bennet, and Sherman (1991) identified several themes when they examined the work of successful teachers of "at risk" children. It is important to note that while the term "at risk" is often associated with urban children, it may be more useful to reflect upon the characteristics of schools or other urban institutions that serve to place students at risk (Dilliard 1994). Bearing this in mind, the authors found that successful teachers of such students create a place of belonging, institute an academic program with clear components and expectations, interrupt the academic program to address individual student problems, are adept in coaching strategies for students, and place high demands and expectations on students. In their discussion of indicators of success, Peterson et al. stressed the varied dimensions of being "at risk" and the diverse strategies that need to be utilized by teachers. They found that the teachers they studied held different perspectives regarding what was most important to emphasize when working with students considered at risk and what was the best indicator of student achievement. This suggests that a specialized urban teacher knowledge and practice base will encompass a repertoire of perspectives and approaches.

Sandoval, Reed, and Attinasi (1993) stress two overarching themes as critical philosophical underpinnings of the successful urban teacher. First, all children can learn in spite of overwhelming environmental, cultural, and economic challenges. Second, caring, knowledgeable teachers can make a difference in the lives of urban students. Their teacher education program, the Urban Teacher Education Program (UTEP), stresses pedagogical practices more than content knowledge. Effective urban practitioners utilize a range of teaching strategies to reach every student, as opposed to relying heavily on direct instruction and seatwork evident in many urban schools (Brookhart and Rusnak 1993), and embrace a pedagogy of empowerment rather than a pedagogy of poverty (Haberman 1991).

The effective schools literature suggests that urban teachers have to be able to concentrate on the improvement of comprehension and other basic skills, allow for alternative types of learning experiences (Levine and Eubanks cited in Levine and Lezotte 1995), focus on higher-order cognitive development and students' personal development, and establish high expectations for their students (Levine and Lezotte 1995).

Haberman (1991) describes core teacher acts, in contrast to discrete teacher behaviors, exhibited in exemplary urban schools. He notes that such acts are usually identified by observing student actions as opposed to teacher actions and that in such situations, students are

- involved in issues they deem meaningful
- involved with explanations of human differences
- encouraged to see the big picture (concepts, ideas, generalization, principles), not just isolated information bytes
- involved in the planning of their educational experiences
- involved in applying the ideals of justice, equity, and fairness to their world
- engaged in real-life experiences
- working in groups that are heterogeneously organized
- asked to question widely held viewpoints and relate new ideas to ones previously learned
- involved in revisions of their work
- engaged with technology
- encouraged to reflect on their lives and how they develop perspectives.

Haberman posits that successful urban teachers must be able to work collaboratively with other teachers, school administrators, mentors, students, teacher preparation programs, parents, and community activists to improve urban education. He suggests that they be interested in and willing to initiate collaborative school-based and community working relationships (Haberman 1993).

Work documenting the successful teaching practices of black teachers (Delpit 1995; Foster, cited in King 1993; Ladson-Billings and Henry, cited in King 1993, for example) and of teachers of black students (Ladson-Billings 1994) is relevant to this discussion because of the large percentage of urban school students who are black and because of the association many make between the term "urban" and black. This body of research shows that successful teachers of black students share teaching perspectives and practices that include teaching rigorous academics as well as providing students with the knowledge necessary to equip them to fight racial oppression; being openly affectionate toward students; offering collective encouragement and praise; fostering the themes of social and personal responsibility; and incorporating the students' home and community cultures into the classroom.

It is not insignificant that urban students respect teachers who set high standards for their behavior and academic performance and who demonstrate a personal interest in them (Noguera 1995). Most urban schools have at least one teacher who fits such a description, yet too often that teacher is isolated and unable to practice teaching in a way that includes collaboration, growth, and development (Noguera 1995).

Teachers who work in urban schools must not only be prepared to work with all students but must also be keenly interested in working with any population of students. I frequently hear teachers and teacher educators express an interest in working with urban schools, but only those that serve diverse student populations or that do not practice tracking. Indeed, specialized urban schools, such as schools with creative programs, are frequently in great demand by parents, students, teachers, and teacher educators. Yet many students in urban areas attend schools that are not diverse or multicultural and are predominantly black or Latino. Many others attend schools that offer a more traditional or standardized curriculum and do not have the resources necessary to provide innovative programs. What happens to these schools and the students who live in them? Thus, exacerbating the fact that the majority of beginning teachers seek employment in suburban school districts, is, apparently, the creation of a hierarchy of urban schools that ultimately results in making an excellent education for the majority of urban school students even more remote. Clearly, a specialized urban teacher knowledge and practice base must take into account all of the varied types of urban schools, including those that are the beneficiaries of attention and resources as well as those that are not.

Urban school structures and urban teachers must be prepared not to model themselves according to or succumb to the deficit view of urban life. Urban teachers must use their teaching practice to challenge such perspectives so that the strengths and wonders of all their students can be uncovered. Urban teachers need to be committed to creative and superior teaching in schools with few resources as well as be empowered to work for school equity (for example, demanding equitable resource allocation formulas for all public school districts whether urban or suburban).

Urban school teachers must also explore ways to build upon their culture as a way to reach students who share a culture similar to that of the teacher, determine ways to learn about the cultures of students who do not share the culture of the teacher, and experiment with ways of building upon the background experiences of each student as a way to expand the repertoire and effectiveness of one's teaching strategies.

Such contextual realities and challenges, life experiences, and urban teaching requirements can no longer be viewed as obstacles to school success or teacher success, but rather as knowledge that needs to be used explicitly in the planning of appropriate school curricula and practices, including teacher evaluation. Because our nation's ills, such as inequality, racism, school hierarchies—even within urban school systems—are compounded by urban settings, it becomes apparent that urban teaching will necessarily have to be more than simply good teaching. We begin to acknowledge that the contextualized nature of urban school environments necessitates the presence of teachers who believe that all students can learn, who are committed to the life success of their students through a meaningful education, and who are willing and supported to develop curricula and instruction that take into consideration the lived urban lives of their students.

TOWARD A CONCEPTUALIZATION OF URBAN TEACHER EVALUATION PRACTICE

TEACHER: Let's talk about projects in students' folders—how do we get humanities credit? If they do four projects, they get 80 or 85? Three projects, 74 or 76? Two for 65? Only one, they get 50?

ANOTHER TEACHER: This is absurd! What are we doing? We are trying to change the system and conform to it at the same time.

BOB: This is emblematic of the system. Early failure means you never see progress. We need to set aside class time and faculty time to discuss portfolios and how we are going to assess student work within the contract we establish with them. Let's end with something positive.

ANN: Kids are talking about the wonderful time in math!

OLDER MATH TEACHER: Kids are coming to math!

SOCIAL STUDIES TEACHER: Several kids caught on to problem solving today.

NATALIE: In my class, kids passed a hat for goggles for the one kid to afford getting into the lab. They are really becoming a community.

BOB: I'm learning about their culture, they are educating me.

MARSHA: We are educating each other. (Fine 1994: 9)

The above conversation on assessment and student learning by a group of teachers who work in one of Philadelphia's developing charter schools is illustrative of the kinds of conversations needed among teachers and school communities interested in improving the instructional and evaluation process. Particularly in light of the realities of urban schools as well as the research that points to the need for and development of a discrete urban school teaching practice, work on guidelines for the evaluation of urban school teachers must be integral to the development of that practice. That we don't completely understand how to connect the situational determinants of the urban context with the practice of teaching means that evaluation can be very helpful in this area. The critical need for urban school students' academic success and the fact that so many urban schools leave a lot to be desired in terms of positive learning environments and school achievement outcomes means that we must move beyond the notion of using evaluation simply to determine which schools or teachers are succeeding and which are failing. Evaluation must be used as one of many tools to assist teachers in their process of development, as a way of enhancing growth as opposed to measuring growth or competence.

Relevant Research on Teacher Evaluation

Research suggests that the teacher evaluation process must be improved, although there is little consensus on how to do so. Teachers support a good evaluation process, with even the most motivated teacher responsive to the acknowledgment of effectiveness (Peterson, Deyhle, and Watkins 1988). Teacher performance is context dependent, complex, and variable, and schools need to employ an evaluation process that documents and acknowledges the contributions that teachers actually make and that accommodates diversity in performance (Peterson, Deyhle, and Watkins 1988). Most school districts require a probationary period for new teachers but fail to provide them with concrete developmental assistance (Ornstein 1988), even though most teachers report that they learned the most through actual teaching practice (Lortie 1975). Lortie also adds that teachers perceive the psychic rewards of the teaching profession to be the most fulfilling.

Good teacher evaluation strategies can help document a wide range of positive practices. Peterson, Deyhle, and Watkins's research (1988) describes a teacher evaluation process in Utah where teachers conceptualize their contributions and merits, and document their value to the school community. This process allows for a more individualized account of performance that takes into account the unique contributions a minority teacher might make. Utah teachers also must choose from among four of the following data sources—peer observation, peer review of materials, student reports, parent surveys, teacher tests, documentation of professionalism, student achievement data, systematic evaluation, administrator reports, or other customized data sources. A teacher may choose to keep a log in which she chronicles the ways she works collegially and meaningfully with members of the school community to document aspects of her professionalism. A panel of teachers, parents, and administrators then evaluates the teacher based on his or her portfolio of work. In the evaluation of urban teachers, we would do well to follow such a model, because it allows for diverse perspectives and multiple manifestations of teachers' work to be addressed.

Ultimately, urban teacher evaluation practices that are responsive to the realities and perceptions of urban school contexts, that are informed by the research on good urban teaching practice, and that are connected to ongoing teacher learning processes are necessary. Given teacher shortages and teacher attrition in urban schools and the realities affecting many urban people who were not successful in school (one-third of all black males currently has a relationship with the penal system, for example), teacher evaluation in urban schools must principally be viewed as a method to improve teaching practice in urban schools so that increasing percentages and numbers of urban school students can be successful.

Evaluation Tied to the School Philosophy

An evaluation process inextricably linked to the improvement of the teaching process must be articulated as part of the philosophy of schools and teacher education institutions. This will enable teachers not to fear the process and to explore openly what they know and perceive about urban school contexts so as to develop, improve, and evaluate their teaching practice accordingly. Any lack of preparation or limited knowledge of urban settings can be acknowledged without penalty—to students or teachers—if teachers' learning about how to teach in the urban context is incorporated as an integral part of the evaluation process. Such a philosophy must also acknowledge the reality that many students as well as faculty may reside in occupied urban territories and many schools will be located within them. While this cannot be an excuse for low expectations, it should be taken into account in terms of the development and implementation of a process of instruction that relates to the lived experience and realities of the school community. The majority of teachers—European American and of color—will not have been prepared by their teacher education programs for the multifaceted nature of diversity and/or urban realities and will also need to be engaged in an evaluation process that guides and develops their professional practice in this area. Finally, evaluation practices must be tied to the educational community, the urban community, as well as to the collective (and collaborative) school-urban community's understandings of reality and success.

Support for Teachers

The convergence in urban school settings of inferior working conditions, limited resources, overcrowded classrooms, and students who can and desperately need to learn suggest that teachers who are going to be successful will need to be supported. While support is a word that is widely used in relationship to teaching and teacher development (Fullan and Hargreaves 1992; Lieberman 1995), it takes on an urgent overtone for the urban teachers, who will need to be members of a school team or process that supports their efforts and operates under the assumption that experimentation and change are needed in order to improve urban teaching practice. Teachers require opportunities to share what they know, to consult with others about problems or practice, and to observe one another teaching (Darling-Hammond 1995b). Below are two examples where teachers' interpretations of the community where they work reveal the different kinds of knowledge, dispositions, and experience that can inform practice. They are also indicative of the types of experiences that may need to be supported so that decisions on how to teach can be cogent. Consider first:

> A short drive up Martin Luther King Boulevard in South Los Angeles presents a stark contrast to the usual images of that city: beaches, palm trees, and Beverly Hills. This is Watts, a terrain of black, nightmarish kaleidoscopic images within an atmosphere of ugly xenophobia, palpable tension, and violence bearing witness to the consequences of the lethal linkage of economic decline, cultural decay, and political lethargy in American life. (Kanpool and Yeo 1995: 78)

Then consider how, as I read the above passage for the first time, I contrasted it with my own story of a person of color who chooses to live in "occupied territories" (south side of Chicago, Harlem, Washington Heights). Driving through these areas on my way to teach, I simultaneously think about the beauty of the people, the immense needs of these communities, and the hope that is present through education and community-based efforts. In Harlem, I think about my relatives and predecessors and the need to continue in the struggle that they worked and sacrificed for.

These two vignettes of teachers reflecting their beliefs have important implications for urban teacher practice and evaluation. Beliefs and experiences do make a difference. Each of these experiences might result in quite distinct but important teaching contributions. The kind of support that Kanpool and Yeo might need would be very different from the kind of support that I would need. For instance, they might need help in coming to see the beauty or strength of urban landscapes—and their inhabitants—that may at first glance be obscured. I might need conversations that would first affirm my experiences and urban perspectives and then empower me to act in ways that are consistent with and that build upon that wealth of experience. An evaluation process must be designed that simultaneously evaluates the contributions that teachers make within needy and resource-poor school contexts and measures what teachers may still need to learn about the realities of many urban communities.

Principals need to support teachers in this endeavor (Leithwood 1992; Lieberman 1995) and teachers need to support each other. Developing a teaching practice, figuring out what works, and sharing what one learns has to occur in an environment where everyone is focused on development, improvement, and empowerment. The notion that the purpose of evaluation is ultimately to improve teaching is not new. Teacher development as encouraging "growth in practice" needs to be strongly associated with urban teacher evaluation.

INCREASING STUDENT OUTCOMES

All work on school improvement must focus on the goal of the education and success of students. At the very least, the evaluation process for teachers in urban schools must embody:

- the teacher learning process
- the student learning process
- an emphasis on student outcomes and high expectations for all
- a multifaceted approach to teaching and evaluation
- a process whereby teachers try to internalize and enact the positive themes described in the research reviewed for this chapter
- the belief that all students can learn
- the idea of experimenting to improve practice
- the notion that if urban schools are failing students then they are also failing teachers.

This evaluation process must include the opportunity for teachers to envision their teaching practice within an urban setting and to engage in individual as well as collaborative assessment with their colleagues and students. All these considerations and components coupled with a multidimensional and flexible assessment model as described in the work of Peterson, Deyhle, and Watkins (1988) may help provide a framework for the evaluation of urban school teachers.

Ultimately, the purpose of urban teacher evaluation must be to help and support teachers to:

- improve their teaching practice
- facilitate student success and achievement
- identify the positives in their work, their schools, and their students
- integrate urban contextual realities into their teaching practice
- learn from what is working and what is not
- always have hope that their practice and their work can be done in a more meaningful manner and result in the highest levels of student success and teacher satisfaction.

The fact that my professional practice was affected by helicopters swirling around my window indicates that the contextual realities outside of and within urban schools cannot be ignored. That we are beginning to explore how to be successful in urban schools and how to change the structure of urban schools to allow for innovative, effective practice is encouraging. To do this on the widespread basis that is necessary, teaching and evaluation improvement must be situated on the belief that all students can and must learn and that teaching practice must be developed and evaluated based on Herculean, collaborative, and genuine efforts in this direction.

POSTSCRIPT

Recently, I was entering my neighborhood by car with my daughter, Ayanna-Grace, who is almost two. Helicopters fly overhead—too close for comfort—and she smiles, looking up out of the window, and says "Mama, plane, plane, plane." The joy and excitement that she feels and that I share with her because of her new knowledge and ability to express that knowledge is temporarily tempered. I begin to think, if only she knew why the helicopters are in our neighborhood all of the time, if only she knew all of the political realities, if only it were different, if only planes were in our neighborhood for a different reason. . . . But, then I stopped myself and realized: But she will know these realities. . . . I will teach them to her. Then, maybe, she will decide to incorporate these realities, to build upon these realities, to help make these realities better in her development into and practice as a caring, grounded-in-reality, change-focused human being.

NOTE

1. Many terms are used to describe or further categorize the term urban. These words include, but are not limited to, inner city, central city, and great city. This chapter will utilize the term urban and incorporate a collective understanding of these terms. The term "of color" will be used to describe the collective experiences of blacks, Latinos, native Americans and Asian Americans.

REFERENCES

Austin, T., and P. Fraser-Abder (1995). Mentoring mathematics and science preservice teachers for urban bilingual classrooms. In T. M. Bey and S. H. King (eds.), Mentoring urban teachers: Facilitating professional development. Special Issue. *Education and Urban Society 28*(1); 67–89.

Ayers. W. (1994). Can city schools be saved? *Educational Leadership 51*(8); 60–63.

Bey, T. M., and S. H. King (eds.) (1995). Mentoring urban teachers: Facilitating professional development. Special Issue. *Education and Urban Society 28*(1).

Brookhart, S. M., and T. G. Rusnak (1993). A pedagogy of enrichment, not poverty: Successful lessons from exemplary urban teachers. *Journal of Teacher Education 44*; 17–26.

Council of Great City Schools (1993). *Diversifying our great city school teachers: Twenty year trends.* Washington, DC: Author. (ERIC No. ED 372 140.)

Darling-Hammond, L. (1990). Teachers and teaching: Signs of a changing profession. In W. R. Houston (ed.), *Handbook of research on teacher education*, 267–90. New York: Macmillan.

——— (1994). *Standards for teachers*. 34th Charles W. Hunt Memorial Lecture presented at the annual meeting of the American Association of Colleges for Teacher Education, Chicago, February.

——— (1995a). Inequality and access to knowledge. In J. A. Banks (ed.), *Handbook of research on multicultural education*, 465–83. New York: Macmillan.

——— (1995b). Policy for restructuring. In A. Lieberman (ed.), *The work of restructuring schools*, 157–66. New York: Teachers College Press.

Darling-Hammond, L., and A. L. Goodwin (1993). Progress toward professionalism in teaching. In G. Cawelti (ed.), *Challenges and achievements of American education*, 19–52. 1993 Yearbook. Alexandria, VA: Association for Supervision and Curriculum Development.

Delpit, L. (1995). *Other people's children*. New York: New Press.

Dilliard, C. B. (1994). The power of call, the necessity of response: African world feminist voices as catalysts for educational change and social empowerment. *Initiatives 56*(3); 9–22.

Dilworth, M. E. (1990). *Reading between the lines: Teachers and their racial/ethnic cultures*. Teacher Education Monograph No. 11. Washington, DC: Eric Clearinghouse on Teacher Education and American Association of Colleges for Teacher Education.

Fine, M. (1994). *Chartering urban school reform: Reflections on public high schools in the midst of change*. New York: Teachers College Press.

Foster, M. (1989). *Recruiting teachers of color: problems, programs and possibilities*. (Monograph of the Far West Holmes Group). Tempe: Arizona State University.

——— (1990). The politics of race: Through African-American teachers' eyes. *Journal of Education 172*(3); 123–41.

——— (1993). Education for competence and community and culture: Exploring the views of exemplary African American teachers. *Urban education 27*(4); 370–94.

Fullan, M., and A. Hargreaves (eds.) (1992). Teacher development and educational change. In M. Fullan and A. Hargreaves (eds.), *Teacher development and educational change*, 1–9. Washington, DC: Falmer.

Gonzales, G., and A. G. Picciano (1993). QUEST: Developing competence, commitment, and an understanding of community in a field-based, urban teacher education program. *Equity and Choice 9*(2); 38–43.

Haberman, M. (1988). *Preparing teachers for urban schools*. Bloomington, IN: Phi Delta Kappa Educational Foundation.

——— (1991). The pedagogy of poverty versus good teaching. *Phi Delta Kappan 73*(5); 290–94.

——— (1993). Predicting the success of urban teachers (The Milwaukee Trials). *Action in Teacher Education 15*(3); 1–5.

Kanpool, B., and F. Yeo (1995). Inner city realities: Democracy within difference, theory and practice. *Urban Review 27*(1); 77–91.

King, S. H. (1993). The limited presence of African American teachers. *Review of Educational Research 63*(2); 115–49.

———— (1995a). Personal conversation with my preservice students who undergo field placements in suburban schools through Hofstra University.

———— (1995b). Personal conversation with fourth-grade student who attends public school in Washington Heights, New York City.

King, S. H., and T. M. Bey (1995). The need for urban teacher mentors: Conceptions and realities. In T. M. Bey and S. H. King (eds.), Mentoring urban teachers: Facilitating professional development. Special Issue. *Education and Urban Society 28*(1); 3–10.

Kozol, J. (1991). *Savage inequalities.* New York: Crown.

———— (1995). *Amazing grace: The lives of children and the conscience of a nation.* New York: Crown.

Ladson-Billings, G. (1994). *The dreamkeepers: Successful teachers of African American children.* San Francisco: Jossey-Bass.

Ladson-Billings, G., and A. Henry (1990). Blurring the borders: Voices of African liberatory pedagogy in the United States and Canada. *Boston Journal of Education 172*(2); 72–88.

Leithwood, K. A. (1992). The principal's role in teacher development. In M. Fullan and A. Hargreaves (eds.), *Teacher development and educational change,* 86–103. Washington, DC: Falmer.

Levine, D. U., and E. Eubanks (1989). Organizational arrangements at effective secondary schools. In H. J. Walberg and J. J. Lane (eds.), *Organizing for learning,* 41–49. Reston, VA: National Association of Secondary School Principals.

Levine, D. U., and L. W. Lezotte (1995). Effective schools research. In J. A. Banks (ed.), *Handbook of research on multicultural education,* 525–47. New York: Macmillan.

Lieberman, A. (1995). Restructuring schools: The dynamics of changing practice, structure and culture. In A. Lieberman, *The work of restructuring schools,* 1–17. New York: Teachers College Press.

Lortie, D. (1975). *Schoolteacher.* Chicago: University of Chicago Press.

MacFarquahr, N. (1995). Newark schools focus on restoring discipline. *New York Times,* September 25, p. B3.

Marquardt, F., C. Fountain, B. Gutknecht, and A. Stoddart (1994). *Collaborating to improve teacher education and school reform in urban settings.* Paper presented at the Conference of the U.S. Department of Education, NCES, Arlington, VA. July. (ERIC No. ED 377 178.)

Meier, D. (1995). *The power of their ideas.* Boston: Beacon Press.

Mesa-Bains, A., and J. H. Shulman (eds.) (1991). *Teaching diverse students: Cases and commentaries.* San Francisco: Far West Laboratories.

National Commission on Excellence in Education (NCES) (1983). *A nation at risk.* Washington, DC: U.S. Government Printing Office.

Natriello, G., and K. Zumwalt (1993). New teachers for urban schools? The contribution of the provisional teacher program in New Jersey. *Education and Urban Society 26*(1); 49–62.

Noguera, P. (1995). Coming to terms with violence in our schools. In D. Levine, R. Lowe, B. Peterson, and R. Tenorie (eds.), *Rethinking schools: An agenda for change*, 209–14. New York: New Press.

Ornstein, A. C. (1988). The changing status of the teaching profession. *Urban Education 23*(3); 261–79.

Peterson, K. D., B. Bennet, and D. F. Sherman (1991). Themes of uncommonly successful teachers of at-risk students. *Urban Education 26*(2); 176–94.

Peterson, K. D., D. Deyhle, and W. Watkins (1988). Evaluation that accommodates minority teacher contributions. *Urban Education 23*(2); 133–49.

Sandoval, P., C. Reed, and J. Attinasi (1993). Professors and teachers working together to develop instructional teams in an urban teacher education program. *Contemporary Education 64*(4); 243–48.

Stallings, J. A., and L. F. Quinn (1991). Learning how to teach in the inner city. *Educational Leadership 49*(3); 25–27.

Steinberg, J. (1995). Students learn to live with less. *New York Times*, September 10, p. 6.

Torres-Guzman, M., and A. L. Goodwin (1995). Urban bilingual teachers and mentoring for the future. In T. M. Bey and S. H. King (eds), Mentoring urban teachers: Facilitating professional development. Special Issue. *Education and Urban Society 28*(1); 48–66.

Weiner, L. (1993). *Preparing teachers for urban schools*. New York: Teachers College Press.

Wilson, W. J. (1987). *The truly disadvantaged: The inner city, the underclass, and public policy*. Chicago: University of Chicago Press.

Zumwalt, K. K. (1986). Working together to improve teaching. In K. K. Zumwalt (ed.), *Improving teaching*, 169–86. Alexandria, VA: Association for Supervision and Curriculum Development.

Chapter Ten

DILEMMAS OF ASSESSMENT AND EVALUATION IN PRESERVICE TEACHER EDUCATION

Nancy Dubetz, Steve Turley,

and Martha Erickson

In this chapter we focus on a set of dilemmas we confront as teacher educators as we strive to make assessment and evaluation equitable, inclusive, and useful to our students in ways that value their emergent and individual constructions of good teaching practice and at the same time are consistent with program performance expectations. To define dilemma, we draw on the work of Lampert (1985), Cuban (1992), and Katz and Raths (1992). We see a dilemma as a recurring need to choose between alternatives, none of which is perfect and all of which lead to trade-offs. Because dilemmas are unsolvable, making decisions around dilemmas requires principled deliberation, which often can be a messy process. Dilemmas around assessment and evaluation in teacher education emerge naturally from our efforts to shape our practice by a set of guiding principles. For us, the principles that shape our decisions about how to assess and evaluate students are:

1. evaluative standards and outcomes must be explicit and public
2. standards and outcomes must be applied equitably, i.e., fairly and consistently
3. assessment and evaluation practices must be directly linked to standards and outcomes
4. the voices of all those who participate in the process of assessment and evaluation must be heard
5. assessment must be intimately connected with instruction
6. assessment and evaluation practices must include a variety of teaching styles and unique approaches.

While the principles are fairly straightforward on a theoretical level, translating them into practice produces perplexing dilemmas. As Cuban (1992) points out, choices often result in tensions between professional, organizational, and personal expectations. Indeed, we have found this to be true in our efforts to make our assessment and evaluation practices fair and inclusive for our preservice student teachers. The dilemmas that we describe in this article grow directly out of our attempts to adhere to the principles listed above when in a real-world context that does not always support them. In this chapter we discuss five dilemmas that we face as teacher educators. These dilemmas are: (1) defining our roles as educators of students and gatekeepers to the profession; (2) establishing educational outcomes that are broad enough to accommodate a diverse set of definitions of good teaching among participants, yet specific enough to establish boundaries between appropriate and inappropriate practices; (3) balancing program accountability with individual autonomy in a setting where multiple individuals participate in the interpretation of standards and outcomes; (4) advocating the use of alternative assessment and evaluation instruments while also adhering to the expectations of the traditional, grade-based educational community in which we are embedded; and (5) applying generic criteria to diverse students in diverse student teaching contexts.

This chapter is a synthesis of a series of audiotaped conversations around assessment and evaluation in preservice teacher education that we began in the fall of 1994. Brief excerpts from the original conversations serve as introductions to each section in order to provide the reader with specific stories of our practice that illustrate some aspect of a given dilemma. In discussing the dilemmas we attempt to differentiate between assessment and evaluation. We view assessment as an ongoing process in which we collect descriptive information to "feed back" to students. For us, evaluation involves summative judgment of our students' use of this information. The distinction we make is similar to that made by Chittenden (1991). However, we also recognize that there was overlap in the use of the terms in our conversations at times.

DEFINING THE ROLES OF GATEKEEPER AND EDUCATOR

MARTHA: In my gatekeeper role during the application process, I look primarily for evidence that the candidate will be able to successfully survive the rigors of the program, but I also look for what the candidate will bring to the program and the profession. I think we all look more carefully at applicants who bring a diversity of experience, background, or perspective. We know the program itself, as well as the profession, is enriched by the talents and skills of those who enter it. Remember Justine, the artist? She continually challenged us to focus more intently on the arts. Those kinds of challenges are good for us as a program in that they force us to be more responsive to student interests.

The problem I have when I review applications concerns my own personal preferences or perspectives. For example, I strongly believe that children benefit when there are male teachers in nursery and elementary schools. I value the decision men make when they choose to become elementary school teachers rather than high school teachers. I also believe the profession benefits when individuals come to teaching from other career fields. I value the determination that career-changers show as they redefine themselves and their dreams. Because of these personal values, my approach to these applicants changes. Instead of asking if this is a solid match between program and applicant, I find myself taking an advocacy role, looking for reasons why the program is the right setting for them to reach their goals. It is the fact that my values come into play that makes these decisions an ethical issue for me.

NANCY: Is your concern that you are not being fair?

MARTHA: That is part of it.

When prospective students first apply to a teacher education program, we assume our gatekeeping role. At this time we evaluate applicants on their written qualifications—their recommendations and their past performance as students as evidenced by their university transcripts; we assess their writing ability in a writing sample. All of this is done in an effort to determine their suitability as students in the teacher education program. As gatekeepers evaluating qualifications for entry into the profession, we also ask certain questions that help us determine an applicant's potential for success as a teacher. For example, does the individual demonstrate a commitment to becoming a teacher? Does s/he seem to be genuinely interested in working with children? Finally, we look for a diversity in life experience across applicants to support our commitment to valuing different teaching models for children. As can be seen in the excerpt of our dialogue above, this last decision is the most problematic, in that we risk seeming tentative and unfair in our choices.

Once students are accepted into the program, our task becomes how to help them succeed as students of teaching and as teachers of children. During student teaching, our role is as educators whose primary task is nurturance and support as we help them find their teaching voices. By the end of this experience, the circle closes and we become gatekeepers again who must determine whether the student is ready to be recommended for state licensing. The dilemma that emerges from this shift in roles is that the roles can get confused and overlap, which makes assessment as a collaborative enterprise (Henning-Stout 1994) extremely difficult, if not impossible. In our role as educators, we want students to see us as partners in helping them to define their identities as teachers during the assessment process; indeed, they must do so in order to be active participants in the assessment of their own work. However, students often interpret our role to be one of a gatekeeper from beginning to end, and it becomes difficult to convince them that we can be partners and advocates for them as well as evaluators of their work. Some students seem unable to view us in these dual roles; knowing that we hold evaluative power that can open or close the gate they want to pass through may be too powerful an image in our students' minds for us to counteract. If students are consciously aware of us as evaluative gatekeepers, they cannot see us as educators using assessment in a descriptive, nonevaluative way as a tool to help them formulate teaching identities and improve their practice. Thus, a dilemma grows directly out of our attempts to invite students into the evaluation process while at the same time serving as gatekeepers to the teaching profession; from their perspective, we assume two roles that seem to contradict rather than complement each other. The two roles that we assume as teacher educators—the role we play as gatekeepers to the profession, and the role of educator or facilitator of student learning—become problematic and contradictory. The tension is between the assessing, or the "sitting beside" and coaching (Herman, Aschbacher, and Winters 1992)—i.e., being a set of eyes for student teachers and being able to give them useful feedback on their work—and the evaluating, which is the valuing of student work along a quality continuum.

Our work is further complicated by the time constraints of the student teaching experience. At a predetermined point in time during that experience we are obligated again to assume the gatekeeper role. It is then we must decide how our students are articulating and analyzing their images of teaching and whether these images fit within the confines of what we have established as appropriate standards. This time frame has been determined by a source outside our teacher education programs, e.g., the university or state education departments. We find ourselves constrained by a time frame that is based on group norms rather than on individual development, or geared to bureaucratic rather than individual needs. With some student teachers, we find ourselves resisting the move from the role of educator to the role of gatekeeper. If we resist and choose to continue in the role of educator by extending a student's teaching experience, our support becomes an added burden to our already full workload, which continues to build with the arrival of a new cohort of students. Thus, we find ourselves in the dilemma of not being able to fulfill all of our responsibilities equally well. As Hargreaves (1994: 11) points out, such choices may be "ethically defensible and practically workable," but they are never perfect.

ESTABLISHING EDUCATIONAL OUTCOMES FOR TEACHING PERFORMANCE

STEVE: When we evaluate our students, who or what are we comparing our students to? Are we taking each of our individual students and looking at her own merits, or are we comparing her to her cohort? To other students we've known in the past? Are we comparing her to what our standards of a good teacher are? Are we comparing her to teachers? I think it's a very sticky issue because I think we tend to do a lot of comparing of students, and as much as we would like to say we get away from this, it's one of the things we do. It's one way we value things, by comparing X to Y.

NANCY: Evaluation seems to me more fair when you have a set of criteria. But we establish our criteria through a process of supervisors sitting around a table and sharing personal stories about individual students in classrooms.

STEVE: You are absolutely right. Telling stories is heavily comparison oriented. I never thought of it in that way. I want to hear your stories of your students because it helps me think about my students relative to these others. So in a sense, we are comparing students with each other.

NANCY: But the good thing about stories is that they provide context. You get to hear all of the contextual factors that might be affecting a particular student teacher, which to me is better than a decontextualized list of criteria.

MARTHA: My problem is that these stories only occur after supervisors have made sense of what is happening. It's not fair to the students. I would like the supervisors to have critieria up front to inform their work as they enter the setting.

Although we define our approach to teacher education as one that recognizes the multiplicity of good teaching and, therefore, values the importance of principled eclecticism in teacher preparation, we believe participants must develop a shared understanding of general outcomes. In the absence of clearly articulated, clearly defined public standards or expectations, we can only rely on our own histories to determine what is appropriate, and practice driven by personal histories is by nature often tacit and subjective. Even when we have an understanding of the purpose and ethos of a program, the subjectivity of our own sense of it is very salient. Thus, we attempt to establish criteria that define the individual who is ready to become a teacher and apply these criteria to individual cases. Because we expect such outcomes to be explicit and public, we must establish a process whereby this can be realized. The dialogue above illustrates one such approach and the inherent tensions it creates.

In our current contexts, supervisors who are most closely connected to the student teachers and their teaching contexts define what counts for good teaching; they assess and evaluate students, drawing on their professional knowledge and an ethos within a particular preservice program. We see this as developing a "shared subjectivity," or a shared sense of what a student teacher should be like at the crucial gatekeeping time at the end of their teacher education experience. We suggest there is value in having supervisors share stories of their students throughout the evaluation process, because individual supervisors start to make connections with what other supervisors are experiencing, which leads to the "shared subjectivity" mentioned earlier. Sharing stories of supervision experience is a powerful device both for reaching a common understanding of program expectations and for individual growth as well. However, as illustrated in the dialogue above, while the sharing of individual stories can support the principle of valuing diversity of teaching philosophies and teaching contexts, it can also result in a kind of "norming" that does not meet our need to create criteria that are fair and equable. Furthermore, because the selection of evaluation criteria is informed by the personal histories of the many individuals who participate in the process, it is not uncommon for tensions among views of good practice to emerge during such discussions. Hargreaves (1994) refers to them as opportunities for dilemma resolution. These opportunities encourage supervisors of student teachers to "discuss principles and approaches to practical problems whose solutions are uncertain and unclear" (Hargreaves 1994: 12). These conversations invite discussion around different theories of good teaching that are grounded in individuals' experiences as teachers of children and teachers of adults. Not surprisingly, such discussion often involves debate and disagreement, and true consensus is not possible.

The process of making standards and outcomes explicit is further complicated by the fact that we are nested in larger communities of teacher evaluation, and standards developed within such communities must be considered in our efforts to establish our own standards. We operate in a context that includes both state and professional accrediting and licensing bodies, each of which seeks to be a definitive player in promoting widely accepted standards for the assessment of teaching. Our efforts to establish program standards must accommodate both local and national purposes as they are promoted by such groups as state departments of education, the National Council for the Accreditation of Teacher Education (NCATE), the Association of Teacher Educators (ATE), and the National Board for Professional Teaching Standards (NBPTS). Thus, standard setting is not solely an individual process, even though the interpretation of standards might be.

INTERPRETING OUTCOMES: PERSONAL AUTONOMY VS. PROGRAM ACCOUNTABILITY

MARTHA: I remember one student whose vision of herself as teacher did not mesh at all with the realities of classroom life as any of us know it. Do you remember Sarah? We could have the most incredible conversations about the nature of creativity, or the political dimensions of a unit on garbage, or the ethics of using behavior modification techniques in the classroom. I was her supervisor for one term and I remember clearly feeling that she was facilitating my growth and development as a supervisor and teacher educator. But what she could not do was make herself conform to the role of classroom teacher. Classroom time had no meaning for her. Going to gym when the kindergarteners were in the middle of a really good discussion on feelings just because the clock said so? No way. Plan a lesson when the children had ideas that were so much more interesting to them than any she could think up? Nope. It took her the entire day to make one batch of "stone soup" with four children because she wanted each to explore every little facet of observing and preparing the vegetables for the soup as well as understanding the very process of cooking itself on each vegetable in the boiling water over time. It was an amazing experience for those chosen few. But, Sarah had no idea why her cooperating teacher would not permit her to spend the next six school days repeating this experience for the rest of the children. These kinds of incidents continued to occur. It took me awhile, but I finally understood what Sarah meant when, in response to my question about her decisions to do this or that, she would answer, "Well, I wanted to see what would happen if . . . " Her image of teaching was teacher-as-anthropologist. She saw herself studying the fascinating world of children and how they think. She was not studying how to facilitate their learning. Nancy, you worked with Sarah in her upper grade placement. Did working with older children make a difference?

NANCY: No. Sarah's cooperating teacher and I had the same reaction you had to her view of teaching. While we could clearly see her interest and commitment to children's learning, we were concerned about her total disregard for the school context in which she was teaching.

The tensions that surface in the establishment of common standards and outcomes often reemerge in their interpretation by the participants who are involved in the assessment and evaluation process—the students, the supervisors, the cooperating teachers. Even when standards are clearly defined, we cannot help but draw on our own set of beliefs and understandings about what good teaching is to interpret them. If we collectively establish a set of standards, we must accept that to some degree the individual who is doing the evaluating will exercise a certain degree of autonomy in interpreting them. We see this as a question of balancing personal autonomy with program accountability. For us, the dilemma of where to locate the power to make evaluative decisions is at the heart of the larger conversation about standards or benchmarks of any kind.

Given the potential power of individual decision making in the evaluation process, we need to explore carefully how collective or shared knowledge is used by supervisors, cooperating teachers, and faculty to evaluate student teachers. For example, in the teacher education programs each of us works in, student teachers do not explicitly participate in establishing the outcomes for teaching performance, yet they do participate in the interpretation of these outcomes during conversations with their supervisors. As said earlier, we believe that the voices of all those who participate in the process of assessment and evaluation must be heard. However, when we encounter a situation such as that presented by Sarah, where student voice and supervisor's voice are so divergent, we are forced to ask ourselves: Who should own the evaluation process? Whose voice should dominate and why? Can we value the diverse perspective on teaching that a student like Sarah embraces while closing the gate to her becoming a teacher?

Like the student teachers, cooperating teachers are crucial to assessment since they regularly provide feedback to the student teacher, but they are often left out of the evaluation loop. They *appear* to be in the loop because they complete final, or summative evaluation forms. However, only in a case where we've asked the teacher to help us work with a student teacher about whom we have concerns does the cooperating teacher role become central to the evaluation process, and only then at the discretion of the university supervisor. The decision to put more trust in the professional judgment of the supervisor and less in the cooperating teacher when it comes to the evaluation of student teacher performance reflects a regularity of many teacher education programs.

Even with supervisors, however, we must accept that standards that have been collectively established will be interpreted individually at some level. In *A License To Teach*, Darling-Hammond, Wise, and Klein (1995) suggest establishing national standards for characteristics or dispositions for teachers that can be demonstrated through prescribed activities and assignments. But at some point it comes down to interpreting performance, or artifacts of performance such as a portfolio, along a continuum of quality from good to bad, appropriate to inappropriate, or whatever terminology we choose to use to interpret quality. In our experience, there is great ambiguity in the interpretive process. We accept it as a necessary trade-off in order to avoid the dangers of creating standards that are so specific that we are following checklists of discrete behaviors, in which the whole becomes invisible as the pieces take priority. If we deny or try to remove the interpretive discretion inherent in the evaluation process, we end up deskilling the evaluator and ignoring the importance of context in making evaluative decisions. We also risk sending the message to students that teaching is a set of discrete behaviors rather than a highly complex activity (Katz and Raths 1992). If teaching were only a science, there would be certain "truths" that are observable and generalizable. If good teaching were rooted in certain "truths," all we would have to do is identify them and teach them to a prospective teacher. But teaching is also an art, and like art, the qualities that we use to define good teaching are context specific and may in fact emerge during the process of teaching itself (Eisner 1994a). Like art, teaching is "guided by educational values, personal needs, and by a variety of beliefs or generalizations that the teacher holds to be true" (Eisner 1994a: 154). Recognizing this is crucial to understanding the relationship between what student teachers believe and how they teach, and this recognition is important if we are to value their emerging views of teaching in our assessment and evaluation of their work.

ALTERNATIVE EVALUATION VS. LETTER GRADES

NANCY: I find it so hard to assign grades to portfolios.

MARTHA: Let me tell you how it played out for us with the student teaching portfolios. We were very excited about the idea of using an old format, but having students do the work in two phases—having the working collection followed by the selected pieces that reflect growth over time. But we had to get it into the syllabus before we had time to establish the criteria, so the idea was that we as a staff would develop the criteria. What happened is that we never came together to establish the criteria until the end of the semester. The idea was that we wanted the students to know what the criteria were, but we didn't do that. So we decided to make the portfolio a pass/fail grade, and that was a total cop-out. We then set a goal that we would have the students set the criteria in the spring at the beginning of the semester.

NANCY: So students would have ownership over the process.

MARTHA: Right. The problem came when bringing the topic of assessment to the beginning of the semester meant rethinking the entire spring semester curriculum, since the topic had traditionally come in the second half of the semester. Because of other priorities and time contraints, assessment got pushed to the very end again. We haven't been able to decide when to do it, much less how to do it.

NANCY: I don't know if this is any consolation, but I have been doing showcase portfolios for two semesters, and I have very specific criteria that were established by me and the students. There is a very explicit explanation about what is to be included and what students are being evaluated for. There is a set of options that they can write about in their introduction to the portfolio, and there is an explanation of the variety of assignments they can include. But even as explicit as it is, it's very hard for me not to read the portfolios, knowing all that has gone into them, and not give them all an A. I find it difficult to assign a letter grade to this alternative form of assessment that gives me so much information about my own teaching as well as their learning. Last semester I gave mostly As, and I ask myself if I am really using the portfolios to differentiate between exceptional work, satisfactory work, and unsatisfactory work. I think it's difficult to do.

MARTHA: It's almost as if the more you know about a person, the harder it is to put a grade on it. You don't want to oversimplify all the work by labeling it with a grade.

Many teacher education programs use alternative forms of assessment and evaluation of students that encompass multiple measures: teaching performance; ability to articulate practice orally (with supervisor, with cooperating teacher, with program faculty in class); ability to articulate practice in writing (journals, reflection papers, student teaching portfolios, academic assignments); and performance in college course work (which is evaluated by a variety of instructors in courses whose content may be loosely connected). Because we see teaching as a complex practice that can be manifested in a variety of ways, we want our assessment practices to reflect this complexity and variety as well.

One might assume that the use of alternative forms of evaluation should not be problematic at the university level. However, even though students are engaged in a variety of different kinds of learning and they are being assessed and evaluated in a variety of ways, this complex process in many teacher education programs is translated into an A, B, C, D, or F, or a Pass or Fail, grade because we are still nested in a traditional, grade-focused, evaluation community. The grade becomes the only information that the university sends to the public to "describe" these student teachers' work. Program faculty use letter grades from college coursework as a way of deciding whether to accept students into the program. It's one of the ways teacher educators evaluate—in their roles as gatekeepers—whether aspiring teachers get through that first gate. Given this context, we face a huge challenge helping students buy into an alternative evaluation process. For the most part, they have only experienced a grade-based system, and thus are sometimes resistant to alternative forms of assessment, particularly when these are translated into, and thus reinforce, grades as the ultimate measure of one's success. Even as teacher education faculty, we frequently find ourselves discussing evaluation in ways that reflect our own struggle to release ourselves from old ways of thinking. For example, we find ourselves debating such issues as grade inflation, what constitutes an A grade or a Passing grade, and to what degree our evaluation should be norm based or criterion based. Such issues are reflected in the dialogue above. These discussions around assessment are crucial to improving our own practice as preservice teacher educators; however, they are extremely labor intensive and time consuming, and we sometimes find ourselves either moving to change our practice with new forms of assessment that are less than clear in our own minds, or conforming to old measures because we have been unable to resolve our debate within the limited time that we have.

APPLYING GENERIC CRITERIA TO DIVERSE STUDENTS IN DIVERSE STUDENT TEACHING CONTEXTS

MARTHA: Working as a supervisor with Mary Chen helped me to understand the potential impact of culture on the dynamics of learning how to teach and on the dynamics of all kinds of classroom interactions. Mary was always respectful when talking to the cooperating teacher and to me. She listened attentively to every question, comment, and suggestion we made. She took copious notes. She agreed with everything we said. But she never offered ideas of her own, and she never deviated from any planned activity no matter how the children were responding to what she was doing with them. She couldn't seem to "read" the class and be flexible. She could not talk easily about the decisions she made when working with the children. She seemed to be always saying, "Tell me what to do and how to do it, and I will do exactly as you say." Even though it seemed to me that I was seeing her behavior in terms of an "Asian" approach to teaching and learning, I still expected to be able to establish the kind of collaborative relationship I like to have with all the students I work with. I wanted her to be a partner in the process of working together to make sense of her developing teaching practice. I did not want her to be a recipient of my "wisdom" or "knowledge" of how to teach. Her respect for my role as expert is not solely an Asian characteristic, but looking back I think I should have acted on it as a cultural marker, though it's very hard to talk in those terms, the danger being that stereotypes are easily reinforced.

I remember how hesitant and unsure I was of my abilities that working with Mary made me. How difficult it was for me to give up my "western" perspective, which seemed to say here I am as your supervisor and I am going to help you see this classroom the way I see it so you can teach the way I think you should be able to teach this group of children. Then I want to see you demonstrate your ability to successfully put my conception of teaching into practice. And she could not do it. Of course, I read it as would not do it. I think back now and it still hurts, especially since I thought that living and teaching in Taiwan had necessarily made me a more culturally responsive teacher educator. I should have been respectful of her need to be told, to be given a model to follow that conformed to her vision of good teaching. If she had had some successes with the children, we would have had a foundation of experience to build on. As an early childhood specialist, I know the importance of starting with the individual learner's needs. But I just couldn't see it. I couldn't see beyond my own perspective then.

And that is always something I'm going to be working on. I guess one of the key learnings for me in this experience is that it helped me to give myself permission to talk about issues of cultural diversity in my assessment and evaluation, even while knowing that I could give offense.

As supervisors, our decisions must take into account how the unique relationship among participants inform assessment and evaluation when applying generic evaluation criteria to a particular situation. The dynamics of the interactions among all the participants cannot be anticipated, despite the time a program spends trying to match settings and individuals. It is one of the reasons why "good" teachers in "good" classrooms can sometimes still be problematic for "good" student teachers and "good" supervisors. A symbolic interactionist perspective seems useful here (Blumer 1969). In one sense, the work we do as teacher educators is about the quality of the interactions we have with all the participants in the process of developing beginning teachers. Focusing on relationships adds a layer of complexity to the valuing process we engage in when we assess and evaluate student teaching performance. We must account for a possible tension between the student teachers' expectations and the way they experience the reality of particular classrooms. Not all students are alike in their ability to look beyond their preconceptions to explore new ideas generated in diverse settings. Nor is such tension unique to students. Everyone who has supervised student teachers can share stories of struggling with discrepancies between expectations of what a good learning environment is for a particular student teacher and what the cooperating classroom turns out to be. Our challenge is to reconcile these differences in our assessment and evaluation practices in order to provide helpful feedback to the individual student and evaluate her or him fairly.

Diane Holt-Reynolds (1991) writes about how important yet difficult it is for us as teacher educators to learn to listen to preservice teachers' "internal conversations" about teaching, which are shaped by their life experience as students and serve as powerful lenses through which they come to understand their work. As teacher educators, we have our own internal conversations to contend with, as illustrated in Martha's story at the beginning of this section. Lortie (1975) begins to capture the context of these conversations with his idea of the apprenticeship of experience that we all possess by having gone through sixteen-plus years of kindergarten to undergraduate school. As Martha's story so clearly illustrates, we also make sense of current experience through the lens of the cultures to which we belong. Thus, when we establish or apply generic evaluation criteria, we must ask ourselves: How do we account for that diversity of apprenticeship and biographical experience each player—student teacher, cooperating teacher, university supervisor, or faculty—brings to the table? How conscious are we of that background when we work with our student teachers, individually or collectively, as faculty and supervisors? Thus, autobiography functions as a critical component of assessment and evaluation.

While we acknowledge that our personal histories as supervisors influence our interpretations, we must also acknowledge that the histories of students influence our assessment and evaluation practices, particularly in a context where students are encouraged to participate in the evaluation process. In our educator role, we recognize that each student teacher enters a preservice program already holding a unique vision of herself or himself as a teacher. These images are carried into their first years of teaching and can have a positive or negative impact on teaching experience, depending on how fully aware the student teachers are of these images (Bullough, Knowles, and Crow 1991). Each of us has worked over the years with student teachers who enter their student teaching experience with a vision of themselves that does not mesh at all with the realities of classroom life as we see it. We believe that in our role as educators (as distinct from our role as gatekeepers) we should use our assessment practices to help our student teachers articulate their visions in relation to the context in which they are working. Making these views explicit helps students analyze the relationship between their images of teaching and what they observe happening in classrooms. It can lead them to question these images. As teacher educators we use a variety of means to help students unearth from their own autobiographies their tacit beliefs about teaching and learning; these tools can include reflection papers linking prior and current school experience, philosophy statements, and journals.

However, autobiography is difficult to assess and evaluate when using generic criteria that are designed to apply to all situations in an effort to be public and fair. Questions arise such as whether we should assess students, on some level, for membership in a group or solely for their unique selves. Our students come to us as participants in multiple cultures. What are the implications of looking at a student's progress in becoming a teacher in terms of his or her membership in an ethnic, religious, or linguistic group? How do their backgrounds inform their images of themselves as teachers? We can tease out some of the personal history and knowledge prior to student teaching by reading written autobiographies and asking probing questions on placement applications or in interviews, but it is difficult to define how these qualities should be factored into our assessment of their teaching.

LOOKING AT THE WHOLE

In writing about dilemmas we face as teacher educators, we have been forced to look beyond the narrow confines of our day-to-day tasks to seek a broader understanding of the factors that impact on our work. We have found it necessary to look at the whole of our work to explain how particular choices we make lead us into particular dilemmas. Eisner (1994b) links paying attention to "wholes" in works of art with addressing the entirety of a school as it undergoes evaluation. We believe a similar approach is important when assessing and evaluating student teachers: What is the entire situation in which the student is embedded, and how do we bring to bear our informed connoisseur's knowledge in our assessment of their work?

Complexity and diversity have been continuing themes in our discussion. Our work is made complex by the many participants involved—students, cooperating teachers, supervisors, college faculty; the different contexts in which students learn; and the different evaluation communities in which we are all embedded. In a people-oriented profession such as teacher education, where a range of personal histories and idiosyncratic approaches must be recognized and valued, the context of our evaluation and assessment practices is constantly changing.

We recognize that dilemmas similar to those described in this chapter are being faced by educators who are seeking to reform assessment and evaluation practices in K–12 schools. It seems important that we as teacher educators share with our students the dilemmas we face as teachers of adults to prepare them for the dilemmas they'll face as teachers of children in schools as they strive to make their own assessment and evaluation practices equitable and inclusive. We need to help them understand the nature of dilemmas and how principled teaching can lead into them. They need to see that the decisions they will make in their own classrooms will not be about the right choice or the wrong choice, but about the best choice for a particular child or group of children in a particular context at a particular moment. The diversity of people and cultures and the multiplicity of perspectives and relationships they will experience as classroom teachers suggest that there cannot be hard-and-fast rules.

REFERENCES

Blumer, H. (1969). *Symbolic interactionism.* Englewood Cliffs, NJ: Prentice Hall.

Bullough, R. V., J. G. Knowles, and N. A. Crow (1991). *Emerging as a teacher.* New York: Routledge.

Chittenden, E. (1991). Authentic assessment, evaluation, and documentation of student performance. In V. Perrone (ed.), *Expanding student assessment,* 22–31. Alexandria, VA: Association for Supervision and Curriculum Development.

Cuban, L. (1992). Managing dilemmas while building professional communities. *Educational Researcher 21*(1); 4–11.

Darling-Hammond, L., A. E. Wise, and S. P. Klein (1995). *A license to teach: Building a profession for 21st-century schools.* San Francisco: Westview.

Eisner, E. W. (1994a). *The educational imagination: On the design and evaluation of school programs.* 3d ed. New York: Macmillan.

——— (1994b). *Cognition and curriculum reconsidered.* New York: Teachers College Press.

Hargreaves, A. (1994). *Development and desire: A postmodern perspective.* Paper presented at the Annual Meeting of the American Educational Research Association, New Orleans, LA., April.

Henning-Stout, M. (1994). *Responsive assessment: A new way of thinking about teaching.* San Francisco: Jossey-Bass.

Herman, J. L., P. R. Aschbacher, and L. Winters (1992). *A practical guide to alternative assessment.* Alexandria, VA: Association for Supervision and Curriculum Development.

Holt-Reynolds, D. (1991). *The dialogues of teacher education: Entering and influencing preservice teachers' internal conversations.* East Lansing, MI: National Center for Research on Teacher Learning.

Katz, L. G., and J. Raths (1992). Six dilemmas in teacher education. *Journal of Teacher Education 43*(5); 376–85.

Lampert, M. (1985). How do teachers manage to teach? Perspectives on problems of practice. *Harvard Educational Review 55*(2); 178–94.

Lortie, D. C. (1975). *Schoolteacher: A sociological study.* Chicago: University of Chicago Press.

Chapter Eleven

EDUCATING THE RAINBOW: Authentic Assessment and Authentic Practice for Diverse Classrooms

A. Lin Goodwin and Maritza B. Macdonald

Authentic assessment of what a person thinks, feels, knows, and is able to do is unreliable when the language of assessment is different from the language of the person under assessment, when the assessment tasks lack meaning and cultural relevance for those being assessed, when pedagogy and curricula are poorly aligned with assessment methodology, and when the primary goal of assessment is to measure what learners don't know as opposed to finding out the ways in which they are capable so as to appropriately point them in new instructional directions. If assessment instruments and processes exhibit these difficulties, at best they are unsuitable, at worst they can be cruel and damaging to the children who must undergo them, because the end results will invariably show children in the least positive light. In such cases, issues of ethics and morality, as well as validity and reliability, become paramount because the lives of children are at stake.

Authentic assessments[1] are often described as meaningful and comprehensive measures of what learners know and are able to do. Unlike standardized tests, which are efficient, norm-referenced instruments that separate learning from testing and require learners to produce distinct and correct answers on cue (Wiggins 1993), authentic assessments are characterized by continuous observations of learning, depth and breadth of response, cycles of revision and refinement, students' engagement in self-assessment, and connections between what is being assessed and real-world issues and questions (Einbender and Wood 1995). Standardized testing has a long history of disadvantaging youngsters who are poor or are members of visible racial/ethnic groups (Carter and Goodwin 1994; Darling-Hammond 1995; Garcia and Pearson 1994; Gould 1981; Oakes 1985). Thus, there is a great deal of optimistic anticipation, even in the face of scant evidence, that assessments that represent alternatives to traditional multiple-choice testing will bring about more equitable educational outcomes for children of color (Garcia and Pearson 1994; Gordon and Bonilla-Bowman 1996).

This chapter is about meeting the needs of children, particularly those who represent racial, cultural, linguistic, and social groups that are marginalized in U.S. society and whose experiences are seldom honored by educational institutions. Thus, when we speak of children in this essay, it is these children we are most concerned about and focus on. Our chapter is founded on two basic premises: (1) that if authentic assessment is to result in positive outcomes for diverse school populations, it must happen in the context of shared language, shared meaning, and shared beliefs; and (2) that authentic assessment is dependent upon authentic practice. We define authentic practice as culturally relevant pedagogy (Irvine 1991; Ladson-Billings 1994) that holds children's heritage and home languages in high esteem and centers curriculum and instruction on these qualities and histories. We believe also that authentic practice is grounded in basic assumptions: the right of every child to a rich and meaningful education; the responsibility of schools and teachers to interrupt negative and harmful patterns of behavior in educational and societal contexts that demean and marginalize children of color; the role schools must play in introducing children, especially poor children and children of color, to "cultures of power" (Delpit 1995); and the worthiness of all children. Our discussion begins by first describing why shared language, meaning, and beliefs are central to authentic assessment and what authentic practice looks like in the presence of these important processes. We then share three vignettes of practice that illuminate the kinds of questions teachers can ask themselves when they are working to support the learning of culturally and linguistically diverse children. We end with some final thoughts on authentic assessment.

SHARED LANGUAGE

The idea of shared language can be taken literally—authentic assessment in the context of language difference is not about assessing a child's ability to understand English but about recognizing the ways in which students make sense of the world and derive meaning from the lessons they experience. Language plays a key role in assessment, whether we are talking about traditional or alternative assessments (Sylvan 1994), and many of the newer, alternative assessments tend to "rely heavily on students' ability to read and write standard English" (Garcia and Pearson 1994: 373; see other chapters in this volume by Hilliard, and Savitch and Serling). Indeed, "schools generally do not value skills in any language but standard American English" (Au 1993: 128) and perceive "languages spoken by subordinate groups [as] inferior or 'broken' versions of [the] dominant-group language" (129). In fact, the inability to speak standard English is oftentimes equated with low levels of cognitive functioning; linguistically diverse children are often then relegated to the lower or nonacademic tracks and offered watered-down curricula (Moll 1991) even while their bilingualism is used as a "scapegoat" for their poor academic achievement (Cummins 1995). It follows then that children whose first language is other than English or children who are bidialectical will not suddenly perform at levels higher than they did previously if authentic assessments fail to take into account their language needs and strengths.

We acknowledge that teachers who speak the home language of the children with whom they work are at a decided advantage when there is a language difference. However, the lack of a common spoken language does not absolve teachers from their fundamental responsibility to provide a meaningful education. Language differences should not interfere with teachers' interactions with all children; communication and understanding involve more than similar language. What should teachers do? First, teachers must fully comprehend the sociopolitical context within which language operates. Thus, they must aim to provide children "with discourse patterns, interactional styles, and spoken and written language codes that will allow them success in the larger society" (Delpit 1995: 29). This is not to suggest that an "English only" climate should permeate the classroom; "proficiency in standard American English should be seen as a goal, *not* as a prerequisite to becoming literate" (Au 1993: 129). Instead, children's home languages should be used as foundations for instruction in mainstream forms of expression. Cummins (1995) and others call this the "additive" versus the "subtractive" approach to literacy, where children are encouraged to develop proficiency in both home and school languages. Doing this requires that teachers see children as more than their language "problem" (see Smith and Goodwin in this volume) and recognize that children are multiply intelligent (Gardner 1983), have many fully developed and yet-to-be-tapped capacities, and are already good thinkers and reasoners in their own languages (Au 1993). Consequently, bilingualism, bidialecticalism, and facility in a language other than English should be seen as positive traits that add depth and quality to classroom instruction and benefit monolingual as well as other bilingual children.

Authentic practice with children who are ELLs (English Language Learners—see Genishi in this volume) involves providing children with multiple opportunities to explain their world—through movement, art, talk, storytelling, building, creating, and the like—and supporting them to then use language, both home and new, to explain what they have done. It also means reconfiguring the classroom so that a variety of interactional styles can be accommodated and children are encouraged to communicate without the discomfort of being singled out (Au 1993; Duran 1994; Jordan 1985). However, changes in classroom interaction patterns must not result in children having fewer encounters with their teacher even while they increase interactions with their peers. Individual conferences enable both teacher and child to become more intimate and to teach each other and engage in cultural exchange. Authentic practice also means being explicit about language as cultural capital, that there are ways of speaking that this society prizes and that enable academic and economic success. In her book *Other People's Children*, Lisa Delpit witnessed a Native Alaskan teacher of Athabaskan

Indian students speaking very explicitly about the differences between "Formal" or "Village English" and "Heritage Language or English" spoken by the children. She then proceeded to deliberately develop the children's formal English while simultaneously respecting and building upon their home vernacular.

Finally, authentic practice entails inviting parents, families, and communities to participate in literacy instruction. Stories, tales of lived experiences, community and real-life issues, discussions about important events and traditions that include those who play significant roles in the lives of children can all become classroom texts as children expand and recreate their worlds. This kind of openness to personal storytelling (Miller and Mehler 1994) gives "audibility to numerous voices seldom heard before . . . [and penetrates] the so-called 'cultures of silence'" (Greene 1988, cited in Dyson and Genishi 1994: 4).

Authentic assessment can emerge naturally within an environment that attends to the instructional strategies outlined above. If children are provided multiple ways to demonstrate knowledge, then teachers are given multiple inroads to children's thinking and capabilities. Authentic literacy assessment sees children as whole and so examines their language in similarly complete ways not by simply focusing on grammatical errors and spelling (although these skills are critical) but also by taking note of meaning making, comprehension, and the ability to extrapolate from classroom texts in order to relate new understandings to other situations. The authentic assessment of ELLs and bidialectical children demands that they be allowed and supported to use their home language as a conceptual scaffold for ideas expressed in the mainstream language. Children can compose books in their own languages, create their own translation dictionaries, use their home languages to grasp and then explain the essence of text as a way to bridge the distance between home and unfamiliar vocabulary.

Teachers who engage in authentic practice and assessment are able to do so because they are cognizant of the many variables that must be considered when assessing second-language learners. Issues of time, comfort levels, and authority must be taken into account; linguistically and culturally diverse children will benefit from additional time to complete assessments and assignments, and they will need to feel comfortable with the adult with whom they are working. Teachers also need to be aware of different culturally based rules of authority governing adult-child relationships. Many children from diverse cultural groups may be taught to defer to adults, to wait until they are asked to speak, or to respond only to the question that is asked. Behaviors such as offering opinions, speaking without invitation, interrupting to insert one's own thoughts, or embellishing responses is more typical of white, middle-class discourse. Thus, in assessing children who not only are speakers of languages other than English but also may be operating according to different cultural norms, teachers will need to use sensitively phrased questions and keen listening in order to allow children's knowledge to surface. Finally, since many children who are second-language learners are also immigrants, assessment that is authentic acknowledges aspects of the immigrant experience that may affect achievement and children's sense of themselves.

Aspects of this experience include such things as isolation, culture shock, the push-pull of assimilation, vulnerability, feeling uprooted, balancing two cultural realities, and silence as a self-protective measure (Igoa 1995). The flexibility, variety, and adaptability (Garcia and Pearson 1994) of authentic assessment does allow teachers to design assessments that can separate second-language competency from competency in other areas and can provide insights into children's learning over time through the use of numerous modalities. Because authentic assessments have the potential to be both comprehensive and personal, they help to ensure that children's feelings, fears, and levels of confidence are taken into account, and they allow teachers to tap into the rich cultural knowledge base that children of color possess.

SHARED MEANING

Shared meaning connotes the existence of mutual understanding between teachers and students, between school and home communities, between the culture of the classroom and the cultures that children bring into the classroom. If teachers and students do not speak the same cultural language, their ability to share meaning is diminished. In the absence of continuous communication between school and home communities, there exist few opportunities for meaning sharing and exchange. When the culture of the classroom is foreign to and rejects the cultural heritage of students, then students are silenced, and shared meaning making is impeded. In the absence of shared meaning, authentic assessment cannot help but be hampered by teachers' inabilities to come to know children intimately or to meet their educational needs appropriately.

There has been much written about the need for more "minority" teachers to instruct the growing numbers of "minority" children (Goodwin 1991; King 1993). Despite recruitment efforts to attract more teachers of color, the fact remains that the teaching profession continues to be predominantly white, and that European Americans are teaching children of color in increasing numbers (Dilworth 1990; Fuller 1992; Grant and Secada 1990; Research About Teacher Education Project 1990). Thus, all teachers, those from the dominant group as well as those from visible racial/ethnic groups, must necessarily be culturally responsive (Irvine 1991). We do not assume that white teachers are not able to reach culturally and linguistically diverse learners or that teachers of color automatically are (Delpit 1995), but wish to underscore the deliberate measures teachers must take to ensure that they value, learn about, and understand the culturally diverse children they teach.

Numerous investigations have sought to discern the mediating influence of race and culture on visible racial/ethnic-group children's ways of knowing and sense making. Huber and Pewewardy (1990) conducted an extensive review of research examining cultural cognitive styles that concluded with the notion that different racial and ethnic groups display numerous cognitive, learning style, and communicative preferences. Researchers and scholars have theorized that the differential school experiences and academic achievements of children of color may be attributed to a mismatch between the culture of the school and the home cultures of pupils. This concept has been variously described as "bicultural ambivalence" (Cummins 1986), "cultural discontinuity or incongruence" (Nieto 1992), and an absence of "cultural synchronization" (Irvine 1991). These theories raise the possibility that culturally and linguistically diverse children may learn in culture-specific ways and may require instruction that capitalizes on their learning styles and strengths rather than emphasizes their "deficits." These theories also suggest that

> the manner in which children of color receive, manipulate, transform, and express knowledge, as well as their task and modality preferences and the ways in which they interact and communicate with others, may not be well explained by mainstream learning theory traditionally grounded in White children's ways of knowing. (Carter and Goodwin 1994: 319)

Notwithstanding the growing body of evidence that supports the idea of culturally grounded learning styles (cf. Dunn and Griggs 1990; Gay 1991; Irvine 1991; Ramirez and Castenada 1974; Shade 1982), it would be unwise for teachers to rush to categorize children according to learning style preference or to use these theories as rigid indicators of how culturally diverse children learn, simply because much of what we now know is inconclusive and untested (Carter and Goodwin 1994; Ladson-Billings 1992). The lesson teachers can and should take from this body of literature is that they will need to build cultural bridges that span home and school communities so that children experience greater continuity between these two contexts and are not forced to "enter school having to unlearn or, at least, to modify their own culturally sanctioned interactional and behavioral styles and adopt those styles rewarded in the school context if they wish to achieve academic success" (Fordham 1988: 55). One of the best examples of this is the Kamehameha Elementary Education Program (KEEP), where ethnographic data gathered from Hawaiian children's home communities were used to achieve "cultural compatibility . . . a school program compatible with the culture of Hawaiian children *in ways that . . . make the program educationally effective*" (Jordan 1985: 109). Substantive research documenting this effort has indicated that Hawaiian children's achievement levels rose as a consequence.

What does this all mean in terms of authentic practice? Primarily, it means that teachers must take it upon themselves to immerse themselves in the community and must define the classroom as an extension of the community as opposed to apart from it (see Smith and Goodwin in this volume). It also means that teachers should allow children's families and caregivers to teach them about the children. Too often, schools and educators establish themselves as the sole experts about children and learning, forgetting that the children they teach are connected to an entire group of people who know these children best and to a way of life that matters to each child. In addition, teachers who engage in authentic practice understand that different ways of knowing can only be nurtured and supported by different methodologies, a wide range of activities, differentiated instruction, deep caring for the uniqueness of each child, and the creation of an inviting classroom family (Purkey and Novak 1984) that values the contribution of each member. Finally, authentic practice is based on curricula that incorporate the cultural experiences of children. Typically, however, this is taken to mean adding ethnic heroes and literature to a curriculum grounded in European American cultural and intellectual traditions, or celebrating "ethnic" holidays in isolation (Banks 1988; Goodwin forthcoming). In contrast, a curriculum that embodies cultural inclusion and social activism is "developmentally appropriate and culturally authentic. . . . [It] integrate[s] multicultural education into different academic disciplines,. . . creates an awareness of how student evaluation and assessment is interpretive and contextual, and it includes parent participation" (Grant and Gomez 1996: 10). Sleeter and Grant term this approach "Education that is Multicultural and Social Reconstructionist" (Sleeter and Grant 1987) because it uses the lives of students and of visible racial/ethnic-group people as starting points for discussions about oppression and emphasizes the empowerment of learners to bring about social change in their own lives and the lives of others.

Curricula and classroom practices that accentuate multiple viewpoints and ways of knowing as well as the empowerment of students of color must be accompanied by assessments that acknowledge that there are many routes to similar outcomes, and that knowledge is situational and culturally bound. A vignette illustrates this point best.

> Lena's classroom has been studying animals and the discussion has turned to zoos. For one of the assignments, children use drawings to depict their definitions of "zoo." One child, Kavemuii from Namibia, draws animals in a big, open, green, and gold field. The other children notice and begin to tease him, saying that he doesn't know anything about zoos. Lena notices and begins a discussion about how zoos came to be and why Kavemuii's drawing is so different from those of the other children. Through the discussion, the children come to understand that countries like the United States build zoos to house animals that are not indigenous to the country; zoos are designed to display animals in habitats that are made by humans and in areas that are inhabitable to animals. In Kavemuii's experience, animal habitats are very different; "zoos" are the open plains where animals live free and not in cages.

This incident illustrates how knowledge is personal, contextual, and cultural. If Lena had not been a skilled practitioner, Kavemuii would have had to endure the mockery of the other children, he would have been told that his definition of zoo was incorrect, and he would have gradually learned not to trust his own knowledge. Authentic assessment in a culture of shared meaning and shared meaning making assumes that children possess much knowledge. The purpose of instruction and assessment is to support them first to reveal what they know and then to guide them to compare, relate, or apply what they know to new information and experiences. Authentic assessment should enable children to demonstrate knowing in a variety of ways and cautions against relying unduly on single modes of expression to the exclusion of other means. Last, authentic assessment enables children to integrate what they know through tasks that connect them personally to content and allows them to ask their own questions through critical inquiry. Authentic assessment in a culture of shared meaning requires that teachers first assume that they may not know and will need to use observation, close listening, and careful questioning to gather more information before they deem children's responses as incorrect.

Shared Beliefs

Finally, authentic assessment is dependent upon shared beliefs in children's inherent capacities to learn and achieve academic success, in students' communities and families as rich resources and equal partners in the educational process, and in the ultimate responsibility of education professionals and institutions to serve as advocates to ensure educational equity for and access to all children, notably poor children and children of color. If schools and educators subscribe to deficit views of children and their families, attribute learners' shortcomings to social or background variables, and fail to be accountable for the academic progress and development of all children, then authentic assessment cannot be possible.

Much has been written about teacher expectations and the detrimental effect that low or inappropriate expectations can have on student achievement (Brophy and Good 1986; Good and Brophy 1984; Irvine 1991; Ortiz 1988). Indeed, there is a growing body of literature that describes the relationship between teacher beliefs, assumptions, attitudes, and preconceptions and teacher behavior (Clark and Peterson 1986; Goodwin 1994; Goodwin in press; Rios 1996). There is also ample evidence that children of color are less likely to have positive experiences in schools or with teachers (Aaron and Powell 1982; Fine 1991; Garibaldi 1988; Nieto 1992; Simpson and Erickson 1983), are more likely to be assigned to the lowest academic or special education tracks (College Board 1985; Goodlad 1984; Hilliard 1990; Oakes 1985), and are frequently subjected to undemanding, unenriched curricula (Collins 1982; Garcia and Pearson 1991; Moll 1991; Oakes and Lipton 1990; Walsh 1987). What seems clear is that a teacher's belief in children's capacity to learn and worthiness has a bearing on the quality of instruction children receive. While children of color should be perceived as efficacious, capable, and unique by their teachers, in reality they are more typically seen as incapable, inferior, and invisible. This is implicit in the labels assigned to children of color (and their families)—at risk, limited English proficient, disadvantaged, culturally deprived, developmentally delayed, dysfunctional, underclass—and the less-than-high-class education they are offered.

Authentic practice and assessment are possible only when teachers believe that children who are culturally and linguistically diverse can and must learn, are fully capable, and will benefit from instruction that is meaningful and rich with powerful ideas. Families and communities send the best children they have to schools; children enter kindergarten curious and ready to learn; mothers and fathers believe in their children and in their potential to achieve; teachers have to share these beliefs and assume responsibility to make positive things happen for children in school. Too often, children are blamed for their own failures, for their poverty, for their lack of facility with English; too often poor, working-class parents are defined as uncaring, unsupportive, or disinterested in education. Teachers can and will find many convenient reasons for children's lack of success, unless they look closely and critically at themselves and their own practices and assume that they are the ones who must do something differently—not the children. This is not easy, and it means "being willing to see [oneself] in the unflattering light of another's angry gaze. It is not easy but it is the only way to learn what it might feel like to be someone else and the only way to start the dialogue" (Delpit 1995: 46–47). What is clear in the end is that in the absence of shared beliefs, shared language and shared meaning will elude us.

PORTRAITS OF AUTHENTIC PRACTICE AND ASSESSMENT

The three vignettes we present below describe teachers whose habits of observation, recording, and searching for repeated evidence before making judgments help them assess students' capabilities and strengths. Each of these teachers seems to reject a one-size-fits-all approach to assessment. Each in different ways tries to build scaffolds that help students move from the familiar to the new. Andrew deals with language differences, Jennifer with individual versus group work, while Miguel searches for balance between performance demonstrations and written/visual demonstrations of knowledge. We see in their approaches that they are keeping a close eye on the students rather than emphasizing one particular method of assessment.

Vignette One

Andrew, who teaches a combined first- and second-grade class, is concerned with literacy issues for children who speak languages other than English. He has a strong belief in the teacher's role as translator of culture, of language, and of institutions for newcomers. He acts on the belief that if these students' encounters with a new language and culture are positive, they will more likely be able to demonstrate what they bring from their previous experiences and they will find their place in a new setting. His own family traveled a great deal when he was a child, and as a result issues of socialization into a new setting are central to his teaching.

Last year, Andrew had students who had recently immigrated from Russia, China, and several Spanish-speaking countries. He describes his approach to assessment in the following way:

I have to determine early in the year what these students bring in relation to literacy in their home language. I want to know if they recognize symbols, words, or labels for different concepts in their languages. I know basic greetings in several languages, and whenever possible I introduce these students to other children or adults in the school who also speak their language. In the first month of school I try to create an atmosphere of curiosity about language, symbols, letters, and sounds for all of my students. Students who are not new to this country, as well as those who are, need to become comfortable with trying out new sounds, exploring new situations, and being able to show what they already know. Based on my observations during the first weeks when I try to "catch them" reading pictures, symbols, or words, I try to support what children already know while simultaneously fostering curiosity about what they have yet to know. For me it is about creating an environment where they all can find themselves. For example, last year I decided to get a series of picture dictionaries in the various languages spoken by children in the class. I bought picture dictionaries in Russian/English, Spanish/English, and Mandarin/English. After the first week of school I realized I had to order a book on Cantonese pronunciations because one of the Chinese students spoke Cantonese and I have only had experience with Mandarin. I want students to see that languages are written using various types of alphabets and characters, that words are written in different directions, some from left to right, others from top to bottom, and some from right to left. I have found that the students develop an awareness about directionality and about the various alphabets. When speaking some Asian languages it is important also to pay attention to tonality, because words that are pronounced the same way change in meaning according to the tone that is used.

Last year I introduced the different dictionaries at one of our whole class meetings and I displayed them in the library area of our classroom. I always have a composition notebook where I write down any evidence of literacy I observe in the first three weeks. According to my notes, my first observations of Maura and Ivan, the two Russian students, describe them using the Renyi Russian-English Picture Dictionary. The next day before class started I observed them finding pictures of classroom items and then copying the Russian and the English labels on pieces of paper. From those lists I concluded that they were interested in learning the English names of these familiar objects. Later on in the day I gave them construction paper and I modeled making a sign for the "Library." They made signs for the teacher, the desk, and the board and tacked them around the room. Then, several English speakers volunteered to make signs in Russian. Two weeks later Maura is teaching three English-speaking girls how to say the days of the week in Russian and she is learning them in English. They asked me to photocopy certain pages from the dictionary to take home, and one day they cut out photocopied pages to put together sentences. At the end of the month we had an alphabet strip with letters in three languages. In my notes I have listed the names of students who made comments and observations about the two rows of alphabets with similar letters such as in English and Spanish. Maura taught us all to say the names of the thirty-three Russian letters and Ivan continued to make labels in English words. By November I had gathered a great deal of information about the new English learners' level of literacy in their own language, how they were using what they already knew about language to build their English skills, and how they were progressing in English. I also have recorded the English-speakers making associations with and contrasts about the names of letters, their shapes, and their sounds, and the most reassuring thing was that all children transgressed language barriers to work as a group as they decoded each other's meanings.

Vignette Two

Jennifer focuses on observing and recording students' interpersonal and intrapersonal preferences as a way to determine how her fourth-grade students approach individual and group tasks. Jennifer's class is racially and culturally heterogeneous, and she has found that Gardner's (1983) perspectives on interpersonal and intrapersonal preferences serve as lenses through which she can assess how diverse children approach different situations. During the early part of the year, she gives students choices for doing tasks, playing, or working alone or with others. She takes notes of their responses. She notices how some children always choose to work alone while others like to be with someone else. She notices how when some children need help, they go and ask someone else, while others will only approach her. She writes down what they do on the playground, who plays with whom, and the kinds of activities children seem to prefer. She pays attention to gender, language, and race so as to discern if these variables are relevant in the interactions children do and do not engage in. She also notices the children who ask questions in the middle of a lesson to clarify something they do not understand and keeps track of the ones who will ask questions only after she has made statements such as, "If there is something you don't understand, please ask now because you might have some difficulty doing the assignments." She works at finding a balance between what she perceives as an overwhelming emphasis on group work in the elementary grades and the importance she places on individual work.

In talking about her emphasis on assessing inter- and intrapersonal preferences, Jennifer explains the following:

I think that in the upper elementary grades, students need to know what they can accomplish on their own and what they can accomplish with others. I also like them to develop ways of searching for answers and asking for help. I find that I have to model how to do this, but unless I first assess how children work if left to their own devices, I won't know how best to help them. I think that sometimes there is such emphasis on putting children in groups that it is easy to overlook children's ideas and personal interests in content. I try to assess what intellectually intrigues the children and then I help them work independently or in groups related to that interest. To do this, I schedule regular individual conferences with students so that they can just tell me about themselves, how they feel school is going for them, what they feel they are doing well, and what they need to work more on. Later on in the year I help them work within groups across interests; this structure enables my students to inform one another, exchange perspectives, and come to see each other as valuable resources. I like to see students work on individual projects and balance that personal passion with group tasks. However, I don't feel anymore that group work is the most appropriate for all students and at all times. That would be using the same method for all the students, and losing track of the individual student.

Vignette Three

Miguel, who teaches Californian sixth graders, believes in multiple forms of learning and of demonstrating knowledge. He uses a three-modality approach: paper-and-pencil journal entries, researching factual information, and model making for any project or assignment he gives. Like Jennifer, who reacts to the overemphasis on group assignments, Miguel reacts to what he perceives as an overemphasis on performances and demonstrations. His pupils are primarily Mexican and Filipino American, and his experiences with these learners have shown him that they know and learn in diverse ways. Thus, requiring children to demonstrate knowledge in just one way privileges some who may feel more comfortable with or who have had more practice in certain forms of expression, and excludes others. He feels that if each assignment or project encompasses the three modalities, it is then possible to honor those who do well in presentations as well as those who do better with written and visual forms.

In describing how he had assigned a project on the study of Ohlone Indians to his students, Miguel explained that he had asked them all to use multiple sources to find twenty facts about the group, to depict something (through building, drawing, story writing, etc.) of importance to the group, to write about why they think it is important to study this community, and what they would like to ask a member of this particular community if they had the opportunity. All students had to complete all four parts of the assignment because Miguel feels strongly that children all need to be guided to develop important skills and to become more confident about working in different ways. However, students were then given a choice of how to present their findings and new understandings, first to classmates and later to family members, who were invited to their more polished presentations. The choice was an oral presentation or a museum exhibit that would allow viewers to independently access information without a verbal presentation. For Miguel, these assessments and choices gave students the opportunity to present their knowledge in ways that were better for them. The opportunity to practice their presentations and receive feedback enabled students to do their best work and helped them understand the value of revision and different points of view. Miguel explained that, in time, these individual assignments become the foundation for experimenting in other areas. Later, students work together to combine their expertise and support one another in trying out new behaviors that may be less familiar or comfortable but so much easier to attempt once children have achieved some success and confidence.

A Final Word on Authentic Assessment

Each of the vignettes represents a real teacher who is striving to do two things: (1) learn as much about students as possible and (2) provide students with multiple entry points to learning. For these teachers, children are empowered by knowing and doing, and so teachers define their role as providing the supports and structures necessary to help children behave and see themselves as learners who are in control of the learning process. Much has been written about different kinds of authentic assessments—portfolios, performances, demonstrations, exhibitions. These are all worthwhile activities that enable students to reveal what they know in numerous ways. However, in the absence of authentic practice undergirded by deep knowledge of students, these activities will be hollow. Thus, what is most critical for teachers to understand when working with children in general, and diverse learners in particular, is that "assessment is an attitude before it is a method" (Chittenden 1991: 29). Authentic assessment begins with teachers making it their business to purposefully watch, listen to, talk with, and think about the children in their classrooms. By observing, recording, informally monitoring, conferencing with, and interviewing their students, teachers initiate an ongoing process that uncovers who learners are and what they know, and that leads to opportunities for teachers and children to build shared language, meaning, and beliefs. But it is more than simply gathering data about children; it is allowing children to get inside you so that you can never look at them in other than the most caring and positive ways. In the end, Lisa Delpit says it best: to be this kind of authentic practitioner "takes a very special kind of listening, listening that requires not only open eyes and ears, but open hearts and minds. We do not really see through our eyes or hear through our ears, but through our beliefs" (1995: 46).

NOTE

1. This chapter uses the term authentic assessment to depict holistic assessments that are embedded in classroom contexts and enable children to demonstrate learning by integrating and applying knowledge and skills to real-world tasks. However, it is important to acknowledge that a variety of terms exist in the literature that are either used interchangeably with or are presented as examples of authentic assessment. These include: performance assessment, alternative

assessment, portfolio assessment, situated assessment, dynamic assessment, curriculum-embedded assessment, and assessment by exhibition (Garcia and Pearson 1994).

REFERENCES

Aaron, R., and G. Powell (1982). Feedback practices as a function of teacher pupil race during reading groups instruction. *Journal of Negro Education 51*; 50–59.

Au, K. H. (1993). *Literacy instruction in multicultural settings*. Fort Worth, TX: Harcourt Brace College Publishers.

Banks, J. A. (1988). *Multiethnic education,* 2d ed. Boston: Allyn and Bacon.

Brophy, J. L., and T. L. Good (1986). Teacher behavior and student achievement. In M. C. Wittrock (ed.), *Handbook of research on teaching*, 3d ed., 328–75. New York: Macmillan.

Carter, R. T., and A. L. Goodwin (1994). Racial identity and education. In L. Darling-Hammond (ed.), *Review of Research in Education*, vol. 20, 291–336. Washington, DC: American Educational Research Association.

Chittenden, E. (1991). Authentic assessment, evaluation and documentation. In V. Perrone (ed.), *Expanding student assessment*, 22–31. Aleaxandria, VA: Association for Supervision and Curriculum Development.

Clark, C. M., and P. L. Peterson (1986). Teachers' thought processes. In M. C. Wittrock (ed.), *Handbook of research on teaching*, 3d ed., 255–96. New York: Macmillan.

College Board. (1985). *Equality and excellence: The educational status of Black Americans*. New York: Author.

Collins, J. (1982). Discourse styles, classroom interaction and differential treatment. *Journal of Reading Behavior 14*; 429–37.

Cummins, J. (1986). Empowering minority students: A framework for intervention. *Harvard Educational Review 56*; 18–36.

——— (1995). Underachievement among minority students. In D. B. Durkin (ed.), *Language issues: Readings for teachers*, 130–59. White Plains, NY: Longman.

Darling-Hammond, L. (1995). Inequality and access to knowledge. In J. A. Banks (ed.), *Handbook of Research on Multicultural Education*, 465–83. New York: Macmillan.

Delpit, L. (1995). *Other people's children*. New York: New Press.

Dilworth, M. E. (1990). *Reading between the lines: Teachers and their racial/ethnic cultures*. Teacher Education Monograph No. 11. Washington, DC: American Association of Colleges for Teacher Education.

Dunn, R., and S. A. Griggs (1990). Research on the learning style characteristics of selected racial and ethnic groups. *Journal of Reading, Writing, and Learning Disabilities International 6*; 261–80.

Duran, R. P. (1994). Cooperative learning for language-minority students. In R. A.

DeVillar, C. J. Faltis, and J. P. Cummins (eds.), *Cultural diversity in schools*, 145–60. Albany: State University of New York Press.

Dyson, A. H., and C. S. Genishi (1994). Introduction: The need for story. In A. H. Dyson and C. S. Genishi (eds.), *The need for story: Cultural diversity in classroom and community*, 1–10. Urbana, IL: National Council of Teachers of English.

Einbender, L., and D. Wood (1995). *An authentic journey: Teachers' emergent understandings about authentic assessment and practice*. New York: National Center for Restructuring Education, Schools and Teaching.

Fine, M. (1991). *Framing dropouts: Notes on the politics of an urban public school*. Albany: State University of New York Press.

Fordham, S. (1988). Racelessness as a factor in Black students' school success: Pragmatic strategy or pyrrhic victory? *Harvard Educational Review 58*; 54–84.

Fuller, M. L. (1992). Teacher education programs and increasing minority school populations: An educational mismatch? In C. A. Grant (ed.), *Research and multicultural education*, 184–202. London: Falmer.

Garcia, G. E., and P. D. Pearson (1991). Modifying reading instruction to maximize its effectiveness for "all" students. In M. S. Knapp and P. M. Shields (eds.), *Better schooling for the children of poverty*, 31–60. Berkeley, CA: McCutchan.

———— (1994). Assessment and diversity. In L. Darling-Hammond (ed.), *Review of Research in Education*, vol. 20, 337–92. Washington, DC: American Educational Research Association.

Gardner, H. (1983). *Frames of mind*. New York: Basic Books.

Garibaldi, A. M. (1988). *Educating Black male youth: A moral and civic imperative*. New Orleans: New Orleans Public Schools.

Gay, G. (1991). Culturally diverse students and social studies. In J. P. Shaver (ed.), *Handbook of research on social studies education*, 144–56. New York: Macmillan.

Good, T. L., and J. Brophy (1984). *Looking in classrooms*, 3d ed. New York: Harper & Row.

Goodlad, J. I. (1984). *A place called school*. New York: McGraw-Hill.

Goodwin, A. L. (1991). Problems, process and promise: Reflections on a collaborative approach to the minority teacher shortage. *Journal of Teacher Education 42*; 28–36.

———— (1994). Making the transition from self to other: What do preservice teachers really think about multicultural education. *Journal of Teacher Education 45*(2); 119–30.

———— (in press). Historical and contemporary perspectives on multicultural teacher education: Past lessons, new directions. In J. King, E. R. Hollins, and W. Hayman (eds.), *Meeting the challenge of diversity in teacher preparation*. New York: Teachers College Press.

———— (forthcoming, March 1997). Multicultural stories: Preservice teachers' conceptions and responses to issues of diversity. *Urban Education 32*; 1.

Gordon, E. W., and C. Bonilla-Bowman (1996). Can performance-based assessments contribute to the achievement of educational equity? In J. B. Baron and

D. P. Wolf (eds.), *Performance-based student assessment: Challenges and possibilities.* Ninety-fifth Yearbook of the National Society for the Study of Education. Part I, 32–51.

Gould, S. J. (1981). *The mismeasure of man.* New York: Norton.

Grant, C. A., and M. L. Gomez (1996). *Making schooling multicultural.* Englewood Cliffs, NJ: Merrill.

Grant, C. A., and W. G. Secada (1990). Preparing teachers for diversity. In W. R. Houston (ed.), *Handbook of research on teacher education,* 403–22. New York: Macmillan.

Greene, M. (1988). *The dialectic of freedom.* New York: Teachers College Press.

Hilliard, A. G., III (1990). Misunderstanding and testing intelligence. In J. I. Goodlad and P. Keating (eds.), *Access to knowledge,* 145–58. New York: College Board.

Huber, T., and C. Pewewardy (1990). *Maximizing learning for all students: A review of literature on learning modalities, cognitive styles and approaches to meeting the needs of diverse learners.* (ERIC No. ED 324 289.)

Igoa, C. (1995). *The inner world of the immigrant child.* New York: St. Martin's.

Irvine, J. J. (1991). *Black students and school failure.* New York: Praeger.

Jordan, C. (1985). Translating culture: From ethnographic information to educational program. *Anthropology and Education Quarterly 16;* 105–23.

King, S. H. (1993). The limited presence of African American teachers. *Review of Educational Research 63*(2); 115–49.

Ladson-Billings, G. (1992). Culturally relevant teaching: The key to making multicultural education work. In C. A. Grant (ed.), *Research and multicultural education,* 106–21. London: Falmer.

——— (1994). *The dreamkeepers: Successful teachers of African American children.* San Francisco: Jossey-Bass.

Miller, P. J., and R. A. Mehler (1994). The power of personal storytelling in families and kindergartens. In A. H. Dyson and C. S. Genishi (eds.), *The need for story: Cultural diversity in classroom and community,* 38–56. Urbana, IL: National Council of Teachers of English.

Moll, L. C. (1991). Social and instructional issues in literacy instruction of "disadvantaged" students. In M. S. Knapp and P. M. Shields (eds.), *Better schooling for children of poverty,* 61–84. Berkeley, CA: McCutchan.

Nieto, S. (1992). *Affirming diversity.* New York: Longman.

Oakes, J. (1985). *Keeping track: How schools structure inequality.* New Haven, CT: Yale University Press.

Oakes, J., and M. Lipton (1990). Tracking and ability grouping: A structural barrier to access and achievement. In J. I. Goodlad and P. Keating (eds.), *Access to knowledge,* 187–204. New York: College Board.

Ortiz, F. L. (1988). Hispanic-American children's experiences in classrooms: A comparison between Hispanic and non-Hispanic children. In L. Weis (ed.), *Class, race, and gender in American education,* 63–86. Albany: State University of New York Press.

Purkey, W. W., and J. M. Novak (1984). *Inviting school success,* 2d ed. Belmont, CA: Wadsworth.

Ramirez, M., III, and A. Castaneda (1974). *Cultural democracy, bicognitive development and education.* New York: Academic.

Research About Teacher Education Project (1990). *RATE IV: Teaching teachers: Facts and figures.* Washington, DC: American Association of Colleges for Teacher Education.

Rios, F. A. (1996). *Teacher thinking in cultural contexts.* Albany: State University of New York Press.

Shade, B. J. (1982). Afro-American cognitive style: A variable in school success? *Review of Educational Research 52*; 219–44.

Simpson, A. W., and M. T. Erickson (1983). Teachers' verbal and non-verbal communication patterns as a function of teacher race, student gender, and student race. *American Educational Research Journal 20*; 269–88.

Sleeter, C. E., and C. A. Grant (1987). An analysis of multicultural education in the United States. *Harvard Educational Review 57*; 421–44.

Sylvan, C. E. (1994). Assessment in a multilingual school: The International high school. *Educational Forum 59*; 74–80.

Walsh, C. (1987). Schooling and the civic exclusion of Latinos: Toward a discord of dissonance. *Journal of Education 169*; 115–31.

Wiggins, G. P. (1993). *Assessing student performance.* San Francisco: Jossey-Bass.

Chapter Twelve

LANGUAGE, CULTURE, AND THE ASSESSMENT OF AFRICAN AMERICAN CHILDREN

Asa G. Hilliard III

Teaching and learning are rooted in and are dependent upon a common language between teacher and student. Language is rooted in and is an aspect of culture. Culture is nothing, more nor less, than the shared ways that groups of people have created to use and define their environment. All people, every group of people on the face of the earth, have created culture. Therefore, they have also created language, which is included in culture. Children all over the world learn to speak the language of their cultural group at about the age of two. Teaching and learning is a worldwide phenomenon. The teaching function and the learning function have occurred in every culture on earth. It is natural and not the exclusive property of any group or groups. Teaching and learning—the transmission of cultural heritage—is as old as the human family. All cultures are intellectually complicated and cognitively demanding.

Teaching and learning are also rooted in environments that are shaped by politics. For example, the United States was created as a slave nation, complete with deliberate designs to prevent the education of slaves. The designs included measures that would curtail the behavior of teachers and learners, as well as measures that would create certain beliefs to justify that curtailment. For example, the belief in and the ideology of white supremacy have led to the development of an ideology that says that genetically, whites are intellectually superior and people of color inferior. This thinking has resulted in a greater segregation of students in schools and disproportionate placement of people of color in certain categories of special education (College Board 1985; Goodlad 1984; Guthrie 1979; Hilliard 1990, 1996; Oakes & Lipton 1990).

A review of the documents that show just how pervasive was the influence of such academic disciplines as history, geography, religion, biology, psychology, anthropology, sociology, and linguistics in the creation and teaching of racist beliefs (Carter and Goodwin 1994; Chase 1977; Kamin 1974). The legacy of these beliefs remains with us today, often wearing the cloak of scientific legitimacy. Africans were said by some historians to have had no history, by linguists to have had inferior language, by political scientists to have had poor self-government, by psychologists to have had low intelligence, by biologists to have had inferior genes, and by theologians to have had no soul—among other things (Guthrie 1976; Hegel 1831; Turner 1969). These views were enshrined in the scientific literature of recent decades. They were taught in universities and colleges. And so, through no fault of the slaves, unprovoked, systematic, and pervasive oppression was instituted and maintained with the help of those many in education who were most responsible for freedom (Anderson 1988; King 1971; Spivey 1978).

LANGUAGE, CULTURE, OPPRESSION, AND AFRICAN AMERICANS

And so, we have before us today culture and pedagogy issues, one of which is the issue of culture and assessment. Valid assessment is thought to be a part of the design of valid pedagogy; yet this is a culturally plural society with political problems based on culture. That issue must be handled in terms of a total context. Language, culture, history, and oppression are inextricably linked together where African American children are concerned. To attempt to analyze assessment practice by reference to language or culture alone will doom such analyses to failure. Indeed, it might well result in data that support beliefs and behaviors which would make matters worse than they already are for African American children. It is the purpose of this essay to identify certain important language issues and to suggest prerequisites for the constructs of valid assessment.

It cannot be denied that African American children are not achieving at optimal levels in the schools of the nation. Neither can it be denied that there is a need for African American children to learn languages and content other than that which many have already learned up to now. The real problem we are forced to confront is this: Can we be explicit about how professional practice can be made to perform the normal and expected function of facilitating the natural healthy learning processes of children? In particular, how can the assessment process be purified so as to operate in the service of African American children rather than against them?

I speak of African American children and not "minority," "at risk," "disadvantaged," "culturally or otherwise deprived," or even "Black," except as it is equivalent in meaning to African American. The reasons for this are scientific rather than either ideological or political. Of the terms above, only "African-American" suggests the need to refer to children's *antecedents, ethnicity,* and *cultural environmental experiences* for explanations and interpretations of a group of people. For example, what are the historical antecedents of a "minority"? I intend to show that it is the failure of scholarship to take history and culture into account that distorts scientific study. Failing to deal with the existence of oppression and its impact will result in a further distortion of study.

Perhaps it is the limited cultural experience of so many U.S. scholars that renders cultural data "invisible." Perhaps at a deeper level there is some white guilt about racial oppression, including oppression through the invalid use of tests, and a sense of impotence to change the systems that serve those ends at the base of the problem of how to make the healthy and normal experiences of African Americans visible to investigators, without the typical retreat to assumptions of pathology among the children. For many years now, there are those of us who have charged that mass-produced standardized professional tests and materials are ill suited to the needs of most African American children, in part because certain false assumptions are made about the children and their culture. Basically, the erroneous core assumption is that African American children are nothing more than incomplete copies of Western European white children. When it is recognized that African American children have a unique culture, that culture is usually seen as inferior to the Western European culture. It is these general ideas that cause gross errors to be made in testing and assessment in four areas in particular:

1. in testing the "mental ability" of African American children
2. in testing the speech of African American children
3. in testing the language of African American children
4. in testing the reading ability of African American children.

These errors are made because most professionals are ignorant of certain basic linguistic principles and of the history of American English and African American speech (Cohen 1969; D'Andrade 1995; Hilliard 1983; Hoover, Politzer and Taylor 1995; Shuy 1977). Therefore, professionals make mistakes when dealing both with English and with African-English. Let's look at this more closely.

Misconceptions About Common American English

1. English is immaculately conceived and is a pure language.
2. English is superior to other languages.
3. English is a fixed or permanent language.
4. English is essentially the same in all English-speaking countries and in the United States.
5. English in America is uninfluenced by African language.
6. English is language, not simply a language.

The President's Commission on Foreign Language Study has already sounded the alarm about the poor language preparation of Americans and about the poor attitudes Americans display toward other languages. Few Americans have been taught such simple things as how English really came to be. Were its true evolution widely known, chauvinistic attitudes toward language might be dismantled.

According to Fromkin and Rodman (1993), Romans invaded Britain in the first century A.D. and dominated Germanic Celts, the previous conquerors of Britain. Britain's northern tribes, the Scots and the Picts, were attacking the

Celtic invaders at the time that the Romans arrived, but Rome prevailed. And as the power of Rome declined during the fifth century, the Romans left Britain. The Celts then sent for Germanic Jutes (Teuton mercenaries) to repel their old enemies, the Scots and the Picts. In 449 A.D., the Jutes helped to defeat the Scots and the Picts and having won, decided to dominate their cousins the Celts with the help of other Germanic tribes, the Angles and the Saxons. It is from the Angles and Saxons and the linguistic soup already present in the British Isles that English was born.

Meanwhile, the Celts left for Wales, Cornwall, and France, and themselves began to speak Welsh, Scottish, Gaelic, and Breton. For the next 600 years or so, English, as spoken by the Germanic conquerors of Britain at varying times, evolved, even as the German spoken in Germany continues to evolve to the point where emerging English and German, one of its parent languanges, are no longer mutually intelligible. (Franklin and Rodman 1993)

In 1066, William the Conqueror invaded and conquered Britain and established French as the national language. English was still the language of the masses, but it was influenced by French. By 1500, British English began to be quite similar to the English that is spoken in England today. And so, what is now English emerged as a polyglot language from the remnants of Celts, Latins, Germanic Jutes, Angles, Saxons, and finally the French.

The result is a language that is largely Germanic in grammar and largely Romance in vocabulary. In fact, we could with some merit argue that English is "nonstandard German." This is hardly a pure or immaculately conceived language, nor is it permanent or fixed. It would be difficult to demonstrate its superiority to any other language. Indeed, it was the linguist and scientist Benjamin Whorf who observed after learning the Hopi Indian language that it was more suitable for sophisticated scientific thought than was his native English. We will deal with the African influence later.

What we are left with, then, is that English, common American English, is simply a language of convenience. As a common language, it is efficient for the nation. Yet, the approach to teaching English in our schools seeks to establish standards for aesthetics and to establish a national cultural heritage based on it. Instead of thinking of "standard" as common or ordinary, "standard English" is thought of as a standard of quality. The effect of this thinking is to subordinate any alternative and to label that alternative as inferior.

Misconceptions About African American Language

To refer to the language of most African Americans as "non standard English" is to mislead people, since the implication is that all that is involved is a variant of English. And yet, like English, the language spoken by African Americans is a fusion of languages *that cannot be understood apart from an appeal to historical origins and to the oppression of slavery.* Winifred Vass (1974) has shown that about 49.1 percent of the Africans who were enslaved were sent to South America, and 42.2 percent were sent to the Caribbean and to the Greater and Lesser Antilles.

About 1.8 percent were sent to Europe and its island environs. The remainder, about 6.8 percent, went to the United States, Mexico, Canada, and Central America. It is important to know that the 4.5 percent of the total trade that came to the United States came mostly during the last fifty years of the slave trade, when by the end of the slave trade, West Africa had been heavily depopulated. Therefore, Africans were brought to the United States from Angola, with many Africans coming through Angola from as far away as Mozambique and South-East Africa on the coast. Thus, during the heaviest years of African enslavement in the U.S., the primary source of people was from the core band of Bantu language culture, and the Africans who were brought to the United States were speakers of one or more of the Bantu languages. Further, one of the principal features of the Bantu family of languages is that they covered the largest part of the African continent. In addition, a well-known characteristic of Bantu languages is something that those who know them have called the "Bantu dynamic." That is to say, these languages exert a powerful influence on other languages. They tend to have tenacity and staying power. It is the retention of the "Bantu dynamic" that is picked up by Lorenzo Turner (1969), who showed how features of African languages, far from being lost during enslavement, were retained in the speech of the Sea Islanders in South Carolina.

Winifred K., a resident of Zaire for over forty years and fluent in Tshiluba, a Bantu language, has described the Bantu dynamic:

> The cultural picture of the Bantu emphasizes a strong oral tradition which places supreme ethnographic value on an individual's ability to communicate impressively. The conquering process begun by metal spears was continued by a gift of speech so forceful that it was adopted by successive ethnic groups, which continued to exist as separate cultural and physical entities within the total Bantu pattern. The Bantu speech dynamic has asserted itself in a new setting, transported to this continent by Bantu-speaking slaves. The Afro-American has retained the deft canny power of communications which has enabled him to "use language in the contests of the situations," to "manipulate and control situations to give himself the winning edge." (Vass 1974: 102)

As Vass has shown, this Bantu dynamic is not limited in its impact to the African continent. In fact, the most highly visible oral culture in America today is the speech of lower-class African Americans.

> Today, Africans and Afro-Americans are a race of gifted speakers, though the motives for unexcelled speech performance have changed from the motive of sheer physical survival to motives expressing the deep psychological needs of the human personality. Completely uninhibited in his efforts to imitate a strange speech, the Bantu-speaking slave brought from Africa had the inner will to expression and the sensitivity to the

human situation which furnish the basis for the greatest potential that every Afro-American has today, his own personal share of the Bantu past. Conscious of it or not, black and white Americans are the inheritors today of a rich cultural contribution: the tough, lusty, good-natured, and uncannily perceptive part of our speech which is our Bantu Heritage. (Vass 1974: 103)

Vass documents the Bantu retention in the speech of both black and white Southerners. She identifies the names of many southern cities today that are Bantu in origin and also locates many Bantu words in the vocabulary of Southerners. She decodes such familiar songs as *Polly Wolly Doodle* and *Here we go Loop de Loop,* which are shown to be freedom songs that are from the Bantu. (see also Alleyn 1971; Turner 1969)

Having lived in West Africa for six years, I can attest to a similar dynamic among people there. Liberia is a west African nation of 26 languages, virtually all a part of the Bantu family of languages. It is a common saying in Liberia, "Never let a Liberian man talk for himself in court. If you do, you will lose." I am witness to the fact that it is common for young children to recognize and speak two or more African languages and some English as well. I saw no evidence that "large lips and tongues," as early linguists had said, "were physical impediments to speech" (Turner 1969: 6). I saw no evidence of genetic or linguistic inferiority among the thousands of African children that I observed in and out of school all over Liberia. I did find a strong oral culture where even young children are frequently excellent public speakers. These examples in Liberia of a powerful oral language, like that described by Vass, show the Bantu dynamic in action, the power of speech exhibited. It is clear that early linguists spoke out of their own ignorance of African language and culture, much the same as many did and still do about the language of African Americans.

This historical, political, and cultural information is important when we learn that many of the things which cause African American children to be labeled as "poor readers," "dumb" (low intelligence), or as "speech impaired" are the retained features of Bantu speech or speech from other African language families mixed with or fused into a form of common English (Alleyne 1971; Turner 1969; Vass 1974). Ironically, some varieties of common English—i.e., white Southern speech—also are influenced by the Bantu dynamic. It is important to note that the African retention in the language of African Americans covers all the features that go to make up language—i.e., vocabulary, phonology, grammar, etc. (Smith 1978)

So, it should be clear that we are really talking about two amalgams when we speak of English and African American speech. To realize this is to reduce the professional problem considerably. The language spoken by many African Americans should simply be regarded as a "foreign" or "semiforeign" language and not as "pathological" or "deficient." The prime test of the "normalcy" of the language of a child is to compare the child's language to the environment within which it was learned. This simple test seems to have been overlooked by many test makers and linguists alike.

From the minimal information presented above, it should be clear that any linguists or other students of the language of African Americans will have serious deficiencies in their professional preparation if they are ignorant of the African cultural linguistic antecedents.

THE PRACTICAL CONSEQUENCES OF A REORIENTATION

Much of the language and many constructs in testing and assessment must be redefined or eliminated! These assessment practices are inconsistent and incompatible with and contradictory to valid cultural-linguistic principles. (Rowe 1991; Salomon 1995) Yet testing and assessment, as we now see them in education, are rooted in and dependent upon language.

Let's take a look at some constructs that will prove to be absurd under the light of cultural-linguistics analysis:

- "basic word" list
- word "difficulty"
- "vocabulary"
- "general information"
- standardized "beginning and ending sounds"
- standardized "comprehension"

Standardized test makers assume that there is, in general, a unique correct answer to a given question or problem. If there is not a unique answer, if there can be multiple answers, then the scoring and analysis system disintegrates. This matter is fundamental! What I am asserting is a basic threat not only to biased testing and assessment of African American children, but to the very foundation of testing and assessment for any child. The results of standardized testing favor children who speak common American English simply because these children are able to respond to questions that are couched in a familiar language based upon familiar experiences. Since the "right children"—upper class, wealthy—tend to get the top scores, it is assumed that the I.Q., reading, speech, language acquisition, and other tests are valid. Test makers have no way of taking the achievement results of a privileged child and separating that part of the scores which is due to the student's special skill and that part which is due simply to growing up in the common white American culture. Because the results come out "right" or appear to have "face validity," the basic assumptions about what the testing and assessment process is supposed to be doing are left unexamined. Let's examine this more closely:

What are the criteria for the establishment of a "basic word list"? Is a basic word list something that all Americans can be expected to have had an equally likely chance to encounter? Is a basic word list a random sample of vocabulary from the total possible vocabulary pool? Does a basic word list represent necessary vocabulary for communication in English? Can there be more than one basic word list? Is the basic word list simply a matter of the identification of words that have a high frequency of use? What does it mean not to be in possession of a knowledge of vocabulary in the basic word list?

In a study by Kersey (1970), the Dolch Common Noun List and the Dolch 220 Word List were compared to a word list from a population of Seminole Indian children. The children's words came from stories used by third and fourth graders. The Seminole word list contained 67.7 percent of the words on the Dolch 220 Word List. But it also contained 149 service words that were not on the list. The Seminole word list contained 63.2 percent of the words on the Dolch Common Noun List plus 189 nouns that were not on the Dolch list. How is the educator to explain this? Is one list better than another? Is a child smarter if he or she knows one or the other list? In short, the meaning of "basic word list" is ambiguous, with fatal results for standardized testing. To treat a single basic word list as universally valid is absurd.

Let's examine the concept of "word difficulty." Is a word difficult only because a few people know it? Is a word easy because many people know it? On many standardized test items, difficulty is determined by statistical methods. Yet it is not clear just what the nature of the difficulty is. The assumptions about difficulty are not explicated. Therefore, what is being tested, difficulty or familiarity?

What about "vocabulary"? Notice the word "vocabulary" is unqualified. Is it a Chicago vocabulary, a Bronx vocabulary, a Boston vocabulary, a Tennessee vocabulary? Is there a universal American vocabulary? If not, do we measure a person's vocabulary, or do we simply try to determine if a person has learned a particular vocabulary? Are we measuring vocabulary ability—the ability to learn words? What is the linguistic rationale for expecting all Americans to have identical vocabularies? What are the criteria for item selection for a vocabulary test? What is a vocabulary test?

I could go on with a similar treatment of "general information," "beginning and ending sounds," and "comprehension." However, the point should be clear: the constructs are ambiguous and the specifications or items are arbitrary! Therefore, the mass production of standardized tests and assessment procedures to measure the behaviors implied by the constructs is in reality the production of mass confusion.

In general, we are faced with a rampant, unbridled ethnocentricism among the designers of standardized tests and assessment procedures for use with populations of diverse cultural groups (Hilliard 1995). If tests are designed only as achievement measures, are content valid, and if the content is agreed to by clients, then there is little to concern us. It is only when the detection of pathology is implied that we must call for superior accountability in testing. The cure for this ethnocentric malady must address the ethnocentrism more than the study and analysis of African American children. William Labov's classic article, "The Logic of Non-Standard English" (1970), is an excellent piece of work in which he proves that "nonstandard English," meaning "African American language," has a logic. He didn't need to prove it to those who speak it. They have not changed. His work teaches the scholars who apparently have had a difficult time understanding African American speech.

URGENT NEEDS

It should be clear by now that "band-aids" will not do. It will take more than lay knowledge to respond to the fundamental issues. That means that cultural linguists who are familiar with linguistics and with the language of African Americans must be a part of an in-depth evaluation of how language is used in assessment and in the instructional process to see if is scientifically appropriate. This principle applies to professional practices whith any ethnic group. We have major changes to make in the whole system of education. Some of them are as follows.

There is an urgent need for systematic cultural-linguistic review of all testing and assessment devices that are used with African Americans. No existing instruments have been subjected to such a review by professionals who are competent in African American cultural linguistics.

There is an urgent need to provide full and competent descriptions of the language that is spoken by African Americans. This language must be described in its historical and cultural context, and not as a simple contrast to common American English.

There is little need to teach teachers specific techniques for teaching the African American child. Teachers must be taught so that their total orientation toward language and cultural linguistic principles represents the best that we now know about the subject. It is not the bag of tricks but the general attitude of a teacher that is important. If an African American child is seen as language deficient, we can show that the behavior of the teacher actually changes toward that child as compared to "normal" children. He or she will engage the child in communication less and pay less attention to the child (e.g., see Aaron and Powell 1982; Irvine 1991; Simpson and Erickson 1983). *It is this teaching behavior and not the language of the child, no matter how different, that creates the problem for learners.* (Johnson and Clement 1973; Nimnick and Johnson 1973)

It is one thing to say that the language context of African Americans must be taken into account in the teaching/learning process. It is quite another to know what to do about it. Both linguists and successful teachers and school leaders—those who are successful with African American children—must be provided with the time to develop and articulate their theories of positive and empowering pedagogy. (One example is the work of Ladson-Billings 1994.) We need no "Black language kits." The child's language presents no pedagogical problems. Cultural-linguistics review can show that this is true.

If chimpanzees (Warshoe at the Yerkes Primate Laboratory) can be taught to do American Sign Language, and if a chimpanzee can teach another chimpanzee to sign, and if a gorilla (Koko at Stanford) can earn a 90 on a human I.Q. test, then one would think that any human being could be taught the simple task of reading. All humans are capable of so much more.

Septima Clark is the creator of "freedom schools" in eleven southern states. These schools were responsible for teaching reading to 12 million potential voters who were illiterate. In a short period of time (Clark seems to suggest about two or three years), the number of illiterates was reduced from 12 million to about 12,000, radically altering voting patterns in the south. I asked Septima Clark how she was able to accomplish such a feat. She responded, "I generally avoided using regular trained teachers." As a teacher educator, I was stunned. "Why would you do that?" I asked. She answered that often people who saw themselves as highly educated projected the idea to her students that they regarded themselves as better than the students. "Their education got in the way." Surely, there is a lesson in this for us, as we ponder the nature of our interventions to come.

CONCLUSION

Who teaches error in linguistic understanding? How do they do it? It is done in many subtle ways in everything from linguistic departments, to English classes, to teacher behavior, and to the mass media. We are faced with nothing less than the need to re-educate our nation to the truth about language. The public in general is not equipped to understand the language issues. We have a major communication problem, especially since so few professionals understand language issues either. There is no quick fix. It is important to conceptualize the problem in its broadest scope. We need no more analyses of the African American child. We need to renovate the system that teaches error. We have the tools to do the job. Do we have the will?

REFERENCES

Aaron, R., and G. Powell (1982). Feedback practices as a function of teacher pupil race during reading groups instruction. *Journal of Negro Education 51*; 50–59.

Anderson, J. D. (1988). *The history of black education in the South: 1860–1935.* Chapel Hill: The University of North Carolina Press.

Alleyne, M. C. (1971). Linguistic continuity of Africa in the Caribbean. In H. J. Richards (ed.), *Topics in Afro-American Studies*, 118–34. New York: Black Academy Press.

Carter, R. T., and A. L. Goodwin (1994). Racial identity and education. In L. Darling-Hammond (ed.), *Review of Research in Education*, vol. 20, 291–336. Washington, DC: American Educational Research Association.

Chase, A. (1977). *The legacy of Malthus.* New York: Knopf.

Cohen, R. (1969). Conceptual styles, culture conflict, and non-verbal tests of intelligence. *American Anthropologist 71*(5); 828–57.

College Board. (1985). *Equity and excellence: The educational status of Black Americans*. New York: Author.

D'Andrade, R. (1995). *The development of cognitive anthropology*. New York: Cambridge Unversity Press.

Fromkin, V., and R. Rodman (1993). *An introduction to language*. New York: Holt, Rinehart and Winston.

Goodlad, J. I. (1984). *A place called school*. New York: McGraw Hill.

Guthrie, R. (1976). *Even the rat was white*. New York: Harper and Row.

Hegel, G. W. F. (1831). *The philosophy of history* (J. Sibree, trans.). Buffalo, NY: Prometheus.

Hilliard, A. G., III. (1983). Psychological factors associated with language in the education of the African American child. *Journal of Negro Education 52*(1); 24–34.

——— (1990). Misunderstanding and testing intelligence. In J. I. Goodlad and P. Keating (eds.), *Access to knowledge*, 145–58. New York: College Board.

——— (ed.) (1995). *Testing African American Students*. Chicago: Third World Press.

——— (1996). Either a paradigm shift or no mental measurement: The non-science and nonsense of *The Bell Curve*. *Cultural Diversity and Mental Health Journal 2*(1); 1–20

Hoover, M. R., R. L. Politzer, and O. Taylor (1995). Bias in reading tests for black language speakers: A sociolinguistic perspective. In Hilliard, Asa G. III (ed.), *Testing African American students*, 51–68. Chicago: Third World Press.

Irvine, J. J. (1991). *Black students and school failure*. New York: Praeger.

Johnson, J. A., and D. C. Clement. *Incongruences between experience bases of lower income urban black children and experiences requisite to success in schools*. In G. P. Nimnick and J. A. Johnson (eds.), *Beyond compensatory education: A new approach to educating children*, 95–109. San Francisco: Far West Laboratory for Educational Research and Development.

Kamin, L. (1974). *The science and politics of I.Q.* New York: Wiley.

Kersey, H. A., Jr. (1970). The Federal day school as the acculturation agent for Seminole Indian children. Paper presented at the annual meeting of the American Education Research Association, Minneapolis. April (ERIC No. ED 039 988)

King, J. (1971). *Pan Africanism and education: A study of race, philanthropy and education in the southern states of America and East Africa*. Oxford: Clarendon Press.

Labov, W. (1970). The logic of non-standard English. In F. Williams (ed.), *Language and Poverty*, 153–89. Chicago: Markham.

Ladson-Billings, G. (1994). *The dreamkeepers: Successful teachers of African American children*. San Francisco: Jossey-Bass.

Nimnick, G. P., and J. A. Johnson (1973). *Beyond compensatory education: A new approach to educating children*. San Francisco: Far West Laboratory for Educational Research and Development.

Oakes, J., and M. Lipton (1990). Tracking and ability grouping: A structural barrier to access and achievement. In J. I. Goodlad and P. Keating (eds.), *Access to knowledge*, 187–204. New York: College Board.

Rowe, H. A. H. (ed.) (1991). *Intelligence, reconceptualization and measurement*.

Australian Council for Educational Research. Hillsdale, NJ: Lawrence Erlbaum.

Salomon, G. (1995). Reflections on the field of educational psychology by the outgoing journal editor. *Educational Psychologist 30*(3); 105–08.

Shuy, R. W. (1977). Quantitative linguistic analysis: A case for and some warnings against. *Anthropology and Education Quarterly 1*(2); 78–82.

Simpson, A. W., and M. T. Erickson (1983). Teachers' verbal and non-verbal communication patterns as a function of teacher race, student gender, and student race. *American Educational Research Journal 20*; 269–88.

Smith, E. (1978). The retention of the phonological, phonemic, and morphophonemic features of Africa in Afro-American ebonics. Fullerton, Seminar Paper 43, CA: Department of Linguistics, California State University, Fullerton.

Snyderman, M., and S. Rothman (1990). *The IQ controversy: The media and public policy.* New Brunswick, NJ: Transaction.

Spivey, D. (1978). *Schooling for the new slavery: Black industrial education, 1868–1915.* Westport, CT: Greenwood.

Turner, L. (1969). *Africanism in the Gullah dialect.* New York: Arno.

Vass, W. K. (1974). *The Bantu speaking heritage of the United States.* Los Angeles: Center for Afro-American Studies, University of California.

Chapter Thirteen

MOVING THE MOUNTAIN: Assessment and Advocacy for Children

Beatrice S. Fennimore

We pass through this world but once. Few tragedies can be more extensive than the stunting of life, few injustices deeper than the denial of an opportunity to strive or even to hope, by a limit imposed from without but falsely identified as lying within.

—Steven J. Gould, *The Mismeasure of Man*

Children depend on adults to help them discover all the capability and potential they possess. The unjust use of testing and assessment[1] denies many children full knowledge of their own power to learn and grow. Children, especially those who are thus cheated, are not in a position to advocate for themselves; only adults committed to justice can press their needs forward in school and society. These advocates are willing to become the protective voices of children soundlessly lost in a maze of inappropriate institutional practices.

The concept of child advocacy is central to the improved treatment of children in schools and society. It emerged in a number of books and articles in the United States in 1969, and was strengthened at that time by the powerful impetus of the civil rights movement (Melton 1983; Westman 1979). Westman (1979) described child advocacy as the assumption of responsibility for promoting and protecting the developmental needs of both an individual child and children in general. He identified the general aims of child advocacy as knowing every child, knowing what each child needs, and making sure those needs are met. While educators have continued to focus on child advocacy as an important issue (Fennimore 1989; Goffin and Lombardi 1988; Jensen and Chevalier 1990), their efforts have been frustrated by the progressively worsening social and economic conditions of children. The fact that American children are nonvoting minors with few constitutional rights, and thus not a forceful part in our political system, continues to make child advocacy an altruistic and highly complicated adult endeavor (Melton 1983).

Child advocacy often represents an ethical and personal call to assume responsibility for "other people's children." This call is taxing and time consuming; it may also carry professional or political risk. Teachers, for example, may fear that acting as advocates for children in school politics might affect decisions involving their own tenure or retention. Many potential advocates hesitate to add more stress to the problems they already encounter as professionals in undervalued or underpaid human service positions. In spite of these and other potential drawbacks, child advocacy continues to bridge the awareness of the barriers children face and hopeful efforts to expand their resources and opportunities. It is also a potential impetus for the formation and implementation of responsible and humane public, social, and educational policies (Fennimore 1989). The protection of children, and a vision of their improved futures, makes advocacy an important and personally rewarding endeavor.

LINKING ASSESSMENT AND ADVOCACY

Child advocacy is best conceptualized in this chapter as standing up for the needs and rights of children (Goffin and Lombardi 1988) so they can reach their optimal personal growth and development in school and society (Fennimore 1989). Since the full potential of any individual cannot be known in childhood, optimal growth is protected only by offering all children as many opportunities as possible. Teachers who are advocates might ask two simple questions about any assessment technique: (1) Will the results of this procedure enhance or limit the current educational opportunities of this child? (2) Will the institutional implications of this procedure open or close doors to the future development and education of this child? The answers to these questions are often found in the analysis of how children are described and treated by their teachers, and the analysis of their placement in school and subsequent exposure to curricular opportunities.

While promising new forms of assessment—such as portfolio construction and qualitative criteria linked to instruction—are emerging in education (Perrone 1991), old and difficult problems persist. These problems generally fall into four conceptual areas: (1) the appropriate role of assessment in a democratic society, (2) the need to acknowledge unequal school resources that have an effect on assessment outcomes, (3) the ways in which some assessment procedures legitimize classification and subsequent differential allocation of resources and opportunities, and (4) the relationship between assessment practices and racial or socioeconomic segregation of students. Advocates have the dual role of defending egalitarian principles in new forms of assessment while also resisting assessment that reflects discriminatory policies and practices.

1. The Appropriate Role of Assessment in a Democratic Society

Advocacy for fair assessment is central to the concept of democratic schooling. All children are well served by democratic schools that protect their right to excellence in education; all children are harmed in some way by discriminatory school practices. Even the children who are "winners" in school sense the precarious nature of their advantage. Fear created by the danger of falling into low-status classifications with fewer resources can fuel the beginnings of scapegoating and discrimination among children. The democratic imperative to prepare students for citizenship requires a modeling of justice within the educational institution. Some critics of American public schools suggest that efforts to democratize educational opportunities have reduced the level of academic excellence. Others argue, however, that current massive school failure is the long-term consequence of meritocratic school practices that have created distinctly different opportunities for learners and then have rationalized school failure by pinpointing deficiencies in children, families, and communities (Bastian, Fruchter, Gittell, Greer, and Haskins 1985). Such meritocratic practices include obvious differences in funding and school resources between schools (often in the same district) that serve more and less advantaged children (Kozol 1991). They might also include the design of magnet, gifted, or other special school programs that have limited admission based on criteria neither available nor fair to all children (National Coalition of Advocates for Students 1988). Any situation in which more advantaged or higher achieving children are given a greater chance to succeed, and then are assumed to be superior because they do succeed, raises ethical questions about educational policies.

Whenever objectively measured achievement matters more than individual development, the full range of knowledge and intuition in our diverse student population is not explored (Hilliard 1990; National Coalition of Advocates for Students 1991). This lack of interest in diverse skills and abilities is particularly troubling in a social climate where the recent publication of *The Bell Curve* (Herrnstein and Murray 1994) heralded a renewed acceptance of genetic explanations of intelligence and arguments of genetic inferiority in some racial groups (Banks 1995). Educational focus on competitive school rankings based on standardized tests blurs both a commitment to equal educational opportunity and an honest appraisal of discriminatory school practices (National Coalition of Advocates for Students 1991). School meritocracy and differential opportunity based on assessment weaken the democratic focus of public education.

2. The Need to Acknowledge Unequal School Resources That Have an Effect on Assessment Outcomes

Advocates cannot overlook the continuing need to rectify inequities of resources and opportunities in American schools. These inequities inevitably affect assessment outcomes—many of which have high stakes for children. The

National Coalition of Advocates for Students states: "It is still true in America that the income level of a child's family is a major determinant of the quality and quantity of education that child receives" (1988: 8). According to Shor:

> The most glaring social inequality is the greater amount of money invested in the education of richer students at all levels. . . . [C]hildren of poor and working-class families still have much less invested in their educations. (1986: 412)

Oakes (1985) reminds educators that the children who have the least of everything in general often get the least in schools, and that their experiences outside school are reinforced by differential treatment inside schools. Twelve years of compulsory education, the central social opportunity for the success of many children, can be thwarted by disadvantages within the school itself. Kozol (1991) cites vast differences in the educational opportunities of American children, and reminds educators that America has not fulfilled its moral commitment to the *Brown* decision of 1954. The large number of American children currently affected by poverty, discrimination, violence, and other social dilemmas (Children's Defense Fund 1995) also face significant risks within the schools themselves. Some of these "risks" include inappropriate educational designations and consequential stigmatization, inadequacy of resources and education, and separation from more advantaged peers (Gartner and Lipsky 1993). Educators who are advocates should not be tolerant of circumstances in which children are shortchanged by social institutions and then blamed for the resulting academic deficiencies. Fair practice in assessment demands an equal opportunity to become one's best and most competent self.

3. The Ways in Which Some Assessment Procedures Legitimize Classification and Subsequent Differential Allocation of Resources and Opportunities

Assessment takes on high-stakes meaning when it is linked with classification and placement in the context of American education. Kirp (1974) states that stigmatization and educational ineffectiveness are two adverse effects of school classification. Exclusion by school placement, according to Kirp, becomes inseparable from other social adversity and makes it difficult to actually isolate the cause of harm in the life of a child. Stigmatization can cause the child to be shunned "without reference to the personal qualities which complicate the labeling process. Individual differences are subsumed under the common, negatively perceived attributes" (Kirp 1974: 296). The pervasive "at risk" label, which was created to predict possible future problems (hopefully to be avoided with current remediation) has become a poorly defined and negative classification in many schools. Added to those with the at risk designation are many children in special education placements, "slow groups," and "bottom tracks" that embody separation and low expectation. Fine (1993) describes this situation as carving out, severing, denying connection to, and then promising to "help" children in need.

The intention may be good, but the act of labeling is in itself disabling (Ginott 1972). What is lost is the sense of the multidimensional child (Mercer 1974) who has the right to full cultural identity, personal respect, the opportunity to change, and access to hope embodied in a complete education. In the long run, all children are shortchanged by systems of school classification that disregard the hope and promise of human complexity and resiliency.

4. The Relationship Between Assessment Practices and Racial or Socioeconomic Segregation of Students

Kirp, in the 1974 publication of *The Rights of Children*, a special issue of the *Harvard Educational Review,* placed school classification in the context of educational and social segregation. He questioned at that time the persistence of tracking in the absence of strong support from educational research (Jones 1972) and presence of evidence of harm by misclassification and stigmatization (*Hobsen v. Hansen* 1967). Advocates must continue to question the relationship of classification and tracking to what Kirp refers to as the "unintended consequence of a policy whose premises are meritocratic" (1974: 311)—continued segregation of poor and minority children. In fact, more than twenty years after Kirp's publication, educators must face up to strong evidence that classification and tracking have substituted for explicit segregation by class and race in the public schools of America (Carter and Goodwin 1994; Goodlad 1984; National Coalition of Advocates for Students 1988). Has an America never entirely supportive of the egalitarian premise that all children have the right to an equal and excellent public education (Hilliard 1991) looked the other way while the segregating mechanism of tracking has provided the rationale for widespread school inequity? It is certain that advocacy for fair assessment must address issues of just distribution of resources and principles of democracy within the context of classification, tracking, class, and race in the United States.

CONCEPTUALIZATIONS RELATED TO ASSESSMENT THAT MUST CHANGE

Advocates must resolve to move beyond discussion of the problematic relationship of school assessment to inequality to a more productive identification of concepts surrounding assessment, which must be challenged and permanently changed. This section focuses on four assumptions that require substantive alteration in educational theory and practice: (1) the assumption of importance, permanency, and durability in the use of I.Q. scores, (2) the assumption that sorting of children by ability is a valid function of public education, (3) the assumption that there is one correct approach, method of completion, or response in many academic tasks, and (4) the assumption that equality and excellence are competing rather than codependent aspirations in public education.

The first assumption that must be challenged is one validating the fundamental importance of I.Q. scores in educational institutions. Intelligence tests were developed in the early 1900s to offset judgments of children based on impression and prejudice (Boehm and White 1982). Murray (1993) considers I.Q. tests to be a systematic combination of other measures that by themselves are of limited interest and use. He says that while I.Q. tests are predictive of school grades, the level of predictablilty indicates that other factors are also important. Information gleaned from I.Q. testing can be useful in the total plan of school assessment and planning, but those scores do not give adequate recognition to the fact that children are highly competent at some things (though perhaps not at others), that the tests do not measure adaptive behavior, and that they do not explain why a child may have done poorly on the test. Schools that accept I.Q. scores at face value (or that are required to do so by state or federal guidelines) may disregard the dynamic and uneven nature of human growth (Kirp 1974). Assumptions that the child will not change, or that the school need not change, strengthen the view that intelligence is inherited and fixed. It is troubling indeed that such assumptions are so often combined with racist or classist beliefs or practices. Whatever the educational contribution of I.Q. scores may be, evidence of their use to downgrade, disregard, disrespect, or segregate in schools should be considered an unacceptable threat to human rights. While direct evidence of such abuse is often difficult to document, indirect evidence may exist when schools continue to sort and separate students—sometimes as early as first grade (Goodlad 1984)—through the use of tests that are known to consistently segregate them along socioeconomic and racial lines (National Coalition of Advocates for Students 1988). Indirect evidence might also be found in school responsiveness to pressure from advantaged parents who openly support tracking as a means of separating their own children from those who are different or less advantaged, or in descriptive language about children that routinely denigrates the potential of less-advantaged children or fails to question the validity of their consistently lower I.Q. scores (Page 1991).

The assumption that sorting students by ability is a valid function of public education must also be challenged. The responsibility of the school is to open the greatest number of opportunities to students. When labeling and sorting take precedence over access, opportunities are unnecessarily withheld from children. Therefore, classification and tracking are at odds with the most important service provided by the educational institution—exposure to unexplored opportunity. A shift of focus from sorting to access would provide many more students with the chance to surprise and engage their teachers with unanticipated strengths and interests. Acceptance of the importance of academic exploration combined with a willingness to keep an open mind to the *possibility* of growth supports lively and important questions in school: What can this child do now? How can we help him or her to do it? What would happen if this child had a chance to try this task? If the child has failed, how could we rearrange the opportunity and offer it again? (An educator with a mind closed to possibility assumes that ability level rarely changes, that there is little use in trying to assist the child in reapproaching tasks formerly out of reach, and that school failure always reflects negative qualities in children rather than inappropriateness of the design or teaching of the curriculum.)

The willingness of teachers to wonder about hidden ability could diminish some common effects of tracking: public identification of children's disabilities or perceived weaknesses, open differences in valuing of students, and judgments of a permanent nature about a student's potential (Oakes 1985). The determination to seek out strengths in children would deter a particularly damaging effect of tracking—the predictable ebbing of opportunities for disadvantaged, less-advantaged, or diverse students (Darling-Hammond 1995). Fewer doors would close before children could even peek inside, and those students who failed on some tests would still have access to tasks they might later be able to successfully master (Diez 1993).

The current educational focus on authentic assessment can represent a potent support for disadvantaged children, whose access to opportunities is blocked by traditional standardized testing (Fennimore 1995). Authentic assessment is situational rather than abstract, evaluative rather than predictive, and focused on real accomplishment instead of assumed ability. Examples of authentic assessment are portfolios of work in process or completed, information from parents and other sources, recorded observations of teachers, self-reports of students, and other significant evidence of active learning (Leavitt and Eheart 1991). Constant analysis of substantive and relevant data in the classroom can lead to a wider variety of creative and interactive opportunities for children. If schools were to embody a climate of *suspense* (as opposed to certainty) concerning the abilities of children, more freedom would exist for students to define their own limitations, interests, abilities, and future aspirations. The only real certainty in learning environments is that children can never master challenges that are withheld or hidden from them.

The third educational assumption to be challenged is that there is one correct approach, method of completion, or response in most avenues of academic inquiry. There is no question that important knowledge and skills in academic subjects must be mastered. However, they need not be mastered by all children at the same time or in the same ways. Equally important to knowledge and skills are children's feelings and their dispositions to persist in tasks and to go on learning (Katz and Chard 1994). Students who can explore, take risks, reflect comfortably on mistakes with an eye toward improvement, and try several approaches to problems can eventually fulfill their potential. Such academic opportunities are often in direct contrast, however, to traditional teacher focus on large group instruction based mainly on preparation for multiple-choice standardized tests. The philosophy of developmentally appropriate practice (Bredekamp 1987) assumes that school expectations should be based on best-available information about child development and a *constructivist* approach to learning (Fennimore 1995), in which knowledge is progressive, temporary, cultural, social, and often not an objective concept. The learner is not evaluated with single (and often simplistic) standardized outcomes. Instead, he or she is expected to demonstrate understanding of complexities, possibilities, and discrepancies that emerge in the process of study (Brooks and Brooks 1993). When depth of thought, persistence in effort, and continuous progress on a flexible timeline are central goals of schooling, the nature of assessment and the concept of academic success will inevitably change. A shift of focus in forms of assessment has the power to liberate the hidden ability and potential of many children who are marginalized in our current educational system. Their teachers might form a more comprehensive understanding of their strengths and thus be more willing to value them for their developmental complexities and resilience in the face of disadvantage. In addition, greater excitement about emerging capacities in all children would enrich school environments with higher expectations for consistent success in a diverse group of students.

The final challenge ahead is the assumption that equity and excellence are competing rather than codependent aspirations in public education. As long as a large number of educators and parents believe that students must be tested and grouped so the "best" can have access to excellence, equity will be a peripheral and elusive educational goal. Nieto (1992) states that the worthwhile educational program must focus on two central concerns: How can we raise the attainment of all students and thus provide them with an equitable and equal education, and how can we give all students the opportunity to become critical and productive members of a democratic society? A school system in which a significant number of children are failing or lacking in basic learning resources has not reached an acceptable level of competence.

Excellence requires not only equal access to resources and opportunities but also an indication that the talents and skills possessed by each student are valid starting points for education (Nieto 1992). Educators who wonder if such positive indications exist in their schools can ask the two questions identified at the beginning of this chapter: (1) Will the results of assessment procedures enhance or limit the current educational opportunities of this child? (2) Will the institutional implications of this procedure open or close doors to the future development and education of this child? Early assessment should direct the school to identify resources and methods that will help the child to achieve excellence; it should not constitute permission to lower school accountability for success when the child has barely begun. For example, a school district giving readiness tests to kindergarten students should plan to meet their identified needs through adaptation of curriculum and availability of support services. This would be in direct contrast to the practice of labeling some incoming kindergarten children as "learning delayed" and then either excluding them from school or placing them in a segregated classroom that will lower current and long-term expectations for their school success.

The critical first step in education is not rigid evaluation of the status of the child; rather, it is the reduction of obvious inequalities that lead to unequal outcomes (Coleman 1990). Thus, the most important focus of a school district that identifies "achievement deficits" in a large number of incoming students should be making sure that those children get equal resources, equal access to excellent teaching, and equal opportunities for success. This is in direct contrast to placing the children in lower tracks, which tend to justify inequitable distribution of resources. The goal of designing feasible approaches to help each child to reach his or her highest potential is the next indispensable step. Public schools deserve to be considered excellent only when the failure of any child is unacceptable and enthusiasm for the success of every child is consistently in evidence.

THE MOUNTAIN CAN BE MOVED: ADVOCACY AND ASSESSMENT

Advocates should believe that something can be done, that change is possible, and that efforts for children are important whether or not immediate success is in evidence. Advocacy, like any effort to change and grow, is developmental in nature, and its social gains are often delayed and later occur out of sight of those who first envisioned them. Advocates who encounter the difficulties of political resistance should be strengthened with the knowledge that they are lifting painful problems from the shoulders of silent children (Fennimore 1989). Educators, unlike the students who suffer inequity and injustice in schools, are in a position of power. The remainder of this chapter focuses on three areas of advocacy for educators who are willing to use their power and are committed to utilizing assessment as a basis for change in schools. These areas are: (1) the role of individual advocates in the classroom, (2) the role of advocates within the school, and (3) the role of advocates in society. Each role is intertwined with the others in any effort to change the ways assessment is conceptualized and utilized in education. Central to each of the three roles is advocacy for change in conceptualization of human intelligence and visualization of the rights and potentials of all children.

The Role of Individual Educators

Advocacy is a philosophy that guides the beliefs, words, and professional behaviors of teachers.[2] Not even expert implementation of teaching strategies and complete coverage of school curriculum are sufficient for successful teaching in our complex social world. A commitment to equity and justice for all children is essential to dedicated teaching, because only teachers can bring equity to life in the classroom. Their determination to do so will help them resist social forces that appear to make the failure of some children permissible. If the *will* of the teacher is not centered on creating a successful learning environment for all students, that lack of determination will weaken any effectiveness of method and materials. It is the responsibility of the teacher to *care* (Noddings 1992) and, when necessary, to struggle alongside the child in order to create a humane climate and equitable opportunity.

A fair and positive use of school assessment is central to the struggle for equity. Oakes (1985) recognizes that schools appear intractable and that change appears futile when so many social forces seem to conspire to keep things the way they are. The teacher who would be an advocate must develop a vision of social justice. Sockett writes that "the human desire to be just and to cooperate in the maintenance of a just society is something humans have to do or they will be somehow morally stunted" (1993: 82). Sockett identifies three moral aspects of teaching: caring about the truth, having courage in troubled circumstances, and encouraging children in powerful ways to overcome their fears and setbacks. Each of those moral aspects can help educators to change ways of conceptualizing and utilizing assessment. A great number of teachers in America know it is true that at least some children in their schools are misrepresented or mistreated because of standardized test scores. If they *care* that dispositions are harmed or that opportunities are unfairly withheld, the moral impetus for advocacy exists. Such advocacy will initiate teacher responsibilities beyond the remunerated position and may reduce the comfort of full acceptance by professional peers in the school (Fennimore 1989). Courage is required to maintain the sense that advocacy is the moral duty of caring educators. Courage and caring strengthen the efforts of teachers to resist inappropriate use of assessment and unfair labeling and classification of children. Courageous and committed teachers can struggle to help children harmed by years of lowered expectations to see their strengths and overcome the fear of new challenges. New and creative forms of assessment can free hidden aspects of intelligence and desire to learn. Every classroom act of encouragement and discouragement is an act of morality that has resounding ramifications in the lives of children.

Sockett (1993) reminds teachers that they still recall good and bad educators from their own childhood days. The bad, spiteful, ineffective, lazy, or inefficient teachers who made us dislike subject matters remain in our memories. Also remaining are the inspirational memories of good, enthusiastic, efficient, passionate, fair, and concerned teachers who touched us by caring for us as individuals. Such memories are based far more in emotions than in pedagogy. All teachers who are advocates can focus on the power of emotional communication to engender hope and resilience in children. How could we question the power of emotion and encouragement in school when the memories of our own teachers have lasted a lifetime?

Individual educators who are advocates must ascertain their sources of choice and power in the classroom. Even when standardized tests are used in school districts, teachers can determine ways in which they will or will not allow scores to change their attitudes and expectations. Their own skill, judgment, and enthusiasm outweigh the value of tests in many classroom decisions (National Coalition of Advocates for Children 1988). Bowman says teachers can create many emotionally stressful experiences when "they do not remember their own childhood passions, misunderstandings, and errors in judgement" (1989: 447). Teachers can use their own childhood memories to guide compassionate dialogue with students. ("Were you so excited about this that you made a mistake?" "I think you just misunderstood the directions—can you tell me what you thought they were?") Furthermore, teachers can reduce stress by working on the same assessment tasks in front of students, demonstrating how easy it would be for them to make a mistake, and sharing tips on successful completion of those tasks. Teachers give emotional as well as academic support when they teach students how to take tests or master other assessments, and allow students to repeat some assessments until they are successful (Berger 1991).

All teachers who are advocates can ascertain and improve their habits of descriptive language about student ability in the classroom. It is not uncommon for teachers, including many who believe they are not exhibiting prejudice in school, to openly describe their students as "low" or "not bright" or "delayed." The way children are talked about matters very much, because it is through language that educators shape beliefs and behaviors. The assessment of developing children must always be considered a question rather than a conclusive statement. Discussion based on assessment can indicate current levels ("He scored at a rather low level on his reading achievement test") while raising questions ("I wonder if a different book would help?") and emphasizing school accountability ("I really must work with him to improve his skills this year"). Prejudice and stereotyping always betray the ethics of teaching, so teachers must be on guard against discriminatory functions of assessment in their schools. One way to do this is to actively vocalize the new strengths and abilities that the children who attract low expectations have shown on new or creative assessments. At the same time, teachers can move more assessment activities closer to the actual work of children and link them to "larger educational and social purposes" (Perrone 1991: 164). One educational and social purpose that teachers can embrace is preparation for future democratic citizenship, responsible work, and service to others. Students will be more inclined to believe the promise of democracy when they perceive the fairness of the opportunities they receive in school.

The Role of Advocates in Educational Institutions

Institutional policy is affected not only by those who create it but also by all who implement it. Designations of leadership and authority exist, but the climates of schools are shaped by the beliefs, intentions, and commitments of teachers as well as administrators. Current trends toward school restructuring, deregulation, and school-based management create new opportunities for educators on all levels to have a personal influence on the outcomes of education (Fennimore 1995). Assessment, a policy as well as an educational issue, is deeply bound to social and political trends. Advocates for fair assessment and equitable school opportunity need to focus on the institutional as well as the individual level.

Sockett (1993) suggests that a profoundly disturbing feature of our current educational system is that it does not take the needs of each child seriously. The systems that have been created to accommodate children who fall into categories, including compensatory and special programs, can be impersonal. Failure of children, once anticipated by labeling or placement in programs, can become automatic. Why, asks Hentoff (1989), is there no outrage against a system that produces this much spoiled human material? Perhaps outrage is absent or invisible because educators feel powerless, parents feel overwhelmed, and students feel anonymous. Existing systems will not change quickly. Persistent advocates, who empower students as they attempt to improve structures of education, can begin to overcome the problem of dehumanization in school.

Advocates can take an important step toward elimination of dehumanizing policies in schools by modeling an open mind toward intelligence and scrupulously avoiding discussion of child ability with peers in terms of numerical scores. The refusal to accommodate single-dimensional views of intelligence will challenge others to consider new conceptualizations of human intelligence. Advocates should also avoid the deficit language about children that has drenched the field of education. Many educators appear blind to the damaging effects of descriptive language ("crack baby," "broken home," "project kids," "socially and emotionally disturbed," "welfare mother," "learning delayed") that devalues children and supports low expectations. The habit of continually describing children in terms of their "deficits" indicates a damaged and troubled relationship between the school and the child (Page 1991). Advocates in schools should also avoid negative descriptions of specific groups or classes of children ("low group," "bottom class on the grade level"). These descriptions negate individual talents, ignore individual efforts, and support inflexible assumptions about ability. Advocates who change the way they themselves talk about children, and who encourage others to do so, will have an impact on school climate. They can "wonder aloud" if certain children have really "failed" or if they have rather been thwarted. The roles that outdated and inflexible views of human intelligence have played in shaping school opportunities can then be openly explored (Lipsky and Gartner 1989). Advocates in institutions can also promote the idea that *schools* are deficient or "at risk" if they cannot meet the needs of diverse students.

While new forms of assessment are being designed and utilized, the traditional standardized test continues to play a major role in schools. Many educators feel torn between the excitement of new ideas and the rigidity of continued testing. High-stakes tests continue to drive major decisions like admission, promotion, graduation, funding, and placement in remedial or "gifted" classes (National Coalition of Advocates for Students 1991). How can advocates address this problem, particularly when test scores are required by or connected to governmental sources of funding? The answer lies in two parts: discovering avenues to humanize an impersonal system of categorization of children, and continuing to articulate problems with the use of tests to designate school opportunities. The National Coalition of Advocates for Students (1991) argues that tests continue to pose the following problems: they reflect faulty assumptions about how children learn, often fail to provide diagnostic information, and continue to reflect or support racial, cultural, or economic bias. Institutional advocates can thus get into the habit of asking persistent questions about assessment. What is the relationship of this test to best available knowledge about how children learn in this age group? What diagnostic information has been provided, and how is it going to be utilized to help the child? Why does this test persistently support the tracking or grouping of children by race or socioeconomic status in this school?

Advocates in institutions will inevitably find assessment linked to tracking and grouping issues. In the absence of a strong research base supporting homogeneous grouping of students (Oakes 1985), advocates may be able to argue successfully for smaller creative projects involving heterogeneous groups of children. Such projects might include planning school social events, engaging in community service, or studying readily available phenomena in the school or community without substantive added expense. Efforts to end well-established systems of tracking continue to be more volatile and to encounter strong arguments that "tests" indicate the need for differentiated opportunities for students. These arguments are most frequently put forth by those whose own children or students are benefiting from the top tiers of inequitable systems. Madaus and Tan (1993) suggest the following advocacy focus for changes in assessment: all assessment techniques should be monitored, educational delivery standards should be in place for all students, poorly based generalizations about students should be avoided, and equitable testing opportunities should be available across the United States. These areas of focus can support institutional advocacy in several ways:

1. Educators can examine assessments used in the district, research possible problems or limitations of those instruments, and suggest better assessments when appropriate.
2. Educators can monitor district and school response to test scores that indicate the need for remediation and support—do students at risk for stigmatization or labeling receive appropriate services and remediations?
3. Educators can monitor inappropriate generalization of responses to test scores in their schools (such as inflexible tracking or ability grouping).
4. Educators can compare assessment opportunities in their school districts with national trends and make recommendations for change or improvement.

It has previously been stated that many new forms of authentic assessment could help children to demonstrate their interests and strengths. However, advocates in institutions must observe the implementation of new assessments carefully. As long as solidified testing and tracking systems exist in schools, the mere addition of some authentic assessment is unlikely to dissolve inequities. Advocates, therefore, must take two tacks as they try to shape the implementation of new assessments within schools. First, they should argue for dismantling the old sorting structures and building new forms of heterogeneous and cooperative grouping of students (Slavin 1987). Second, they should examine new assessments to be sure they will hold high expectations and fair opportunities for all children. Schools with poor morale and ebbing resources may retain the same low expectations for children based on different assessments. The purpose of all assessment should be to determine levels of achievement, to design better-informed approaches to education, and to create more educational opportunities for each child. Also, assessment should discover what the child has learned, not whether the child has learned specific things. Institutional advocacy must seek to foster the strength of public education to care, connect, and respond to the needs of a diverse student population (Noddings 1992). The only acceptable result of that response is a high level of school success leading to a promising future for every child.

The Role of Advocates in Society

The political use of I.Q. and other standardized tests to create or defend social policy should be the major focus of advocates. Public opinion about human intelligence and education should not be shaped by psychometric instruments consistently shown to favor one advantaged group over many others. Educational advocates should be concerned about the recent expansion of norm-referenced standardized tests for political purposes of officials, administrators, or others of influence. Educational testing in the political context tends not to be used to justify greater efforts to meet the needs of all children. Rather, scores are used to place children on a bell curve—a public ranking that inevitably places some children at the bottom (National Coalition of Advocates for Students 1988). Political pressure on teachers to raise test scores skews the climate of the classroom and changes the meaning and intention of education (Genishi 1992). Public castigation of educators for low scores, or the threat of loss of funding, creates anger in schools toward children who do not do well on single measures. The result can be "exclusion of some, the extrusion of others and the 'dumbing down' of the curriculum for yet others" (Lipsky and Gartner 1989: 157). Anxious teachers who are scapegoated for low test scores may in turn attribute their failures to the many identified disabilities in their students—poverty, broken families, or low self-esteem (Macchiarola and Gartner 1989).

Advocates must be concerned about the recurring emergence of the issue of biological determinism, which possesses "evident utility for those in power" (Gould 1981: 21) to retain the status quo. Educators cannot afford to be naive about segments of the public that intend to retain the control and power they now possess. The "winners" in discriminatory school districts often seek to justify meritocratic policies (which often do serve them very well) with the argument that quality is diminished when children of different abilities are mixed. These may also be the most educated and powerful parents in a school district, who have the greatest influence with administrators and school boards. Authentic assessments that demonstrate credible abilities in children who traditionally land at the bottom of school sorting systems may be viewed as a threat by those who stand to lose their current advantage from kindergarten through college admissions. Only strong, articulate, persistent advocacy can chip away at this complex maze of resistance. Advocates must change the mind of the public about the nature of intelligence, the use of tests, and the democratic purpose of schooling.

Steven Jay Gould (1981) notes that the original advance of Stanford Binet testing became a multimillion-dollar industry. The testing industry today is selling 100 million tests a year (Genishi 1992) within a lucrative state-level market. Pressures on schools related to scores are great, but there is little political impetus to properly evaluate the scores and their impact on schools (National Coalition of Advocates for Students 1991). Advocates may find it useful to uncover and publicize the amount of money spent in districts on tests compared to other services for children, and to trace the actual provision of services for children who score low on tests. It would be informative also to track the number of days spent on testing and the ways in which testing disrupts other scheduled learning opportunities. The public may have little idea of the amount of funding designated for tests or the actual follow-up in terms of educational intervention. Likewise, the public may not understand the present and future economic advantages of utilizing authentic assessments to widen opportunities available to all children. Advocates can play a critical role in educating the public about the financial and human costs of inappropriate testing and the advantages of humane and equitable assessment.

Access and equitable opportunity are the final key areas for advocates in society. Original support for widespread testing was based on the claim that education is better when the abilities of children are identified. Ample evidence now demonstrates that testing works to the disadvantage of many. Advocates need to identify arenas in which they can publicly challenge test makers and test users to demonstrate the validity of the claim that they are helping children. For example, companies that produce tests and participate in exhibits at major educational conferences can be asked to participate in an open dialogue with educators at those conferences about the relationship of their tests to positive outcomes for children. Local or state committees that select tests and assessments for school districts can ask representatives of testing companies to meet with them to document positive outcomes of their products. How do the tests ensure fair assessment and educational equity? Advocates can argue for new definitions of "what counts" as school success (Howe 1994), and resist the distribution of resources based on the so-called tested ability of children. The three immediate steps to relieve overt forms of discrimination based on school testing would be: reduction of gross extremes of racial separation, flexibility in all tracking schemes, and relief of the deprivation experienced by children in "low" or segregated tracks (Kirp 1974). It is the combination of advocacy for the reduction of current discrimination and induction of new and equitable forms of assessment that can move the needs of all children forward.

It is important at the end of this chapter to return to Sockett's discussion of courage as central to the moral practice of teaching. He warns that intellectual passions can be crushed by educational institutions because "the weight of social control seems inexorably opposed to the variations of the human spirit" (1993: 75). The courageous teacher, Sockett says, attacks the institutional framework that stultifies, oppresses, and misleads. While traditional views of the teaching profession may not include political and social activism, it seems now that advocacy must permeate the practice of teachers. Cochran-Smith writes: "To alter a system that is deeply dysfunctional, the system needs teachers who regard teaching as a political activity and embrace social change as part of the job— teachers who enter the profession not expecting to carry on business as usual but prepared to join other educators and parents in major reforms" (1995: 494).

Assessment of school children in the United States places mountainous barriers in the paths of many. It thwarts student potential through labeling, tracking, classifying, separating, excluding, or lowering the expectations of those who teach them. The solution to this persistent and seemingly intractable problem, which is complicated by prejudice and discrimination, requires visible and determined action. First of all, educators must acknowledge and resist the ways in which assessment is used to retain and legitimize social, political, and educational inequality. Second, they must embrace vigorous change in the ways they construct meaning from assessment and in the ways assessment affects their daily treatment of children. Finally, they must identify and model professional behaviors, including the use of descriptive language about the abilities of children, that defend human potential and protect children from institutional abuse.

Commitment to such actions may encounter powerful resistance from those who benefit from the advantaged tiers of an unequal system and others who accept the current educational sorting system as valid. Educators who strive to change the nature and role of assessment in schools must therefore attend to the political as well as the educational nature of their efforts. Their advocacy must be based on well-established professional ethics, a personal will to improve the opportunities of children, the ability to care deeply about what happens to children other than one's own, and a passion for justice for a highly diverse and challenged child population. The children of America are waiting for teachers with wisdom and vision of such strength that the mountains in their paths can finally be moved.

NOTES

1. The term "assessment" is used throughout this chapter to identify any form of testing or evaluation that influences educational opportunities and outcomes for children. The term "test" is used to identify norm-referenced standardized examinations used for specific purposes in school systems.
2. The term "teacher" is used in this section to indicate any educator, including academic professors, whose attitudes toward assessment scores are influential in classroom practice.

REFERENCES

Banks, J. A. (1995). The historical reconstruction of knowledge about race: Implications for transformative teaching. *Educational Researcher 24*; 15–25.

Bastian, A., N. Fruchter, M. Gittell, C. Greer, and K. Haskins (1985). *Choosing equality: The case for democratic schooling.* Philadelphia, PA: Temple University Press.

Berger, R. (1991). Building a school culture of high standards: A teacher's perspective. In V. Perrone (ed.), *Expanding student assessment,* 32–39. Washington, DC: Association for Supervision and Curriculum Development.

Boehm, A. E., and M. A. White (1982). *The parent's handbook on school testing.* New York: Teachers College Press.

Bowman, B. T. (1989). Self-reflection as an element of professionalism. *Teachers College Record 90*(3); 44–51.

Bredekamp, S. (ed.) (1987). *Developmentally appropriate practice in early childhood programs serving children from birth through age eight.* Washington, DC: National Association for the Education of Young Children.

Brooks, J. G., and M. G. Brooks (1993). *In search of understanding: The case for constructivist classrooms.* Washington, DC: Association for Supervision and Curriculum Development.

Carter, R. T., and A. L. Goodwin (1994). Racial identity and education. In L. Darling-Hammond (ed.), *Review of Research in Education,* vol. 20, 291–336. Washington, DC: American Educational Research Association.

Children's Defense Fund (1995). *The state of America's children yearbook.* Washington, DC: Author.

Cochran-Smith, M. (1995). Color blindness and basket making are not the answers: Confronting the dilemmas of race, culture, and language diversity in teacher education. *American Educational Research Journal 32*(3): 493–522.

Coleman, J. S. (1990). *Equality and achievement in education.* Boulder, CO: Westview.

Darling-Hammond, L. (1995). Inequality and access to knowledge. In J. A. Banks and C. M. Banks (eds.), *Handbook of research in multicultural education,* 465–83. New York: Macmillan.

Diez, M. E. (1993). Probing the meaning of assessment. In *Essays on emerging assessment issues,* 5–11. Washington, DC: American Association of Colleges for Teacher Education.

Fine, M. (1993). Making controversy: Who's "at risk"? In R. Wollons (ed.), *Children at risk in America,* 91–110. Albany: State University of New York Press.

Fennimore, B. S. (1989). *Child advocacy for early childhood educators.* New York: Teachers College Press.

——— (1995). *Student-centered classroom management.* Albany, New York: Delmar.

Gartner, A., and D. K. Lipsky (1993). Children at risk: Students in special education. In R. Wollons (ed.), *Children at risk in America: History, concepts and public policy,* 157–82. Albany: State University of New York Press.

Genishi, C. (ed.) (1992). *Ways of assessing children and curriculum.* New York: Teachers College Press.

Ginott, H. (1972). *Teacher and child: A book for parents and teachers.* New York: Macmillan.

Goffin, S. G., and J. Lombardi (1988). *Speaking out: Early childhood advocacy.* Washington, DC: National Association for the Education of Young Children.

Goodlad, J. I. (1984). *A place called school: Prospectus for the future.* New York: McGraw-Hill.

Gould, S. J. (1981). *The mismeasure of man.* New York: W. W. Norton.

Hentoff, N. (1989). Anonymous children/diminished adults. In F. J. Macchiarola (ed.), *Caring for America's children,* 137–48. New York: Proceedings of the Academy of Political Science.

Herrnstein, R. J., and C. Murray (1994). *The bell curve: Intelligence and class structure in American life.* New York: Free Press.

Hilliard, A. G., III (1990). Misunderstanding and testing intelligence. In J. I. Goodlad and P. Keating (eds.), *Access to knowledge,* 145–58. New York: College Board.

———— (1991). Equity, access and segregation. In S. L. Kagan (ed.), *The care and education of America's young children: Obstacles and opportunities,* 199–213. 90th Yearbook for the National Society for the Study of Education. Chicago: University of Chicago Press.

Hobsen v. Hansen, 269 F. Supp. 401 (D.D.C. 1967).

Howe, K. R. (1994). Standards, assessment and equality of educational opportunity. *Educational Researcher 23*(8); 27–33.

Jensen, M. A., and Z. W. Chevalier (1990). *Issues and advocacy in early education.* Boston: Allyn and Bacon.

Jones, R. (1972). Labels and stigma in special education. *Exceptional Children 38*; 560–61.

Katz, L. G., and S. C. Chard (1994). *Engaging children's minds: The project approach.* Norwood, NJ: Ablex.

Kirp, D. L. (1974). Student classification, public policy and the courts. *Harvard Educational Review. The Rights of Children.* Reprint Series No.9; 282–327.

Kozol, J. (1991). *Savage inequalities.* New York: Harper Perennial.

Leavitt, R. L., and B. K. Eheart (1991). Assessment in early childhood programs. *Young Children 46*(5); 4–9.

Lipsky, D. K., and A. Gartner (1989) Overcoming school failure: A vision for the future. In F. J. Macchiarola and A. Gartner (eds.), *Caring for America's children,* 149–58. New York: Proceedings of the Academy of Political Science.

Macchiarola, F. J., and A. Gartner (1989). Failing America's children: Responsibilities and remedies. In F. J. Macchiarola and A. Gartner (eds.), *Caring for America's children.* New York: Proceedings of the Academy of Political Science.

Madaus, G. F., and A. G. A. Tan (1993). The growth of assessment. In G. Cawelti (ed.), *Challenges and achievements of American education,* 53–79. Washington, DC: Association for Supervision and Curriculum Development.

Melton, G. B. (1983). *Child advocacy. Psychological issues and interventions.* New York: Plenum.

Mercer, J. R. (1974). A policy statement on assessment procedures and the rights of children. *Harvard Educational Review. The Rights of Children.* Reprint Series No. 9; 328–44.

Murray, F. B. (1993). A convergence of flawed measures of teacher ability: Or how many wrongs does it take to make a right? In *Essays on emerging assessment issues*, 13–19. Washington, DC: American Association of Colleges for Teacher Education.

National Coalition of Advocates for Students (1988). *Barriers to excellence: Our children at risk*. Boston: Author.

——— (1991). *The good common school: Making the vision work for all children*. Boston: Author.

Nieto, S. (1992). *Affirming diversity: The sociopolitical context of multicultural education*. New York: Longman.

Noddings, N. (1992). *The challenge to care in schools. An alternative approach to education*. New York: Teachers College Press.

Oakes, J. (1985). *Keeping track. How schools structure inequality*. New Haven, CT: Yale University Press.

Page, R. N. (1991). *Lower-track classrooms*. New York: Teachers College Press.

Perrone, V. (1991). Moving toward more powerful assessment. In V. Perrone (ed.), *Expanding student assessment*, 164–66. Washington, DC: Association for Supervision and Curriculum Development.

Shor, I. (1986). *Culture wars: School and society in the conservative restoration, 1969–1984*. Boston: Routledge.

Slavin, R. E. (1987). Developmental and motivational perspectives on cooperative learning. *Child Development 58*(9); 1161–67.

Sockett, H. (1993). *The moral base for teacher professionalism*. New York: Teachers College Press.

Westman, J. C. (1979). *Child advocacy. New professional roles for helping families*. New York: Free Press.

Chapter Fourteen

ASSESSING TEACHER PERFORMANCE IN A DIVERSE SOCIETY

Ana María Villegas

The United States is becoming increasingly diverse, as can be seen from the racial and ethnic composition of the school-age population. Students of color comprised 25 percent of elementary and secondary school enrollments in 1980, and about 31 percent in 1990. By the year 2030, students from racial and ethnic groups are expected to account for over half of the school-age population (Educational Research Service 1995). Those entering the teaching profession, now and in the future, must be prepared to teach culturally heterogeneous classes.

In contrast to the changing student population, gains in the proportion of racial and ethnic minorities among teachers has been minimal over the same time period. Specifically, people of color comprised 9 percent of the teaching force in 1981, and about 13 percent in 1993 (National Center for Educational Statistics 1993). In the years to come, the already few numbers of racial and ethnic minority teachers could drop dramatically unless active steps are taken to recruit more people of color into teaching (Darling-Hammond 1990; Smith 1992).

This prediction is based largely on the continued high high school dropout rate among students of color, which limits the numbers eligible for higher education (King 1993; Waters 1989); the inability of teacher education programs to attract and graduate students of color (Coley and Goertz 1991; Kirby and Judson 1993); and the widespread use of teacher competency tests, which has excluded a disproportionately high number of minority candidates (Darling-Hammond 1990; Dilworth 1990; Garcia 1986; Graham 1987; Smith 1992). According to Smith (1992), these tests are culturally biased. Whatever the reasons, the striking discontinuity between the cultural background of teachers and their students deprives all students of minority role models (Bass de Martinez 1988; Carnegie Forum 1986; Garibaldi 1989; Hidalgo and Huling-Austin 1993; King 1993) and limits the cultural knowledge and expertise available within the profession (Irvine 1990; Villegas forthcoming).

Developing a responsible teacher performance assessment system in the current demographic context is a delicate enterprise. The task demands a clear vision of what prospective teachers need to know and be able to do to teach students successfully from diverse cultural backgrounds. At the same time, proactive steps are required to make certain the assessment does not discriminate unfairly against teacher candidates, especially candidates from racial and ethnic minority groups.

This chapter discusses how Educational Testing Service (ETS) dealt with issues of diversity in designing Praxis III: Classroom Performance Assessments of The Praxis Series: Professional Assessments for Beginning Teachers™. Praxis III was developed by ETS primarily for use in decisions made by states or local agencies empowered to license teachers. Because the assessment generates detailed information about a candidate's performance in specified domains of teaching, it has been found useful for professional growth purposes both at the preservice level and during induction programs for beginning teachers.

I have organized the chapter into four sections. First, I present the culturally responsive vision of teaching that guided the development of Praxis III. I then describe Praxis III, showing how both the methods used to collect teacher performance data and the criteria used to evaluate teacher performance flow from the adopted vision of teaching. This is followed by a discussion of equity-related issues inherent in performance assessment, especially when the results rely heavily on the assessor's professional judgment, as Praxis III does. I conclude the chapter with a brief comment about the potential contribution of Praxis III to the field of education.

DEFINING TEACHING

In developing its vision of teaching, ETS staff first considered what research in cognitive science says about the learning process. A review of this research showed that learning is not the simple act of accumulating new facts and skills, as is popularly believed. In order to move beyond rote memorization to achieve understanding, students need to reorganize or reconfigure what they already know about a topic or concept (Resnick 1989; Tharp and Gallimore 1988; Vygotsky 1978), while simultaneously building on the learning strategies that are familiar to them (Moll 1986, 1988; Villegas 1991). Both what a student believes to be true about the topic at hand and how he or she interprets new information and approaches learning profoundly influence what is learned. Put differently, students' prior knowledge and experiences—both personal and cultural—are critical resources for learning.

By extension, teaching entails assisting students to build bridges between what is already familiar to them and the new content and skills to be learned. A salient characteristic of an effective teacher, therefore, is the ability to help students connect learning in school to their everyday life experiences both within and outside school. Because classrooms often include students from diverse backgrounds, teachers need a repertoire of instructional procedures that can accommodate such diversity. Equally important, teachers must be skilled in selecting from this repertoire those instructional procedures that are appropriate to the students and the situation rather than rigidly following fixed scripts. Thus, successful teaching necessarily entails making thoughtful decisions that are guided by theory and research, practical knowledge, and ethical considerations. This view of teaching, which ETS adopted, is described by Dwyer and Villegas (1991) in a document entitled *Guiding Conceptions and Assessment Principles for The Praxis Series: Professional Assessments for Beginning Teachers*™.

Cognizant of the growing diversity of the student population and the importance of having all students be treated equitably by their teachers, ETS gave special attention to what teachers need to know and must be able to do to be effective in our multicultural society. To this end, I conducted a comprehensive review of the professional literature on multicultural education (see Villegas 1991). In that review, I argued that responsive teachers, first and foremost, need a positive attitude toward diversity and a favorable disposition toward students from diverse backgrounds. They also must understand that learning always occurs in a cultural context. Furthermore, they need to know how to familiarize themselves with the background experiences of students in their classes. Even more critical, responsive teachers must be able to use their understanding of the sociocultural dynamics of teaching and learning as well as their knowledge of the students in the class to make learning accessible to all. These principles of responsive teaching were infused throughout the Praxis III assessments and are discussed next.

Openness Toward Diversity

To be responsive to their students, teachers must be favorably predisposed toward diversity. This entails respecting individual and cultural differences, believing that all students are capable of learning, and having a sense of efficacy. These attitudes provide the basis for a meaningful relationship between teacher and students.

Schools and classrooms generally are not organized to accommodate diversity, whether individual or cultural. As traditionally structured, schools assume that all children bring a similar socialization, one that corresponds closely to the experiences of the dominant group in our society (Heath 1983; Michaels 1981; Philips 1983). Youngsters who enter school with ways of learning that differ from the expected norm often are seen by educators as "deficient." Unfortunately, when teachers hold a deficit view of a child, they lose the ability to make accurate assessments of that child's strengths and limitations because they tend to emphasize what the youngster cannot do, rather than what he or she is capable of doing well (Hilliard 1989; Moll 1986; Villegas 1988). To capitalize on the strengths students bring to class, teachers must respect and appreciate differences. They must accept all students as learners who already know much, and who have experiences, concepts, ideas, and language that can be built upon and expanded to help them learn even more.

Responsive teachers believe that all students are capable of learning, and they hold high expectations for each pupil, regardless of background (Brophy 1982;

Delpit 1988; Gallimore 1985; Irvine 1990; Moll 1988; Tikunoff 1990). The power of teacher expectation on student behavior is well documented. Teachers who believe students can learn convey this confidence in numerous ways, such as by maintaining high performance standards and by encouraging the student to excel. In turn, their students tend to live up to those expectations and to do well academically.

Teachers who see themselves as capable of making a difference in their students' learning are more likely to have academically successful students (Brophy 1982; Brophy and Good 1986; Irvine 1990). When teachers have a sense of efficacy, they accept responsibility for teaching all students. Rather than blaming the children and their home conditions for academic difficulties, responsive teachers seek ways of restructuring learning activities to meet the children's needs.

Awareness That Teaching and Learning Occur in a Sociocultural Context

Responsive teachers know that the classroom is not a neutral setting in which all students have equal access to academic content and are able to display freely what they know. It is useful to think of the classroom as a community with its own culture, or patterned way of life (Villegas 1988). In many classrooms, verbal participation is required constantly of students. Implicitly, teaching and learning are equated with talking, and silence is interpreted as the absence of knowledge. Students are questioned in public and required to bid for the floor by raising their hands. Speaking in orderly turns is the rule. Display questions prevail. Individual competition is valued over group cooperation. Topics tend to be introduced in small and carefully sequenced steps, with the overall picture emerging only at the end of the teaching sequence. Unfortunately, the home and community upbringing of some children does not prepare them for the sociocultural demands of this classroom. When teachers fail to see that the organization of the classroom influences student learning, they invariably set some youngsters at a decided disadvantage.

Responsive teachers are vigilant of the sociocultural dynamics of their own classrooms. They understand that embedded in their practices are implicit rules that govern what counts as knowledge, how stories are told, how access to the floor is gained, how members of the class are to interact with one another, and how knowledge is demonstrated, among other things. To create an inclusive classroom community, one in which all students are given access to learning, teachers must first become aware of the sociocultural demands embedded in their classroom activities. Then they must use this insight to the benefit of all students—including making explicit to the youngsters the sociocultural demands of the classroom in order to avoid miscommunication in cross-cultural settings. It also entails modifying the organization of classroom life to build on the ways of learning and interacting that are familiar to the different students in the class.

Learning About the Students

Because teaching entails helping students to build bridges between what they already know and the new knowledge to be acquired, it is critical that teachers become familiar with their students' background knowledge and experiences. This familiarity should not be limited to school knowledge; responsive teaches must also have a clear understanding of the way life is organized in the communities in which the children live. For example, to make the culture of the classroom inclusive of all students, teachers need to know how the children use and display knowledge, tell stories, and interact with peers and adults at home and in their communities. They also must find out about the students' lives outside school, including the youngsters' knowledge of and beliefs about topics that are relevant to the curriculum.

When learning about the students' community experiences, teachers must exercise caution. It is important to keep in mind that individual differences exist within any single group, and that community life changes constantly. To avoid the pitfall of stereotyping, teachers must resist pre-established notions of groups. All Latino children, for example, do not learn best in cooperative group settings. While many Latino children prefer cooperation over competition, there are some who thrive in competitive situations. For this reason, it is best for teachers to know procedures they may use to acquaint themselves with the specific students in their classes. These procedures include making home visits, talking with parents, consulting with other teachers, conferring with community members, and observing children in and out of school.

Using Information About the Students in Planning, Implementing, and Evaluating Instruction

Awareness of the sociocultural dynamics of their classrooms and knowledge of the personal and cultural resources students bring to school will have limited payoff unless teachers can translate their insights into pedagogical practices. Because teaching must build upon and modify students' prior knowledge, responsive teachers select and use instructional materials that are relevant to students' experiences outside school (Hollins 1989), design instructional activities that engage students in personally and culturally appropriate ways (Garibaldi 1992; Irvine 1990), make use of pertinent examples or analogies drawn from the students' daily lives to introduce or clarify new concepts (Irvine 1992), manage the classroom in ways that take into consideration differences in interaction styles (Tikunoff 1985), and use a variety of evaluation strategies that maximize students' opportunities to display what they actually know in ways that are familiar to them (Moll 1988; Ortiz and Maldonado-Colon 1986). It should be emphasized that all students must be helped to meet high standards of achievement. Research shows, however, that there are different paths to this goal. Strict adherence to one type of teaching strategy will invariably disadvantage some students in the class. Instead, responsive teachers need a repertoire of instructional approaches that includes skills in direct instruction as well as in management of cooperative learning—e.g., group projects, peer centers, reciprocal teaching.

The four principles of responsive teaching discussed above apply to all students, not just to youngsters from racial and ethnic minority groups. Traditionally, schools have favored students from the dominant group in our society, and this bias still permeates current practices, as evident in the continual use of ability grouping and instructional tracking despite considerable research showing that children from nondominant groups are negatively impacted by these practices (e.g., Ekstrom and Villegas 1991; Oakes 1992, 1985; Slavin 1990, 1987). The critical challenge to educators today is finding ways of restructuring learning to build on the strengths of all students, not just some. This challenge cannot be met without a favorable disposition toward diversity, a proper grasp of the culture of the school and classroom, and a clear understanding of the personal and cultural resources children bring to school, together with the skill to translate this knowledge in teaching.

A RESPONSIVE ASSESSMENT SYSTEM

Praxis III is informed by the vision of responsive teaching described above. The system assumes that the teacher is a thoughtful practitioner whose job it is to tailor instruction to the students in his or her class, building on what the youngsters know while simultaneously stretching them beyond their known world. This section first describes the instruments and procedures used in Praxis III to collect performance data. Then, it details the criteria used to evaluate teacher performance.

The Assessment Process

Praxis III combines several methods to collect teacher performance data, including classroom observations and semistructured interviews. A full assessment consists of several cycles, each centered on the direct observation by a trained assessor of an instructional event or lesson taught by the beginning teacher in his or her own class. Prior to the initial observation, the beginning teacher is asked to complete a *class profile*, which elicits information about the students registered in the class, general classroom routines, as well as a visual representation of the classroom. The assessor uses this form to learn about the classroom context. After the initial assessment cycle, the teacher only needs to update the form to reflect changes in the class.

Prior to each observation, the beginning teacher completes an *instructional plan* for the specific event or lesson to be observed. The form asks the teacher to specify the learning goals for the event, describe how the goals will be attained, and explain how he or she will evaluate whether the goals were met. This document enables the assessor to review the planned strategies for purposes of formulating appropriate questions to ask during the preobservation conference with the teacher.

During the *preobservation conference*, the assessor discusses the instructional plan with the teacher candidate. This conference, which uses a semistructured interview format, gives the teacher an opportunity to discuss how the features of the plan build on students' prior knowledge and experiences. A subset of the questions asks the candidate to describe the specific procedures she or he has used in learning about the students' background relative to the planned lesson.

The heart of the assessment cycle is the *classroom observation*. All observations are announced, and the exact date and time are agreed upon by the teacher candidate and assessor. Throughout the observation, the assessor takes descriptive notes on the actions of both the teacher and students. Full scripting is not required or encouraged. Instead, the assessor is trained to focus on the type of classroom behavior that is relevant to the Praxis III assessment framework, which is described later in this chapter.

Following the observation, the assessor has a second conference with the teacher. The primary purpose of the *postobservation conference* is to provide the beginning teacher with an opportunity to reflect on the instructional event and evaluate its effectiveness, explain any deviations from the instructional plan, and suggest what she or he would do differently and/or similarly if given the chance to teach the lesson again to the same students. Some of the questions in this interview are designed to glean insight into the teacher's communication with the students' parents or guardians, and consultation with other teachers or school professionals regarding the pupils' development.

As this description shows, both teacher interview and classroom observation data play a critical role in Praxis III assessments. Semistructured interviews give insight into the teacher's thinking and decision making. These interviews are needed because Praxis III assumes that teachers are reflective practitioners who must tailor their teaching to the students in the class. Classroom observations yield information about the teacher's ability to execute an instructional plan. At the same time, they ground conversations with the teacher in the realities of a specific classroom and during a specific instructional event, thereby enabling the well-trained assessor to probe the teacher's explanations of the event in the contextualized manner called for by the guiding conception of teaching.

The Teaching Criteria

Teachers who participate in Praxis III assessments are evaluated on nineteen criteria that cluster into four areas or domains: (A) organizing content knowledge for student learning; (B) creating an environment for student learning; (C) teaching for student learning; and (D) teacher professionalism. The specific criteria comprising each domain are summarized in Table 14.1. The discussion that follows illustrates how equity and diversity concerns were infused throughout the assessment framework.

Organizing Content Knowledge for Student Learning

The criteria in this domain focus on the candidate's understanding of the subject matter for instructional planning purposes. Is the teacher's grasp of the subject matter sufficient to specify clear learning goals for an instructional event? Can the teacher sequence instructional activities and design instructional materials that advance the learning goals? Is the teacher able to devise an evaluation plan to determine whether the students have attained the specified goals?

For a lesson to be effective, the learning goals, instructional methods and materials, and evaluation strategies must be appropriate to the students in the class, as suggested by criteria A2, A4, and A5. Praxis III searches for evidence that the teacher tailors instruction to the students in the class. Such tailoring demands that the teacher be familiar with his or her students, as indicated in criterion A1—becoming familiar with relevant aspects of students' background knowledge and experiences. This important criterion is assessed primarily through a review of information contained in the instruction profile for the given lesson, and elaborated upon during the preobservation interview with the teacher. In judging the teacher's competence in this area, Praxis III looks at the strategies the candidate uses to learn about the students in the class, and what he or she knows specifically about the students' prior knowledge of and interest in the instructional topic.

The preobservation interview includes probing questions that seek to determine how the teacher's familiarity with the students' background knowledge and experiences has influenced his or her choice of materials and learning activities. Answers to these probes reveal how much importance the teacher attributes to the children's background experiences in planning instruction.

Evaluating students is critical to the learning process, as criterion A5 indicates. Teachers need this information to give students feedback about their work and to redirect their learning if necessary. Additionally, this information gives teachers insight into their own instructional effectiveness. Because reliance on a single method of evaluation is likely to create a disadvantage for some children, Praxis III seeks evidence that the teacher plans to use a variety of strategies to evaluate his or her pupils. These strategies might include informal observations of students, examination of students' work products, close attention to students' answers to oral questions or comments during class discussions, and analysis of students' scores on written tests, among other things.

Creating an Environment for Student Learning.

The criteria in this domain focus on the teacher's ability to create an inclusive classroom community that supports student learning. To accomplish this, teachers must actively promote fairness, engage in meaningful relationships with their students, and communicate challenging expectations to each student (see criteria B1, B2, and B3). To determine the teacher's competence in these three areas, Praxis III asks assessors to review their observational and interview data with the following questions in mind: In what ways does the teacher help students have access to learning? Are certain students or groups of students excluded from the lesson? In what ways does the teacher attempt to relate positively to students? In what ways does the teacher help the students feel valued in the class? Does he or she see individual and cultural differences as strengths to draw on, and how is this conveyed? Does the teacher show by word or action that all students are capable of meaningful achievement? Are the learning expectations for the students

Table 14.1 — The Praxis III Criteria

Domain A — Organizing Content Knowledge for Student Learning	Domain B — Creating an Environment for Student Learning	Domain C — Teaching for Student Learning	Domain D — Teacher Professionalism
A1: Becoming familiar with relevant aspects of students' background knowledge and experiences	B1: Creating a climate that promotes fairness	C1: Making learning goals and instructional procedures clear to students	D1: Reflecting on the extent to which the learning goals were met
A2: Articulating clear learning goals for the lesson that are appropriate for the students	B2: Establishing and maintaining rapport with students	C2: Making content comprehensible to students	D2: Demonstrating a sense of efficacy
A3: Demonstrating an understanding of the connections between the content that was learned previously, the current content, and the content that remains to be learned in the future	B3: Communicating challenging learning expectations to each student	C3: Encouraging students to extend their thinking	D3: Building professional relationships with colleagues to share teaching insights and to coordinate learning activities for students
A4: Creating or selecting teaching methods, learning activities, and instructional materials or other resources that are appropriate for the students and that are aligned with the goals of the lesson	B4: Establishing and maintaining consistent standards of classroom behavior	C4: Monitoring students' understanding of content through a variety of means, providing feedback to students to assist learning, and adjusting learning activities as the situation demands	D4: Communicating with parents or guardians about student learning
A5: Creating or selecting evaluation strategies that are appropriate for the students and that are aligned with the goals of the lesson	B5: Making the physical environment as safe and conducive to learning as possible	C5: Using instructional time effectively	

challenging, yet still within their grasp?

Within the Praxis III framework, teachers must establish, communicate, and maintain classroom routines and procedures (criterion B4). Such organization lets students know what is expected of them in different learning situations, how they are supposed to act, and how to get help when they need it. In brief, this organization constitutes the culture of the classroom. Because differences in interaction styles can lead to miscommunication, Praxis III seeks evidence that the teacher candidate makes as clear as possible to the students what is expected of them in different learning situations. Because these expectations are typically established early in the year, the assessor often must infer their existence from the behavior of classroom participants. Assessors are trained to play close attention to whether the classroom community runs smoothly. Instances in which the flow of classroom life is disrupted provide the occasion for the teacher and/or students to make explicit the hidden sociocultural demands of the classroom. When a student's actions do not conform to expectations, does the teacher first rule out the possibility of failure in communication before concluding that the student is either misbehaving or academically incompetent?

It should be emphasized that Praxis III does not preclude student involvement in establishing classroom rules. In fact, such involvement is viewed favorably, as long as all students in the class have input into the decisions.

Evidence for the various criteria in this second Praxis III domain is derived primarily from two sources, the classroom observation and interviews with the teacher. The preobservation interview asks the teacher to talk about the culture of the classroom, focusing on both behavioral rules as well as more subtle expectations about what counts as knowledge and the appropriate ways of displaying academic competence. By observing the actions of the teacher and students, the assessor gains insight into the behavioral rules and sociocultural expectations embedded in the various learning activities. The assessor notes any instances in which the flow of classroom life is disrupted—either by behavioral or academic difficulties. These instances are then discussed in the postobservation interview with the teacher.

Teaching for Student Learning

The five criteria in this domain concern the teacher's ability to help students gain access to instructional content. This entails examining the strategies the teacher uses to: make learning expectations clear to the students; render content comprehensible to the students; encourage students to extend their thinking; monitor students' understanding of the content, providing feedback and adjusting learning activities as needed; and use instructional time effectively. Because the criteria focus on the quality of the interactions teachers have with their students, for this portion of the assessment data are derived primarily from the classroom observation. The postobservation interview allows the assessor to raise questions about the observed actions.

From an equity perspective, the task of the assessor relative to this teaching domain is to determine whether the specific strategies used by the teacher in the observed lesson provide access to learning for *all students*, not just some. How does the teacher, for example, help students of different backgrounds (e.g., ethnic groups, language groups, males and females, students with exceptionalities) understand the instructional procedures? Does the teacher use examples from the youngsters' lives outside the school to make content comprehensible? Does the teacher challenge students' thinking in ways that are relevant to their experiences? Are there patterns of exclusion in the way the teacher monitors student understanding and provides feedback? Are all students given meaningful work to do?

Teacher Professionalism

Professional teachers have a number of responsibilities that extend beyond their work in the classroom but are still related to it. For one thing, they must reflect on their practice. Beginning teachers cannot be expected to implement perfect lessons. In fact, the perfect classroom performance is rare even among highly competent and experienced teachers. For this reason, all teachers must cultivate the ability to reflect on their performance in class with the goal of learning from experience. Praxis III acknowledges the importance of teacher reflection in criterion D1, evidence of which is sought during the postobservation interview.

Professional teachers also must believe they can make a difference in the lives of their students (see criterion D2). Teachers with a sense of efficacy persist in the search for strategies that will enable students who are experiencing learning difficulties to overcome the problems. In Praxis III, assessors seek out evidence of this commitment to students' learning primarily during the postobservation interview, which asks the teacher to suggest specific actions for working with individual students or groups who were observed having difficulties in the lesson.

As members of a profession, teachers must build relationships with colleagues for the purposes of sharing instructional insight (criterion D3). Additionally, professional teachers must communicate routinely with parents or guardians about student learning (criterion D4). Evidence for these two criteria also comes from the postobservation interview with the teacher.

To summarize, Praxis III assumes that teachers are professionals who on a daily basis must make a myriad of decisions regarding how best to teach the students in their classes. The Praxis III system also assumes that to be responsive, teachers must help the students build bridges between their prior knowledge and experience and the new content and skills to be learned. As such, responsive teachers need to learn about their students' experiences and to draw on this knowledge in teaching. They also must create classroom communities that are inclusive of all students, and use a flexible teaching style to make academic content accessible to all. None of this can be accomplished, however, if teachers do not accept diversity nor hold both themselves and their students accountable to high standards of performance.

As the description of the teaching criteria shows, Praxis III is a high-inference assessment system. That is, the system acknowledges that competent teaching is displayed in many different ways, depending on the context. For example, some of the ways a teacher can make content comprehensible to his or her students include having the youngsters do library research, engaging the class in discussions, getting students to question each other in small groups, providing direct explanations of concepts to the class, or using analogies to clarify confusing ideas. This contextualized view of teaching, while ideal for accommodating classroom diversity, also makes the system highly dependent on the professional judgment of the assessor, thereby introducing an external threat to the validity of the system. The next section discusses this and other equity-related concerns, and how ETS addressed them in Praxis III.

HIGH-INFERENCE PERFORMANCE ASSESSMENT— EQUITY CONSIDERATIONS

Without a doubt, the most valid way to assess teaching competence is to engage candidates in the activity of teaching. This does not mean, however, that performance assessment is inherently more equitable than paper-and-pencil tests, as some have come to believe. While having greater face validity than conventional tests, performance assessment must contend with a set of interpretive problems that can arise from cultural and other types of bias (Long and Stansbury 1994). This is especially true in high-inference systems that rely on assessor judgment.

A Look at the Problem

The major danger of high-inference assessment systems is that, unless carefully monitored, the cultural assumptions and personal biases of the assessors might influence their judgment of the candidate's professional decisions and actions. A hypothetical example will help illustrate this point. Teachers in the Kamehameha Early Education Project, a well-documented educational program that has produced consistently good academic results with Polynesian children in Hawaii, are asked to allocate turns at talk during reading lessons in ways that resemble the rules for participation in the "talk story," a recurrent speech event in the children's home community (see Au 1980; Au and Jordan 1981). Specifically, the teacher encourages students to build joint responses during story time, either among themselves or together with him or her. This strategy of collective turn-taking parallels the joint construction of a story by two or more individuals, which is typical of the talk story. Joint turn-taking, however, contrasts markedly with the one-speaker-at-a-time rule that prevails in traditional classrooms. Lacking familiarity with this feature of Hawaiian culture, an assessor might view negatively the collective turn-taking strategy described in the above example. From the assessor's cultural vantage point, the lesson could appear disjointed or even chaotic. This might lead him or her to assign a low rating to the teacher in the area of classroom management, when in fact the instructor is being responsive to the students by building on the children's cultural experiences.

Similarly, assessors who have a strong preference for a teacher-centered instructional style might find fault with student-centered classroom lessons. Conversely, those who prefer to have students take considerable control for their learning could view teacher-directed instruction negatively.

Assessors are not the only source of bias in performance assessments. Biases can also be built into the methods used to collect performance assessment data. For example, the teacher interviews used in Praxis III may seem like straightforward activities in which the interviewer elicits specific information from the interviewee. This deceptively simple task can become terribly complex, however, when the interviewer expects direct answers to his or her questions, but the interviewee has learned from her or his culture to avoid giving direct answers because it is considered impolite. Thus, differences in communicative norms may cause miscommunication and could ultimately lead to misinterpretations about a candidate's knowledge and skills.

The point of the examples given above is that teacher evaluation, like teaching, occurs in a sociocultural context. Built into this context are tacit expectations regarding how candidates are to display their pedagogical expertise. When left unexamined, these expectations can become a major source of problems in performance assessments.

How Praxis III Guards Against Problems of Interpretation

Praxis III uses a variety of strategies to guard against problems of interpretation, the most salient of which is a rigorous five-day training program for assessors. The program is designed to prepare trainees to conduct both the classroom observation and the accompanying interviews with the teacher, review and code the data, and make evaluative judgments about teacher performance. Training activities make extensive use of videotaped classroom lessons and interviews with teachers to give trainees practice with the system. Additionally, trainees are required to complete at least one full assessment cycle in an actual classroom setting and to discuss their experiences with colleagues in the training program. To become certified as a Praxis III assessor, a trainee must demonstrate the ability to carry out an assessment professionally and reliably. To be admitted to the training program, a candidate must have extensive and recent teaching experience.

As part of their training, potential assessors participate in a variety of activities designed to sensitize them to the cultural dynamics of classrooms. For example, one of my papers (see Villegas 1991) is used as a stimulus for small group discussions of responsive teaching. As a follow-up, trainees are asked to generate examples of responsive and nonresponsive teaching behaviors for selected Praxis III criteria. In another activity, videotaped segments are used to analyze the cultures of two strikingly different classrooms. Throughout all this, trainees are helped to understand that good teaching practice is context specific and is highly influenced by the students, the subject matter, and the situation.

The assessor program also prepares trainees to monitor the intrusion of their own cultural assumptions into the judgments they will make about teacher candidate performance. One of the most useful discussions on this topic follows a videotape of an African American teacher instructing a class of mostly African American students. Invariably, the tape produces strong opinions about the teacher's competence. Usually, some of the trainees see the teacher as cold, distant, and overly focused on discipline. From these impressions they often infer that the instructor has poor rapport with the students. The trainees are generally surprised to learn that the teacher in the videotape is considered superior by her colleagues and has meaningful relationships with the students in her class. In fact, what some assessors in training describe negatively as an authoritarian teaching style is precisely one of the salient qualities that makes this teacher effective with the students. This incident gives the leader of the training session an opportunity to engage the participants in a thoughtful discussion of how assessors' preferences in teaching styles, unless monitored, can distort the assessment results.

Because evaluation in cross-cultural settings is especially complex, assessors in training are cautioned to search for multiple pieces of evidence from their data, especially when inclined toward giving a low rating to the teacher candidate for any single Praxis III criterion. Furthermore, if during a classroom observation the assessor sees what might be considered a questionable practice, he or she is trained to probe the teacher's rationale for this practice during the postobservation interview and to take this information into account in arriving at a judgment about the candidate's competence. The teacher might have a convincing reason for behaving as he or she did in the classroom, that the assessor might miss unless it is explained. This use of the postobservation interview allows assessors to monitor, at least to some extent, the intrusion of their biases into the assessment.

Another strategy intended to protect teacher candidates from assessor bias, especially when Praxis III is used in making licensure decisions, is to require the licensing agency to conduct multiple assessment cycles of any single candidate, each involving a different assessor. For example, ETS requires that a minimum of three assessments be conducted whenever Praxis III is used to license a teacher. ETS encourages licensing agencies to conduct additional assessment cycles if resources permit it. Still another precaution licensing agencies might take to avoid potential miscommunication deriving from cultural differences (although it is not a precaution required by ETS of Praxis III users) is to have at least one assessor on the team working with the candidate be of his or her racial/ethnic background. While membership in the same group does not eliminate the possibility of miscommunication, it might at least help flag gross misinterpretation of a candidate's actions and explanations.

Last, as a service to teacher candidates, ETS provides an orientation session to Praxis III prior to their participation in the assessment process. This orientation provides a thorough explanation of the criteria used to assess teaching performance and the methods used to collect performance data. Praxis III was not designed to surprise candidates with trick questions. The system is public and accessible to all.

CONCLUDING COMMENTS

With Praxis III, ETS has taken a bold step toward advancing a professional view of teaching. Grounded in a context-specific and culturally responsive model of teaching, Praxis III requires that teacher candidates tailor their instruction to particular situations, instead of merely implementing tightly prescribed procedures. This conception of teaching and the high-inference assessment system that it calls for have the potential for upgrading the competence of the teaching force and ultimately for improving the educational experiences of all students, including the increasing numbers of students from racial and ethnic minority groups.

Departures from traditional views of teaching and conventional methods of testing teacher competence have posed a new set of equity challenges. Chief among these challenges is finding effective strategies for guarding against assessor bias and for preventing miscommunication derived from cultural differences between the assessed and their assessors, as described in this chapter. ETS has responded to these challenges decisively. It has developed a rigorous training program for assessors, one that includes numerous activities designed to guard against potential problems of interpretation. ETS also has issued guidelines requiring teacher licensing agencies using Praxis III to conduct multiple assessment cycles of any single candidate, each by a different assessor. Furthermore, ETS provides a comprehensive orientation to Praxis III for teacher candidates designed to give them a clear understanding of the assessment methods and criteria, and to prepare them for the assessment process. Praxis III is currently being used in California on a pilot basis to license teachers who were certified in other states but not in California. California is also using a modified version of Praxis III in its extensive support and assessment program for beginning teachers. Ohio and Minnesota are now preparing to implement Praxes III. But, because this is a relatively new system, it is still too early to tell whether the strategies adopted will allow all candidates—but especially candidates of color, who as a group have experienced difficulties in the past with teacher competency tests—a fair opportunity to demonstrate strengths that might not otherwise surface through more traditional forms of teacher assessment.

REFERENCES

Au, K. H. (1980). Participation structures in a reading lesson with Hawaiian children: An analysis of a culturally appropriate instructional event. *Anthropology and Education Quarterly 11*(2); 93–115.

Au, K. H., and C. Jordan (1981). Teaching reading to Hawaiian children: Finding a culturally appropriate solution. In H. Trueba, G. Guthrie, and K. Au (eds.), *Culture and the bilingual classroom: Studies in classroom ethnography,* 139–52. Rowley, MA: Newbury House.

Bass de Martinez, B. (1988). Political and reform agendas impact on the supply of black teachers. *Journal of Teacher Education 39*(1); 10–13.

Brophy, J. E. (1982). Successful teaching strategies for the inner-city child. *Phi Delta Kappan 63*(8); 527–30.

Brophy, J. E., and T. L. Good (1986). Teacher behavior and student achievement. In M. C. Wittrock (ed.), *Handbook of research on teaching*, 328–75. 3d ed. New York: Macmillan.

Carnegie Forum on Education and the Economy, Task Force on Teaching as a Profession (1986). *A nation prepared: Teachers for the 21st century*. Washington, DC: Carnegie Forum.

Coley, R. J., and M. E. Goertz (1991). *Characteristics of minority test takers*. Princeton, NJ: Educational Testing Service.

Darling-Hammond, L. (1990). Teachers and teaching: Signs of a changing profession. In R. W. Houston, M. Haberman, and J. Sikula (eds.), *Handbook of research on teacher education*, 267–90. New York: Macmillan.

Delpit, L. D. (1988). The silenced dialogue: Power and pedagogy in educating other people's children. *Harvard Education Review 58*(3); 280–98.

Dilworth, M. E. (1990). *Reading between the lines: Teachers and their racial/ethnic cultures*. Teacher Education Monograph No. 11. Washington, DC: ERIC Clearinghouse on Teacher Education and American Association of Colleges for Teacher Education.

Dwyer, C. A., and A. M. Villegas (1991). *Guiding conceptions and assessment principles for The Praxis Series: Professional Assessments for Beginning Teachers*[TM]. Princeton, NJ: Educational Testing Service.

Educational Research Service (1995). *Demographic factors in American education*. Arlington, VA: Author.

Ekstrom, R. B., and A. M. Villegas (1991). Ability grouping in middle grades mathematics: Process and consequences. *Research in Middle Level Education 15*(1); 1–20.

Gallimore, R. (1985). *The accommodation of instruction to cultural differences*. Paper presented at the University of California Conference on the Underachievement of Linguistic Minorities, Lake Tahoe, CA, May.

Garcia, P. A. (1986). The impact of national testing on ethnic minorities with proposed solutions. *Journal of Negro Education 55*(3)1; 347–57.

Garibaldi, A. M. (1992). Preparing teachers for culturally diverse classrooms. In M. E. Dilworth (ed.), *Diversity in teacher education: New expectation*, 23–39. San Francisco: Jossey-Bass.

Garibaldi, A. (ed.) (1989). *Teacher recruitment and retention: With a special focus on minority teachers*. Washington, DC: NEA.

Graham, P. A. (1987). Black teachers: A drastically scarce resource. *Phi Delta Kappan 68*(3); 598–605.

Heath, S. B. (1983). *Ways with words: Language, life, and work in communities and classrooms*. London: Cambridge.

Hidalgo, F., and L. Huling-Austin (1993). Alternate teacher candidates: A rich source for Latino teachers in the future. In Tomas Rivera Center, *Reshaping teacher education in the Southwest—A forum: A response to the needs of Latino students and teachers*, 13–34. Claremont, CA: Tomas Rivera Center.

Hilliard, A. (1989). Teachers and cultural styles in a pluralistic society. *NEA Today 7*; 65–69.

Hollins, E. (1989). *A conceptual framework for selecting instructional approaches and materials for inner-city black youngsters.* Paper commissioned by the California Curriculum Commission, Sacramento, California.

Irvine, J. J. (1990). *Beyond role models: The influence of black teachers on black students' achievement.* Paper presented at Educational Testing Service, Princeton, NJ, May.

———— (1992). Making teacher education culturally responsive. In M. E. Dilworth (ed.), *Diversity in teacher education: New expectation*, 79–92. San Francisco: Jossey-Bass.

King, S. H. (1993). The limited presence of African-American teachers. *Review of Educational Research 63*; 115–49.

Kirby, S. N., and L. Hudson (1993). Black teachers in Indiana: A potential shortage? *Evaluation and Policy Analysis 15*(2); 181–194.

Long, C., and K. Stansbury (1994). Performance assessments for beginning teachers. *Phi Delta Kappan 76*(4); 318–22.

Michaels, S. (1981). Sharing time: Children's narrative style and differential access to literacy. *Language in Society 10*; 423–42.

Moll, L. C. (1986). Writing as communication: Creating strategic learning environments for students. *Theory into Practice 25*(2); 102–108.

———— (1988). Some key issues in teaching Latino students. *Language Arts 65*(5); 465–72.

National Center for Education Statistics (1993). *Schools and staffing in the U.S.: A statistical profile 1990–91.* Washington, DC: U.S. Office of Education.

Oakes, J. (1985). *Keeping track: How schools structure inequality.* New Haven: Yale University Press.

———— (1992). Grouping students for instruction. In M. C. Alkin (ed.), *Encyclopedia of Educational Research*, 562–68. 6th ed. New York: Macmillan.

Ortiz, A. A., and E. Maldonado-Colon, E. (1986). Reducing inappropriate referrals of language minority students in special education. In A. C. Willig and H. F. Greenberg (eds.), *Bilingualism and learning disabilities*, 37–50. New York: American Library Publishing Company.

Philips, S. U. (1983). *The invisible culture: Communication in classroom and community on the Warm Springs Indian Reservation.* New York: Longman.

Resnick, L. B. (1989). Introduction. In L. B. Resnick (ed.), *Knowing, learning, and instruction: Essays in honor of Robert Glaser*, 1–42. Hillsdale, NJ: Erlbaum.

Slavin, R. E. (1987). Ability grouping and student achievement in elementary schools: A best-evidence synthesis. *Review of Educational Research 57*; 293–336.

———— (1990). *Achievement effects of ability grouping in secondary schools: A best-evidence synthesis.* Madison, WI: National Center on Effective Secondary Schools.

Smith, G. P. (1992). *Recruiting minority teachers.* Paper presented at a major symposium of the annual meeting of the American Association for Teacher Education.

Tharp, R., and R. Gallimore (1988). *Rousing minds to life: Teaching, learning, and schooling in social context.* Cambridge: Cambridge University Press.

Tikunoff, W. J. (1985). *Applying significant bilingual instructional features in the classroom.* Rosslyn, Virginia: National Clearinghouse for Bilingual Education.

———— (1990). *Toward a pedagogy of authentic second language development.* Keynote address at the annual meeting of the New York State Association for Bilingual Education, New York.

Villegas, A. M. (1988). School failure and cultural mismatch: Another view. *Urban Review 20*(4); 253–65.

———— (1991). *Culturally responsive pedagogy for the 1990s and beyond.* Trend and Issues Paper No. 6. Washington, DC: ERIC Clearinghouse on Teacher Education.

———— (forthcoming). Increasing the diversity of the U.S. teaching force. In B. J. Biddle, T. L. Good, and I. F. Goodson (eds.), *The international handbook of teachers and teaching.* Dordrecht, The Netherlands: Kluwer Academic Publishers.

Vygotsky, L. S. (1978). *Mind in society.* Cambridge: Harvard University Press.

Waters, M. M. (1989). An agenda for educating black teachers. *Educational Forum 53*(3); 267–79.

Chapter Fifteen

ASSESSING the DIALOGUE of TEACHERS in a MULTICULTURAL CLASSROOM: A Difficult Struggle

Valerie Ooka Pang

At the end of the every semester I hear teacher education professors moan in the hallowed halls of academe, "I hate giving grades! Let the students have whatever grade they want!" Then I see a wild-eyed professor frantically run down the hall out of the building screaming, "I need a sabbatical!"

Assessment is one of the most difficult aspects of teacher education. I struggle with assessment every semester because it is a complex task that involves appraising content and pedagogical knowledge, instructional skills, social interaction skills, and attitude. Comprehensive teacher assessment includes a whole list of duties and responsibilities that I feel must be reviewed within the context of equity. How fairly does the teacher treat each student? What attitudes does the teacher hold about different groups of children? What efforts is the teacher making in curriculum and instruction to reach and motivate all students? These are extremely important questions, yet ones not easily measured. By raising important questions such as these in class, it is possible to gain access to teachers' conceptions of and responses to issues of equity. Unfortunately, in many teacher education classes, lecture is the primary form of instruction. Yet I find that dialogue is one of the most important instructional strategies one can use with adult learners. In this chapter I will explain why dialogue is important in teacher education and examine the complexities of assessing discourse. For the purpose of this chapter, I will look particularly at assessing teacher dialogue in teacher education classes. Those of us who work with teachers cannot witness their classroom practice on a constant or continuous basis. However, we have access to their thinking, dispositions, and beliefs through their classroom conversations. In fact, my experience has been that through the assessment of teacher dialogue, we are provided with critical insights into the ways in which teachers perceive children and the ways in which they approach compelling or controversial issues.

TEACHER ASSESSMENT: A NATIONAL CONCERN

On the national level, accountability is a widespread concern. The National Board for Professional Teaching Standards (NBPTS) was established in 1987 to create a national policy on teacher assessment and to develop new teacher assessment procedures (Baratz-Snowden 1993). Professionals in the field as well as in the general community believe teachers need to meet rigorous standards before being granted initial or permanent teaching certificates. In response to this, NBPTS has developed a teacher assessment procedure that incorporates interviews and portfolio materials, examines performance through simulations, and conducts a measure of content area knowledge. NBPTS felt that it was important to measure not only the content knowledge of teachers but also their performance in the classroom and how they make decisions about situations that arise in schools. While the NBPTS standards apply to the advanced certification of experienced teachers, the Interstate New Teacher Assessment and Support Consortium (INTASC) is working to address intial teacher certification, preparation, and induction. Also established in 1987, INTASC aims to develop performance-based standards that "describe what teachers should know and be able to do . . . placing more emphasis on the abilities teachers develop than the hours they spend taking classes" (INTASC 1992: 3). In considering these standards, the INTASC task force is also considering a variety of alternative assessments, including portfolios.

Portfolios have become a key aspect of teacher assessment because they allow for the examination of both pedagogical knowledge and teaching skills. For example, Wolf, Whinery, and Hagerty (1995) recommend that videos of lessons be included in portfolios so that an assessment of teacher skills embedded within the classroom context can be viewed as part of the collection. They believe portfolios should be a starting point for conversations about teacher practice in small groups of four or five teachers in a school or university class. Cruickshank and Metcalf (1993) suggest that teacher abilities can also be assessed through on-campus experiences using microteaching and simulations. Microteaching allows a peer group to assess a teacher's lesson and her/his ability to present information clearly and to adapt to the needs of the students.

Sometimes I ask teachers to create portfolios. These portfolios may include educational artifacts like lesson plans, journal notes, research papers, student work, and self-reflection pieces on philosophy and goals. Still, I find that many of our assessment measures, even those that are more performance based, fall short because they do not look at interactions between teacher and students or assess the quality of dialogue a person contributes to class discussions.

THE IMPORTANCE OF DIALOGUE

I believe dialogue is one of the most important methods of instruction for teacher educators. Dialogue is exciting, challenging, and thought provoking. I use an issues-centered approach to teacher education. Since teachers generally dominate the "conversation" in their classrooms, it is all the more important in teacher education classes to continually stress the inquiry method. I think modeling dialogue in university classes provides an example of a crucial teaching strategy. Teachers learn to be more concise and thoughtful when a room full of their peers is ready and able to respond to them. And by listening carefully to what teachers say, I gather valuable insights into how mindful teachers are to listen and respond to their students.

One of the questions I asked myself when I began teaching at the university level was, "How can I develop a community of learners where everyone works together to create a free and just society?" I chose Paulo Freire's philosophy of problem-posing education (1971); thus much of my class is devoted to dialogue and group work. Why? Change in teachers must come from within; this occurs only when teachers have had many opportunities to share, discuss, challenge, and reflect on educational issues like student expectations, academic tracking, bilingual education, cultural assimilation, white privilege, and Afrocentric curricula. Once in a while I lecture, but I believe when teachers are forced to tackle difficult issues in small and large groups, they must explain and sometimes defend their viewpoints, and this engages them in the process of learning. Teachers, then, share in the leadership and the responsibility for their own learning and the growth of the community.

In contrast, many university and K–12 classrooms are founded upon what Freire called the banking approach to education, where students are passive learners who receive and memorize information so that they can recite it back to the teacher (Freire 1971). This passive role conditions students to accept the status quo. When schools, whether K–12 or university level, act like factories, students are taught not to challenge or to create new ways of thinking; they may blindly accept the unfairness of society (Carnoy 1974: 1991).

Many educators believe teachers should be encouraged to develop and express their "voice" (Delpit 1995; Giroux 1988; Sleeter and Grant 1988). I believe most teachers need to be challenged to cultivate their voice and that this can happen when they have opportunities to engage in dialogue about crucial educational issues. In a shared learning process, teachers ask one another many questions that force them to clarify their values. They also ask me difficult, soul-searching questions.

In modeling a classroom dedicated to dialogue, I aim to create mini-"think tanks" of people who are committed to working together. The classroom can reflect a democratic community in which each person is an active and reflective learner. I hope the atmosphere says to each teacher, "You are a precious and worthy person. All of us in the class need your input to develop. Help us be the best people we can be." I want each teacher to create the same kind of atmosphere in her/his classroom.

During the first class session, I begin memorizing the names of all the teachers. Learning the names quickly tells each person that she or he is an important member of our class family. In addition, knowing their names allows me to encourage their participation in discussions. This important first step helps me to create strong interpersonal relationships with the teachers in my classes.

Since I believe in "problem-posing" or issues-centered education, I try to create a classroom in which we trust and respect one another, a place of caring (Noddings 1984). It is a safe place where mistakes are the "fertilizer of success." It may take time for some teachers to find their own "voice" and to express it. I explain to teachers that we need the input of every person because we will not grow as a learning community unless we help one another see new aspects of issues.

ASSESSMENT OF SOCIAL INTERACTION AND ATTITUDES

In a teacher education class, I have many opportunities to witness discourse skills. Though alternative assessments like portfolios may be effective in examining content knowledge, lesson planning, and philosophical reflections, portfolios may not show how teachers interact with their colleagues, parents, and students. I build my teacher education classes upon dialogue as the major method of instruction (Pang 1994). It helps me find out: What do people say? Does what they say show a commitment to our national values of equity, freedom, and justice? How do they deliver their thoughts? In their interactions and discussions, do teachers see themselves as part of a large interconnected community? What growth does the teacher show? Is there evidence that the teacher is looking at issues from many viewpoints? Is the teacher able to place the needs of the community above his/her own?

Barber (1992) has spoken of our civic bankruptcy, how we have become a nation of individuals who see themselves almost exclusively as private people with responsibilities only to family and career. I listen for verbal responses and watch for interactions of teachers that demonstrate a sense of community. I believe it is crucial that they understand their destiny is linked to their colleagues and to their students (Pang, Gay, and Stanley 1995). We do not teach because we are sacrificing our lives for others. Hopefully we teach because we are helping to create a better society for ourselves, our families, and our neighbors. One of the most disturbing events in a classroom of teachers is to hear a teacher in one situation espouse the virtues of equality, freedom, and community while in another instance refuse to listen to a colleague.

In summary, as teachers engage in dialogue, I listen for statements from teachers that provide me with a sense of the following:

1. Is the teacher respectful to herself and to others when she answers or engages in group activities?
2. Does the teacher respond to the others' views in a thoughtful manner, or is he only waiting for his turn to respond?
3. Does the teacher show a commitment to the community of learners by listening to the response of all colleagues, even those who may disagree with her? Can she put herself in someone's "shoes" and look at the issue from another's viewpoint? Can she do this when a person is a nonmajority group member?
4. Does the teacher give his honest views of the issue being discussed? Is the teacher speaking from personal views or just espousing education jargon or what is considered acceptable?
5. Does the teacher see herself as part of a large community where she has the responsibility to contribute to the well-being of the whole, sometimes in lieu of her own personal needs?
6. How does the teacher relay information about his students? Is he supportive of their abilities and concerned about their needs?

Let us now look at a dialogue teachers in my class had about race. I used the O.J. Simpson verdict as a starting point for a discussion on racial tensions, which led to dialogue about how cultural experiences shape the way people view life. Many times I notice it is easy to overintellectualize a topic. However, by using controversial topics that evoke emotional responses, I believe I am likely to get responses that more accurately represent what teachers really think and believe. In the area of racial issues, it is difficult to find topics in which teachers are willing to share their true feelings. Often I have found teachers not to say what they think in fear of appearing to be racist or closed minded. However, in terms of the O.J. Simpson trial, it was difficult to find anyone who did not feel strongly about the outcome. This event easily initiated powerful and passionate conversations around race, racial equality, racism, and equity and caused people to articulate their own beliefs and values. Shaver and Strong (1982) remind us that education is a lifelong commitment to growth, but that it is only through the continual review of our values that can we move ahead. By talking with each other, teachers can reflect upon what other people have said and reconstruct their views. Dialogue becomes an important avenue for self-reflection.

The O.J. Simpson Verdict

The day the verdict was read, teachers came to class extremely agitated. I could feel emotional conflict in the air. Some of the teachers were extremely mad. Others were ecstatic. I asked the teachers to wait a week to discuss the case. I felt that a week would give them distance from the initial announcement so they would be able to view the issue with logic and reason. Here is a portion of their conversation.

I began: "I noticed that several of you came to class ready to burst. Before we begin, I hope that we can have a respectful conversation. I think it is an opportunity for all of us to look at the verdict from each other's viewpoints. Please address how you felt about the verdict and answer this question, 'What did you learn from the O.J. Simpson verdict?'"

Charlotte jumped in right away saying, "Oh man! He was guilty. He shouldn't have gotten off."

John (in a sarcastic tone) said, "O.J. is the million-dollar man who killed his wife and got away with it."

Andrew sat calmly and commented. "I was happy to see O.J. get away with it. I know this sounds bad, but there have been so many black men who have been put in jail for things they didn't do. I was happy that he got off."

Evan seemed somewhat puzzled by Andrew's comments and asked, "What do you mean? He killed two people. How can you say you were happy?"

Andrew replied, "I know that you won't understand, but as a black male, I know that the system is not fair. We are always afraid the police will stop us or pick us up for things we didn't do. That's just how it is. I was happy O.J. got off. I don't know if he was guilty or innocent."

No one said anything for a moment.

Then Peter commented, "The media coverage of the trial was shocking. The media promoted mistrust between the races."

John looked around and observed, "I saw the verdict as a class thing. He was a wealthy man—that's why he got off. The justice system is tied to wealth—money can buy freedom. I also saw an interview of a black man. He defended the verdict as a racial verdict because the black jurors couldn't go back to their community with a guilty verdict. I am just telling you what I heard on TV."

A few teachers looked at John as if to reply, but they waited for their turn to speak.

Charlotte allowed softly, "I was upset with the whole system and how the case was handled. Two people are dead. I couldn't believe what was printed in the *Star* and *National Inquirer*. The kids brought those newspapers to school."

Robert defiantly said, "I took the newspapers away from the kids because I didn't feel it was appropriate. The pictures were bloody and not for school."

Christine firmly reminded us, "Remember that there are two people dead. Where are the kids going to go? There's no closure to this. Who did it?"

Victoria interjected carefully, "If he was guilty he should fry. But I don't think O.J. could have done it. Let me make it clear—he's done nothing for me or the black community. I am amazed at the things that go on—planting evidence, framing people. He couldn't have cleaned up all that blood. O.J. couldn't have done it. We need to make our own analysis and not jump to conclusions."

Sherlie reminded us, "We know how husbands clean up after themselves. I don't think O.J. did it."

One of the male teachers looked up, but did not say anything.

Robert said in a matter-of-fact tone, "O.J. became white. He was accepted by the white society. He wasn't really part of the black community. I don't think he did it either. He didn't have time to do all that they said he did."

Henrietta said, "It comes down to education. The jury was hand picked. What was their level of education? I don't think they were very educated and that's why the verdict was not guilty. I don't want to say anything more, but it is very important who serves on the jury. I don't think the jurors were very smart."

Robert looked at Henrietta, "I don't want to be disrespectful, but are you saying that just because most of the jurors were black that he got off?"

Henrietta made a nervous laugh, "I just wanted to point out that the jurors were not that educated and so didn't have the skills to make a complicated decision. I didn't say anything about the jurors being black."

John shook his head as if in disbelief. He wanted to reply, but seemed to be holding back.

Ron raised his hand and said, "This was not a racial issue as much as it was a murder trial. Two people were murdered. People need to get a life. Some people watched it every day. Their lives revolved around the trial. It was a soap opera."

Helen explained, "I have a sixth-grade class made up of African American and Latino students. They wrote an essay on their opinion of the verdict before it was read. I didn't tell them what I thought. In my class, one-third of the children believed O.J. was not guilty, while two-thirds thought he was guilty. My kids are mostly minority."

Christine told the class, "My class discussed the jury and the responsibility of juries. My kids wanted to know what the jurors thought."

Helen commented, "The jurors argued. They were sequestered for too long of a time. They got real tired and wanted to get out of there. Their verdict may have been different if they hadn't been isolated for such a time."

Patty spoke with quiet conviction, "I can't speak for everyone in the black community, but I think about the times when African American males have not gotten fair treatment. We have to carry an ID. This is really a racially divided issue. Our personal experiences shape how we act and what we think. I told my teenage son if the police stop him, then he is to answer the officer's questions politely, but he is not to get out of his car. He should be very careful. He is not to trust the officer. I did not tell my son when he was growing up that the police officer is his friend."

Dustin sadly observed, "I was surprised at my own racist reaction when I heard the verdict over the radio. I didn't think it was right for this *black* man to get away with it. I was embarrassed about my own feelings. I work with people in the prison system and most of my clients are African American. I didn't think I was really prejudiced."

Charlotte asked, "Why did O.J. run away? He acted like he was guilty."

Victoria responded, "When a black man sees the police, he runs."

Robert looked at the teachers around the room and stated, "I learned from watching everything that it was a complex issue. I watched how the judge responded and he seemed to be impartial. There were many things involved in the case, and I believe race was one of the major issues. And remember we weren't part of the jury. What we saw was filtered by the media."

At this point I jumped in to change topics. "Now I want to move the discussion away from the O.J. verdict to what impact does race have in society? How about in our classrooms?"

Victoria spoke first, "I believe that race places a very big part in schools. Look at all the examples that Lisa Delpit writes about in her book [*Other People's Children*]. I felt that for the first time an author really understood what I was feeling. I feel good when I read the book."

Robert interrupted, "I also found Delpit to give examples of things that have happened in my life. I really liked this book. I have felt the isolation in schools and society. She's not making this stuff up."

Patty again quietly spoke, "I believe that people have different experiences in society that shape the way we think. The O.J. verdict shows that. We need to understand that happens in our classrooms too. When most of the teachers, where we teach, are white and most of the kids are of color, their experiences are going to be different. Delpit wrote about the frustrations of many teachers of color and that they have been silenced."

Julia finally was able to interject, "Culture and language are important in a child's life. There are many white teachers who know that. Much of our staff is white and speak Spanish and some of us live in Barrio Logan too. We see parents working hard and wanting their children to get a good education. Yet there are so many barriers for children and their parents. I don't know if O.J. was guilty, but race does make a difference and we are trying to provide our kids with more options in life. That's why we work so hard in our school. We know that race is a barrier in life."

Andrew spoke up, "I don't think many teachers really understand how important race and culture are in this society. For me, I can never be anyone else besides a black male. Don't get me wrong, I like being a black male, but I don't have any choice either because of my skin color. Look at me, everyone knows I'm black. How would you like to be followed when you go shopping? This happens to me all the time. At school, most of the books and materials are written by whites and about white accomplishments. I would like to see more of a balance. Though I think we, teachers, try to bring in more information, the entire system is organized on the history and ways of western society."

Ron shot up his hand and said, "Wait a minute. I teach a lot of black history. My kids really respond to it. I get it in, but I also teach the stuff that we must cover."

Andrew replied, "That's my point. Did you teach black history to make the curriculum more interesting for your students of color and still teach the same concepts like "pull yourself up from your bootstraps" and that western imperialism was good for the growth of the United States as a nation? Or did you talk about how everyone did not benefit from industrialization?"

Charlotte ended the conversation, "All of this shows we have a long way to go. All of us. The racism that came out after the verdict was horrible. We live in an imperfect system and we must work together to change things so we really live in a fair society. But what is fair? That will take another long discussion too."

This had been a heated discussion of an extremely complicated topic in which issues of democracy, the social justice system, the police, racism, domestic violence, wealth, and schools were intricately woven.

Of the twenty-five teachers in the class, fifteen were European Americans. All of the European American teachers sat at a table where there was at least one other European American. Six educators were African American and five always sat together at the middle table. There were two Mexican American teachers who sat together at another table and across from two European American males. Another Mexican American teacher sat with her husband and a European American female colleague in the corner. The only Asian American sat at a table that included the sixth African American and a European American woman. The teachers chose seats just as their students do: they chose to sit next to people they knew and felt most comfortable with.

This graduate class in multicultural education was held on-site at an elementary school in a predominantly Latino and African American section of the city. About 90 percent of the teachers taught bilingual classes or in an inner-city school. Most of the teachers had approximately ten years of experience. Some had been teaching for thirty years, while a few had only several years of experience. All were elementary grade teachers.

Why Was the Dialogue Important?

This was a challenging group of teachers. The teachers had strong opinions about teaching and were frustrated by a lack of services for many of their students. Unfortunately, the teachers had few opportunities to develop their voices or to come together as a community and tackle difficult issues. One of the teachers mentioned that there had been no in-depth discussion about controversial topics in any of their six previous classes, which included science methods, language arts, math methods, and educational psychology.

Why did I encourage teachers to discuss the O.J. verdict? The classroom is often a microcosm of society. Teaching does not occur in a vacuum; we teach in a social context and are influenced by our social milieu. The perception of the O.J. Simpson case was an example of how the experiences of European Americans and African Americans and other people of color may differ. People may disagree about the meaning of the same pieces of information. For example, some teachers felt the lack of fit of the gloves was important. Other teachers believed the DNA evidence was more important.

Cultural differences were evident in class. Five of the six African American teachers believed O.J. was innocent. Most of the European American teachers thought he was guilty. I believe their cultural glasses influenced what they thought. Many of the African Americans had grown up with what they termed "a healthy distrust" of the police. They themselves had been stopped or their family members pulled over by the police for little or no reason. The European American teachers disagreed vehemently about the integrity of the police. They felt the police were credible and reliable.

I moved the discussion toward equity in society and in schools. Most of the European American teachers believed that, for the most part, African Americans have the same rights as they do. However, most of the African American teachers disagreed immediately. They felt that many European American teachers did not understand how they had a privileged place in society. For example, most of the school books are written by white authors and the system is based on white values, and children are encouraged to write but not to learn how to perform. The written word is more important than oral tradition. There is little movement incorporated in the school day. Most days students sit at desks and work.

Then I asked, "Do we live in a racially divided society?"

Most agreed. Before the verdict, the European American teachers felt that though there are problems in the United States, the racial problems are not that deeply seated. However, after the verdict, the European American teachers were surprised at the response of the African Americans in class. They felt the African American teachers supported the black jurors because of skin color and did not look at the evidence in the O.J. Simpson case. Several of the European American teachers felt the court system had let them down. Many African Americans saw the reaction of some European Americans as racist. I heard one teacher say, "O.J. was acquitted by a court of law. They made those rules. Now when those rules do not work for them, they [European Americans] want to change them." Other African American heads were nodding in agreement.

In the discussion of the verdict, a strong undercurrent of emotion emerged. This issue struck at fundamental values and beliefs, and the teachers were willing to share their honest opinions. In the first section of the dialogue, I felt we heard comments that arose from their personal values. The teachers acknowledged that the class was clearly divided by race. The African American speakers (Andrew, Robert, Victoria, Sherlie, and Patty) talked about a society that was racist and inequitable to blacks, while several European Americans (Charlotte, Peter, Henrietta, Helen, and Ron) disagreed with the verdict and voiced their displeasure with the jury system, the media, and how money was used to buy the not guilty verdict. Most of the African Americans in class seemed to be speaking from personal experiences with racism. Several European American teachers commented upon the lack of experience of the jurors and how they were not well educated. The African American teachers were stung by those comments and the assumptions undergirding them, since a majority of the jurors were black. The European American teachers were uncomfortable speaking up because they did not want to appear to be racist. It took courage for all the teachers to share their views of the controversial case and verdict.

One European American male, Dustin, reflected upon his own reaction to the verdict. He said he was surprised at his own racism considering he has chosen to be a teacher in prisons. His comment demonstrated how he was attempting to rid himself of barriers that may act as obstacles to his commitment to his present and future students, many of whom are men of color.

Patty, an African American female, also surprised the class. She candidly and poignantly explained why many African Americans are suspicious of the police and how her experiences as a person of color and the mother of children of color have taught her that the actions of individuals and institutions often threaten her and those whom she loves, and that equality is a goal we strive for but have yet to attain in the United States.

As I reflected upon their comments, I saw that the racial divide was as wide as the Mississippi River is long.

In the second portion of our discussion, when I shifted the conversation to how race impacts schools and our readings, European American teachers were more distant and talked about teacher values and teacher knowledge. Most European American teachers did not have the same emotional connection with the reading material as did the African American and Latino teachers. In discussing how race impacts our schools and society and asking for examples from our readings of Delpit's text, their comments were more general. Ron and Charlotte, though obviously committed to all children, did not provide real depth. As European Americans, Ron seemed to be defensive and Charlotte did not seem to want to tackle the issue. In contrast, Victoria, Robert, and Patty explained to the class that they have felt the same isolation and frustration as the African American teachers and students Delpit writes about in her book. Andrew pointedly described his pain of being overlooked in the classroom and how the contributions of African Americans have been glaringly missing from school curriculum. This observation supports Sleeter's (1995) finding that it is difficult for European American teachers to really come to grips with social oppression, because it is difficult for these teachers to place themselves in an unequal context and look at the social system that benefits them.

For European American teachers, race did influence schooling. They believed that discrimination was an unfortunate aspect of American society. However, their experiences with discrimination were minimal, and their responses came primarily from an emotional distance. In contrast, their African American colleagues cited many instances where race had impacted their lives as children and as teachers.

The class discussions benefited everyone. African American teachers had the opportunity to voice their concerns with racism in the classroom and in schools and to talk about how many of their children were not being provided with the best education. In one discussion, a Latina talked about the racism she saw in schools. About midsemester, after we read the chapter by Delpit where she explained many teachers of colors' frustration with the system, a Latina teacher talked about how when she first began her teaching career twenty years ago, no one would talk to her for two years because she was the only bilingual teacher.

Teachers would ignore her in the lunchroom and at faculty meetings. However, she was determined to make it as a teacher because she saw the many needs of Spanish-speaking students. She stuck it out. As she finished her discussion, most of her colleagues had tears in their eyes, both males and females. She was a caring person and they were shocked at how she had been treated by others, but were also touched by her commitment and quiet courage.

European American teachers also expressed their frustrations with the system and gained a better understanding of why teachers of color felt excluded and isolated from their colleagues. The African Americans, European Americans, as well as the other teachers in the class were trying to mend the huge gap between themselves. However, in a sixteen-week class the conversation among colleagues could only begin.

As the semester came to a close, I did see movement in most teachers; they attempted to move away from their personal biases and to understand how society as a large institution creates inequities. African Americans expected European Americans to challenge a system they saw as racist. European Americans realized that their personal claim to equity did not release them from their responsibilities as members of a society that discriminates. Further, European American teachers were willing to listen to the concerns of teachers of color, while teachers of color were also careful to listen to their colleagues and not overgeneralize. I saw more mingling among the groups during the breaks and after class. There was more cross-cultural talking. All the teachers realized the importance of working together to create bridges and linkages with each other and that this took respect and trust. Respect and trust can be the shapers of powerful conversations, but they have to be earned by each teacher. However, there are few teachers who are unwilling to share their heartfelt beliefs with others who are sincerely listening and want to grow. Such authentic dialogue enabled tacit beliefs to emerge and supported self-examination. Teachers were able to place private beliefs alongside public commentary. This meant that when teachers' personal and professional beliefs were not in sync, others could sense and sometimes see the inconsistencies. The notion of congruency between implicit and explicit beliefs becomes an added dimension of teacher dialogue. In the next section I will talk about why this is an important aspect of assessment.

When Personal Values and Professional Beliefs Do Not Match

In assessing teachers I look for congruency between personal values and professional beliefs. Sometimes what teachers say may not really represent what they believe. Let's look at a slice of another conversation where the dialogue ended abruptly.

One evening a discussion about gay and lesbian culture arose. I felt most teachers were working at listening to each other. Those whose religious values conflicted with the lifestyles of gays and lesbians carefully framed their comments and, with much effort, stayed calm in the discussion. For example, a fifth-grade teacher asked, "I am very religious and so I am opposed to gays on those grounds, however I also believe that we are all children of God. Can you explain how old you were when you felt that you were gay? Have you told your parents?" In turn, the gay and lesbian teachers in class were challenged not to take some comments personally or to act defensively.

At the end of an intense discussion, a male heterosexual teacher, John, looked at a gay colleague and pointed a finger at him saying, "I can't believe you would waste our time talking about this issue. I got nothing out of the discussion." The colleague appeared calm though his voice shook slightly, "I think it is important that you know there are gay and lesbian students in your classes, especially those in high schools, who are wrestling with their sexual orientation. Many young people consider suicide. Mental health specialists believe that almost 30 percent of adolescent suicides are linked to sexual orientation." I then interjected that I felt it was important that we speak to each other with respect. I reminded the teachers that we could disagree in our beliefs, but that we should not attack the person with whom we disagree.

In this case I felt John had not exhibited effective interpersonal communication skills. His tone was hostile and condescending. I was disturbed by this because he did not treat the other teacher with dignity and respect. I realized that John's ideas have been reinforced by the power structure of our nation. His views represented those of many Americans; why should he change his view when he has so much evidence that schools and society agree with his views? What bothered me the most was that though he often stated his belief in equity for all, his comments about gay and lesbian issues did not seem to match his espoused theories. Though I realized John does not have to agree with his colleague, I expected him to be cordial and respectful. His personal beliefs and values did not always corroborate with his teacher beliefs and knowledge. I wondered how he would treat a gay student in his high school physical education class. What messages would he, the teacher and role model, convey about gay and lesbian issues?

As I assessed the interaction between John and his colleague, I used the following questions:

1. How have this teacher's comments progressed from the beginning of the semester to the end of the term?
2. In situations where the teacher disagrees with another person, does the teacher move away from blaming others for differences in opinions?
3. Does the teacher really listen to opposing viewpoints and attempt to understand another's perspective? Or is the person only waiting for her/his turn to speak?
4. Can the teacher see the issue in a broad social context rather than only from his/her individual viewpoint?

In utilizing these questions as guidelines, I felt that John had moved little from his initial comments at the beginning of the class. John, a European American, had grown up in the Pacific Northwest. He had talked early in the semester about how he thought African American males did not work hard or care about self-development. This was the reason he believed so many were incarcerated. No matter what other colleagues said to him, John contended that the system was, for the most part, fair and that anyone had the same chance he did in society. By the middle of the term, he seemed to see society in a slightly broader way. John spoke up about how it must be extremely frustrating to be a person of color continually having to prove oneself.

I believe John was trying to view society from other vantage points besides his own. However, his attack on his gay colleague demonstrated not only his fear of the topic but also the fact that he had missed the importance of his civic responsibility of honoring and respecting each person. He seemed to have moved slightly toward accepting the views of some people of color, yet he was not able to transfer that respect to another group. He still erected barriers during dialogue; his movement forward was minimal.

Teacher Education: Assessing Teacher Effectiveness

Teacher dialogue is important in that it can provide teachers with opportunities to reevaluate what they are doing and challenge them to design new programs that may be more effective in reaching students in the classroom. Though this chapter focuses upon teacher dialogue, I want to point out that the assessment of teachers should also include teacher effectiveness with students. This is a major problem with teacher education courses. Though our aim is to assist teachers in becoming more effective, unless we spend many hours in the classroom observing how teachers interact with their students, we do not know what impact we are making in our inservice and graduate classes.

Some teacher educators ask teachers to videotape themselves. I believe this is a helpful strategy and can illuminate the discussions teachers have with their students. These videos can be used as centerpieces of teacher dialogue. One of the limitations of videos, however, is that it may not be possible to witness the warmth or undercurrent of anxiety teachers and students may feel. Interactions are like works of art. Though it is possible to reprint a painting in colorful books, the reproduction usually does not have the vibrancy or depth of the real piece of art. It is not possible to copy art and preserve its feel and the emotions the piece may evoke from the viewer.

I believe it is important for teachers to relate effectively and respectfully to parents, students, and colleagues. I think the following aspects of teaching are important ones to consider when weighing teacher effectiveness:

1. How well does the teacher develop an interpersonal relationship with each student? (For example, does the teacher know each student's name and does the teacher engage each student every day in verbal conversation or through nonverbal communication such as eye contact?)
2. Does the teacher listen to the student? Does the teacher hear the student's comments and questions and appropriately respond to them?

3. Does the teacher treat each student fairly? Does the teacher provide each student with positive strokes and constructive feedback?
4. Does the teacher deal effectively with cultural conflicts that arise in class? For example, when a teacher is accused of being racist by a student of color, does the teacher know how to deal with the comment (Valli 1995)?
5. Is the teacher's curriculum culturally relevant and effective (Irvine 1992)? Are the students learning? Are they interested and engaged in the learning process?
6. What does the teacher do to encourage a sense of community and collaboration between students? Do students listen to each other? How do they treat one another?

The answers to these questions can be addressed in teacher dialogue sessions. These questions delve into the value orientation of teachers and are important to the dialogue process.

CONCLUSION

How did I assess teacher dialogue in a graduate class on multicultural education? I examined the remarks teachers made throughout the semester. I looked for logical and insightful comments shared in an atmosphere of respect and honor. I also listened for congruency between personal values and teacher beliefs. Did the teacher provide an honest view of the issue? Was there consistency between emotional attitudes and teacher beliefs, or did the teacher seem to espouse one belief in one situation but act or speak in a contradictory way in another? This was an important aspect of the criteria I used. When I assessed teachers, they did not have to agree with my political or value orientations, but their statements did need to be honest and sincere. Unfortunately, the comments of the teacher named John were not consistent from one discussion to another. There are teachers who hold the same beliefs as John and yet are trying to make themselves available to new perspectives and information. Other teachers may be confused and discuss their frustration and feelings of perplexity. I looked for comments that demonstrated a movement toward understanding diversity in the community rather than an overriding concern with being right.

Teachers are faced with difficult decisions every single day. Children bring their hopes, frustrations, and problems to school. Some of their lives are shaped by issues of poverty, depression, abuse, and divorce. Teachers must be able to dialogue with their peers about the social and academic complexities found in teaching. They must continually reflect upon their ability to reach and teach each child. In order to do this, I believe dialogue is one of the most important avenues of teacher education. Most teacher education textbooks do not talk about real situations. The theoretical and philosophical foundations of education are important, but only if they serve to make teachers more effective. Through dialogue, teachers have the opportunity not only to bring in their experiences but also to shape the direction of the discussion. Few public school classrooms are democratic, as are few teacher education classes. However, by using dialogue and an issues-centered approach to teacher education, it is possible to create a classroom that is real and challenges teachers to move forward, to create more effective and culturally affirming classrooms.

To stimulate dialogue, I used Lisa Delpit's insightful book (1995), *Other People's Children*. Delpit challenges teachers to look at their personal belief systems and how those systems shape their behaviors as a teacher. Since Delpit writes about topics that some consider controversial, teachers in the class had difficulty at first talking with each other about the issues she raises. They initially directed their comments only to the people at their table. Often they selectively listened to one another. The racial divide was severe. However, as the semester continued, the teachers did find "common ground" and realized that their goal of assisting all children to be their best was the link that helped them relate to and listen to each other honestly. Though our educational rhetoric supports democratic discourse, engaging in meaningful dialogue and assessment of that conversation is a difficult struggle. In future classes I hope to encourage teachers to assess their own dialogue. And I believe that assessing teacher dialogue helps me to understand how effective I am as a teacher educator just as I believe it is crucial for teachers to see that assessment has little to do with grades but is primarily about their ability to become the best teacher possible.

One final note. At the beginning of this chapter, the teacher education professor could be seen frantically running out of the building. The professor was reported missing and later found making noodles for a small health-food restaurant in Tahiti where he would never have to assess another person again.

NOTE

The author would like to acknowledge the assistance of David Strom and Joseph Hawkins in preparing this manuscript.

REFERENCES

Baratz-Snowden, J. (1993). Assessment of teachers: A view from the National Board for Professional Teaching Standards. *Theory into Practice 32*(2); 82–85.

Barber, B. (1992). *An aristocracy for everyone: The politics of education and the future of America.* New York: Ballantine.

Canroy, M. (1974). *Education as cultural imperialism.* New York: David McKay.

Cruickshank, D. R., and K. K. Metcalf (1993). Improving preservice teacher assessment through on-campus laboratory experiences. *Theory Into Practice 32*(2); 86–92.

Delpit, L. (1995). *Other people's children.* New York: New Press.

Freire, P. (1971). *Pedagogy of the oppressed.* New York: Herder and Herder.

Giroux, H. A. (1988). *Teachers as intellectuals: Toward a critical pedagogy of learning.* Granby, MA: Bergin and Garvey.

Interstate New Teacher Assessment and Support Consortium (INTASC) (1992). *Model standards for beginning teacher licensing and development: A resource for state dialogue.* Washington, DC: Council of Chief State School Officers.

Irvine, J. J. (1992). Making teacher education culturally responsive. In M. Dilworth (ed.), *Diversity in teacher education,* 79–92. San Francisco: Jossey-Bass.

Noddings, N. (1984). *Caring: A feminine approach to ethics and moral education.* Berkeley: University of California Press.

Pang, V. O. (1994). Why do I need this class: Multicultural education for teachers. *Phi Delta Kappan 76*(4); 289–92.

Pang, V. O., G. Gay, and W. B. Stanley (1995). Expanding conceptions of community and civic competence for a multicultural society. *Theory and Research in Social Education 23*(4); 302–31.

Shaver, J., and W. Strong (1982). *Facing value decisions.* New York: Teachers College Press.

Sleeter, C. (1995). Reflections on my use of multicultural and critical pedagogy when students are white. In C. Sleeter and P. L. McLaren (eds.), *Multicultural education, critical pedagogy, and the politics of difference,* 415–37. Albany: State University of New York Press.

Sleeter, C., and C. Grant (1988). *Making choices for multicultural education: Five approaches to race, class, and gender.* Columbus, OH: Merrill.

Spring, J. (1991) *American education: An introduction to social and political aspects.* 5th ed. White Plains, NY: Longman.

Valli, L. (1995). The dilemma of race: Learning to be color blind and color conscious. *Journal of Teacher Education 46*(2); 120–29.

Wolf, K., B. Whinery, and P. Hagerty (1995). Teaching portfolios and portfolio conversations for teacher educators and teachers. *Action in Teacher Education 17*(2); 30–39.

Chapter Sixteen

PARENTS AS ALLIES FOR ALTERNATIVE ASSESSMENT

Jennifer J. Robinson

INTRODUCTION

In order for alternative assessment to permanently replace standardized methods of evaluation, public support must be garnered. Parents head the list of potential supporters who are critical to the success of this most recent innovation (Bridge 1976; Fullan 1982). As states and school districts have adopted research-based practices that differ from what parents remember from their school days, some reactions have been negative and critical. This conflict between parental beliefs and school practices may be disillusioning and frustrating for both parties as they struggle to sustain good relationships to provide children with the best possible education. In fact, it has been said that, as schools and parents have attempted to create shared meanings regarding the goals and purposes of education, they have been "worlds apart" in their views, resulting in a lack of meaningful, productive interaction (Lightfoot 1978).

To ensure support for newer instructional strategies, schools and districts should provide parents with a thorough understanding of these innovations and attempt to involve parents throughout the stages of adoption (Dodd 1996). Research on parents' perspectives (Ames 1993; Johnson 1991; McGilvray-Rivet 1992) suggests that much of parental opposition stems from preconceptions, lack of information, or misinformation.

WHY PARENTS RESIST

Parents tend to generate their beliefs about education based upon their own past experiences, which serve as guiding influences over decisions and actions (Goodwin 1987). When it comes to images of schooling and assessment, parents generally retain schema that reflect an approach steeped in years of standardized testing. Despite the fact that test scores, letter grades, and percentiles provide only narrow interpretations of student achievement, parents express more comfort with these types of indicators than with more complex and alternative measures. While parents admit to having limited knowledge about grading and how to assess learning, they question the value of change.

In a recent study (Robinson 1996) in which parents from New York City were asked their views regarding changes in grading policies, most parents admitted having difficulty expressing their opinion because they lack general knowledge about assessment. According to these parents, assigning grades is the territory of the teacher; however, parents expressed a desire to understand how assessment works so that they can consider the implications of current practice and the ramifications of change.

Some parents struggle with new concepts of assessment because alternative assessment means different things to different people. There is no standard definition. Assessments described as alternative are often very different from one another, and some similar assessments use other labels such as performance, authentic, or outcome based. Where parents are looking for a solid indication of a child's educational attainment and mastery of traditional subject matters, alternative assessment appears vague and open ended.

Parents worry that educators will not be able to assess performance accurately and fairly. With some emphasis on outcomes related to changes in attitudes and habits of mind, parents fear that teachers will forsake the teaching of rigorous academics for softer, affective issues such as self-esteem. Without a clearly defined means to measure true change or growth in attitudes, some parents mistrust the subjectivity in this type of assessment (Hooten 1995).

A related misconception is the belief that alternative assessment is synonymous with values education. The recent outcry against outcome-based education from many conservative parents reflects a concern that student evaluations will be based upon a particular set of values. According to these parents, alternative assessment supports moral relativism, and there is fear that student assessment will depend upon the degree to which liberal philosophies are embraced, rather than purely upon academic achievement (Hooten 1995). Parents who choose not to fight against school policies and practices that conflict with their perspectives have already begun seeking alternate ways to educate their children including in private, parochial, and home schools.

Ensuring high standards for all learners is another concern. Parents tend to place their confidence in standardized test scores that measure their child's progress in light of other children of the same age and grade level. Performance assessments, however, move us beyond comparative interpretations and not only tell us what children know; they also tell us what we need to do to help students gain deeper understanding. Designing assessment criteria that can be transferred across subject matter yet are general enough to allow students opportunities to practice content knowledge is challenging but helpful in determining the quality of students' learning (Diez and Moon 1992). When students are aware of the criteria by which their work will be judged, and when learning experiences are designed to prepare students to demonstrate their learnings and not just regurgitate facts, assessment becomes a means by which teachers, parents, and students can discuss the process of learning.

The advent of alternative and authentic assessment has brought a shift in how teachers group and educate students. Many alternative assessment models lead to inclusive rather than exclusive grouping patterns, a definite obstruction to the traditional tracking system. While parents concede that the "factory" model of schooling is ineffective, they are just beginning to understand how other models (untracking, for example) might benefit students. The flexibility of performance assessment allows all students to demonstrate mastery of a common set of requirements. Alternative assessment measures, in which students demonstrate their knowledge of content in varying ways and in varying time periods, help to eliminate the need for tracking and support the notion that untracked classes can benefit all students of all achievement levels.

In light of challenges to the traditional conception of student evaluation, parents and teachers should find comfort in the promise of alternative assessment. First, asking the question, "What should students know and be able to do?" forces an expansive examination of the curriculum. Teachers reconsider their goals for instruction and they focus on making learning experiences more relevant (Diez and Moon 1992).

Second, when students are required to demonstrate mastery of subject matter through complex tasks that approximate real-life situations, they develop greater appreciation for school and for inquiry. Thinking skills improve as well.

Alternative assessment strategies that invite parent participation—such as student-led conferences—foster discussion between teachers and parents about the nature of learning and the purpose of assessment. Such dialogue opens communication and helps reduce anxiety regarding academic achievement.

When children are viewed as "critically involved in defining their own learning," parents and teachers are "relieved of some of the pressure within to produce results in children" (Lightfoot 1978: 79). Instead, parents and teachers see that their role is to "provide the environments for learning and present the child with an array of intellectual tools and strategies" (79). A perspective that embraces alternative assessment allows the integration to "take place within the child in his own time" (79).

WHAT PARENTS WANT

Research suggests that parents expect the school to initiate contact when there is a change in policy or practice (Epstein 1986; Robinson 1996). Parents want to be informed and included in decisions regarding changes and additions to the school curriculum and policies. At issue is maintaining open lines of communication that include all families (English and non-English-speaking) in the process.

When conflict arises between parents and educators, resolution needs to be found in a way that respects the rights of all concerned. Educators, district administrators, and policymakers need to answer specific questions regarding alternative assessment (Hoge 1995) in order to gain support from all—even the most resistant—parents:

1. *How will specific outcomes be measured?* Parents deserve to know how affective learning is assessed (e.g., attitudes or character traits such as honesty, ethical judgment) and what exactly will be measured.
2. *How is a particular outcome scored?* Quality performance assessment necessitates that educators design good criteria by which to judge the quality of the performance. This allows for fine gradations of excellence to be determined. These criteria should be clear to students and to parents.
3. *Who decides what the standard will be?* When a standard is determined, parents have a right to know who is responsible for setting the standard (the local district, superintendent, or the community) and how that standard will be followed.
4. *How will the child's attitudes be reoriented?* Parental concerns that home values may be challenged are real. Educators must be ready to clarify how attitudes will be assessed and how to collaborate with parents to identify values that are universally acceptable.
5. *What if parents and the state disagree on the standards?* How will these differences be resolved? The question here is, who ultimately has authority over the child . . . the parents or the state?

As broad community involvement is cultivated, the impact of dissident minority groups will lessen, and the democratic practice of involving parents in school decision making will become a viable solution.

BEYOND THE BAKE SALE: HOW TEACHERS AND PARENTS CAN WORK TOGETHER

Historically, "good" parent involvement has been defined by the school as fund raising, running bake sales, and chaperoning. Parental involvement includes supporting the work of the classroom teacher by helping with homework at home, by implementing special events such as class parties, pictures, and the like, or by volunteering to help with field trips, class plays, . . . etc. While these types of involvement are meaningful and useful, it is also true that parents have historically been excluded from the decision making and governance processes in schools and from framing and defining their own modes of "good" involvement. Not until recently has there been a widespread effort to involve parents in meaningful collaboration with teachers and administrators around substantive issues of curriculum and governance (Comer 1980; Fine 1993).

Two distinct ideologies, reflected in approaches to parent participation, have implications for the ways in which social and cultural diversity facilitate parental involvement. These perspectives have implications for alternative assessment.

Proponents of "accommodation" believe low-income and non-European families should accommodate the learning situations subscribed to by the schools. The "home curriculum" (belief systems, values, and practices that children bring with them from home) must be modified by the efforts of parents and teachers to conform to the academic conditions of schools that are heavily influenced by white middle-class values (Ascher 1987).

Proponents of mutual adaptation argue that most schools and assessment practices are designed to best meet the needs of white middle-class students and do not reflect the lifestyles, values, or experiences of urban or non-European families. Furthermore, there is a good deal of natural learning that occurs in the home that teachers take time neither to learn about nor to understand (Ascher 1987). In mutual adaptation, it is just as important to retain the integrity of the home culture as it is to introduce the child to the dominant culture. In fact, just as parents can learn new approaches to parenting, teachers can learn from parents new ways to teach and assess learning that will be more harmonious with how children learn in the home. Through such culturally responsive pedagogy (Villegas 1991), better quality contact between home and school helps to cultivate successful home-school relations and success for children.

Mutual adaptation (Ascher 1987) for parent involvement moves all parties beyond surface conversation and into the integration of home culture into the existing curriculum in a way that helps to contextualize assessment for students and teachers. Since knowledge of the student is a prerequisite to effectively integrating assessment and instruction (Cohen 1995), educators may see some advantage in enlisting the perspectives of the parent who may offer a different interpretation of assessment results.

Teachers can utilize parental knowledge as a way to design and interpret authentic assessment. Formative types of performance assessment can begin to engage parents and teacher in meaningful conversation that might affect the manner in which instruction is conducted.

Authentic assessment can be a mutual responsibility whereby the teacher and parent examine progress and learning as a process, not as a destination. As parents bring their understanding of the child, and teachers bring an understanding of curriculum, parents and teachers can forge a relationship that engages them in conversations about what has been, is, and will be best for future learning.

Involving parents in the assessment process will undoubtedly be met with mixed reactions, especially since few parents have the experience or the time to participate at this level. While not all parents have the time, interest, or capacity to be among the decision makers, all parents deserve an explanation. In the New York study, there was some resistance to parental involvement in curricular decision making. Several parents said they lacked the skill and knowledge to offer sound suggestions. Others confirmed their interest but stated that this level of decision making might not be for all parents.

Teachers can facilitate parental involvement by creating a neutral zone within which questions and concerns can be discussed (Vondra 1996). Rather than prepare a defensive strategy, teachers should listen first. Developing the ability to listen is the first step toward opening communication.

Active listening is beneficial for several reasons. First, it allows all parties the opportunity to develop a respect for the perspective of others. Very often, teachers and parents are prepared to do battle before listening to each other. Second, listening ensures a thorough understanding of all points of view. Listening allows an opportunity to search for common ground, a position of commonality whereby productive discussion and problem solving around the issues can occur. As real communication begins to happen, honest discussion about the benefits and challenges of alternative assessment can take place.

The issues surrounding alternative assessment are complex. Some of the latest research on performance assessment confirms the difficulty of implementation (Guskey1994). For example, teachers at the same grade level in a school may use different performance tasks to assess student progress. This can be confusing to parents, who do not understand how different types of assessment can satisfy the same standard. In some communities, districts have developed a bank of assessment tasks with accompanying criteria for teachers' use. These generic assessments can then be tailored to specific content. In another district, "anchor tasks" are being used by teachers in every school in addition to their own assessments as a means of establishing parity without uniformity (Cohen 1995).

There are other challenges. Designing effective performance tasks is not easy. Authentic assessment tasks must be *contextualized* so that they reflect the knowledge and skills needed in the world at large. Students should be required to apply their knowledge and skills through tasks that *engage their thought processes at high levels.* Good activities should *relate to the content* of what is being assessed, not merely be engaging to students.

Educators should be honest with parents about communicating the emerging and evolving nature of alternative assessment. As curriculum becomes more integrated, performance assessment must reflect multiple disciplines, and complex rather than simple criteria must be developed (Cohen 1995). In cases where students are permitted a choice among well-designed alternatives, there is greater freedom and opportunity to express learnings through media that are reflective of personal learning styles. In communities of wide socioeconomic and cultural variation, a diverse group of assessment alternatives that maintain high standards should reflect the learning styles and needs of all the children represented therein.

This chapter has explored parents' concerns regarding alternative assessment measures and has presented strategies to educators for a more collaborative approach. Establishing consistent, open communication with parents is critical to vital home-school relationships and to success for students. Parents who learn the whys, hows, and wherefores of alternative assessment prior to and during implementation can provide the support necessary to sustain and institutionalize this innovation.

References

Ames, C. (with Madhab Khoju and Thomas Watkins) (1993). *Parents and schools: The impact of school-to-home communications on parents' beliefs and perceptions.* Report No. 15. Baltimore: Johns Hopkins University, Center on Families, Communities, Schools and Children's Learning.

Ascher, C. (1987). *Improving the school-home connection for poor and minority urban students.* ERIC/CUE Trends and Issues Series, No. 8. New York: Columbia University Teachers College, ERIC Clearinghouse on Urban Education.

Bridge, G. R. (1976). Parent participation in school innovations. *Teachers College Record 77*: 366–84.

Cohen, P. (1995). Designing performance assessment tasks. *Education Update 17*(6): 1–8.

Comer, J. P. (1980). *School power.* New York: Free Press.

Diez, M. E, and J. C. Moon (1992). What do we want students to know? . . . and other important questions. *Educational Leadership 49*(8): 38–41.

Dodd, A. W. (1996). Involving parents, avoiding gridlock. *Educational Leadership 53*(7): 44–46.

Epstein, J. (1986). Parents' reactions to teacher practices of parental involvement. *Elementary School Journal 86*(3): 277–94.

Fine, M. (1993). Ap(parent) involvement: Reflections on parents, power, and urban public schools. *Teachers College Record 92*(2): 177–84.

Fullan, M. (1982). *The meaning of educational change.* New York: Teachers College Press.

Goodwin, A. L. (1987). *Teaching images: Unlocking preservice student teaching beliefs and connecting teaching beliefs to teaching behavior.* Unpublished doctoral dissertation, Teachers College, Columbia University, New York, NY.

Guskey, T. R. (1994). What you assess may not be what you get. *Educational Leadership 51*(6): 51–54.

Hoge, A. (1995). What you can do. *Citizen 9* (8): 4.

Hooten, J. (1995). Outcome-based deception? *Citizen 9* (8): 1–4.

Johnson, D. (1991). Parents, students and teachers: A three-way relationship. *International Journal of Educational Research 15* (2): 171–81.

Lightfoot, S. L. (1978). *Worlds apart: Relationships between families and schools.* New York: Basic Books.

McGilvray-Rivet, S. J. (1992). *Puerto Rican parents and an urban school.* Unpublished doctoral dissertation, Boston University, Boston, MA.

Robinson, J. (1996). *From the parents' perspective: Parent involvement in an urban elementary school.* Unpublished doctoral dissertation, Teachers College, Columbia University, New York, NY.

Villegas, A. (1991). *Culturally responsive pedagogy for the 1990s and beyond.* ERIC/CTE Trends and Issues Series, No. 6. Washington, DC: ERIC Clearinghouse on Teacher Education.

Vondra, J. (1996). Resolving conflicts over values. *Educational Leadership 53*(7): 44–46.

Chapter Seventeen

TOWARD AN EDUCATION OF CONSEQUENCE:
Connecting Assessment, Teaching, and Learning

Vito Perrone

Student assessment is a critical aspect of the educational encounter. At its best, it provides teachers with important knowledge of students and their growth as learners, informs ongoing curricular and pedagogical practice, is a basis for helping students reflect on their own learning, and serves as a window for parents into the power of the teaching-learning exchange that involves their sons and daughters. Without careful attention to assessment, the educational limitations for students and teachers are large. In so many ways, this is the central message of this book.

Moving to "assessment at its best," however, has proven over the years to be far more difficult than expected. Assessment has most often been reduced to various norm-referenced and criterion-referenced tests, essentially sampling processes aimed at determining what students have retained of fairly discrete subject matters, mostly secondhand versions of students' modes of thinking and meaning making. Such efforts have fostered relatively low levels of teaching and learning while assuring, as Deborah Meier suggests, that "accountability is mostly a myth."[1]

Getting closer to students, having access to what they can actually do, seeing their learning over time, systematically and thoughtfully, is the challenge that many teachers have put before themselves in recent years as they have explored portfolio assessment and the use of exhibitions of performance. These efforts to move beyond the unsituated tests that have been so dominant in the last several decades are beginning to take hold in increasing numbers of schools.[2] This book accounts for many of these fresh efforts to alter the assessment landscape, moving toward "assessment at its best."

It is important to note, however, that some of the emerging discourse about assessment is similar to that which surfaced alongside the progressive education reform period earlier in the century.[3] Teachers then, as now, were engaged in discussions about "documenting children's learning," making "real work" the focus of attention in assessment, getting closer to students' understandings, their meanings, helping students make learning their own.[4] And yet such directions didn't come to dominate the educational landscape. We should pay attention to that history.

What seems clear is that these older progressive changes in the ways assessment was thought about and practiced demanded a major shift in the teaching-learning encounter. It was not merely a change in the form of tests being used or the ways students were graded. It had more to do with students assuming much more active roles, becoming the primary workers, engaged in content issues that mattered to them; a curriculum that was flexibly organized and called upon students to actually demonstrate their understandings, with uncoverage as opposed to coverage of content assuming prominence; and teachers learning to live with more uncertainty, being willing to alter—generally slow down—their pace, accepting the fact that students might pursue different directions, different topics, possibly learn different things. The shift in patterns and responsibilities was large. What we should learn from the earlier experience is that a more productive system of assessment only makes sense if the teaching-learning exchange itself is equally powerful. Why develop, for example, portfolios of students' work if the work students are asked to complete is primarily sets of worksheets? Why record student presentations if the presentations are on topics about which the students had little choice and have little interest? Why ask students to select "best work" and share with their parents how they selected their work if they haven't had the time or resources to complete work they, in fact, honor and see as important? Having a system-wide spelling list from which there will be a test each Friday, having a standard textbook with unit tests and year-end tests to prepare students for, having a predetermined set of topics to study along with a list of things every child should clearly know, leaves teachers with greater certainty and with less to invent, stay in touch with, observe, respond to. Given the organization of schools, it is not surprising that the less complex patterns of assessment, curriculum, and pedagogy remained dominant in the earlier period, even as teachers and schools here and there pursued more progressive possibilities. Conditions may not now be so different from then.

Many schools today have made portfolio assessment and more performance-oriented exhibitions central features of their curricula. And such directions have become prominent in the educational discourse—dominating, in fact, the literature relating to pedagogy and assessment. Yet the overall volume of tests developed beyond schools continues to enlarge.[5] And even as teachers are encouraged—through the various curriculum frameworks being developed by the states and the standards under construction by various disciplinary organizations—to enlarge their thinking about curriculum and make student understanding more central, there remain countervailing pressures to standardize what students learn. The path to "assessment at its best" remains as difficult today as at earlier periods of time.[6]

When assessment is discussed, whatever the definitions, the matter of *standards* is quickly brought forward. How standards are understood, however, makes a critical difference. One of the serious problems is that standards are usually described and set by persons far away from classrooms. "Students will know X and be able to see X in three different ways by the time they complete grade three" may be thought of as a "high standard." But it may say very little about the power of a student's learning. Reaching such externally delineated standards may come at the expense of standards that are much more important to the students themselves and ultimately to the society.

In all the talk about standards, for example, there is little acknowledgement that children and young people not only *hold* standards but also need to work toward *next* standards, another level. In the best of learning environments, standards have an active, dynamic quality. Anyone who has spent time closely observing children and young people, paying attention to their intentions, knows that there is this active side to standards. Patricia Carini notes in this regard:

> By working as I did for most of my professional life in [the Prospect School], I was mainly in the midst of children playing, talking, drawing and making things together. I was struck with how the give and take among children in a climate that offered plentiful time and materials influenced standards. It was a context in which standards could and did arise. It was a context in which standards could also be altered and reworked. That happened because the children were much in the company of each other and in the company of each other's work. In that physical and active workplace with many projects in the making, an idea or process sometimes gets carried further than that had happened before. What hadn't seemed doable proved through some child's efforts to be possible .[7]

My experience is similar. When the first child writes a novel, novels become possible for others. When the first student uses visuals to buttress an argument, more visuals appear with student exhibitions. When the first student engages in an original scientific experiment, original work becomes common. When the first child makes a hook shot on the basketball court, others quickly follow. In active settings, in which students are encouraged to carry out their work in their own ways, to follow their interests and intentions, to take the time to do good work, the work gets better. In this manner, new and more complex standards are being developed all the time. Most of our educational settings, however, aren't organized to support such possibilities. Until they do, "assessment at its best" will continue to struggle for acceptance.

There is, then, little point in rethinking the assessment process without also rethinking the curriculum—what is taught and learned—and the pedagogy. As I noted earlier, I have seen too many portfolios that are mostly accumulations of simple responses to predetermined questions or writing prompts and lab reports of experiments developed exclusively by others with fairly predictable results. I have also been present for too many exhibitions in which the content has come directly from a textbook and clearly didn't relate to a serious student interest or commitment.[8]

In relation to changes in teaching-learning practices, it needs to be acknowledged that much that has existed in the assessment area has worked against teaching-learning practices that are geared toward intellectual challenge, serious writing—what is being described as "teaching for understanding." That is why we need assessment practices that are *different* (and I prefer different to alternative). The commitment to these more powerful teaching-learning directions, a point I will keep stressing, demands, however, far more than merely *beginning* a different path for assessment, although, that, too, needs acknowledgement. In settings where the different assessment processes aren't tied to powerful curriculum content and pedagogy, portfolios (to include exhibitions and performances) will fade rapidly as something tried, another thing about which to remark, "It didn't work."[9]

As a means of making the foregoing more clear, I will offer some thoughts about writing and writing assessment—in part because writing has been in the vanguard of the change in pedagogical and assessment practices. Various teacher scholars (such as Don Graves, Peter Elbow, and Nancy Atwell, among others) and programs such as the National Writing Project and the Bread Loaf School of English have been particularly active in promoting pedagogical and assessment practices in which student authorship is taken seriously, writing workshops are daily occurrences, students come to understand the power of collective thought through the encouragement of peer conferencing and engagment in evaluation of their own writing, and teachers understand more fully that writing is a process and a meaning-making, interpretive activity. In this regard, Elbow notes that "portfolio assessment . . . is ideal for inviting students and teachers to be allies in the assessment process. Portfolio assessment takes the stance of invitation. . . ."[10] I like very much the idea of teaching and learning and assessment as invitation. Writing may be the best entry to such a stance.

Where writing activities match our best understandings of writing practice, portfolios have often come to mean something. They have been "measures" of students' growth, vehicles for self-evaluation on the part of students, means for parents to see their children's work over time, a basis for teacher conversations about standards, the meaning of good writing. In these circumstances, good practice and the presence of portfolios are fully complementary, naturally connected, reciprocally powerful. While the portfolios in such settings have been useful in parent discussions, they have not yet become in most settings a basis for accountability—a way of reporting to a community beyond the school, attending to the political agenda that surrounds schools in a large way. For purposes of accountability, writing assessment—even in relation to good pedagogical directions—is still not too far removed from the current technology of standardized testing. Students *do* write for the various district and state tests that have emerged around writing, and this is an improvement, but their writing tends to be unsituated, disconnected from their ongoing work in a powerful classroom. It is usually about one task, a single piece of writing. It is hardly a process that is likely to bring forth children's best and most committed efforts or guarantee much teacher or public understanding of children's writing.

Those who are encouraging active writing programs make clear that serious writing for children (as well as for adults) takes thought and time. It is almost never unsituated, far removed from personal experience or interest, disconnected from an individual's way of interpreting the world. They recognize, further, that in settings where children's ongoing school experience is rich, where teachers read a great deal to children, giving emphasis in writing to authorship and personal style, where active learning is promoted, where the world is permitted to intrude, to blow through the classroom, children have much more to talk and write about. In this sense, writing is not something apart; it has a context, and that context is important to understanding the writing that is actually produced. Unfortunately, most current writing assessment efforts, even when they actually ask students to write, make little connection to contextual matters.

The best person to judge particular children's writing, who can address constructively their progress as writers, their writing biographies as it were, is in most cases the teacher closest to them. That shouldn't surprise anyone. It is the classroom teacher who is in the best position to know, for example, the questions a particular child has been raising about various aspects of classroom learning, and to refer, when reading a piece of writing, to previous pieces of writing, to the particular book the child is currently reading, to the genres or authors that the child is most inclined toward at the moment, to a painting just completed, to a trip recently taken, to the new baby sister in the home, to the spring flooding across the community's many glacial lakebeds, to the special meadow colors, to the classroom's human mosaic. Because this particular teacher's reading eye and thought are responsive to the surrounding context, never really separate from the text under development, she can bring about, not surprisingly, an interpretation. It is that teacher, deeply involved with the child as writer, who knows the next question to raise, when to push and when not to, who can judge the meaning and quality of a piece of that child's writing. It is this outlook that should govern our perspectives about assessment issues as a whole.[11] An example that has stayed with me for a long time relates to Judy Egan, a teacher Don Graves worked closely with in New Hampshire. It is drawn from her article "Thirty-Two Going on Eight."[12] The subject of Judy's exposition is Heather, an eight-year-old, though Heather in this case is also the prism through which Judy sees her own writing (an aspect of the article I will not discuss, though it is fully expressed in the title of her article). Judy writes:

. . . this tall eight year old (in my class now for two years) possesses strong will and determination. Heather is definitely in control of herself and, thus, her writing . . . (2)

Heather's writing patterns had always intrigued me. I recalled thinking what an enigma she was because I was unable to predict her writing mood of the day. Just when I'd think that I'd hit upon a motivator—zap, it would no longer be successful and Heather would refuse to write. Yet other days there was no stopping her. . . . Heather was in control of her own writing. I've only begun to understand this. . . . (2–3)

Heather is now enjoying writing more. She has gained confidence in her abilities as a writer as she has become more aware of herself through her audience. Her topic choice has expanded to allow her to expose herself as a person. (3)

Judy then describes having seen Heather's doll collection, suggesting in the process that she might want to write about it. Heather responds: "But I have so many! It would just be too long!" (3) Judy's fuller text proceeds as follows:

The following day and for approximately the next fifty, Heather did not write about her doll collection. She continually told me she intended to. I remember pushing, probing, interviewing—all to no avail. She'd work on other pieces but it was obvious through their lack of content, detail and Heather's own lack of enthusiasm that her mind was elsewhere. The doll collection kept coming up (but nothing was started). . . . Weeks passed. More stories were started but never finished. I was finding it difficult to stay in the background but I tried to have confidence in Heather. On March 7th, two months after my initial interview with her, she skipped across the room to hand me a small booklet. Five blank pages lay beneath a cover where she had scribbled, *My Doll Collection,* by Heather.

Now she had made a commitment, yet for the next few days there was always an excuse. "I just CAN'T go in writing today." "I have other plans." "Do I have to?" "It's not a good day for writing." I remember thinking at times that Heather was just being lazy, (hoping) to find easy way out....My encouragement and conferencing brought few results, perhaps a line or two but seldom more.... Given the choice of another topic, I only received, "Nah, I WANT to do my doll collection." (3–4)

The days continued to pass by and then, just as anticipated, Heather literally bounced into the classroom one early April morning at 8:15, forty-five minutes before the start of the school. She went directly to the workboard where the children are assigned the first activity of the morning. Finding her name tag elsewhere, she demanded, "But Mrs. Egan, I HAVE to go in writing first today. I have it all planned out!" Over time and through experience, I learned these days weren't to be taken lightly. No matter what my plans for Heather, I would allow her to take control of her morning. The school bell rang—she marched into the writing area—*My Doll Collection* out of her folder—pencil moving—add an illustration—conference—revise—rewrite. Three pages were completed when, to Heather's dismay, lunch stopped the morning's activities. The next two days followed a similar pattern until on Friday she uttered a desperate plea, "I HAVE to finish my book today—before the weekend. I just have to get it out of my head!" Once in the writing area, Heather elicited help, "I need a conference NOW. I have all these ideas to still put in. YOU know how many dolls I have. I feel like my brain is going to explode!"

Judy described at this point her conferencing with Heather to help her bring focus to the writing project as well as the assistance she received from other classmates.

[An hour later], she was beaming beside me, "Guess what, Mrs. Egan? I finished it, I FINALLY finished it. What a relief!" Bending down to meet her outstretched arms, I took the small book from Heather. She read it to me and then, conferencing it together immediately, she made a few final revisions. Heather's book is now published in its final form between the covers chosen months earlier. . . . Completed on April 16th, three months after the topic found its place in her mind, it has been a little over one month since the piece had been actively started. (4)

The story is wonderful, full of detail and obvious commitment. I have provided below a couple of paragraphs—essentially one fourth of the work—to give a flavor of the writing.

MY DOLL COLLECTION

By Heather Thomas

(Dedicated to my Mom)

My auntie and Grandad went to different countries. But my Grandad is dead. He was dead when my Mom was around 7 years old. What does that have to do with it? They brought back dolls from different countries. I have a lot of dolls. I have a favorite doll. She is from China. She had to have a hair transplant. I play dolls with my brother. Darryl was pulling her hair and it came out.

HOLLAND

I have a Holland doll. She is pretty. She has a hat that looks weird. It comes up and it makes a point and it makes a curl. She has a blue apron and dress. Her hat is made out of lace. She is pretty. She has blonde hair and when she lays down her eyes close. She has wooden shoes. They are neat. (5)

What would Heather have produced had she been forced to write on April 1st at 10:00 A.M.? What would the judgment have been of a reader sitting in some state capitol or national testing service office to Heather's blank page or to her one or two uninspired lines? How would Judy Egan have felt about it? Would her confidence have been undermined? In the context of Judy Egan's classroom, Heather grew as a writer, producing work honored because it was contextual, responded to by a person who knew Heather and her work over time. And it was this close understanding that gave to Judy Egan the confidence to support this particular child as she did. And with each piece in Heather's portfolio Judy could tell a story, provide a context.

Implicit in the foregoing example is the understanding that teachers who are deeply committed to being in a position to describe the growth of their children in writing—or in any other learning/subject area, for that matter—are persons who honor children's work as the products of thought and capable of evoking thought. They are authentic readers. While I know that I may have overstressed the point, I did so out of a belief that any talk of assessment that doesn't understand the importance of teachers being close to their student writers/learners and the surrounding context is doomed intellectually. It will certainly not lead to any lasting change.

This brings me, in regard to writing, to questions about assessment that go beyond where we are. Having already acknowledged the centrality of the classroom setting, the classroom teacher, and work over time, my principal alternative direction is quite obvious. It is rooted in carefully organized and considered classroom documentation. Classroom teachers can, for example, systematically preserve copies of drafts of children's writing as well as finished pieces in a portfolio. Two to three pieces a month provide a reasonable collection. Reviewing them periodically can inform a teacher's ongoing efforts to assist particular children, which, of course, is an important purpose of the portfolio. At year's end, the accumulation—organized chronologically—can be carefully reviewed with some of the following questions serving as a framework: Over time, what are the salient features, dominant motifs? How much invention? What about complexity? Choice of topics? Discourse frameworks? Connections to ongoing academic and social strengths? Diversity of word use? Voice? Use of conventions? Such a review can be enormously revealing, often providing a perspective missed in the course of addressing work that stands alone. Such a portfolio is almost always revealing to parents, bringing the kind of overview, that large picture, that parents often miss as they interact with their children about the school experience.[13] Having the work over time can also assist children themselves in bringing careful self-evaluation, more solid interpretation, to their own efforts as writers. That kind of opportunity ought not be missed. This kind of classroom-based review can address concerns about the ongoing support of individual children, and it can inform further ongoing instructional practice. It can also serve as a way for a teacher to describe children's growth over the course of a year as well as to inform more fully the children's subsequent teacher or teachers.

For purposes of a larger schoolwide review, randomly selected children from each classroom in a school might be asked to select five or six pieces of their writing to be read by groups of teachers in the school as a whole—providing the readers with a statement of context for the individual works. At the level of the school, using such samples as a base, knowing that they were written within the instructional program itself and not apart from it—not as a forced, unsituated exercise—should provide readers with more confidence about describing, for example, the writing of fourth graders in this Thomas Jefferson Elementary School. And they should be able to do it with good authority.

Further, and importantly, by forming in the school as "a community of readers of writing," the teachers involved in this schoolwide review can actually enlarge greatly their understandings of writing, very likely becoming in the process better teachers and facilitators of writing. If assessment efforts don't produce these kinds of results, it is quite clearly a failed and faulty exercise.

While I have focused on writing, what I have outlined could as easily have been about science, mathematics, or social studies. Regarding the notion of teachers coming together as communities of readers of children's writing, it should be obvious that teachers can also come together as communities of readers of children's understandings of history as demonstrated in their completed projects and performances. Such communities are vital to change in school.

In closing this account and book, I wish to stress again the importance of tying assessment to powerful learning. Learning that matters is not inert; it has an intimate quality, it can be seen in the world—is, in fact, useful in some fashion that can be understood. The period of Reconstruction in American history is not, for example, just about a debate between conciliators and radicals; it has much to do with the way the United States developed socially, racially, and economically. What if Reconstruction had proceeded differently? Would race relations have taken a different direction? It is out of such questions that authentic content is constructed. Content needs to be at least this powerful to cause us to engage in an equally powerful mode of assessment.

In settings in which students are engaged in work they care about, in relation to questions that matter to them, that move them along in their mastery of a topic, an idea, a formulation, a design, they also tend to know how they are doing, whether their work is at a beginning stage or quite far along. They are capable in such circumstances of sophisticated self-evaluation. This is what we should want. Again, powerful content and self-assessment are reciprical.

We have, I believe, a chance to make a difference in the schools, to assure that children and young people receive an education of power and consequence. Movement toward assessment practices that "invite students and teachers to be allies," to draw on Peter Elbow, is an important beginning. Connecting that alliance to a powerful curriculum and to a more inquiry-oriented pedagogy of understanding will help us get to the schools we need.

NOTES

1. Presentation at the North Dakota Study Group Meeting, February 16, 1995.
2. I note "dominance" here as a reminder that students are subjected to more tests today than ever before and that the tests have a greater impact on students and their educational opportunities than was the case in earlier decades.
3. It is important when engaged in discussions of educational change to acknowledge earlier efforts that are related. Too often, what is currently viewed as reform is spoken about as "new," not tried before.
4. L. Cuban (1993), *How Teachers Taught: Constancy and Change, 1890–1990.* (New York: Teachers College Press).
5. W. Haney and G. Madaus (1989), "Searching for Alternatives to Standardized Tests: Whys, Whats and Whithers," *Phi Delta Kappan* 70: 683–87.
6. I understand that there is considerable optimism about portfolio assessment, but I also see the continuing power of tests and the belief that what students should know, year by year and course by course, needs to be specified, made more explicit. There remains too much distrust in the capacity of teachers in local schools to construct curricula in relation to their own students and to engage in assessment that can be understood easily beyond a school community.
7. P. Carini (1994), "Stories of Experience with Evaluation and Standards," Grand Forks, ND: University of North Dakots, North Dakota Study Group on evaluation, p. 4.
8. Regarding the power of academic content, I have been asking college students regularly for the past eight years to think about a piece of work they completed in their K–12 schooling that they believed was "something wonderful," that they honored as being "the best work they could do," that they thought was "worthy of saving," and "were eager to share with a parent, grandparent, others." Most have been unable to bring forward any work that approximated such a description. Some have had one or two examples. In the settings we should strive to create, such work should be more common, the products of powerful pedagogy and assessment.
9. I should note, however, that Linda Nathan's research in two schools involved with the Coalition of Essential Schools concludes that teachers' commitments to make use of portfolios affected the ways they thought about and developed curriculum, approached the teaching and learning exchange (pedagogy), and interacted with, related to, students. She argues, in this regard, that portfolio assessment can help cause pedagogical and curricular change. That assumption is certainly worth more examination. See L. Nathan (1995), *Portfolio Assessment and Teacher Practice,* unpublished doctoral thesis, Harvard Graduate School of Education.
10. P. Elbow. (1991), Forward to P. Belanoff and M. Dickson (eds.), *Portfolios: Process and Product* (Portsmouth, NH: Boynton/Cook), xvi.
11. I realize that I have outlined in some respects an ideal context—a thoughtful teacher, who has a materials- and language-rich classroom, has come to know

her/his students well and takes writing seriously. I believe, however, that this ideal is more possible than not, that it could become more the norm if we made such an end a priority, providing to teachers the support they need to be the thoughtful practitioners most teachers wish to be.

12. J. Egan (November, 1981), "Thirty-two Going on Eight," *Insights* 14 (3), 2–8.

13. I meet many parents who, because they see their children's work one piece at a time, lose perspective about their children's growth as writers. Seeing a year's worth of writing, organized chronologically, provides a far different view. Change is typically more evident, and a genuine, constructive parent-teacher conversation is more possible.

CONTRIBUTORS

MARGARET BORREGO BRAINARD is an instructor in the Preservice Program in Childhood Education at Teachers College, Columbia University. After working as a classroom teacher, special educator, and administrator for sixteen years, she is currently working on her doctorate in teacher education. Her research interests include alternative assessment, the inclusion of special needs children in the regular classroom, and the theory-building strategies of beginning teachers.

MARGUERITE M. CLARKE has a Bachelor of Education Degree from St. Patrick's College, Ireland, and received a Master's in Bilingual and Multicultural Education from California State University in Chico in 1991. After teaching in California, Ireland, and Japan, she received a Fulbright scholarship in 1995. Currently, she is a Boisi Fellow and a doctoral student in the Educational Research, Measurement and Evaluation program at Boston College. Her research interests include issues in testing and assessment, as well as policy research related to national and international educational trends.

LINDA DARLING-HAMMOND is currently William F. Russell Professor in the Foundations of Education at Teachers College, Columbia University where she is also Co-Director of the National Center for Restructuring Education, Schools, and Teaching (NCREST) and Executive Director of the National Commission on Teaching and America's Future. She is actively engaged in research, teaching, and policy work on issues of school restructuring, teacher education reform, and the enhancement of educational equity. She is author or editor of six books, including *Professional Development Schools: Schools for Developing a Profession, A License to Teach: Building a Profession for 21st Century Schools,* and *Authentic Assessment in Action.*

As Chair of New York State's Council on Curriculum and Assessment, she has helped to fashion a comprehensive school reform plan for the state that supports curriculum and assessment for more challenging learning goals linked to professional development and greater equity in opportunities to learn. As Chair of the Model Standards Committee of the Interstate New Teacher Assessment and Support Consortium (INTASC), she has helped to develop licensing standards for beginning teachers that reflect current knowledge about what teachers need to know to teach diverse learners to these higher standards.

NANCY DUBETZ is currently an Assistant Professor in the Department of Elementary Education at the State University of New York in New Paltz. Her research interests include the study of teacher education, teacher thinking, and second language learning and teaching. She and a colleague are presently engaged in a self-study of their experiences as two first-year teacher educators.

STEPHEN C. ELLWOOD, IV, is a doctoral candidate in the Department of Curriculum and Teaching at Teachers College, Columbia University. He recently received an Ed.M. in Curriculum and Teaching. Prior to attending Teachers College, he received an Ed.M. from the Harvard Graduate School of Education. He taught in public schools for eight years before attending graduate school. He is currently an instructor in the School of Education, University of Alaska, Fairbanks.

MARTHA ERICKSON, M.ED., is a full-time instructor in the Preservice Program in Childhood Education, in the Department of Curriculum and Teaching, Teachers College, Columbia University. She teaches courses in supervision and preservice teacher education.

BEVERLY FALK is Associate Director at the National Center for Restructuring Education, Schools and Teaching (NCREST) at Teachers College, Columbia University. Her present work there focuses on supporting learner-centered teaching practices through authentic assessment design and development. She is currently involved in helping New York State redesign its curriculum and assessment system.

Dr. Falk has taught in early childhood through graduate education settings and currently teaches courses at Teachers College as well as the City College of New York. She has been the director of an early childhood center, the founding principal of a public elementary school, a program coordinator and consultant for several school districts, and a speaker at numerous conferences and workshops. She is the author of several articles and monographs about learner-centered educational reform initiatives and is co-author, with Linda Darling-Hammond and Jacqueline Ancess, of the recently released book *Authentic Assessment in Action.*

BEATRICE S. FENNIMORE is a Professor in the Department of Professional Studies in Education at Indiana University of Pennsylvania and also serves as an adjunct faculty member at Teachers College, Columbia University. She has focused her work on child advocacy, teacher preparation, multiculturalism, and public school equity issues.

CELIA GENISHI is a Professor of Education in the Program in Early Childhood Education and Chairperson of the Department of Curriculum and Teaching at Teachers College, Columbia University. She is a former secondary Spanish and preschool teacher and teaches courses related to early childhood education and qualitative research methods. Previously she was on the faculty at the University of Texas at Austin and Ohio State University. She is the co-author (with Anne Haas Dyson) of *Language Assessment in the Early Years* and (with Millie Almy) of *Ways of Studying Children*; editor of *Ways of Assessing Children and Curriculum*; and co-editor (with Anne Haas Dyson) of *The Need for Story: Cultural Diversity in Classroom and Community.* She is also author of many articles about children's language, observation, and assessment. Her research interests include collaborative research on alternative assessment, childhood bilingualism, and language use in classrooms.

A. LIN GOODWIN is an Associate Professor of Education and Co-Director of the Preservice Program in Childhood Education in the Department of Curriculum and Teaching, Teachers College, Columbia University. Her research and writing focus on multicultural teacher education, educational equity, transformative teaching, teacher beliefs, and the educational experiences of Asian Americans. Recent publications include, "Teaching and Teacher Education" in the first *Asian American Almanac*, "Making the Transition from Self to Other: What Do Preservice Teachers Really Think About Multicultural Education?" in the *Journal of Teacher Education*, and "Racial Identity and Education" in AERA's *Review of Research in Education*.

Dr. Goodwin also serves as a consultant and staff developer to a wide variety of organizations including school districts, philanthropic foundations, higher education institutions, and professional educational organizations around issues of diversity, educational equity, and multicultural curriculum development.

PAULA HAJAR is an Assistant Professor of Education at Teachers College, Columbia University. From 1971 until 1985 she was a classroom teacher, administrator, and staff developer at several private schools in New York City. In 1993 she received her doctorate from the Harvard Graduate School of Education.

ASA G. HILLIARD, III, is the Fuller E. Callaway Professor of Urban Education at Georgia State University, with joint appointments in the Department of Educational Policy Studies and the Department of Educational Psychology and Special Education. A teacher, psychologist, and historian, he began his career in the Denver Public Schools. He earned a B.A. in Psychology, M.A. in Counseling, and Ed.D. in Educational Psychology from the University of Denver, where he also taught in the College of Education and in the College of Arts and Sciences in the Honors Program in Philosophy. Dr. Hilliard served on the faculty at San Francisco State University for eighteen years. During that time he was a Department Chair for two years, Dean of Education for eight years, and was consultant to the Peace Corps and Superintendent of Schools in Monrovia and school psychologist during his six years in Liberia, West Africa.

He has helped to develop several national assessment systems, such as proficiency assessment for professional educators, and developmental assessments of young children and infants. He is a Board Certified Forensic Examiner and Diplomate of both the American Board of Forensic Examiners and the American Board of Forensic Medicine. He has served as an expert witness in several landmark federal cases on test validity and bias, including the *Larry P. vs. Wilson Riles* I.Q. test case in the 9th Federal District, California, and also in two Supreme Court cases on test bias, *Ayers vs. Fordice* in Mississippi, and the Guardians for the New York City's Police Sergeant's Examination.

Dr. Hilliard is a founding member of the Association for the Study of Classical African Civilizations and serves as its first Vice President. He has conducted many Ancient African History study tours to Egypt, is the co-developer of a popular educational television series, *Free Your Mind Return to the Source: African Origins*, that has been shown in many cities in the U.S. and in several foreign countries. He has produced videotapes and educational materials on African history through his production company, Waset Education Productions.

Dr. Hilliard has written numerous technical papers, articles, and books on testing, Ancient African History, teaching strategies, public policy, cultural styles, and child growth and development. Recently he served with Dr. Barbara Sizemore as Chief Consultant on the *Every Child Can Succeed* television series produced by the Agency for Instructional Technology.

Dr. Hilliard has consulted with many of the leading school districts, publishers, public advocacy organizations, universities, government agencies, and private corporations on valid assessment, African content in curriculum, teacher training, and public policy. Several of his programs in pluralistic curriculum, assessment, and valid teaching have become national models. He has worked on projects with the National Academy of Sciences, and has spoken at the National Aeronautics and Space Administration (NASA), the Smithsonian Institution, and the National Geographic Society.

Dr. Hilliard has served on many boards such as the Agency for Instructional Technology, Zero to Three, Association for the Study of Classical African Civilizations, Public Education Fund Network, American Association of Colleges for Teacher Education, and The Far West Regional Laboratory for Educational Research and Development.

SABRINA HOPE KING is an Assistant Professor at Hofstra University. Formerly at the University of Illinois at Chicago, her work focuses on urban education, black teachers, and the preparation of teachers from all backgrounds to work successfully within the context of diversity.

MARITZA B. MACDONALD, ED.D., Senior Research Associate at NCREST (the National Center for Restructuring Education, Schools and Teaching), Teachers College, Columbia University, is a teacher educator and school-based researcher with a focus on issues of equity, biliteracy, and accountability. Her work expresses her personal and professional concerns with assessments that do not grasp the conceptual and linguistic competence of children for whom English is a new language and the United States a new culture. Her message is to use multiple forms of assessments with a focus on those that appeal to students' nonverbal expressions of their knowledge such as different art forms and culturally relevant content.

GEORGE F. MADAUS is currently the Boisi Professor of Education and Public Policy at Boston College. He is the former Director of Boston College's Center for the Study of Testing, Evaluation and Educational Policy; and the Executive Director of the National Commission on Testing and Public Policy. He has been the Vice President of AERA Division D, and a past President of NCME. He served on the 1974 and 1985 Joint AERA, APA, and NCME Test Standards Committee and on the 1981 Joint Committee on Standards for Educational Evaluation. He was Co-Chair of the APA, AERA, and the NCME Joint Committee on Testing Practices, and served on the subcommittee that drafted the *Code of Fair Testing Practices in Education*. He has been a visiting Professor at the Harvard Graduate School of Education and St. Patrick's College, Dublin, a Fellow of the Center for Advanced Study in the Behavioral Sciences, and is a member of the National Academy of Education.

VALERIE OOKA PANG is a Professor in the School of Teacher Education at San Diego State University. She has published in journals such as the *Harvard Educational Review, Phi Delta Kappan, Theory and Research in Social Education,* and *Multicultural Education.* She is presently working on a book about Asian Pacific American students with Li-rong Lilly Cheng for SUNY Press. Her interests are in multicultural education, teacher education, and Asian Pacific American children.

VITO PERRONE is Director of Teacher Education Programs and a faculty member in Learning and Teaching, at the Harvard Graduate School of Education. He teaches courses in pedagogy, curriculum, and history and writes extensively about such issues as educational equity, progressivism in educational testing, and evaluation.

ANASTASIA E. RACZEK, M.ED., is a doctoral candidate in Educational Research, Measurement and Evaluation at Boston College and is the Boisi Graduate Fellow in Educational Policy at the Center for the Study of Testing, Evaluation, and Educational Policy. She has served as a Teaching Fellow in the Graduate School of Education, Boston College, and as the Graduate Student Representative to Division D (Measurement) of the American Educational Research Association (AERA). Research interests include the use of tests as a public policy; the measurement of social, educational, and economic inequality; and health status assessment.

JENNIFER J. ROBINSON is an Assistant Professor in the Department of Curriculum and Teaching at Montclair State University in New Jersey. Her research interests include parental involvement and minority teacher recruitment.

JULIE HEIMAN SAVITCH graduated from Tufts University with a Master's in Education. Julie was a teacher for six years, during which time she spoke at a number of conferences for the National Council for Teachers of English (NCTE). She has published two articles on the subjects of team teaching and untracking. In September, 1996, Julie began her doctoral work as a Dean's Fellow at the University of Pennsylvania.

LESLIE ANNE SERLING received her M.A. in Early Childhood/Elementary Education from New York University in 1985. She has taught diverse populations in the elementary grades for the past twelve years in New York City and Seattle public schools. To explore inclusion model approaches, Leslie has taught various combinations of bilingual, multi-age, special needs, gifted, and regular education students. She has been an adjunct instructor at Fordham University in New York City and at Antioch University in Seattle. Currently, Leslie is an educational consultant in Seattle.

YVONNE SMITH is a teacher of three-, four- and five-year-olds at Central Park East Elementary School (CPE 1) in East Harlem, New York City. Yvonne has been an early-childhood educator in New York City for twenty-one years and has devoted eleven of those twenty-one years to the children at CPE 1. Her two experiences with private schools, first as a student teacher at Riverside Church Nursery and then as the parent of a daughter who attended City and Country School were, she believes, pivotal in expanding her notions of what was possible in education. Her ideas were further shaped by experiences gained at the Workshop Center for Open Education at City College. Her thinking about teaching young children and about the profession as a whole continues to evolve as a result of her work at CPE, at the Prospect Center with Pat Carini, at the Center for Collaborative Education, and her involvement with the Elementary Teachers Network at Lehman College, with the National Board for Professional Teaching Standards, and with student teachers.

STEVE TURLEY is Assistant Professor of Education and Director of Field Programs in the Multiple Subject Credential Program at California State University, Long Beach. His current areas of interest are teacher preparation, classroom supervision, and the cooperating teacher.

ANA MARÍA VILLEGAS is a professor of education at Montclair State University, where she teaches courses in urban education and supervises student teachers. Prior to joining Montclair in September 1996, she was a senior research scientist with the Division of Education Policy Research of Educational Testing Service, where she conducted research on a variety of issues on access to education, including culturally responsive teaching.

INDEX

CREDITS

"The Road Not Taken" by Robert Frost courtesy of Pocket Books, an imprint of Henry Holt & Co., Inc.

"Invictus" by W.E. Henly courtesy of AMS Press.

Table 14.1, "The Praxis III Criteria," courtesy of ETS. © 1993.